In

In a compelling study of Indian women, Geraldine Forbes considers their recent history from the nineteenth century under colonial rule to the twentieth century after Independence. She begins with the reform movement, established by men to educate women, and demonstrates how education changed women's lives enabling them to take part in public life. Through their own accounts of their lives and activities, she documents the formation of their organizations, their participation in the struggle for freedom, their role in the colonial economy and the development of the women's movement in India since 1947.

"[The author's] clear, vivid narrative is infused with deep sympathy for her subject and prolific scholarship."   *The Times Higher Education Supplement*

"This book is essential reading for everyone interested in Indian women."
Journal of Asian Studies

GERALDINE FORBES is Distinguished Teaching Professor of History and Director of Women's Studies at the State University of New York Oswego. Her publications include *An Historian's Perspective: Indian Women and the Freedom Movement* (1997) and *Positivism in Bengal* (1975) for which she was awarded the Rabindranath Tagore Prize in 1979 for the best book on Bengali culture. She has also edited and introduced *An Indian Freedom Fighter Recalls her Life* by Manmohini Zutshi Sahgal (1994) and *Memoirs of an Indian Woman* by Shudha Mazumdar (1989).

THE NEW CAMBRIDGE HISTORY
OF INDIA

Women in modern India

THE NEW CAMBRIDGE HISTORY OF INDIA

General editor GORDON JOHNSON

President of Wolfson College, and Director, Centre of South Asian Studies,
University of Cambridge

Associate editors C. A. BAYLY

Vere Harmsworth Professor of Imperial and Naval History, University of Cambridge,
and Fellow of St Catharine's College

and JOHN F. RICHARDS

Professor of History, Duke University

Although the original *Cambridge History of India*, published between 1922 and 1937, did much to formulate a chronology for Indian history and describe the administrative structures of government in India, it has inevitably been overtaken by the mass of new research published over the last fifty years.

Designed to take full account of recent scholarship and changing conceptions of South Asia's historical development, **The New Cambridge History of India** will be published as a series of short, self-contained volumes, each dealing with a separate theme and written by one or two authors. Within an overall four-part structure, thirty-one complementary volumes in uniform format will be published. As before, each will conclude with a substantial bibliographical essay designed to lead non-specialists further into the literature.

The four parts planned are as follow:

I The Mughals and Their Contemporaries

II Indian States and the Transition to Colonialism

III The Indian Empire and the Beginnings of Modern Society

IV The Evolution of Contemporary South Asia

A list of individual titles in preparation will be found at the end of the volume.

THE NEW
CAMBRIDGE
HISTORY OF
INDIA

IV.2

Women in Modern India

GERALDINE FORBES

CAMBRIDGE
UNIVERSITY PRESS

PUBLISHED BY THE PRESS SYNDICATE OF THE UNIVERSITY OF CAMBRIDGE
The Pitt Building, Trumpington Street, Cambridge, United Kingdom

CAMBRIDGE UNIVERSITY PRESS
The Edinburgh Building, Cambridge CB2 2RU, UK
40 West 20th Street, New York, NY 10011–4211, USA
477 Williamstown Road, Port Melbourne, VIC 3207, Australia
Ruiz de Alarcón 13, 28014 Madrid, Spain
Dock House, The Waterfront, Cape Town 8001, South Africa

http://www.cambridge.org

© Cambridge University Press 1996

First published 1996
First paperback edition 1999
Reprinted 2004

Printed in the United Kingdom at the University Press, Cambridge

A catalogue record for this book is available from the British Library

Library of Congress Cataloguing in Publication data
Forbes, Geraldine Hancock, 1943–
Women in modern India / Geraldine Forbes.
p.   cm. – (The New Cambridge History of India; IV. 2)
Includes bibliographical references and index.
ISBN 0 521 26812 5 (hc)
1. Women – India – History – 19th century. 2. Women – India –
History – 20th century. I. Title. II. Series.
DS436.N47   1987 pt.4, vol. 2
[HQ1742]
954 s – dc20
305.4'0954'09034   95–41202 CIP

ISBN 0 521 26812 5 hardback
ISBN 0 521 65377 0 paperback

I dedicate this book to those Indian women who have enriched my life by making my research in India an experience with history lived and living history:

"CAPTAIN" LAKSHMI SAHGAL

"COLONEL" LATIKA GHOSH

KALYANI BHATTACHARYYA

KAMALADEVI CHATTOPADHYAY

KRISHNABAI RAU NIMBKAR

KULSUM SAYANI

MANIBEN KARA

MANMOHINI ZUTSHI SAHGAL

RENUKA RAY

ROMOLA SINHA

SHUDHA MAZUMDAR

SMT. AMBUJAMMAL

CONTENTS

ILLUSTRATIONS

GENERAL EDITOR'S PREFACE

The New Cambridge History of India covers the period from the beginning of the sixteenth century. In some respects it marks a radical change in the style of Cambridge Histories, but in others the editors feel that they are working firmly within an established academic tradition.

During the summer of 1896, F. W. Maitland and Lord Acton between them evolved the idea for a comprehensive modern history. By the end of the year the Syndics of the University Press had committed themselves to the *Cambridge Modern History*, and Lord Acton had been put in charge of it. It was hoped that publication would begin in 1899 and be completed by 1904, but the first volume in fact came out in 1902 and the last in 1910, with additional volumes of tables and maps in 1911 and 1912.

The *History* was a great success, and it was followed by a whole series of distinctive Cambridge Histories covering English Literature, the Ancient World, India, British Foreign Policy, Economic History, Medieval History, the British Empire, Africa, China and Latin America, and even now other new series are being prepared. Indeed, the various Histories have given the Press notable strength in the publication of general reference books in the arts and social sciences.

What has made the Cambridge Histories so distinctive is that they have never been simply dictionaries or encyclopedias. The Histories have, in H. A. L. Fisher's words, always been "written by an army of specialists concentrating the latest results of special study". Yet as Acton agreed with the Syndics in 1896, they have not been mere compilations of existing material but original works. Undoubtedly many of the Histories are uneven in quality, some have become out of date very rapidly, but their virtue has been that they have consistently done more than simply record an existing state of knowledge: they have tended to focus interest on research and they have provided a massive stimulus to further work. This has made their publication doubly worthwhile and has distinguished them intellectually from other sorts of reference book. The editors of *The New Cambridge History of India* have acknowledged this in their work.

The original *Cambridge History of India* was published between 1922 and 1937. It was planned in six volumes, but of these, volume 2 dealing with the period between the first century A.D. and the Muslim invasion of India never appeared. Some of the material is still of value, but in many respects it is now out of date. The last fifty years have seen a great deal of new research on India, and a striking feature of recent work has been to cast doubt on the validity of the quite arbitrary chronological and categorical way in which Indian history has been conventionally divided.

The editors decided that it would not be academically desirable to prepare a new *History of India* using the traditional format. The selective nature of research on Indian history over the past half-century would doom such a project from the start and the whole of Indian history could not be covered in an even or comprehensive manner. They concluded that the best scheme would be to have a *History* divided into four overlapping chronological volumes, each containing about eight short books on individual themes or subjects. Although in extent the work will therefore be equivalent to a dozen massive tomes of the traditional sort, in form *The New Cambridge History of India* will appear as a shelf full of separate but complementary parts. Accordingly, the main divisions are between I. *The Mughals and their contemporaries*, II. *Indian states and the transition to colonialism*, III. *The Indian Empire and the beginnings of modern society*, and IV. *The evolution of contemporary South Asia*.

Just as the books within these volumes are complementary so too do they intersect with each other, both thematically and chronologically. As the books appear they are intended to give a view of the subject as it now stands and to act as a stimulus to further research. We do not expect *The New Cambridge History of India* to be the last word on the subject but an essential voice in the continuing discussion about it.

ACKNOWLEDGMENTS

My research for this book was sponsored by grants from the American Institute of Indian Studies, the National Endowment for the Humanities, and the State University of New York. I have used libraries in the USA, England, and India. I am especially indebted to librarians at the India Office and the Fawcett Library in London; the National Library, the Nehru Memorial Library, the Asiatic Society, the All-India Women's Conference Library, the Indian National Archives, and the State Archives in West Bengal, Maharashtra, and Tamilnadu, all in India; and Smith College Library, the Library of Congress, and the Regenstein Library in the USA. Over the years I have benefited from the dedicated service of librarians who have helped me search for books and documents.

I am grateful to the editors of the Cambridge series: Gordon Johnson, Chris Bayly, and John Richards for having faith in my ability to write this volume and for their patience when I asked for extensions of my deadline. Marigold Akland has been a wonderful editor, encouraging and helpful throughout the process, while I am very grateful to Frances Nugent for her diligent copyediting. Gail Minault and Barbara Ramusack both gave this manuscript a careful reading and their comments have been extremely helpful in my revisions. I have asked the advice of a number of colleagues while writing this book and have valued their opinions. I would especially like to thank C. S. Lakshmi, Neera Desai, Joya Chaliha, Sylvia Vatuk, Veena Talwar Oldenburg, Mrinalini Sinha, and Dagmar Engels. I have drawn extensively on their work and ideas as well as the writings of many other fine scholars and I have been helped immensely by colleagues who have read parts of this work and given me copies of their unpublished articles and manuscripts.

There are many other friends and colleagues who have helped me in my research. In India, I would like to mention Maitreyi Krishnaraj, Tota Mitra, Joey Chaliha, Pablo Bartholomew, Tarun Mitra, Aditi Sen, Bharati Ray, and Rana and Manisha Behal. In England Tapan Raychaudhuri, Richard Bingle, and Rosemary Seton have given advice and suggestions. In the USA my friends at SUNY Oswego and Syracuse University have lent me books and articles, listened to my complaining, and told me to get on with it.

The photographs used in this book have been collected from many sources, especially private collections. I have made a good faith effort to trace the photographers who took these pictures but often without success. I am grateful to Smith College and the British Library and to the many individuals who made their collections available to me: Dr. P. C. Mahtab, Shudha Mazumdar, Krishnabai Nimbkar, Mithan Lam, Sevati Mitra, and Renuka Ray. I have also been given permission to include a photo by Pablo Bartholomew.

Throughout the writing of this book, my husband, Sidney ("Skip") Greenblatt, has been by my side: encouraging me, listening to me read out drafts of chapters, making suggestions, and always urging me to get it finished! Perhaps we will now be able to take a vacation without carrying a few chapters of the "Cambridge volume."

ABBREVIATIONS

ABP	*Amrita Bazar Patrika*
AIWC	All-India Women's Conference
BC	*Bombay Chronicle*
BPWC	Bombay Presidency Women's Council
BVA	Bombay Vigilance Association
CPI	Communist Party of India
CS Papers	Cornelia Sorabji Papers (IOOLC, London)
CWMG	*Collected Works of Mahatma Gandhi*
DNB	*Dictionary of National Biography*
DRP	Dr. Reddy Papers (NMML, New Delhi)
DSS	Desh Sevika Sangha (Women Serving the Country)
EPW	*Economic and Political Weekly*
FC	Fawcett Collection (Fawcett Library, London)
GOI	Government of India
IAR	*Indian Annual Register*
IESHR	*Indian Economic and Social History Review*
ILM	*Indian Ladies' Magazine*
INC	Indian National Congress
IOOLC	Indian Office and Oriental Library Collection (London)
ISR	*Indian Social Reformer*
JBC	Josephine Butler Collection (Fawcett Library, London)
JN	Jawaharlal Nehru Papers (NMML, New Delhi)
JWH	*Journal of Women's History*
MR	*Modern Review*
MRS	Mahila Rashtriya Sangha (Women's National Organization)
NCWI	National Council of Women in India
NFIW	National Federation of Indian Women
NI	*New India*
NMML	Nehru Museum and Memorial Library (New Delhi)
NSS	Nari Satyagraha Samiti (Women's *Satyagraha* [truth-force] Organization)
RP	Rathbone Papers (Fawcett Library, London)

RSS	Rashtriya Stree Sangha (National Women's Organization)
RWC	Ruth Woodsmall Collection (Smith College, Northampton, Mass.)
SPL	Social Purity League
WBA	West Bengal Archives (Calcutta)
WIA	Women's Indian Conference
WSIQ	*Women's Studies International Forum* (formerly *Women's Studies International Quarterly*)

A NOTE ON SPELLING

Many Indian names have alternative spellings. In the text I have tried to use the most common or most accepted forms but I have used the original spellings in references in the footnotes.

INTRODUCTION

The first historical accounts of Indian women date from the nineteenth century and are a product of the colonial experience. These accounts tell of an ancient time when women were held in high esteem followed by a long period when their status declined. Then Europeans came on the scene. The foreign rulers, according to these narratives, introduced new ideas about women's roles and capabilities and these ideas were adopted by enlightened Indians. Until recently the history of women in British India has been recounted in this way, that is, as a slow but progressive march towards "modernity" following a long period of stagnation and decline. Both British missionaries and those Indian reformers who welcomed the opportunity to put forth a critique of their own society hypothesized a "golden age" followed by centuries of corruption and betrayal. Salvation came in the guise of European forms of governing, technology, and values. This way of writing about the past, particularly as linear movement through time toward a specific goal, was a hallmark of European history.

Both European-inspired histories and the Indian texts they cited shared a belief in a unique female nature. Indian texts essentialized women as devoted and self-sacrificing, yet occasionally rebellious and dangerous. Texts on religion, law, politics, and education carried different pronouncements for men depending on caste, class, age, and religious sect. In contrast, women's differences were overshadowed by their biological characteristics and the subordinate, supportive roles they were destined to play. Historians were equally essentialist in their portrayal of Indian women. Occasionally Indian texts and historical narratives singled out one woman for special attention but usually this was because her accomplishments were significant by male standards. Topics that were intimately interwoven with women's lives – household and agricultural technology; religious rituals and sentiments; fertility and family size; furnishings, jewelry and clothing; inheritance and property rights; and marriage and divorce – were largely overlooked.

In the 1970s the United Nations focused world attention on the status of women. Member countries were asked to appoint committees that could gather statistics and produce reports on this topic. As India and other countries set up commissions to study the status of women, the UN declared 1975 International Women's Year and 1975–85 Women's Decade.

In India, as in the West, the international mandate was welcomed by a small but determined group of academics already examining questions related to women's status. Historians among this group first turned their attention to the glaring omissions in accounts of politically significant events and only later to studying issues of greatest salience to specific groups of women.

Soon after the systematic study of women's past began, students of history recognized they were witnessing a revolution. Gerda Lerner, an American pioneer in the field of women's history and the first person to hold a chair in women's history, said: "Women have a history; women are in history." Her words became a manifesto. What emerged was a new way of thinking about gender. Instead of accepting feminine identity as natural and essential, historians and other social scientists treated it as constructed. This liberating hypothesis stimulated questions about women's unequal position.

In the West there have been three general approaches to women's history. The earliest of these was additive history, that is, history written after a re-examination of the sources to discover the contributions and role of women. The second approach, genderized history, draws on a feminist perspective to rethink historiography and make gender difference a key to the analysis of social relations. A third approach, contributory history, privileges female agency while recognizing how patriarchy impedes women's actions.

Writing the history of women in a colonial setting presents additional challenges. Colonial histories have narrated the civilizing mission of the British as rescuing Indian women from their own culture and society. Nationalist discourse, according to Partha Chatterjee, resolved the "woman question" by the end of the nineteenth century.[1] If Gandhi revived the "woman question," as I would argue, nationalist historians have concluded that Gandhi brought women into public life and gave them the tools to solve their own problems. But this is too

---

[1] Partha Chatterjee, "The Nationalist Resolution of the Women's Question," *Recasting Women: Essays in Colonial History*, ed. Kumkum Sangari and Sudesh Vaid (Delhi, Kali for Women, 1989), pp. 238–9.

simplistic and ignores the history of women before Gandhi came on the scene. The newer challenges to the task of writing women's history come from the subaltern school, originating in Calcutta, and from historians interested in resistance in everyday life.

The first volume of *Subaltern Studies* appeared in 1982, heralding a new school of history focusing on all non-elite colonial subjects. Borrowing the term "subaltern" from Antonio Gramsci, these historians have explicated the interplay of coercion and consent during 200 years of British rule. In their attempts to explain hegemonic processes, subaltern historians have uncovered and articulated the stories of suppressed peoples. Although they have paid some attention to women, the uncovering of women's subalternity has not been their forte.

It was the subaltern project that led Gayatri Spivak to write her challenging article: "Can the Subaltern Speak?"[2] In this article she states the problem of writing the history of colonial women:

as object of colonial historiography and as subject of insurgency, the ideological construction of gender keeps the male dominant. If, in the context of colonial production, the subaltern has no history and cannot speak, the subaltern as female is even more deeply in shadow.[3]

Spivak warns the uncritical historian to beware of the pitfalls of valorizing "the concrete experience of the oppressed."[4] This way of writing history often constitutes an autonomous subject without due recognition of the dual oppression of colonialism and patriarchy, and the further oppression of Western scholarship.[5] She concludes this essay with a charge to the feminist intellectual to take her work very seriously.[6]

Challenged by the work of James Scott in uncovering the everyday forms of resistance in Southeast Asia,[7] Douglas Haynes and Gyan Prakash have extended this idea to South Asia and to issues of gender. Their aim is to shift the focus away from "extraordinary moments of collective protest" to a "variety of non-confrontational resistances and contestatory behavior."[8] For women's history, this can lead to a way of

[2] Gayatri Chakravorty Spivak, "Can the Subaltern Speak?" *Marxism and the Interpretation of Culture*, ed. Cary Nelson and Lawrence Grossberg (Urbana and Chicago, University of Illinois Press, 1988), pp. 271–313.   [3] *Ibid.*, p. 287.   [4] *Ibid.*, p. 275.
[5] *Ibid.*, p. 295.   [6] *Ibid.*, p. 308.
[7] James Scott, *Weapons of the Weak: Everyday Forms of Peasant Resistance* (New Haven, Yale University Press, 1985).
[8] Douglas Haynes and Gyan Prakash, *Contesting Power* (Delhi, Oxford University Press, 1991), pp. 1–2.

examining women's agency even while they belong to and participate in an oppressive patriarchal society.[9]

Historians of British India are now producing serious monographs on how women experienced colonial rule and how it affected their lives as well how women and the "woman question" affected colonial politics.

There are other ways of writing about gender, especially focusing on the colonial structures that controlled women's lives and analyzing the documents that determined the construction of women in the dominant discourse. These have furthered our understanding of how hegemonic processes work. These studies take as their subject matter not the lives and actions of women but the way women were imagined and represented which in turn influenced how women saw themselves and what they did. New theoretical frameworks, questioning power relationships, language, the observer's gaze, and the dominance of positivist notions, have found gender a compelling subject. This scholarship, when informed by a feminist perspective, contributes significantly to the production of women's history.

This volume belongs to women's history and strives to be contributory in the best sense of the term. I have drawn on women's materials to the greatest extent possible to demonstrate that Indian women have not been as silent as some accounts would have us believe.

At the dawn of women's history as it is now written, Miriam Schneir, in a book entitled *Feminism: The Essential Historical Writings* (1972), stated: "No feminist works emerged from behind the Hindu purdah or out of Moslem harems; centuries of slavery do not provide a fertile soil for intellectual development or expression."[10] Historically this construction of the veiled and enslaved woman has fired the colonial imagination and allowed it to cloak outright exploitation as a "civilizing mission." In the 1930s and 1940s British feminists were eager to help their "little sisters" but remained convinced that imperial rule was benevolent. Post-colonial, cold-war feminists such as Mary Daly have condemned their own patriarchal systems but saved their most vitriolic attacks for third-world men in a form of literary "Paki-bashing."[11] In

---

[9] Nita Kumar, ed., *Women as Subjects, South Asian Histories* (Charlottesville and London, University Press of Virginia, 1994), p. 4.

[10] Miriam Schneir, ed., *Feminism: The Essential Historical Writings* (New York, Vintage, 1972), p. xiv.

[11] Mary Daly, *Gyn/ecology: The Metaethics of Radical Feminism* (Boston, Beacon Press, 1990).

the first place, not all Indian women were behind veils, although certain ideas about modesty and respectability were widely shared. It is equally false to define women's world as one which totally suppresses female agency. To go one step further and declare that Indian women, secluded and not secluded, had no voice is the third act of silencing.

Recent scholarship on women, whether it be women's history or a new questioning of the documents of history, is fueled by the work of archivists and historians locating and saving women's writings and material objects. When I first became interested in women's history in India I was warned about the difficulty of finding sources. That was 1970. Now, a quarter of a century later, I am able to see both how far we have come and how much is left to do. In the early 1970s women's records were not in libraries or archives but in the homes and memories of individuals. Those of us then engaged in research on women's lives uncovered records, documents, journals, magazines, literature, memoirs, letters, photographs, pamphlets, all authored by women. Most important, we met women who were willing to record their oral histories. Researchers collected songs, folk tales, and artistic works, and reread phallocentric documents with a new sensitivity to gender. Research units and documentation centers undertook the task of preserving papers and books that might otherwise have disappeared. The Nehru Memorial Library devoted its attention to acquiring the personal papers of women who had previously been overlooked by libraries and worked to enlarge its significant collection of oral histories. Unfortunately some of the smaller libraries and provincial archives have not preserved valuable collections of women's records and some important private collections have disappeared. SPARROW (Sound and Picture Archives for Research on Women) in Bombay is a recent and heroic attempts to preserve women's documents, especially photographs, films, and recordings.[12] As yet there is no archive or museum devoted to preserving items of women's material culture.

In writing this book I have used a wide range of material produced by feminist scholars, as well as my own notes from years of researching women's history in India. I have been an active participant in the discovery and preservation of women's records and I have read through some private collections which I fear no longer exist. What I think makes this book unique is the extent to which I have been able to draw

[12] Founded in Bombay by C. S. Lakshmi, Neera Desai, and Maitreyi Krishnaraj.

on women's own accounts about the activities they participated in and witnessed. In privileging women's own words, I understand the danger of making them agents of their own destinies. While I have tried to make the reader aware of the constraints which surrounded them, I am influenced by women's perceptions of themselves as agents. The historian has a duty to set personal narratives within a context, but it is also important to recognize that these women constituted themselves as subjects acting in the world.

My object is to privilege women's own accounts so I am focusing, throughout most of this book, on women who were literate. That makes them, by their small numbers, an elite. Unfortunately the term "elite" has been employed to categorize, and then dismiss, women who struggled to become literate. Anandibai Joshi is a case in point. Married at age nine, she endured a difficult life, often filled with privation, abuse, and social ostracism, before she finally came to America, studied at Philadelphia Women's Medical College, and became India's first foreign-trained woman doctor. Haimabati Sen was a child widow who was thrown out of both her brother's home and her brother-in-law's home. That she finally became a medical doctor, trained in the vernacular system, and then wrote a detailed memoir makes her part of an elite in the sense of having obtained higher education and a profession, and writing about her life. But it was not elite status that gave her or Anandibai Joshi this chance. They achieved what they did by sheer force of will. Many of the women who found a voice and left records did not lead privileged lives. They lived and worked within patriarchal societies but were not crippled in the process. I have also utilized nontraditional sources: oral history, women's diaries and letters, songs, pamphlets, literature, and photographs to move beyond the elite and convey the complexity and diversity of India.

I begin this work with male reformers in nineteenth-century India. I have chosen to proceed in this way because patriarchal systems offer women few opportunities until men decide it is time for change. I acknowledge the British as sparking this change. Many of the reforms they proposed had little to do with the deepest needs of the society. However, education was one of the items on the reform agenda that contributed to the emancipation of women. It was not an unmixed blessing since some educational schemes were designed to socialize women to be even more dependent and obedient than previously. Moreover, education often isolated women from their traditional allies within the household. But there is an element of serendipity in education.

Many educated women began to define their own problems. As women's organizations developed, men focused their attention on power politics. If the nationalists solved the woman question it was in terms of their own discourse; the women's discourse about women's problems was alive and well.

I have discussed the women's movement before the nationalist movement because women began asking for their rights before they were brought into the nationalist agitation. The women involved in the women's movement justified their new roles with the ideology of social feminism, that is, they tied their arguments about women's rights to women's obligation to perform traditional roles and serve the needs of the family. Although conventional wisdom credits Gandhi with bringing women into public life, I would argue that they were already there. Gandhi gave them a blueprint for action. Equally important, Gandhi assured their husbands and fathers that these politically active women would not rebel against the family. Feminist demands for equality with men were never fully integrated into the nationalist program even though nationalism was feminized.

I have devoted one chapter to assessing what the new colonial economic scene meant for women. The lack of sources available for this discussion has limited my analysis. There is a crying need for more work in this area. These are difficult topics for researchers, but it is essential historians take steps to uncover more about the lives of the many women employed on plantations, in domestic work and the agricultural sector, as well as in mining, transportation, and the new professions.

Chapter 7 looks at the activities of women from the late 1930s until the early 1950s. The focus is women's activism. By the 1940s women were part of all movements, conservative and radical, and began to view themselves differently. Increasingly they found social feminism wanting and began to borrow from more radical ideological frameworks, especially Marxism and its offshoots. By Independence in 1947 the hegemony of the women's organizations, who claimed to speak for all women, had been destroyed.

The last chapter discusses certain themes in post-Independence India: political involvement, economic participation, and the contemporary women's movement. I argue that the momentous report,

Toward Equality, a report commissioned by the government to examine the status of women since Independence, has had a crucial impact on the contemporary women's movement. The authors of this report have made us aware that the promises of the freedom movement were honored only in laws, regulations, and policy documents. Yet this in itself is no small matter, although it falls far short of Gandhi's promise and what women want. As a historian, I would draw attention to the fact that *Toward Equality* appeared in 1974 – twenty-seven years after Independence. That it appeared at all is a tribute to what had gone before. Other nations that have experienced colonial rule, and many that have not, have not done nearly so well by their women. Not all Indian women benefited from the promises contained in the Constitution but the fact that women are continuing the fight for women's rights is a significant point to make.

The contemporary feminist movement in India is alive and well but divided by a variety of forces that threaten the consensus of the 1980s. The rise of right-wing movements with their women's units is reminiscent of the mobilization of women for the nationalist struggle. The legacy is in the mobilization of women for activities outside the home and confirms that Indian women are no longer excluded from politics or political activities. But this is not a movement for equality for women. Women's involvement in these activities serves a fascist agenda and only empowers those who would scream for the enemy's blood.

I have used the term "feminist" throughout this book knowing full well that Sarojini Naidu and more recently Madhu Kishwar have declared "I am not a feminist."[13] Each of us defines feminist in her own way – I prefer an inclusive definition that would allow me to see feminism in the speeches of Saraladevi Chaudhurani and Sarojini Naidu and in the writings of Dr. Haimabati Sen and Madhu Kishwar. Feminism supports equal rights for women and sees patriarchal society as responsible for their oppression. I would like to quote Veena Oldenburg's comment on her decision to use the word feminist:

Feminism has a long history and is no longer monolithic; multiple feminisms abound, and *feminism is* capable of the same kinds of distinctions one would expect in any analysis of the word *patriarchy.* I define the word *feminist* in its simplest political sense, as a person (and not necessarily a woman) whose analytical perspective is informed by an understanding of the relationship between power and

---

[13] AIWC, Fourth Session, Bombay, 1930, p. 21; Madhu Kishwar, "Why I Do Not Call Myself a Feminist, *Manushi*, no. 61 (November–December, 1990), pp. 2–8.

gender in any historical, social, or cultural context. To me, the argument against using the word *feminist* is weakened by the fact that terms and theories of equally Western provenance – Marxist, socialist, Freudian, or post-structuralist – do not arouse similar indignation and are in fact (over)used as standard frameworks for analyses of Indian society by Indian scholars.[14]

This book is being written in a period of rapid political and social change. The end of the cold war and the breakup of the Soviet Union have contributed to a new climate where nationalism and the liberal ideals of democracy, progress, protest, and dissent are frequently under attack. There are challenges to conventional accounts and at the same time people are looking to history for both explanations of what is happening and validation of their own claims. Within the field of "women's history" other debates are taking place. As conflicting "schools" and new materials become part of our milieu, the charge to the serious historian seems formidable. One might be tempted to abandon history completely but there are those who, like Dipesh Chakrabarty, challenge us "to write into the history of modernity the ambivalences, contradictions, the use of force, and the tragedies and ironies that attend it."[15] In this book I am not so much writing new history as emulating the best historians who were aware of their sources, self-conscious about what they were doing, concerned about evidence that did not always "fit," and tentative in their conclusions. It has been a great pleasure to work on this book and my hope is that it will stimulate others to become engaged in writing history, to include gender in their own conceptual frameworks, or perhaps just admire and enjoy what women have done.

[14] Veena Talwar Oldenburg, "The Roop Kanwar Case: Feminist Responses," *Sati, the Blessing and the Curse,* ed. John S. Hawley (New York, Oxford University Press, 1994), pp. 102–3.
[15] Dipesh Chakrabarty, "Postcoloniality and the Artifices of History: Who Speaks for 'Indian' Pasts?" *Representations,* 3 (winter, 1993), p. 21.

CHAPTER 1

REFORM IN THE NINETEENTH CENTURY: EFFORTS TO MODERNIZE WOMEN'S ROLES

Rammohun Roy's (1772–1833) name is usually listed first among those of nineteenth-century reformers concerned with improving women's status. Historians have called him the "father of modern India," a "champion of women's rights," and a feminist. But his personal relationships with women were far from ideal. He was married three times, at age nine, ten, and twenty-one years. His first wife died soon after the marriage, another died in 1826 and one outlived him. There is no evidence that he looked to his wives for companionship; in fact, there were rumors that his adopted son, Rajaram, was the child of his Muslim mistress.[1] After Rammohun's father's death he argued with his mother, Tarini Devi, and in anger left the family home with his wives and children. The relationship deteriorated even further when Tarini Devi encouraged a nephew to challenge Rammohun's right to ancestral property. The suit began in 1817. Among the court records is an unused document showing that Rammohun was prepared to argue, in front of a judge, that his mother hated him, desired his worldly ruin, and would have even "welcomed his death." Rammohun had developed a set of questions to be asked of his mother if she were called as a witness. He planned to ask if she was so angry at him for refusing to worship her idols that she would lie under oath to destroy him.[2] Rammohun admitted he admired his mother's strength and independence yet he was willing to publicly humiliate her.[3] Examined from this perspective Rammohun seems less than an ideal champion of women's rights. Where were women's voices?

Unfortunately, Tarini Devi left no record of her side of the story. Was her quarrel with her son over religion? Or property? Or was she simply

[1] S. N. Mukherjee, "Raja Rammohun Roy and the Status of Women in Bengal in the Nineteenth Century," *Women in India and Nepal,* ed. Michael Allen and S. N. Mukherjee (Canberra, Australian National University, 1982), p. 165.
[2] "On the Part and Behalf of the Defendant Above Named," *Raja Rammohun Roy Letters and Documents,* ed. Rama Prasad Chanda and Jatindra Kumar Majumdar (Delhi, Anmol Publications, 1987), p. 234. [3] S. N. Mukherjee, "Raja Rammohun Roy," pp. 164–5.

a cantankerous old woman who would not tolerate her son's disobedience? She died in 1822 and like so many of the women of her time what we know about her comes from her son's writings.

Rashsundari Devi (*c.* 1809 –?), a Bengali woman, wrote a story of her life, *Amar Jiban* ("My Life"), that was published in 1868.[4] This detailed memoir revolves around her day-to-day experiences as a housewife and mother. Obsessed with a desire to read, she stole a page from a book and a sheet of paper from her son and kept them hidden in the kitchen where she furtively pursued her education. This is the first autobiography written in Bengali and it is rich in its details of the period when reformers were attempting to change the lives of women. When Rassundari Devi was finally able to write about her own struggle to master simple reading, she commented: "These days parents of a single girl take so much care to educate her. But we had to struggle so much just for that."[5]

Dr. Vina Mazumdar, one of contemporary India's well-known feminist scholars, recalls that one of her great-great-grandmothers performed sati (cremated herself on her husband's funeral pyre) after this custom had been prohibited. Family history records this as a voluntary decision opposed by the woman's sons and grandsons. One granddaughter-in-law refused to accept the blessing of the woman about to become sati. It is this woman – the rebel – who has been remembered by Vina Mazumdar's family as having a strong and vibrant personality.[6]

What we know of the lives of these early nineteenth-century women we know either from memoirs written later, remembered lore, or the accounts of others. The accounts that exist are misleading. We know about Tarini Devi and Vina Mazumdar's ancestresses because of our interest in nineteenth-century social reform. Rammohun Roy was considered one of the greatest reformers, so all details of his life have been recorded. Sati, a custom that pronounced a woman virtuous if she agreed to be burned with her husband's corpse, was strongly opposed by Rammohun Roy. Vina Mazumdar is only one of many Indians whose family history includes a sati story. Because social change – in British terms "social reform" – became such an important issue, our

---

[4] Tanika Sarkar, "A Book of Her Own. A Life of Her Own: Autobiography of a Nineteenth-Century Woman," *History Workshop Journal*, 36, (autumn, 1993), pp. 35–65.

[5] "Rassundari Devi," *Women Writing in India 600 BC to the Present*, 2 vols., vol. 1, 600 BC to the Early Twentieth Century, ed. Susie Tharu and K. Lalita (New York, The Feminist Press, 1991), pp. 190–202, quote from pp. 201–2.

[6] Vina Mazumdar, "Comment on Suttee," *Signs*, 4, no. 2 (winter, 1978), pp. 270–1.

accounts of Indian women in the early part of the nineteenth-century are often imbedded within discussions of sati, child marriage, widow-hood, polygyny, and prohibitions on education. These issues dominate the narrative, leaving us uninformed about women's work and occupa-tions, values and emotional lives, and health and physical well-being. As Lata Mani has so rightly pointed out, the debates over social issues construed women as victims or heroines, denying them complex per-sonalities and agency. Mani writes: "Tradition was thus not the ground on which the status of woman was being contested. Rather the reverse was true: women in fact became the site on which tradition was debated and reformulated."[7]

THE WOMAN QUESTION IN COLONIAL INDIA

In the nineteenth century, the "woman question" loomed large. This was not a question of "what do women want?" but rather "how can they be modernized?" It became the central question in nineteenth-century British India because the foreign rulers had focused their atten-tion on this particular aspect of society. Enamored with their "civilizing mission," influential British writers condemned Indian religions, culture, and society for their rules and customs regarding women.

The British were not the first outsiders with a radically different cul-tural tradition to conquer India. Centuries earlier Muslim dynasties had entered the sub-continent from the northwest and brought to India a new religion and a new way of organizing power relations. But signifi-cant changes that affected the lives of ordinary people first came with British rule. Traditional Hindu society was "decentered" and previous challenges from foreign invaders had allowed it to remain so. The tradi-tional state collected the rents and demanded obeisance but did not inter-fere with the social order. Muslim rule did not significantly alter this structure. But the British, pursuing commercial aims, introduced new relationships and explained their actions within a view of the world that was "clear, precise, instrumentalist, technical, scientific, effective, true, and above all beneficial to all who came into contact with it."[8]

---

[7] Lata Mani, "Contentious Traditions: The Debate on *Sati* in Colonial India," *Recasting Women: Essays in Colonial History*, ed. Kumkum Sangari and Sudesh Vaid (Delhi, Kali for Women, 1989), pp. 117–18.

[8] Sudipta Kaviraj, "On the Construction of Colonial Power: Structure, Discourse, Hegemony," *Contesting Colonial Hegemony*, ed. Dagmar Engels and Shula Marks (London, German Historical Institute London, 1994), p. 31.

The nineteenth century was a time of political, social, and scientific upheaval in Europe. The British regarded their domination of the subcontinent as proof of their moral superiority. In arguments over how to best rule their colonial subjects in India, they were led to discussions of the ideal relationship between men and women.[9] James Mill, in his influential *History of British India* (first published in 1826), argued that women's position could be used as an indicator of society's advancement. The formula was simple: "Among rude people, the women are generally degraded; among civilized people they are exalted." Mill explained that as societies advanced, "the condition of the weaker sex is gradually improved, till they associate on equal terms with the men, and occupy the place of voluntary and useful coadjutors." Having learned about Hindu society through reading Halhed's *Code of Gentoo Laws*, a translation of the Code of Manu, some religious works, and accounts written by travelers and missionaries, Mill concluded: "nothing can exceed the habitual contempt which the Hindus entertain for their women . . . They are held, accordingly, in extreme degradation."[10]

Missionaries concurred. Reverend E. Storrow came to India in 1848 and pronounced Indian disunity a consequence of the low status of women. Storrow's list of strong countries – Israel, Rome, and Western Europe – all derived their courage and virtue from the high position accorded women.[11] Having linked military strength with the status of women, the British concluded that domination of India was natural and inevitable.[12]

Later in the century, as part of the continuous process of legitimating British rule, Sir Herbert Hope Risley characterized the Indian intelligentsia as interested in intellectual and political ideas, but unconcerned with reforming society. Risley was pessimistic about the general progress of India without reform. He concluded his comments:

---

[9] See Mrinalini Sinha, "'Manliness': A Victorian Ideal and Colonial Policy in Late Nineteenth Century Bengal," Ph.D. dissertation, SUNY Stonybrook (1988). Published title: *Colonial Masculinity: the "manly Englishman" and the "effeminate Bengali", in the late nineteenth century* (Manchester, Manchester University Press, 1995).

[10] James Mill, *The History of British India*, 2 vols. (New York, Chelsea House, 1968), pp. 309–10.

[11] Revd. E. Storrow, *Our Indian Sisters* (London, The Religious Tract Society, n.d.), pp. 154–67.

[12] See Francis G. Hutchins, *The Illusion of Permanence: British Imperialism in India* (Princeton, N.J., Princeton University Press, 1967).

History affords no warrant for the belief that the enthusiasm of nationality can be kindled in sordid and degenerate surroundings. A society which accepts intellectual inanition and moral stagnation as the natural condition of its womankind cannot hope to develop the high qualities of courage, devotion and self-sacrifice which go to the making of nations.[13]

The ideas which gained currency among the British rulers of India included humanitarianism, utilitarianism, social Darwinism, and nationalism.[14] Positivist and social Darwinian theory developed rankings of religions and cultures showing India lower on the evolutionary scale than countries of the Middle East or Western Europe. If there were any hope for India, it would follow from the introduction of Western ideas and institutions. Yet few Western critics of Indian society really believed total regeneration was possible. At any rate, a new gender ideology and modification of the actual treatment of women would be the necessary prelude to any positive change.

THE INDIAN RESPONSE

Colonial domination set the change in motion; Indians reshaped the imported ideas and institutions to fit the social and cultural milieu. The historian, Rajat K. Ray, described the impact of imported ideas on the Bengal Renaissance, when intellectuals in eastern India were rediscovering their past and engaging in new intellectual activity, in these terms: "[they] digested and borrowed and inherited elements in such a way that the new culture could not be said to be a pale imitation but was a genuinely indigenous product."[15] The ideology that emerged to redefine gender relations was an amalgam of new foreign ideas, indigenous concepts, and the response of Indian men and women to the foreign presence in their midst.

Not all agreed that gender relations needed modification. A number of Indian intellectuals praised their own culture's treatment of women[16] or compared the conditions of Indian women with those of European

---

[13] Sir Herbert Hope Risley, *The People of India,* 2nd edn., ed. W. Crooke (Delhi, Oriental Books Reprint Corp., 1969), p. 171.

[14] Vina Mazumdar, "The Social Reform Movement in India – From Ranade to Nehru," *Indian Women: From Purdah to Modernity,* ed. B. R. Nanda (New Delhi, Vikas Publishing, 1976), p. 46.

[15] Rajat K. Ray, "Man, Woman and the Novel: The Rise of a New Consciousness in Bengal (1858–1947)," *IESHR,* 16, no. 1 (March, 1979), p. 3.

[16] Tanika Sarkar, "The Hindu Wife and Hindu Nation: Domesticity and Nationalism in Nineteenth Century Bengal," *Studies in History,* 8, no. 2 (1992), pp. 213–35.

women and concluded that females in both countries suffered hardships.[17] Those who accepted the idea that society's ills could be traced to the oppressed condition of women saw female education and female emancipation as the first steps towards progress.[18] But both groups – those who extolled gender relations and those convinced of the need for reform – shared an ideology, later linked to the nationalist project, that separated the home from the world. According to Partha Chatterjee, Indians pursued science, technology, rational economics, and Western political forms while regarding the home as the source of "true identity" that needed protection and strengthening, not transformation.[19]

By the last decade of the nineteenth century there was a recognizable reformist ideology. The shape of this ideology – particularly in its view of women – was retained throughout much of the twentieth century. First and foremost, Indian women were to be pitied. In 1839 Mahesh Chundra Deb spoke to the Society for the Acquisition of General Knowledge about the daily life of young married women:

Suffice it to say that every man who has carefully examined the condition of Hindoo women cannot help pitying the benighted and miserable situation in which they are placed. Not withstanding all their kind attention, their pious and dutiful conduct, their submissive behavior towards their husbands, they frequently meet with severe scoldings and are even sometimes cruelly punished from ungrounded jealousy or a tyrannical whim.[20]

The theme of Deb's speech – the misery of Indian women – echoed the Western critics of Indian society and was repeated in speeches and essays throughout the century. But humanitarianism was only one of the arguments used to urge reform. Inspired and influenced by Western ideas, these reformers were also conversant with their own traditions. Rammohun Roy, Pandit Vidyasagar, Swami Dayananda Saraswati, and many others were trained in Hindu classics and saw India as recovering from a dark age. There had been a "golden age," they argued, when women were valued and occupied positions of high status. This view of the Vedic past had been adopted from the Indologists and was useful to

---

[17] Tapan Raychaudhuri, *Europe Reconsidered* (Delhi, Oxford University Press, 1988), p. 336.
[18] David Kopf, *The Brahmo Samaj and the Shaping of the Modern Indian Mind* (Princeton, N.J., Princeton University Press, 1979).
[19] Partha Chatterjee, "The Nationalist Resolution of the Women's Question," pp. 238–9.
[20] Mahesh Chundra Deb, "A Sketch of the Conditions of the Hindoo Women" [1839], *Awakening in the Early Nineteenth Century*, ed. Goutam Chattopadhyay (Calcutta, Progressive Publishers, 1965). pp. 89–105.

refute Mill's version of India.[21] During this "golden age" women were educated, married only after they had reached maturity, moved about freely, and participated in the social and political life of the time. The power of such an idea may well have stifled serious historical research on women's lives until recently. Uma Chakravarti has argued that for contemporary women this perception of the past "has led to a narrow and limiting circle in which the image of Indian womanhood has become both a shackle and a rhetorical device that nevertheless functions as a historical truth."[22]

Acceptance of a golden age was widespread but explanations of "the fall" differed widely. Some reformers simply commented on wars and invasions, claiming that political disorder inevitably led to restrictions on women's education and mobility. A number of reformers located the decline during the time of the *smritis,* that is, to a period when the vast body of law codes such as the *Manusmriti,* commentaries, epics – most prominently the *Mahabharata* and the *Ramayana* – and *puranas* or stories of the gods were written. These theorists argued that the decline in women's status could be traced to these writings.[23] But most of the reformers blamed Muslim rule. Ignoring the fact that rulers such as Akbar attempted to abolish sati and that Muslim law accorded women a higher status than Hindu law, these writers claimed child marriage, prohibitions on widow marriage, seclusion, and restrictions on female education were responses to the Muslim threat to women's safety.[24]

Both the "golden age" and "dark age" are problematic for historians but these concepts proved useful in the development of an ideology legitimating social reform. In order to persuade his audience that the woman question needed immediate attention, Mahesh Chundra Deb said: "in whatever light, then, we view the situation of the Hindoo women – whether we look to their physical or mental condition – we shall find to our great mortification that it is truly deplorable."[25] It was the postulation of a "dark age" that made this self-criticism palatable. The past had been squandered and change and reform were neces-

---

[21] "Literature of the Ancient and Medieval Periods: Reading against the Oriental Grain," *Women Writing in India,* vol. I, p. 49.

[22] Uma Chakravarti, "Whatever Happened to the Vedic *Dasi?" Recasting Women,* p. 28.

[23] Charles H. Heimsath, *Indian Nationalism and Hindu Social Reform* (Princeton, N.J., Princeton University Press, 1964), pp. 114–15.

[24] "Ideals of Indian Womanhood," *ISR,* 38 (September 24, 1927), p. 56.

[25] Deb, "A Sketch," p. 91.

sary to regain for society its lost vigor. These reformers were not revivalists, they were speaking to the colonial administrators in the language that had gained currency in the contest for moral authority. Colonial officials agreed that religion was central to Indian life, Indian people were slaves to religion, and sati (and many other customs) were religious practices. That the discourse on Indian military weakness versus British success focused on the topic of gender relations to the exclusion of a range of other issues such as trade patterns, technological innovation, the technology and methods of warfare, and dynastic failure is nothing short of amazing. Yet this is what happened.[26]

The discovery of the golden age and of the errors that had led to the fall made it possible for Indians to prescribe change. Once people understood the misery of women and the means of improving the situation, it was simply a matter of will. Pandit Vidyasagar harangued his audience:

Countrymen! how long will you suffer yourselves to be led away by illusions! Open your eyes for once and see, that India, once the land of virtue, is being over flooded [by] the stream of adultery and foeticide. The degradation to which you have sunk is sadly low. Dip into the spirit of your Sastras, follow its dictates, and you shall be able to remove the foul blot from the face of your country.[27]

Reform, actually a return to the past according to most social reformers, was in harmony with both natural law and the dictates of reason. "Evil customs," such as child marriage and polygyny, were not in harmony with nature. Rammohun Roy wrote of women who were "forced upon the pyre," "bound" with ropes so they would perish with their husbands. Vidyasagar wrote of customs which had "hampered the evolution of her [woman's] faculties," and D. K. Karve wrote of a caste widow who "fell victim to the passion of some brute."[28] According to reformers these customs were perverted, twisted, distorted practices born of ignorance and fear and followed without recourse to common sense. The first generation of Western-educated young men had evoked reason as the touchstone for both ideas and action. These later advocates of social reform combined rationalism with their appeal to revive the golden age. According to Vivekananda, there should be no

[26] Lata Mani, "Contentious Traditions," *Recasting Women.*
[27] Isvarachandra Vidyasagar, *Marriage of Hindu Widows* (Calcutta, K. P. Bagchi and Co., 1976), pp. 108–9.
[28] Neera Desai, *Woman in Modern India*, 2nd edn. (Bombay, Vora and Co., 1967), p. 65; Vidyasagar, *Marriage of Hindu Widows*, p. 123; Dhondo Keshav Karve, *Looking Back* (Poona, Hingne Stree-Shikshan Samstha, 1936), p. 45.

hesitation in applying the full panoply of Western analytical methods to the "science of religion." Similarly, Swami Dayananda made it clear that he would not defend "the falsehoods" of the Hindu religion but would unveil them just as he had exposed the errors of other religions.[29] The tests of reason, of course, supported the social system these reformers claimed had existed during the golden age.

CHANGING THE LIVES OF WOMEN

What do we know about women's lives on the eve of this transformation? There are, of course, the records of the reformers (mentioned earlier) but these are tainted by polemics. Constructing a clear picture of the lives of women before colonial rule is difficult, although recent feminist scholarship has added a great deal to our view of the past. The pre-British records include an abundance of prescriptive texts but fewer documents that shed light on the actual lives of women. Tryambakayajvan's *Stridharmapaddhati* ("Guide to the Religious Status and Duties of Women"), translated by Julia Leslie, is the only extant work totally devoted to women's duties. Written in the eighteenth century, before the reformist programs, this text describes the lives of women from the highest ranking, land-holding groups. Unfortunately, "there are no references to women agricultural laborers, market women, or any of the vast army of women who must have been living and working outside the context of the court."[30]

Among the higher castes, the female child spent her youth preparing for marriage. Her marriage to a man of the same caste and ideally higher status was arranged by her parents. Following the marriage ceremony she was sent to her husband's home and required to adjust to their customs. Her husband was to be regarded as "the supreme god among all gods" and served accordingly. The fortunate woman gave birth to sons while issueless women or those who gave birth only to daughters were treated with disdain. The aging woman watched her children mature and marry and accepted the new roles of mother-in-law and grandmother. If her husband died before her, she became a widow with abstemious habits. After his death she was to

---

[29] M. K. Halder, *Renaissance and Reaction in Nineteenth Century Bengal: Bankim Chandra Chatterjee* (Columbia, Mo., South Asia Books, 1977), p. 188.

[30] I. Julia Leslie, *The Perfect Wife: The Orthodox Hindu Woman according to the Stridharmapaddhati of Tryambakayajvan* (Delhi, Oxford University Press, 1989), pp. 3–20.

devote her life to his memory, her impurity could never be removed, and she was to live out her life as the most inauspicious of all creatures.[31] By faithfully performing her duties, a woman helped to maintain an ordered universe.

Historically, women experienced these rules and prescriptions differently depending on religion, caste, class, age, place in the family hierarchy, and an element of serendipity. There were women who lived up to the ideal, but there were also women who rebelled against these prescriptions. The historical record confirms that women found an escape from conventional roles in religion and scholarship, and occasionally through political action.[32] Some women were able to live outside patriarchal households and gain status as courtesans.[33] But the options open to women of extraordinary talent or those unhappy with their lives were limited. Surviving records inform us that a few women became educated, attained fame, and commanded armies but most were denied men's opportunities to acquire knowledge, property, and social status.

By the second half of the nineteenth century there were reform groups in all parts of British India. They focused attention on sati, female infanticide, polygyny, child marriage, purdah, prohibitions on female education, *devadasis* (temple dancers wedded to the gods), and the patrilocal joint family. Their activity acted as a stimulus and encouragement to reform-minded individuals in other areas, and gradually reformist organizations with an all-India identity began to emerge.

MALE REFORMERS

Across India, there is a long list of reformers who undertook major efforts on women's behalf. In Bengal, Iswar Chandra Vidyasagar championed female education and led the campaign to legalize widow remarriage, and Keshub Chandra Sen, a leader of the Brahmo Samaj,[34]

---

[31] *Ibid.*, pp. 273–304.   [32] Tharu and Lalita, *Women Writing in India*, introduction.
[33] For an interesting discussion of this theme, see Veena Oldenburg, "Lifestyle as Resistance: The Case of the Courtesan of Lucknow, India," *Feminist Studies*, 16, no. 2 (summer, 1990), pp. 259–87.
[34] The Brahmo Samaj began with a group of Bengali Hindus who wanted to rethink their religious heritage. In 1815 Rammohun Roy assembled his friends for religious discussions and by 1828 they were meeting for weekly services and sermons as the Brahmo Sabha. Debendranath Tagore (1817–1905), author of the Brahma Covenant and a volume of scriptures and the designer of revised rituals, founded the Brahmo religion. When his followers wanted more dramatic action in the areas of caste equality, temperance, and equality for women, the Samaj split and then split again. By the 1870s it was considered a separate religion.

sought to bring women into new roles through schools, prayer meetings, and experiments in living. By the turn of the century, Swami Vivekananda, the leader of an activist order of Hindu monasticism, was arguing that women could become a powerful regenerative force. In North India, Swami Dayananda Saraswati, the founder of the Arya Samaj,[35] encouraged female education and condemned customs he regarded as degrading to women: marriages between partners of unequal ages, dowry, and polygyny. At the same time, Rai Salig Ram (also known as Huzur Maharaj), a follower of the Radhasoami faith, advocated female emancipation in his volumes of prose, *Prem Patra*. Among Muslims, Khwaja Altaf Husain Hali and Shaikh Muhammad Abdullah introduced education for girls. In western India, Mahadev Govind Ranade founded the National Social Conference to focus attention on social reforms. At the same time, the Parsee journalist Behramji Malabari captured the attention of the British reading public with his articles in *The Times* on the evils of child marriage and the tragedy of enforced widowhood for young women. Dhondo Keshav Karve offered a practical solution with his institutions in Poona to educate young widows to become teachers in girls' schools. In South India, R. Venkata Ratnam Naidu opposed the *devadasi* system while Virasalingam Pantulu worked for marriage reform. Both sought to increase opportunities for female education. Reformers were found throughout India and among all communities. They addressed a number of issues, most of them relating to marriage and the importance of female education.

What is especially interesting about these nineteenth-century reformers is their activism. Their ideas on gender were rooted in personal experience; during their lives they attempted to change those with whom they lived and worked. They were not simply reacting to British pressure – these issues were very real and they responded to them with passion.

To illustrate the efforts of these male reformers, I will sketch the life work of Pandit Iswar Chandra Vidyasagar, from Bengal; Virasalingam Pantulu, a Telugu speaker from Madras Presidency; and Justice

[35] In northern India, Dayananda Saraswati (1824–83) launched a vigorous campaign against popular Hinduism including the brahmin priesthood, rituals, and pilgrimages, and customary prohibitions on widow remarriage and female education. Holding the Vedas infallible, he established the first Arya Samaj (Noble Society) in Bombay in 1875. Within a few years, reformers in Delhi, Lahore, and other North Indian cities had set up independent Arya Samajes.

Mahadev Govind Ranade, from Bombay. These three men were born in the first half of the nineteenth century, were well educated, and had personal experiences which caused them to reflect on the plight of women in Hindu society.

In 1828 eight-year-old Iswar Chandra Vidyasagar (1820–91) walked, with his father, from the village of Birsingha in Midnapur District to Calcutta to seek admission in an English-language institution. The fees at Hindu College were too high for his father to pay so Iswar Chandra was enrolled in Sanskrit College. While studying in Calcutta he lived at the home of a friend whose sister was a child widow. This was Iswar Chandra's first experience of the hardships this custom imposed on women. Sometime later his old guru decided to marry a young girl. Iswar Chandra was enraged and demonstrated his anger by refusing his guru's hospitality. Before a year had passed the guru died and left behind a girl widow with nowhere to go and no means of support.[36] Iswar Chandra vowed then to devote his life to improving the status of Hindu widows and encouraging remarriage.[37]

Iswar Chandra also became an impassioned supporter of female education and an opponent of polygyny. He wrote lengthy tracts substantiating his positions with scriptural citations and historical data. A decline in religion created the environment that allowed contemporary customs to thrive, he wrote. When his opponents protested, he insisted they were misinterpreting scripture and employed a masterful command of Sanskrit to point out their ignorance.

In his first tract on widow remarriage (1855) Iswar Chandra claimed that this practice was permissible in *Kali Yuga* ("The Dark Age"), the age in which he and his contemporaries lived. Two thousand copies of this book were sold in the first week, a reprint of 3,000 soon sold out, and the third reprint was of 10,000 copies.[38] But not everyone was convinced. On the streets of Calcutta Vidyasagar found himself insulted, abused, and even threatened with death.[39] But he pressed on and urged the British to pass legislation that would enable Hindu widows to remarry. To support his request Iswar Chandra collected almost 1,000 signatures and sent this petition to the Indian Legislative Council. The Council received thousands of signatures for and against this measure

[36] Desai, *Woman in Modern India*, p. 69; S. K. Bose, *Iswar Chandra Vidyasagar* (New Delhi, National Book Trust, 1969), pp. 5, 32.
[37] Asok Sen, *Iswar Chandra Vidyasagar and his Elusive Milestones* (Calcutta, Riddlu-India, 1977), p. 60. [38] Bose, *Iswar Chandra*, p. 35. [39] Sen, *Iswar Chandra*, p. 59.

but the members finally decided to support the "enlightened minority." The Hindu Widow Remarriage Act was passed in 1856. Although the value of this Act for improving the lives of women has been questioned, one cannot doubt Iswar Chandra's desire to create a more humane society.

The Remarriage Act did not change the status of widows. Frequently blamed for the husband's death, the high-caste widow was required to relinquish her jewelry and subsist on simple food. Young widows were preyed upon by men who would make them their mistresses or carry them away to urban brothels. But woe to the widow who succumbed to a suitor and became pregnant. In 1881 the court at Surat in western India tried Vijayalakshmi, a young brahmin widow, for killing her illegitimate child. At the first trial she was sentenced to hang but on appeal this was changed to transportation for life and later reduced to five years. This case so angered Tarabai Shinde (c. 1850–1910), a young Marathi housewife, that she wrote *Stri-purusha-tulana* ("A Comparison Between Women and Men"). Vijayalakshmi's case had triggered an intense public discussion about the misfortune of widows and the issue of widow remarriage. For Tarabai, it was clear that this issue was simply a metaphor for the general mistreatment of women. She wrote: "So is it true that only women's bodies are home to all the different kinds of recklessness and vice? Or have men got just the same faults as we find in women?" As for widows: "Once a woman's husband has died, not even a dog would swallow what she's got to."[40] Tarabai Shinde's cry for equality went unheeded in a world where reformers wanted to help women, not accord them equal status.

Vidyasagar lived in a world where the males among *kulin* brahmins, an aristocratic caste with rigid marriage rules, were highly sought after as bridegrooms and able to marry as many women as they wished. As Vidyasagar collected data on this custom, he became horrified by the magnitude of the problem. Using as a sample 133 *kulin* brahmins of Hooghly District, Iswar Chandra revealed the abuses inherent in polygyny. One fifty-year-old man had married 107 times; Bholanath Bandopadhyaya (age fifty-five) had eighty wives; Bhagaban Chattopadhyaya (age sixty-four) had seventy-two wives, and so the

---

[40] Rosalind O'Hanlon, "Issues of Widowhood: Gender and Resistance in Colonial Western India," *Contesting Power: Resistance and Everyday Social Relations in South Asia,* ed. Douglas Haynes and Gyan Prakash (Delhi, Oxford University Press, 1991) pp. 62–108, quotes from p. 93 and p. 96.

documentation continued. Arguing that the practice of *kulinism* was inhuman, Iswar Chandra presented the government with a petition signed by 2,500 persons requesting the legislative prohibition of polygyny. No action was taken and ten years later he presented another petition, this time signed by 21,000 persons. The government, overly cautious about social reform in the wake of the rebellion of 1857, declined to act. Vidyasagar continued his campaign and although he produced anti-polygyny tracts in 1871 and 1873, the issue was dead.[41]

Vidyasagar's third campaign focused on mass education for girls and boys. He had been appointed Special Inspector of Schools for the Districts of Hooghly, Midnapur, Burdwan, and Nadia and was able to use his influence to establish a system of vernacular education in Bengal, including forty schools for girls. J. E. D. Bethune, legal member of the Governor-General's Council, had set up a girls' school in 1849 and it became Vidyasagar's responsibility to guide it through its difficult years. He remained associated with it until 1869.[42]

Despite this great man's efforts, widow remarriage never received the approval of his society, polygyny was not abolished, and the battle for female education had only begun. From the perspective of women's rights, the new law often proved harmful. Remarried women from castes that had traditionally practiced remarriage, were often deprived of their rightful inheritance[43] and those castes were denigrated as inferior.[44] Widow celibacy was lauded by the elite as a hallmark of respectability.[45] Vidyasagar's biographer has written about the elusive nature of Vidyasagar's goals: he strove to introduce fundamental reforms within the colonial context. His proposals proved too radical for many of his contemporaries and although the colonial government criticized Indian customs, they were unwilling to back his efforts for change. Vidyasagar personified the best of the nineteenth-century social reformers; arguing for social change he demonstrated an "untiring will for positive social action."[46]

Kandukuri Virasalingam Pantulu (1848–1919) was born in

[41] Bose, *Iswar Chandra*, pp. 43–7. [42] *Ibid.*, pp. 23–5.
[43] Lucy Carroll, "Law, Custom and Statutory Social Reform: The Hindu Widow's Remarriage Act of 1856," *Women in Colonial India: Essays on Survival, Work, and the State*, ed. J. Krishnamurthy (Delhi, Oxford University Press, 1989), pp. 23–5.
[44] Prem Chowdhry, "Popular Perceptions of Widow-remarriage in Haryana: Past and Present," *From the Seams of History*, ed. Bharati Roy (Delhi, Oxford University Press, 1995), pp. 39–40.
[45] Sekhar Bandyopadhyay, "Caste, Widow-remarriage and the Reform of Popular Culture in Colonial Bengal, " *From the Seams of History*, p. 34. [46] Sen, *Iswar Chandra*, p. 165.

Rajahmundry, the capital of Godavari District, in a Telugu-speaking district of Madras Presidency. Virasalingam, a brahmin trained in classical Telugu, spent his life involved in movements to promote this language for modern education and communication. After he had passed his matriculation, he was appointed a teacher in a government school. Later he became headmaster of the Anglo-Vernacular School at Dhavaleswaram. A member of the Brahmo Samaj and Prarthana Samaj,[47] he published his own journal, *Vikeka Vardhani* ("Journal to Promote Enlightenment") to encourage social reform. Above all, he believed in the necessity of purifying religion by opposing wrong customs and attempting to stop wrong conduct. Purified religion, social reform, and vernacular education would be the three pillars of a regenerated society purged of its evil ways.[48]

Virasalingam made widow remarriage and female education the key points of his program for social change. He opened his first girls' school in 1874 and in 1878 organized a Society for Social Reform. At their first meetings members of the society discussed the importance of the anti-*nautch* movement to wean people from hiring *nautch* (dancing) girls for celebrations, but by 1879 Virasalingam had made widow remarriage the key issue. Rajahmundry celebrated its first widow remarriage in 1881 with Virasalingam performing the ceremony. The town was hostile towards this practice but Virasalingam persisted and before long there was a small community of remarried couples. Virasalingam continued to look for prospective candidates while writing numerous articles about the need for a change in public opinion. In 1891 a Widow Remarriage Association was formed, and thirty brahmin households signed a pledge promising to participate in the ceremonies and marriage feast whenever a remarriage occurred.[49] Eventually the majority of the

---

[47] The Prarthana Samaj (Prayer Society) of Bombay began after the Brahmo Samaj missionary, Keshub Chandra Sen, had visited that city in 1864. Members of this organization believed in an all-powerful God and salvation through worship, and rejected idolatry and the authority of brahmin priests. Religious devotion mandated concern with the world and Prarthana Samajists dedicated themselves to gradual social reform. Even though they rejected conventional Hinduism as a religion, they did not want a break with Hindu society.

[48] *Autobiography of Kandukuri Veeresalingam Pantulu*, trans. Dr. V. Ramakrishna Rao and Dr. T. Rama Rao, 2 parts (Rajamundry, Addepally and Co., n.d.), p. 173.

[49] On Virasalingam see *Autobiography*; Neera Desai, *Woman in Modern India*; Pratima Asthana, *Women's Movement in India* (Delhi, Vikas, 1974); Karen I. Leonard and John Leonard, "Social Reform and Women's Participation in Political Culture: Andhra and Madras," *The Extended Family*, ed. Gail Minault (Columbus, Mo., South Asia Books, 1981), pp. 19–45; "Rao Bahadur Mr. K. Virasalingam Pantulu and His Wife," *ILM*, 2 (September, 1902), pp. 84–5.

prominent citizens of Rajahmundry joined Virasalingam's association.

Virasalingam had a significant impact on female education. When reformers and conservatives debated female education in Rajahmundry the argument took a different form than it had in Calcutta and Bombay where colonial power was evident. Here the language of debate was Telugu and the controversy was conducted without reference to the colonial critique of Indian society. In this context reforms for women were not equated with westernization. The consequences of this movement were far-reaching:

> The widow marriage campaign was the catalyst which initiated . . . the first generation of Western-educated Andhras into social, religious and political reform activities. A symbolic effort to change the status of women, it posed a fundamental challenge to orthodox concepts of women and their role in family and society. The campaign had a major ideological impact upon the development of modern Telugu literature and the nationalist movement in Andhra.[50]

In Bombay, Justice Mahadev Govind Ranade (1842–1901) graduated from Elphinstone College in Bombay and became a teacher and journalist. Like so many other young men of his generation, he questioned the customs and beliefs of his society. In 1869 Ranade joined the Widow Marriage Association, and in 1870 the Prarthana Samaj. At first, he and his colleagues were engaged in "intellectual protest against superficial dogmas untenable for a rational mind," but later they became more interested in social action.[51]

In 1871 Ranade was made a judge in Poona where he joined a group of committed social reformers intent on achieving real change. Soon after he had received this appointment his wife of almost twenty years died. Social reform colleagues expected he would marry a widow. But Ranade's father, anticipating this disaster, moved quickly to arrange a marriage between his thirty-one-year-old son and an eleven-year-old girl. Ranade protested but did not refuse the match. Married to Ramabai, Mahadev became both husband and teacher, mentoring the girl who became one of India's most important social reformers.[52]

In the following years Ranade tried to mediate between a reformist agenda and traditional society. He wanted to encourage widow remar-

---

[50] Leonard and Leonard, "Social Reform," p. 36.
[51] Heimsath, *Indian Nationalism*, p. 179.
[52] Ramabai Ranade, *Himself, The Autobiography of a Hindu Lady* (New York, Longman, Green and Co., 1938).

riage and female education and oppose child marriage, but his personal world, located between tradition and modernity, was fraught with moral ambiguity. Other reformers voiced their disapproval but they were unable to push him towards a more radical stand.

Ranade's reputation as a social reformer rests on his role in building one of the most important institutions for social reform – the National Social Conference (begun in 1887) – and in his philosophy of social change. Firmly believing India had enjoyed a golden age, when women enjoyed a higher status than in his time, he blamed the *smriti* ("remembered" religious literature including law books, epics, and *puranas*) writers for the fall. Only gradual reform, accomplished without radical or wrenching change, could bring about the restoration of the golden age. Ranade argued that evolutionary change was inherently Indian; outside forces could act as a stimulant but the true impetus for change came from "the inner resources of the society itself."[53]

Ranade described the society he hoped to see as changing "from constraint to freedom, from credulity to faith, from unorganized to organized life, from bigotry to toleration, from blind fatalism to a sense of human destiny."[54] He warned his critics that to stand still or work against change would result in decay and possibly the extinction of Indian society.

Every year reformers, working alone or with local organizations, attended the National Social Conference where they learned about initiatives all over the sub-continent. In his role as founder-leader, Ranade recommended four methods of accomplishing social change. His favorite method was using argumentation, especially citing examples of past tradition, to convince opponents that many customs were accretions rather than part of true Indian culture. If the appeal of history was ineffective, he suggested the reformer use a moral argument. It was only after trying to persuade people that reformers should focus on legislation. When all else failed, social rebellion was in order. At the second annual meeting of the National Social Conference in 1889 over five hundred people took a solemn vow that they would support widow marriage and female education, and cease practicing child marriage and the exchange of dowry. This was a significant step, in Ranade's view, towards the identification of reforms for women with an all-India agenda.

---

[53] Heimsath, *Indian Nationalism*, p. 181.   [54] *Ibid.*, p. 187.

After her husband's death, Ramabai wrote a memoir describing her childhood, her marriage to Justice Ranade, her early education at his hands, and their life together until his death in 1901. This memoir, published in the early years of the twentieth century, includes Ramabai's account of her childhood and marriage at age eleven in 1873. The childhood she recalled was not one of terror and anxiety. Raised to regard early marriage as inevitable, Ramabai wrote of how she and other little girls looked forward to the celebrations associated with marriage. When taunted by the women in her husband's household, she kept her peace and admitted that her interest in reading was unseemly in the presence of women with very little education.[55] At least in the way she recalled her life, Ramabai was a dutiful wife even if her "duties" were a departure from the normal tasks of women.

These reformers viewed women as their subjects – to be changed as a consequence of persuasive arguments, social action, education, and legislation. The historian Sumit Sarkar has argued that these reformers were concerned primarily with modifying relationships within their own families and sought only "limited and controlled emancipation" of their womenfolk.[56] Women themselves were not partners in the schemes created for their regeneration; more often they were portrayed as opposed to their own liberation. Without first-hand accounts by these women, their reluctance to change in the ways prescribed by their husbands and fathers could be read as nascent feminist resistance, an intelligent reading of their true interests, or plain and simple opposition to any change. Shudha Mazumdar has related her mother's opposition to Shudha becoming a "boarder" at St. Theresa's School for Girls:

> She felt that my being a boarder would result in many complications, and make it difficult, if not impossible to give me in marriage when the time came . . . To prevent me from becoming a permanent liability on the family, dependent on my brothers in old age, she recommended that to ensure my economic independence it was of paramount importance to execute a deed beforehand in my favor, granting me the rights of a substantial portion of my Father's estate.[57]

But these reformers, like Shudha's father, were unwilling to relinquish the power of the patriarchy or redistribute wealth. They dreamed of a

---

[55] Ramabai Ranade, *Himself*, chapter 5.

[56] Sumit Sarkar, "The 'Women's Question' in Nineteenth Century Bengal," *Women and Culture*, ed. Kumkum Sangari and Sudesh Vaid (Bombay, Research Center for Women's Studies, 1994), p. 106.

[57] Shudha Mazumdar, *Memoirs of an Indian Woman*, ed. Geraldine Forbes (New York, M. E. Sharpe, 1989), pp. 43–4.

world where women would be educated and free from some of the worst customs of the society – child marriage, sati, polygyny. But at the same time, these new women would be devoted to home and family.

THE "NEW WOMAN" OF THE LATE NINETEENTH CENTURY

During the course of the nineteenth century, the pattern of women's lives began to change. In reality the concept of the "perfect wife" was being redefined. First, there were modifications in the appropriate activities for a female at different stages of her life. Second, the appropriate arena for female action was expanded. And third, there was a new and growing approval of individualism.

As a consequence of changes set in motion by the British conquest of India, by the end of the nineteenth century there were a number of women who were educated, articulate, mobile, and increasingly involved in public activities. In the rural setting life was dominated by the household – for both men and women. With increased urbanization and the growth of new professions associated with colonial domination, work was increasingly separated from the home. Paralleling this change was the establishment of new educational, religious and social institutions. As families moved from their village homes to the cities, they increased their contact with "foreigners" and witnessed the erosion of traditional household activity. Like boys of an earlier generation, some of these girls attended educational institutions, social gatherings unrelated to family affairs, and new religious ceremonies. These "new women," as they were called, were part of a modernizing movement which sought to modify gender relations in the direction of greater equality between men and women.[58]

A number of Indian men have written about their lives emphasizing the differences between themselves and their fathers and grandfathers. For example, Brajendra Nath De (1852–1932) was first educated at home, then sent to one of the new schools that taught English. He obtained a scholarship to study in England where he passed the civil service examination, returned home in glory, and began a career which made it necessary to live outside his traditional family home.[59] As one

[58] Ghulam Murshid, *Reluctant Debutante* (Rajshahi, Bangladesh, Rajshahi University, 1983), introduction.
[59] Brajendra Nath De, "Reminiscences of an Indian Member of the Indian Civil Service," *The Calcutta Review*, 127 (1953); 128 (1953); 129 (1953); 130 (1954); 131 (1954); 132 (1954); 136 (1955).

of the first eight Indians appointed to the Indian Civil Service (ICS), Brajendra Nath was considered an excellent example of the "modern" professional class, but his wife had been a child bride and he remained attached to his large joint family with its numerous dependants and obligations. He insisted on educating his daughters and one of them, Saroj Nalini Dutt, led the way in organizing rural women's organizations in the years immediately following World War I.

Many of the "new women" were also educated in their homes and then sent to a girls' school. Parents who cared about female education waited until their daughters were older before arranging their marriages or occasionally allowed young married women to continue their education. Older brides became mothers at a later age and often played a greater role in child-rearing.[60] Often there were opportunities to exercise some choices of their own and consequently their status was far less derivative than had been true for a previous generation.

There were also significant changes in what women could do – often characterized as a movement from the private to the public sphere. But this both overly simplifies the Indian context and overly dramatizes what actually happened. The shift was neither abrupt nor permanent and many women, who briefly attended a school or emerged from purdah to attend a "mixed" function, returned to the household where they continued to live in the more traditional fashion.

Women also experienced increased opportunities for the expression of their individuality. Although women in earlier times were certainly not an undifferentiated group, we do not have sufficient records to go beyond generalizations about their lives. Formal education and particularly the development of publications intended for and written by women gave women a voice. It is impossible to enumerate, let alone locate, all the literature from this period (c. 1850–World War I) but we know that in Bengal women produced almost 400 literary works, ranging from poetry to novels and autobiographies, and twenty-one journals.[61] Through their writings they were able to communicate with each other and develop new social networks.

Saraladevi Chaudhurani (1872–1954), a Bengali woman from the famous Tagore family, is an excellent example of the "new woman."

---

[60] Meredith Borthwick, *The Changing Role of Women in Bengal, 1849–1905* (Princeton, N.J., Princeton University Press, 1985), chapter 5.

[61] Malavika Karlekar, *Voices From Within: Early Personal Narratives of Bengali Women* (Delhi, Oxford University Press, 1991), p. 11.

Her mother, Swarnakumari Devi, was a novelist and editor of a women's journal. Saraladevi was born into an extraordinary family in terms of wealth, prestige, and involvement in the major cultural activities of the day. Saraladevi's education began at home with a tutor, she then attended Bethune College, graduating with honors in English in 1890. She continued studying – French, Persian, and then Sanskrit – in preparation for her MA examination. Remaining at home, she studied music, wrote songs, and wrote for her mother's journal. Her boldest step was to leave home and become a teacher in Maharani's School in Mysore. Saraladevi agreed to marry at age thirty-two and only then because her dying mother asked her to. In 1905 she married Rambhuj Dutt from Lahore, a Punjabi nationalist and member of the Arya Samaj. She had one son and continued her work as an educationalist, a patriot, and a feminist.[62]

Saraladevi was an unusual woman for her time but there were many others, less famous with less freedom, who also took advantage of opportunities to obtain an education and take the first steps towards controlling their own lives.

CONCLUSIONS

The goal of the male reformers was progress. Without social reform to substantially improve women's status, regeneration seemed doomed to failure. Humiliated by their colonial status, Indians of the late nineteenth century were obsessed with the issues of strength and power. They needed an explanation for the weakness that had led to their defeat and an answer to the question of how to build up their strength. If they accepted the nineteenth-century European theory that the status of women was integral to the level and strength of civilization and the European conclusion that Indian customs were degrading to women's status, they gained an explanation for their defeat and a prescription for reform. In Bankim Chandra Chattopadhyaya's patriotic novel *Anandamath* (1882), nationalists were born when they came face to face with a battered and neglected image of the Mother Goddess. Dedicating their lives to the regeneration of the Mother, they took up the slogan, "Bande Mataram" (Hail to the Motherland). In the hands of the great reformer Vivekananda, worship of the Goddess, reverence for

---

[62] Borthwick, *The Changing Role of Women*, pp. 131–3; "Saraladevi Chaudhurani," *DNB*, vol. I, ed. S. P. Sen (Calcutta, Institute of Historical Studies, 1972), pp. 289–91.

the Motherland, and a commitment to female education and improving the status of women became the triple vow of the modern man.[63] But Vivekananda regarded most of the social reform programs of his contemporaries as inadequate to the great task of "national reconstruction." Change was essential but not through reliance on Western guidance, continuous breast-beating about the evils of Hinduism, or leadership by English-educated intellectuals. It must come from the people, guided and educated by the intelligentsia.[64]

The debate over the Age of Consent Act in 1891, an Act to raise the age of consent from ten to twelve, degenerated into a battle for control of Indian women's sexuality. By this time many of the best-educated and influential men were involved with nationalist politics and the "woman question" was no longer a subject on which educated Indians and British rulers could agree.[65] But these issues were not discarded as the "new women" moved forward to set up their own organizations and reorganize social reform priorities. The changes these male reformers proposed could not resolve the "woman question." They had little understanding of women's lives beyond those of women in their own families. Moreover, many of them doubted the efficacy of legal measures even as these changes were enacted. In her review of three recent books published on the history of women in India, Janaki Nair comments on the "limited operation of the 'modernization' paradigm." She writes: "The agenda of 'modernization,' to which both colonialist and nationalist discourse laid claim, did not, indeed could not, include the wider transformation of Indian society."[66] Nevertheless, the steps taken by these respectable and well-educated Indian men linked improving women's status with the modernization agenda. Their campaign set in motion further attempts to establish institutions that would be supportive of a new generation of women leaders.

[63] M. K. Haldar, *Renaissance and Reaction in Nineteenth Century Bengal: Bankim Chandra Chatterjee* (Columbia, Mo., South Asia Books, 1977), p. 188.
[64] Raychaudhuri, *Europe Reconsidered*, p. 338.
[65] Partha Chatterjee argues that the nationalists dispensed with the "woman question" by relegating it to the realm of the spiritual. *Recasting Women*, pp. 233–53.
[66] Janaki Nair, "Reconstructing and Reinterpreting the History of Women in India," *JWH*, 3, no. 1 (spring, 1991), p. 132.

CHAPTER 2

EDUCATION FOR WOMEN

Among the earliest women's memoirs from the nineteenth century are
stories of a passionate desire to learn to read. Rassundari Devi, born *c.*
1809, taught herself to read by stealing precious moments from her
housework and the responsibilities of caring for twelve children. Later,
she described her craving for knowledge:

I was so immersed in the sea of housework that I was not conscious of what I was
going through day and night. After some time the desire to learn how to read properly grew very strong in me. I was angry with myself for wanting to read books.
Girls did not read . . . That was one of the bad aspects of the old system. The other
aspects were not so bad. People used to despise women of learning . . . In fact, older
women used to show a great deal of displeasure if they saw a piece of paper in the
hands of a woman. But somehow I could not accept this.[1]

Rashsundari's progress was slow but she learned to read, to write, and
finally wrote about her own experiences.

Haimabati Sen (*c.* 1866–1932), born a half-century later, recalled her
childhood in Khulna District of East Bengal:

The outer quarters were my resort, that is where I spent all my time; during the
office hours I stayed in the school room. The teacher was very fond of me. I greatly
enjoyed listening to the lessons. But I had no right to education. Though I lived like
a boy in every respect, in matters of education I remained a woman. It is a popular
superstition in our country that women, if educated, have to suffer widowhood;
hence that path was entirely closed for me. But I was inspired by an eager wish God
had planted in my heart.[2]

Fortunately, a sub-inspector visited the school and heard Haimabati
answer the questions her brothers missed. The sub-inspector spoke to
her father and Haimabati became a regular pupil.

Pandita Ramabai (1858–1922) was awarded the title "Pandita" in
recognition of her great learning. Ramabai's first teacher was her
mother. Anant Padmanabha Dongre, Ramabai's father, was a great
Vedic scholar who decided to educate his wife over the objections of

---

[1] *Women Writing in India*, vol. 1, ed. Tharu and Lalita, p. 199.
[2] *From Child Widow to Lady Doctor: The Intimate Memoir of Dr. Haimabati Sen*, trans.
Tapan Raychaudhuri, ed. Geraldine Forbes and Tapan Raychaudhuri, in press.

the community. Ramabai's rigorous education began at age eight and continued until she was fourteen. She memorized the *Bhagavata Purana* and the *Bhagavad Gita*; then studied Sanskrit grammar and vocabulary. At this time her family was traveling from one pilgrimage site to another and Ramabai learned first-hand how various sects practiced Hinduism.[3]

One cannot generalize from these three cases about women's desire to learn. But given conventional notions about the impropriety, even danger, of women's education we can be certain these headstrong women were a minority. In his Report on the State of Education in Bengal (1836) William Adam wrote: "A superstitious feeling is alleged to exist in the majority of Hindu families, principally cherished by the women and not discouraged by the men, that a girl taught to read and write will soon after marriage become a widow." Adam also commented on the fear, shared by Hindus and Muslims, that a "knowledge of letters" might facilitate female intrigue.[4] Because Hindu women were totally dependent on fathers, then husbands, and finally sons for support, they said prayers and performed rituals to insure longevity for these men. If learning to read would lead to a husband's death, then pursuing knowledge was tantamount to suicide. This was a sex-segregated world; men and women did different work and occupied separate spaces. Women interacted primarily with women and it was women who enforced the prohibition against female education. Many of the women who learned to read before the 1870s have reported hiding their accomplishments from other women. Even if mothers were lenient with daughters, mothers-in-law and the other women in the father-in-law's home were seldom as kind. It is difficult to impute motives to the women who vehemently opposed education. Subjects of a harsh patrilineal, patriarchal system, they were not in a position to oppose prevailing codes. Their survival depended on upholding the status quo and an educated stranger in their midst posed an obvious threat. Those women and girls who were eager to learn had no recourse but to look to the men who controlled their lives.

Missionaries began the first girls' schools but their efforts were soon rivaled by Indian reformers. Despite their valiant efforts, there were no

[3] Nicol Macnicol, *Pandita Ramabai* (Calcutta, Association Press, 1926) pp. 11–13; "Ramabai Pandita", *DNB*, vol. III, pp. 457–9.

[4] Syed Nurullah and J. P. Naik, *History of Education in India: During the British Period* (Bombay, Macmillan, 1943), p. 21; Meredith Borthwick, *The Changing Role of Women*, pp. 60–1.

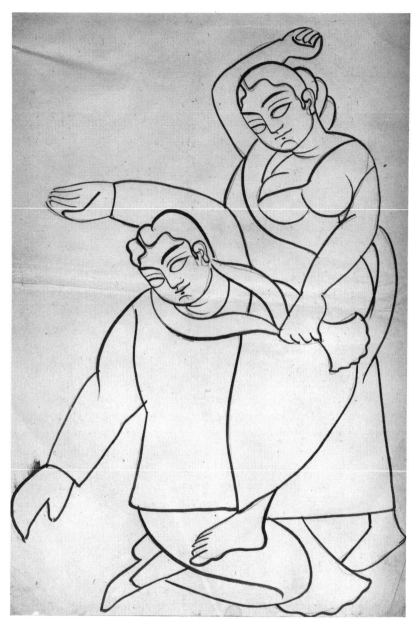

1 Satire on women's changing roles: "Wife assaulting her husband" by
Nibaran Chandra Ghosh, Kaligat, c. 1900

real advances in female education until the second half of the nineteenth century when the government offered financial support. Even then, efforts to organize girls' schools languished until the urban professional elite joined reformers in supporting formal education for girls. In the last quarter of the nineteenth century, institutions proliferated and the number of educated women grew steadily. The debate then turned to what was the most suitable type of education for women. Before the century was over a few women came forward to articulate their ideas about female education. By the twentieth century women were ready to design a curriculum and set up schools for girls.

TRADITIONAL EDUCATION

Traditionally education meant learning to read sacred literature. Among Hindus, members of the priestly caste, brahmins, were learned in all branches of sacred knowledge, while the other twice-born castes (kshatriyas and vaishyas) were given a less rigorous program but also learned practical skills. Shudras and most women were not taught the sacred books but some women were taught to read. Some women from upper-class Vaisnavite families learned to read puranic literature.[5] Muslim girls were expected to learn the Quran and some accounting skills but the strict seclusion observed by upper-class families prohibited their daughters from attending schools. Consequently, what they learned about their religion they learned at home, either from their families or through tutors.[6] At the turn of the century there were only eleven Quran schools for girls in Bengal with 142 pupils.[7]

At the beginning of the nineteenth century, female literacy was extremely low in relation to male literacy. Male literacy, ranging from approximately 6 percent in Bengal to 20 percent in the Deccan, was also low in comparison with Western nations or Japan. Moreover, indigenous schools for boys were on the decline.[8] Boys attended three kinds

[5] Aparna Basu, "Mary Ann Cooke to Mother Theresa: Christian Missionary Women and the Indian Response," *Women and Missions: Past and Present: Anthropological and Historical Perceptions*, ed. Fiona Bowie, Deborah Kirkwood, and Shirley Ardener (Providence, R.I./Oxford, BERG, 1993), p. 190.

[6] Sonia Nishat Amin, "The Early Muslim Bhadramahila: The Growth of Learning and Creativity, 1876–1939," *From the Seams of History*, p. 112.

[7] Usha Chakraborty, *Condition of Bengali Women Around the Second Half of the Nineteenth Century* (Calcutta, Usha Chakraborty, 1963), p. 52.

[8] Aparna Basu, *Essays in the History of Indian Education* (New Delhi, Concept Publishing Co., 1982), pp. 31–2; Nurullah and Naik, *History of Education in India*, pp. 12–13.

of schools: small village schools which taught elementary reading and accounting; higher schools for Hindus, primarily brahmins, which taught Sanskrit grammar, lexicography and literature; and Persian and Arabic schools for Muslims. We do not know how many of these schools there were throughout India, but in Bengal there were approximately 100 traditional institutions per district with a total of 10,800 students. There were 164 Hindu schools in Poona in the 1820s. Aparna Basu, contends that "the state of higher learning among Hindus and Muslims resembled that which existed in Europe before the invention of printing."[9]

Female education was informal and largely limited to practical matters. Women from respectable families often studied classical or vernacular literature as "a pious recreation," and girls from propertied families received some education in keeping accounts.[10] But most females learned only the household arts.

ENGLISH EDUCATION IN INDIA

English education was introduced into India because the East India Company needed clerks and translators. From 1813 the Company set aside some money for education, and after the Charter of 1833 English became the official language. In 1844 Lord Hardinge announced that English-educated Indians would be given preference for government appointments. Free-traders voiced their support for this policy believing it would help develop an Indian population loyal to the British. The missionaries joined the chorus of approval. Eager to convert Indians from influential families, missionaries recognized how much easier it would be with English as the language of professional advancement. Liberals believed in the civilizing influence of Western philosophy and literature. It was only at the end of the century that these men saw the dangerous side of education, that is, its tendency to promote nationalism and political unrest. Then, the government made attempts to control and even curtail education.[11]

Long before the government decided to sponsor English education, Indian gentlemen set up Hindu College in Calcutta. Opened in 1816,

[9] Basu, *Essays*, p. 33.
[10] Kalikinkar Datta, *Survey of India's Social Life and Economic Condition in the Eighteenth Century, (1707–1813)* (Calcutta, Firma K. L. Mukhopadhyay, 1961), pp. 23–4.
[11] Basu, *Essays*, pp. 7–9.

Hindu College was designed to prepare young Indian men for lucrative positions with the East India Company. In the first three decades of the twentieth century Hindu College and similar schools throughout British India depended on the patronage of wealthy Indians and were in direct competition with traditional schools teaching Sanskrit, Persian, and Arabic. As economic patterns changed, patronage for traditional schools disappeared. At about the same time, bright young men decided to study English.[12]

In contrast to support for boys' schools, there was little interest in the education of girls. The colonial government, despite pressure exerted by missionaries and liberals, was unconcerned with female education. The missionaries were interested in female education and schools for girls because, they argued, women needed to be brought into the fold to make conversions permanent. But since men made the decisions, female education was ancillary.[13]

Unmarried female missionaries arrived in India in the 1840s and were assigned to work with women and children. These missionary women, educated and eager to prove their worth, concentrated on converting adult married Indian women to Christianity.[14] They gained entry to households as teachers where they read stories, taught needlework, and attempted to bring their charges to Christ. Rarely were they successful in gaining converts. When it became apparent that these zenana projects were unproductive, the mission authorities substituted girls' schools. Missionary women continued to teach and it was their students, Indian women from Christian families, who became teachers in a number of the new girls' schools.[15]

EARLY SCHOOLS FOR GIRLS

The opening of Hindu College in 1816 was closely followed by the founding of the Calcutta School Society to promote female education. Radha Kanta Deb, the secretary of this society, became a patron of female education and assisted in the formation of the Calcutta Female Juvenile Society (founded in 1819 by Baptists). In 1821, the School

[12] *Ibid.*, p. 14.
[13] Harihar Das, *Life and Letters of Toru Dutt* (London, Humphrey Milford, 1921), p. 8.
[14] Geraldine Forbes, "In Search of the 'Pure Heathen': Missionary Women in Nineteenth Century India," *EPW,* 21, no. 17 (April 26, 1986), pp. ws2–ws8.
[15] Glendora B. Paul, "Emancipation and Education of Indian Women Since 1829," Ph.D. dissertation, University of Pittsburgh (1970).

2 Entrance to Forman Girls' School, Lahore, 1936

Society brought Miss Mary Anne Cooke to Calcutta but could not raise the money to open schools. The Church Missionary Society stepped in, employed Miss Cooke, and opened thirty schools for "respectable" Hindu girls. These schools enjoyed the patronage of Hindu gentlemen and were staffed by brahmin pundits, but they failed to attract girls from the higher castes. The religious instruction deterred prestigious families while pupils from the lower classes or Christian families were lured to the school by gifts of clothing and other items.

The Church Missionary Society was more successful in South India where it opened its first boarding school for girls in Tirunelveli in 1821. By 1840 the Scottish Church Society could claim six schools with a clientele of 200 Hindu girls. By mid-century the missionaries in Madras were instructing nearly 8,000 girls, the majority of whom were Christians, in day schools and boarding schools.[16]

One of the most important schools for girls was the Hindu Balika Vidyalaya opened in 1849 in Calcutta by J. E. Drinkwater Bethune, legal member of the Governor-General's Council and president of the Council of Education. The school was secular, instruction was in Bengali, and the girls were transported in a carriage emblazoned with a Sanskrit verse declaring that a daughter's education was a father's religious duty. Pandit Vidyasagar was appointed school secretary. Bethune persuaded several prominent families to endorse this experiment and by 1850 there were eighty pupils. When Bethune died in 1851, support for the school declined. In 1863 the school had ninety-three girls aged five to seven, three-quarters of whom were from the "lowest class," a clear indication of continuing upper-caste prejudice against female education.[17]

GOVERNMENT SUPPORT OF FEMALE EDUCATION

Lord Dalhousie, Governor-General of India from 1848 to 1856, declared that no single change was likely to produce more important

[16] Dr. (Mrs.) R. Vishalakshmi Neduncheziar, "Education of Girls and Women in Tamilnadu," *Status of Women Souvenir 1973* (Madras, Task Force Sub-Committee on Education, Tamilnadu, 1975), no page numbers.

[17] J. C. Bagal, *Women's Education in Eastern India: The First Phase* (Calcutta, The World Press Private Ltd., 1956), pp. 77–95; N. S. Bose, *The Indian Awakening and Bengal* (Calcutta, Firma K. L. Mukhopadhyay, 1969), pp. 188–9; "Hindoo Women," *Calcutta Review*, 40 (1864), pp. 80–101; "The Bethune Female School," *The Bengalee* (January 13, 1863), p. 13; Borthwick, *Changing Role*, pp. 73–7.

and beneficial consequences than female education.[18] Sir Charles Wood, president of the Board of Control from 1853 to 1855, issued an education despatch in 1854 that detailed a shift in government policy, from providing higher education for the elites to support for mass education in the vernacular. This new focus on a total system of education was to include both sexes. The despatch read:

The importance of female education in India cannot be over-rated; and we have observed with pleasure the evidence which is now afforded of an increased desire on the part of many of the natives to give a good education to their daughters. By this means a far greater proportional impulse is imparted to the educational and moral tone of the people than by the education of men.[19]

The moral and financial support of the colonial authorities was essential to the spread of female education, but did not guarantee schools for girls. Unlike education for males, education for females did not automatically enhance the prestige and financial standing of the family. In fact, the opposite may have been true.

Indian norms and social customs made the British model of schooling difficult, if not impossible. Deeply ingrained notions of sex segregation and, in some areas, of complete seclusion, meant girls had to have female teachers and study in separate institutions. The widely accepted ideal of youthful marriage limited a girl's school-going years. Moreover, the demands on women for food production and nurturing left little time for lessons and studying.

There was a third set of problems associated with the institutions for female education. Indians were unaccustomed to sending their daughters to "schools" yet this was the only practical method of accomplishing the task. Zenana education – education given in the home – was expensive, cumbersome, and largely ineffectual. Schools were the answer but what kind of schools? Who would teach? What would be taught? Which families would choose to send their daughters to school and for how long? If girls were married prior to puberty, could they continue their education as married women? The leaders of Indian society had to respond to these questions – a far more difficult task than providing moral and material support.

[18] Y. B. Mathur, *Women's Education in India, 1813–1966* (Bombay, Asia Publishing, 1973), p. 25. [19] *Ibid.,* p. 29.

REFORMED HINDUISM AND FEMALE EDUCATION

The breakthrough came with the establishment of government schools, such as Bethune's, and schools sponsored by reformist religious institutions. First the Brahmo Samaj, and later the Prarthana Samaj, Arya Samaj, and Theosophical Society all supported female education.

In 1854 there were approximately 626 girls' schools (Bengal: 288, Madras: 256, Bombay: 65, and NWFP and Oudh: 17) with a total of 21,755 students.[20] Obviously these schools were very small and the total number of girls receiving this education was minuscule in relation to the total population. Yet, a shift in attitudes towards female education had taken place.

Indians supported female education because they wanted social and religious reform, or social and financial mobility, or both. The founders of Hindu College and other early schools for boys wanted to advance the opportunities of their own class. In the case of female education, early supporters saw opportunities for social mobility as the demand for educated brides increased. They were also motivated by a desire for social reform, possible only if women as well as men were educated. Many Western-educated Bengali gentlemen undoubtedly wanted to "wean away their own wives and daughters" from various forms of popular culture regarded as licentious and vulgar. This increased the social distance between the "new women" and their less educated sisters and deprived educated middle-class women of an avenue of protest offered by street performers and popular songs.[21] The concern here was not with women as individuals, but with their development as companions to men, as "scientific" nurturers, and as members of civil society.

Members of the Brahmo Samaj, the Bengal-based reform society, led the movement for female education and equality between the sexes. Keshub Chandra Sen, a Brahmo leader, lectured on the importance of female education in 1861 and the following year organized a society for males who supported reforms for women. In 1865, the Brahmo Samaj sponsored the first organization where women met for religious instruction, sewing lessons, and discussions of social issues.[22]

[20] *Ibid.*, p. 26.
[21] Sumantha Banerjee, "Marginalization of Women's Popular Culture in Nineteenth Century Bengal," *Recasting Women: Essays in Colonial History*, pp. 130–1.
[22] Borthwick, *Changing Role*, p. 291.

3 Girls from the Brahmo Samaj by N. B. Pujary, *c.* 1904

The topic of women's education led to a split in the Brahmo Samaj in 1866. That year, Navabidhan (Keshub Sen's breakaway group) welcomed Miss Mary Carpenter to Calcutta. Carpenter's mission was to encourage female education and she was quick to notice the shortage of suitable teachers.[23] She spoke publicly about the problem, presented her proposals to the Governor-General, and helped establish the National Indian Association to promote mutual understanding between Indian and English people. In 1872 Carpenter, Keshub Sen, and another English woman, Annette Akroyd, set up a normal school.[24] Later Akroyd broke with Keshub and worked with another group of Brahmos to established the Hindu Mahila Vidyalaya (Hindu Girls' School). By 1878 this school had merged with the older Bethune School to become Bethune College, an affiliate of Calcutta University. In 1883 Kadambini Basu and Chandramukhi Basu received their BAs from Bethune, becoming the first women graduates in the British Empire.[25]

In Madras it was the Theosophical Society that encouraged female education. Speaking as a leader of the society, Annie Besant (1847–1933) asserted that in ancient times Hindu women were educated and moved freely in society. She urged a return to this "golden age." In England Besant had been identified with women's emancipation since her public lecture on women's suffrage in 1874.[26] Besant had been associated with a number of other movements in England before she read Madame Blavatsky's *Secret Doctrine* in 1889. She then decided to join the theosophists and make India her home. Madame Blavatsky, a founder of the Theosophical Society, viewed child marriage, child widowhood, and sati as perversions of the original Hindu doctrine.[27] When Besant first spoke in India in 1893, she spoke of the greatness of the Indian past and the need to regain that past. Later she focused on specific problems and by 1901 had written an article for the *Indian Ladies Magazine* on the "Education of Women." Besant warned that

[23] Mary Carpenter, *Six Months in India*, 2 vols. (London, Longman, Green and Co., 1868), vol. II, pp. 142–5.
[24] Lord Beveridge, *India Called Them* (London, George Allen and Unwin, 1947), p. 83.
[25] David Kopf, "The Brahmo Idea of Social Reform and the Problem of Female Emancipation in Bengal," *Bengal in the Nineteenth and Twentieth Century,* ed. J. R. McLane (East Lansing, Mich., Asian Studies Center, 1975), pp. 47–50.
[26] Annie Besant, *The Political Status of Women*, 2nd edn. (London, C. Watts, 1885), pp. 1–11 (pamphlet).
[27] H. P. Blavatsky, "Hindu Widow-Marriage," *A Modern Panarion: A Collection of Fugitive Fragments* (London, T. S. Publishing Society, 1895), vol. I, p. 243.

India's fate would be sealed if women were not educated. But Western education was not the answer; it would "unsex" women. Indians should look to their own ideal of womanhood – the Goddess Durga.[28] Besant pledged her efforts to this reform and founded a women's college based on these principles.[29]

In North India female education was encouraged by the Arya Samaj, a reformist Hindu sect which followed the teachings of Swami Dayanand Saraswati. By the end of the nineteenth century, progressive Arya Samajists recognized the importance of involving women in their reform efforts. The Jullundar Samaj opened the Arya Kanya Pathshala (Girls' School) in 1890 with a lady principal in charge.[30]

The Kanya Mahavidyalaya (Girls' Higher School) of Jullundar was opened somewhat later. Both this high school and the elementary girls' school, firmly established by 1892, owed their existence to the efforts of Lala Devraj. He opened his first school for girls in the family home, supported it through the sale of "waste paper," and staffed it with teachers who were partially compensated with food from his mother's kitchen. As public acceptance for the idea of female education grew so did the school's enrollment. Before long a cadre of experienced women teachers and school administrators had designed special instructional materials. This institution occupied a special place in the community and "became a catalyst for various kinds of change relating to women in [the] Punjab."[31]

THE PROGRESS OF WOMEN'S EDUCATION

Between 1849, when Bethune School opened, and 1882, when the Indian Education (Hunter) Commission reviewed the progress of education in India, serious efforts had been made to develop primary schools for girls and teacher-training institutions. Higher education for women and co-education were still contentious issues.[32] Faced with the

---

[28] "Mrs. Besant on Indian Womanhood," *ILM*, 1, no. 7 (January, 1902), pp. 195–7; "Indian Women," *MR*, 25 (1919), pp. 271–2.

[29] Arthur H. Nethercot, *The Last Four Lives of Annie Besant* (Chicago, University of Chicago Press, 1963), pp. 17, 55, 73; "Annie Besant," *DNB*, vol. I, pp. 51–3.

[30] Kenneth W. Jones, *Arya Dharma: Hindu Consciousness in Nineteenth Century Punjab* (Delhi, Manohar, 1976), pp. 104–5.

[31] Madhu Kishwar, "Arya Samaj and Women's Education: Kanya Mahavidyalaya," *EPW*, 21, no. 17 (April 16, 1986), pp. ws9–ws24; Kumari Lajjavati, "A Pioneer in Women's Education," *ISR*, 45 (June 1, 1945), pp. 134–5.

[32] Premila Thackersey, *Education of Women: A Key to Progress* (New Delhi, Ministry of Education and Youth Services, 1970), p. 6.

4 Indian girls at school in Madras, by R. Venkiah Bros, *c.* 1930

fact that 98 percent of school-age girls were not in school, authors of the Hunter Commission Report recommended more liberal grants-in-aid for girls' schools than for boys' and special scholarships and prizes for girls. In the next two decades higher education expanded rapidly; whereas there were only six women in Indian universities in 1881–82, by the turn of the century there were 264. During the same time period secondary school enrollment rose from 2,054 to 41,582.[33]

The story of women's education in the period following the Hunter Commission and the end of the century can be told through the work of three pioneer educationalists – Pandita Ramabai Saraswati, founder of the Sharada Sadan in Bombay and Poona (1889), Mataji Tapaswini who began the Mahakali Pathshala of Calcutta (1893), and D. K. Karve who began a school for widows in Poona (1896). These three examples are particularly significant because they represent efforts to build female schools distinct from those of the religious reform organizations. These were not secular public schools in the contemporary sense; in fact, they were all narrowly caste-, class-, and community-based.

---

[33] Thackersey, *Education of Women*, pp. 1–11; Mathur, pp. 40–4.

These three examples are especially worthy of attention because they highlight the involvement of women in structuring and defining female education.

PANDITA RAMABAI

Pandita Ramabai was truly remarkable as a pioneer in women's education and rebel champion of women's rights. Her father supervised her education and allowed her to remain unmarried. When her father and mother died, Ramabai was sixteen years old, unmarried, and able to read Sanskrit. She and her brother traveled throughout India lecturing on female education and social reform. The Calcutta elite were enchanted and bestowed on her the name "Saraswati" – the Goddess of Learning – and called her "Pandita" because she seemed as learned as other brahmin pandits. Other audiences were outraged and they jeered and booed when she attempted to speak.[34]

Ramabai's brother died in Calcutta and she married his close friend, Bipen Behari Das Medhavi (a shudra by caste). The next year, at age twenty-three, Ramabai gave birth to a daughter. Unfortunately her husband died the following year.

Returning to Poona, Ramabai began to work with reformers to educate women through the Arya Mahila Samaj (Aryan's Women's Society).[35] While in Poona she gave evidence before the Hunter Commission and stressed the urgent need for women doctors and teachers. Determined to learn English and study medicine, Ramabai sought help from members of the Anglo-Catholic Community of St. Mary the Virgin whose mother house was at Wantage in Oxfordshire, England. They were able to give her some assistance while the balance of her expenses were met through the sale of *Stri Dharma Neeti* ("Morals for Women"), her book urging women to take charge of their

[34] Jyotsna Kapur, "Women and the Social Reform Movement in Maharashtra," M.Phil thesis, Delhi University (1989), p. 79.

[35] *The Letters and Correspondence of Pandita Ramabai*, compiled by Sister Geraldine, ed. A. B. Shah (Bombay, Maharashtra State Board of Literature and Culture, 1977), pp. 15–18; Rajas Krishnarao Dongre and Josephine F. Patterson, *Pandita Ramabai: A Life of Faith and Prayer* (Madras, Christian Literature Society, 1969), pp. 6–10; Muriel Clark, *Pandita Ramabai* (London, Paternoster Bldg., 1920), pp. 24–5; "Pandita Ramabai," *Men and Women of India*, 1, no. 6 (June, 1905), pp. 316–19. Meera Kosambi, "Women, Emancipation and Equality: Pandita Ramabai's Contribution to Women's Cause," *EPW*, 23, no. 44 (October 29, 1988), pp. ws38– ws49; Meera Kosambi, *At the Intersection of Gender Reform and Religious Belief* (Bombay, SNDT, Research Center for Women's Studies, Gender Series, 1993).

own lives. Ramabai, her young daughter, and a traveling companion, Anandibai Bhagat, left for England in 1883. Soon after the three of them had settled at Wantage, Ramabai declared she was unwilling to convert to Christianity. Some months later Anandibai committed suicide (the records here become very elusive) leaving Ramabai extremely shaken.

Ramabai was only twenty-five years of age and had already watched her parents, her brother, her husband, and her closest friend die. It was at this time, alone with her small daughter in a strange country, that Ramabai decided to accept baptism.[36] She continued her studies until 1886 when she decided to sail for America to attend the graduation ceremonies of her cousin Anandibai Joshi.

To finance this trip and popularize her cause Ramabai wrote *The High Caste Hindu Woman*. Ten thousand copies of this book were sold before Ramabai had left America. In 1887 Boston admirers set up a Ramabai Association to support her work in India. She traveled throughout the United States and Canada studying educational, philanthropic, and charitable institutions and lecturing to various groups. By May of 1888, she had collected over $30,000 in the name of her association.[37]

In India Pandita Ramabai established Sharada Sadan (Home of Wisdom), a school for widows, in Bombay. This was to be a non-sectarian school where all the caste rules of brahmins were scrupulously observed. It attracted some high-caste Hindu widows, among them Godubai (renamed Anandibai after her marriage to D. K. Karve) but generally the Hindu community remained suspicious of Ramabai's motives.

Ramabai attempted to forestall criticism by forming an Executive Committee composed of reformers who were known as staunch Hindus. This plan did not work and less than one year later Bombay newspapers carried articles critical of Ramabai and her school. When financial problems forced her to move the school to Poona, the newspaper *Kesari* charged her with converting widows to Christianity. Ramabai's admitted crime was allowing widows to attend her personal prayer meetings. By 1893 twenty-five girls were withdrawn. But there was no dearth of widows in need of shelter and before long Ramabai had other students. By 1900 the Sharada Sadan had trained eighty women who were able to earn their own living through teaching or nursing.[38]

---

[36] *Letters and Correspondence*, p. 14.   [37] *Ibid.*, pp. xx–xxi.   [38] *Ibid.*, pp. 257–362.

Ramabai's second school, Mukti, was established thirty miles outside of Poona at Kedgaon following the famine that began in 1897. She began taking women and children who were victims of famine into Sharada Sadan where she fed and clothed them, and enrolled them in her school. Attempting to control the plague, the government placed restrictions on the movement of people; in Poona the city magistrate placed a limit on the number of inmates in Sharada Sadan. Since she could not keep famine victims in Poona, Ramabai took her charges to Kedgaon where she had purchased 100 acres of land. By 1900 this venture had grown into a major institution housing 2,000 women and children attending school and involved in industrial training and production. Financing for Mukti came from an American committee which willingly approved all her schemes.[39]

Given a free hand, Ramabai urged the inmates of her home to become Christians and developed a unique educational program to suit their needs. Her own version of Christianity was doctrinally eclectic, combining ideas she had learned from the sisters at Wantage, and from Roman Catholic, Jewish, and Indian Christian friends. Ramabai saw caste as the great flaw in Hindu society. It led to false valuing of the intellect and denigration of physical work. Caste associations promoted narrow self-interest and inhibited the development of a democratic spirit.

Ramabai designed a remedial curriculum. Literature selected for its emphasis on moral models would engender a spirit of caring; classes in physiology and botany were included to teach students about their own bodies and the physical world in which they lived. Industrial training was included – in printing, carpentry, tailoring, masonry, wood-cutting, weaving and needlework – as well as training in farming and gardening. All students were required to join "unions" or societies such as the Temperance Union or the Christian Endeavor Society in an effort to break down caste barriers and develop new loyalties based on interest. As members of these societies, the children learned simple parliamentary rules and were encouraged to take charge of their own affairs.[40]

Ramabai's educational work impressed contemporaries, but her connection with Christianity has obfuscated her contribution to women's education. An acknowledged Christian when hatred of the

---

[39] *Ibid.*, pp. 342–416.   [40] *Ibid.*, p. 412.

ruling power was growing daily, her work angered some of the most powerful men in western India. Ramabai believed the intensity of their anger was related to the fact that many of her pupils came from the higher castes. She argued that these men would have remained unconcerned if her work were confined to low-caste women.[41]

There were many issues that provoked Ramabai's sharp and unpopular comments. When she heard about the Rukhmabai case, she exploded in angry denunciations of both the British and Indian men. Rukhmabai, married as a child, had been tried and sentenced to prison (but was never imprisoned) because she refused to have a conjugal relationship with her husband (see chapter 3). Ramabai wrote:

Our only wonder is that a defenseless woman like Rukhmabai dared to raise her voice in the face of the powerful Hindu law, the mighty British Government, the 129,000,000 men, the 330,000,000 gods of the Hindus; all these have conspired together to crush her into nothingness. We cannot blame the English Government for not defending a helpless woman; it is only fulfilling its agreement made with the male population of India.[42]

Ramabai's greatest legacy was her effort, the first in India, to educate widows and the pupils she left behind to carry on her work.

MATAJI MAHARANI TAPASWINI

The Mahakali Pathshala (Great Mother Kali School) of Bengal stands in sharp contrast to Pandita Ramabai's schools, with their missionary connection and foreign support. Founded in Calcutta in 1893 by Her Holiness Mataji Maharani Tapaswini, this school and its many branches has been styled a "genuine Indian attempt" at developing female education.[43] This school received no financial assistance from foreigners and employed no foreign teachers. Founders of the institution accepted the "school" model for female education, but opposed co-education and the use of one syllabus for both sexes. Their aim was to educate "girls on strictly national lines in the hope that they might regenerate Hindu society." This was a project consistent with those of nationalist "revivalists," who, in the historian Tanika Sarkar's view, did not automatically oppose reform "in the name of resisting colonial

---

[41] Ibid., p. 257.

[42] Ibid., p. 257; Kosambi, "Women, Emancipation and Equality," pp. ws44–ws45.

[43] Minna S. Cowan, The Education of the Women of India (Edinburgh, Oliphant, Anderson and Ferrier, 1912), p. 113.

knowledge."[44] Despite their differences with the liberal reformers, they too believed in the relationship between progress and female education and looked to a future where Indian women would play a larger role in the affairs of the country.

Gangabai (Mataji Maharani Tapaswini), a brahmin woman of the Deccan who had learned Sanskrit and studied sacred literature, opened her first school with thirty pupils.[45] She had come to Calcutta with a mission: to promote female education in harmony with Hindu religious and moral principles. Unlike Pandita Ramabai, Gangabai believed that Hindu society could be regenerated from within. Her notion of an ideal education for women was translated into a syllabus which included: knowledge of sacred literature and history; an understanding of the myths and legends that spoke of the duties of the daughter, wife, daughter-in-law, and mother; and practical skills such as cooking and sewing.[46] This syllabus was praised by "Hindoo gentlemen of the middle-class" who believed that much of the female education then in existence "demoralized and denationalized" young Hindu women.[47] Cooking lessons were especially popular in light of the prevalent belief that educated girls avoided the kitchen. Financial support for this institution grew rapidly and within ten years there were twenty-three branches with 450 students. As the school expanded it published its own Bengali and Sanskrit textbooks. Gangabai turned more and more to supervision while the actual administration of the school was left in the hands of an illustrious board of trustees presided over by the Maharaja of Darbhanga, Bengal's largest landlord.

This school proved immensely popular. Patrons approved of the emphasis on religious injunctions, domestic skills, and strict purdah. Although the original curriculum included very little formal reading and writing, this gradually changed. In 1948 the Mahakali Pathshala was affiliated to Calcutta University and by that time all that remained of the original curriculum was the performance of a few *pujas* (religious rituals).[48] In

[44] Tanika Sarkar, "Rhetoric Against the Age of Consent," *EPW*, 28, no. 36 (September 4, 1993), pp. 1869–78.
[45] M. M. Kaur, *The Role of Women in the Freedom Movement (1857–1947)* (New Delhi, Sterling, 1968), p. 85. Kaur claims that Maharani Tapaswini was a niece of the Rani of Jhansi. [46] Kaur, *The Role of Women*, p. 145.
[47] "The Mahakali Pathshala," *The Statesman* (February 3, 1985), p. 7.
[48] Latika Ghose, "Social and Educational Movements for Women and by Women, 1820–1950," *Bethune School and College Centenary Volume, 1849–1949*, ed. Dr. Kalidas Nag (Calcutta, S. N. Guha Ray, 1950), p. 146; Cowan, *The Education of Women in India*, p. 113; "The Mahakali Pathshala," p. 7.

the early years of the twentieth century the existence of this school and its popularity were regarded as indicators that the conservative elements of society, at least in Bengal, had given their approval to the concept of female education.[49]

DHONDO KESHAV KARVE

In the 1890s Dhondo Keshav Karve established a number of female schools in Poona. In his autobiography, *Looking Back*, Karve reconstructs his personal history to explain how his experiences led him to build a school for widows in 1896. Other accounts tell the story of Godubai Joshi (later Anandibai), a child widow who became Karve's second wife. She dreamed of setting up a widow's home soon after she became Pandita Ramabai's first pupil. What may well have been the culmination of the life-long dream of two people has been known as "Karve's Home." Anandibai joked about this when she was very old:

Sometimes in fun I tell him that although people call him Maharshi, some of the credit is due to me. For if I had not managed the family affairs and set him free to carry out his public activities, he could not have achieved so much.[50]

Karve's association with reform movements dated back to his college years. After graduation from Elphinstone College he taught mathematics in three different high schools in Bombay before accepting a position at Fergusson College in Poona. There he was elected a life member of the Deccan Educational Society.[51] When his wife died, he decided he would marry a widow and chose Godubai, the twenty-two-year-old sister of his college friend. People in his home town excommunicated him and persecuted his mother. These actions shocked Karve and caused him to question remarriage as a way of helping child widows. At the same time he became increasingly interested in education as a way of assisting widows to become financially independent. In 1896 he opened a shelter for widows that became a school.

The curriculum in this school was designed to make young widows employable and self-sufficient. Because schools for girls were scarce, Karve was asked to admit unmarried girls as well. To accommodate this new clientele, Karve set up the Mahilya Vidyalaya (Girls' School) to

[49] *ILM*, 3, no. 1 (July, 1903), p. 16; *ILM*, 3, no. 6 (December, 1903), pp. 194–5.
[50] D. D. Karve, ed. and trans. *The New Brahmins: Five Maharashtrian Families*, ed. assistance, Ellen E. McDonald (Berkeley, University of California Press, 1963), p. 79.
[51] "(Maharshi) Dhondo Keshav Karve," *DNB*, vol. I, pp. 299–301.

develop "good wives, good mothers, good neighbors." He believed that widows needed an education "that would make them economically independent and would enable them to think for themselves"[52] but unmarried girls needed an education that would reinforce their dependence.

Parvatibai Athavali, Anandibai's widowed sister, played an important role in the growth and expansion of Karve's schools. Married at age eleven, Parvatibai became a widow at age twenty, the third widowed daughter in her father's home. Rejecting all discussion of remarriage, Parvatibai declared her wish to study and "do some work of importance."[53] After receiving her education in Karve's school, she became a teacher and then the superintendent. Parvatibai, a voluntarily tonsured widow, orthodox in her food habits, spoke publicly against widow remarriage.[54] Through her, Karve gained credibility with conservatives who previously characterized him as a radical because of his own remarriage. In her public lectures, Parvatibai insisted a woman's true mission in life was to marry. She supported the curriculum of Karve's school with instruction in the vernacular languages and emphasis on childcare and homecraft. Traditionally, these subjects had been taught by the older women in the households, but the increased complexity of women's work made formal education necessary.[55] Parvatibai warned women against rejecting their "natural roles" to enter the tyrannical market place. Yet she had entered the market place and from her own account not unwillingly. She explained her own life as follows:

I felt that a widow who had one or two children and who had had some actual experience of the happiness of domestic life, if she were able to do some work of importance would not be tempted to enter again into the duties of a married life. In accordance with this idea, I settled on my ideal of life.[56]

In her description of the ideal education for a woman and the ideal life-course, Parvatibai seemed to ignore the lesson of her own life. Like Karve, she regarded public roles for women as an aberration rather than the norm.

Karve spent much of his money on his institutions and even cashed in his life insurance policy of Rs 5,000 to raise funds for the home.

---

[52] Quoted in D. D. Karve, *The New Brahmins*, p. 51.
[53] Parvati Athavale, *My Story, The Autobiography of a Hindu Widow*, trans. Revd. Justin E. Abbott (New York, G. P. Putnam, 1930), p. 30.
[54] Dhondo Keshav Karve, *Looking Back* (Poona, Hinge Stree-Shikshan Samastha, 1936), p. 75. [55] Athavale, *My Story*, p. 133. [56] *Ibid.*, p. 30.

Anandibai, now the mother of his child, was alarmed because she knew that if Karve died she would be refused even domestic employment. Many brahmin widows found employment as cooks or maidservants but if they married a second time they were considered unclean. By her own account Anandibai, "cried, quarreled with him, abused him" but could not get him to budge. Karve was similarly neglectful of their day-to-day needs. Finally Anandibai realized that for survival she would have to seek employment. She completed a course in midwifery and earned enough to provide for the family's needs.[57]

Karve's third institution for women was the Women's University founded in 1916. He had heard of the Women's University in Japan and concluded that this model would be more suitable for India than the Western co-educational university. As president of the National Social Conference in 1915 he said: "we must recognize that both national and social economy require that women should occupy a station of their own distinct from that of men ... but that the office they have to fill is different, though equal – perhaps greater in importance."[58] All courses at the women's university were conducted in the vernacular, special subjects like home science were included, and it was "possible for women to avoid difficult subjects like mathematics and physical science."[59] This institution limped along for the first few years until it was adopted by Sir Vithaldas Thackersey who contributed Rs 1,500,000 in 1920 with the stipulation that the university be named after his mother (thereby becoming Shreemati Nathibai Damodar Thackersey Indian Women's University or SNDT) and relocated in Bombay.[60]

THE EARLY TWENTIETH CENTURY

By the turn of the century the number of schools for girls and school enrollment had risen dramatically. By the end of World War I, there were educational institutions for women in all parts of the country, and enrollments tripled at the school level and quintupled in universities.[61] Parents now had more options: they could choose the type of institution, the curriculum, even the language of instruction. These alterna-

---

[57] Karve, *Looking Back*, pp. 77–82.   [58] *Ibid.*, p. 104.
[59] *Ibid.*, pp. 95–106; D. D. Karve, *The New Brahmins*, p. 56.
[60] G. L. Chakravarkar, *Dhondo Keshav Karve* (New Delhi, Publications Division, Government of India, 1970), pp. 169–87.   [61] Basu, *Essays*, p. 14.

tives assuaged the fears of conservatives and liberals, the religious and the non-religious, those who desired radical change and traditionalists, anglophiles and anglophobes. Institution-builders like Karve had effectively argued that female education was the ideal method of smoothing over the rough spots in the transition from tradition to modernity and his successors continued to echo his reasoning:

In the eyes of men of forethought and ambition, a woman trained on these lines to the profession of wifehood, is a far more desirable companion than an amateur wife. The training which a girl gets in her own home and under her own mother in India is admirable as far as it goes, but modern life has introduced many complexities to deal with for which a regular and systematic training is necessary.[62]

Maharani Tapaswini and K. D. Karve were educating young women from conservative homes to become, as they argued, better wives and mothers in a modern world. To gain the support of conservative communities, they developed curricula dominated by home science and religious lore. And their rhetoric matched their curricula. Karve may have educated young widows to be self-supporting but he was clear that unmarried girls needed to be taught how to become good wives and mothers. Maharani Tapaswini was not at all interested in education for employment.

Pandita Ramabai stands in direct contrast to these two educators. She was critical of her own society and renounced Hinduism to become a Christian. She built a successful school in terms of numbers but she relied for both material and psychological support on foreign missionaries. They sent her money and praised her while her own community ostracized her. Ramabai wanted to make women capable of supporting themselves. It was an appealing idea as long as her focus was lower-class women; upper class/caste families were unwilling to contemplate economic independence for their wives and daughters.

Between 1900 and 1920 "new women," that is, women who were the beneficiaries of the social reforms and educational efforts of the nineteenth century, stepped forward to begin their own schools. They too were aware of conservative attitudes towards female education, but the picture had changed considerably. The demand for female education was growing steadily and what parents wanted, it seemed, was reassurance that these new schools observed "traditional" customs. To illus-

---

[62] "Thackesay (sic) Women's University Convocation," Sir Visvesvaraya's convocation address, June 29, 1940, *IAR*, 1 (January–June, 1940), (Calcutta, Annual Register, n.d.), p. 438.

trate the change I will sketch the educational efforts of two women: Begum Rokeya and Sister Subbalakshmi.

BEGUM ROKEYA SAKHAWAT HOSSAIN

In 1909 Begum Rokeya Sakhawat Hossain (1880–1932) began an institution for Muslim girls in the district town of Bhagalpur, Bihar. She set up this school soon after her husband's death but his relations were offended. Driven out of her home by her step-daughter, Begum Rokeya closed the school and moved to Calcutta where she opened another school, Sakhawat Memorial Girls' School, in 1911. Although this was not the first school set up by a Muslim woman for Muslim girls, Begum Rokeya's systematic and undaunted devotion to this project has earned her the title of pioneer. This school, with Urdu as its language of instruction, was designed and organized for students who observed purdah even though Begum Rokeya wrote and spoke publicly about the evils of this custom.[63]

Begum Rokeya was fortunate, by her own account, in having an elder brother and a husband who encouraged her interest in education. Her elder sister Karimunnessa had not been so lucky. When it was discovered that Karimunnessa had learned to read English, she was sent to live under the watchful eye of her grandmother until her marriage could be arranged. To be on the safe side, Rokeya's elder brother taught her to read English in the dead of night. Syed Sakhawat Hossain, her husband, was a widower who had been educated in the West. He looked to his young wife for companionship and soon after their wedding gave her lessons in English and encouraged her to write essays. At age twenty-one, only three years after their marriage, Rokeya was publishing articles about women's condition. Over the years she wrote a number of articles, short stories, and novels in which

[63] Sources on Begum Rokeya include *Inside Seclusion: The Avarodhbasini of Rokeya Sakhawat Hossain,* ed. and trans. Roshan Jahan (Dhaka, Bangladesh, BRAC Printers, 1981); Ghulam Murshid, *Reluctant Debutante* (Rajshahi, Bangladesh, Rajshahi University, 1983); Amin, "The Early Muslim Bhadramahila," pp. 107–48; Sonia Nishat Amin, "The World of Muslim Women in Colonial Bengal: 1876–1939," Ph.D. dissertation, University of Dhaka (1993); Sonia Nishat Amin, "Rokeya Sakhawat Hossain and the Legacy of the 'Bengal' Renaissance," *Journal of Asiatic Society,* Bangladesh, 34, no. 2 (December, 1989), pp. 185–92; Sonia Nishat Amin, "The New Woman in Literature and the Novels of Nojibur Rahman and Rokeya Sakhawat Hossain," *Infinite Variety: Women in Society and Literature,* ed. Firdous Azim and Niaz Zaman (Dhaka, University Press Limited, 1994), pp. 119–41.

she developed her ideas on the need to awaken women to their oppression and the role of education in this process.

In three of her essays, "Ardhangi" ("The Female Half"), "Griha" ("The House"), and "Borka" (or *burqah* – "The Veil"), Rokeya commented on women's asymmetrical development, lack of economic means, and confinement for the sake of male honor. In "Sugrihini" ("The Ideal Housewife") she pointed out that education would help women fulfill their traditional roles knowledgeably and professionally and hence contribute to the progress of the nation. Additionally, education would make it possible for women to grow and develop in step with their menfolk.

Begum Rokeya's school conformed, in curriculum and purdah restrictions, to the schools for Muslim girls in the Punjab and United Provinces.[64] Emphasis was placed on literacy and practical subjects such as handicrafts, home science, and gardening. The curriculum in Begum Rokeya's school also included physical fitness training. But this was the only deviation from an educational program designed to produce good wives and mothers: companions and help-mates to their husbands and teachers for their children.

The strictest rules of female seclusion were observed in transporting the girls to and from the school and there was only slight modification (curtains replacing closed shutters) when the young pupils vomited and fainted in the hot, airless carriage.[65] Inside the school the girls covered their heads. This was a new form of modest attire, suitable for the modernizing women now entering new spaces where neither the *burqah*, designed as outdoor wear, nor the clothes worn inside the home were suitable. The new head coverings signified concern with both modesty and modernity.

While Begum Rokeya's school conformed to rules of female seclusion, she wrote stinging criticisms of the practice. In addition to her essay on the *burqah*, she wrote *Sultana's Dream* (1905), a short story in which women ran the world and men hid indoors, and *Avarodhbasini* ("The Secluded Ones") (1929), forty-seven serialized reports documenting the custom of purdah. Her satirical writings on female seclusion were meant to inform an audience ignorant of the real tragedy of purdah (her own aunt was killed by a train because she

---

[64] Gail Minault, "Purdah's Progress: The Beginnings of School Education for Indian Muslim Women," *Individuals and Ideals in Modern India*, ed. J. P. Sharma (Calcutta, Firma K. L. Mukhopadhyaya, 1982), pp. 76–97. [65] Jahan, *Inside Seclusion*, pp. 33–5.

would not cry out for help). Seclusion, Begum Rokeya wrote, "is not a gaping wound, hurting people. It is rather a silent killer like carbon monoxide gas."[66] She denied this custom had any basis in the Quran or Shari'ah (the Muslim religious law).

Rokeya's campaign was unpopular. Accused of being both pro-Christian and a Europhile, Rokeya attracted more hostility when she endorsed Katherine Mayo's *Mother India*. But her school remained open, attended by Muslim girls from good families. Apparently her central argument, that neglect of female education would ultimately threaten Islamic culture, struck a responsive chord.

SISTER SUBBALAKSHMI

At about the same time that Begum Rokeya opened her school for Muslim girls in Calcutta, Sister Subbalakshmi (1886–1969) established a school for young high-caste widows in Madras. Sister Subbalakshmi's concern was society's discarded child widows. Her plan was to transform these unfortunate and inauspicious women into useful and valued members of society.[67]

Prior to her own marriage at age eleven, Subbalakshmi had received four and a half years of formal schooling. Her husband died shortly after their wedding and she returned to her parents' home in Rishyiyur, Tanjore District. Her parents decided not to burden her with all the restrictions normally placed on widows and instead arranged to send her to school. Their community reacted so violently that Subramania Iyer, Subbalakshmi's father, decided to move. In Madras, Subramania Iyer taught his daughter English at home and then sent her to a convent school. The nuns' dedication so impressed the young Subbalakshmi that she resolved to devote her life to educating widows. Although she never became a Christian, she was affectionately known as "Sister Subbalakshmi" in recognition of her dedication to her chosen work.

Subbalakshmi completed her matriculation and enrolled in Presidency College, Madras University. As the first Hindu widow in

---

[66] *Ibid.*, p. 20.
[67] Monica Felton, *A Child Widow's Story* (London, Victor Gollancz, 1966); *Women Pioneers in Education (Tamilnadu)* (Madras, Society for the Promotion of Education in India, 1975); interview with Mrs. Soundarain, Madras (January 22, 1976); letter from Rabindranath Tagore to Miss M. F. Prager, Eur. Mss., B 183, IOOLC; interview with Sister Sublakshami (*sic*) (December 10, 1930), RWC, box 28; Malathi Ramanathan, *Sister R. Subbalakshmi: Social Reformer and Educationalist* (Bombay, Lok Vangmaya Griha, 1989).

Madras to study for a BA, she was threatened with excommunication, harassed in the streets, and ostracized in the classroom. By 1911 she had completed her BA degree and was ready to begin her life's work. She set up her first school in her father's home in a Madras suburb and began with a class of four brahmin widows.

Subbalakshmi's interest in helping widows coincided with that of Miss Christina Lynch (later Mrs. Drysdale), the Irish feminist who was appointed inspectress of female education in Coimbatore. Miss Lynch was deeply troubled by the difficulty of finding "suitable" (high-caste) teachers for the schools. At the same time she was aware that Madras had over 22,000 widows between the ages of five and fifteen, many of them brahmins. Meeting with Subbalakshmi's father, Miss Lynch explained that she had worked out a plan whereby the government would support a home for young brahmin widows willing to be trained as teachers. Meanwhile, Sister Subbalakshmi was pursuing the same scheme with her friends and relations. In 1912 the Sarada Ladies Union was formed as a women's club to provide its members with an opportunity to hear lectures, discuss new ideas, and collect money for a brahmin girls' school.

In 1912 the government agreed to support a boarding school for training teachers. The government would pay the rent and give scholarships to three girls; the remainder of the operating expenses had to be met through donations and fees. In order to make this plan more acceptable to critics of education for Hindu widows, Miss Lynch proposed shifting the school from a liberal section of the city to the more orthodox Triplicane. This meant Subbalakshmi had to locate a "home" for the widows. After an extensive search she finally settled on the Ice House, the old warehouse along the beach once used to store ice from Boston. The Ice House was slowly made habitable for the thirty-five girls who by this time had joined Subbalakshmi. As Sister Subbalakshmi commented, "There was a lot of gossip and ill-talk" about the large number of girl widows and female staff who occupied the Ice House without male protection. The presence of so many inauspicious women walking about forced local people to modify their schedules. Subbalakshmi wrote:

I remember how the orthodox elders in a well-to-do family wanted the bridegroom's procession either before 9 a.m. or after 10 a.m. so that there would be no contact (seeing) the widows on their way to school.[68]

[68] By Sister Subbalakshmi, n.d. enclosed in a letter from R. Tagore, Eur. Mss., B 183, IOOLC.

The school's curriculum was set by the government. The aim was to train these women as teachers: first, they were prepared for regular classes, then they completed the syllabus for matriculation, and finally, they entered Queen Mary's College (begun in 1914 as the first college for women in Madras). In 1922 the Lady Willingdon Training College and Practice School, an institution for teacher training, opened with Sister Subbalakshmi as principal. At this institution Sister Subbalakshmi was able to implement some of her ideas on education. The college offered three programs: post-graduate training for potential high school teachers, secondary training for teaching through the eighth grade, and training for elementary teachers. English was emphasized (because teachers who knew English were in demand), some vocational subjects were required to instill the value of working with the hands, a training course in physical education was available and popular, and Hindu and Christian priests offered moral and religious instruction. Before long Sister Subbalakshmi was compelled to open Sarada Vidyalaya, a high school and boarding school for adult widows. This facility was necessary because the Ice House did not accept widows over age eighteen even though the age of marriage was gradually shifting upward and the concept of widows working as teachers was gaining acceptance.

The boarding school was run in strict conformity with orthodox Hindu customs. In the early days of the school, Sister Subbalakshmi denounced remarriage. Her widowed aunt, V. S. Valambal Ammal, was described by a visitor to the home as a woman in "disfigured [shorn hair] condition" wearing a white sari and performing a traditional *puja* (act of worship). Mrs. Drysdale utilized her inspection tours to locate high-caste widows and would often pay the train fare of reluctant fathers who wanted to see for themselves how the institution was run.[69]

Sister Subbalakshmi understood the importance of running the boarding school for widows in accordance with orthodox customs and caste rules. At the same time her own life was one of rebellion against the accepted role for a widow. She defied caste rules by opening a school for the fisherfolk in the area of the Ice House. When she was warned that as a government servant she could not join the Women's Indian Association, Sister Subbalakshmi continued to attend branch meetings while scrupulously avoiding the more public annual confer-

[69] *Ibid.*

ences. When the Women's Indian Association and the All-India Women's Conference began their campaigns in support of the Child Marriage Restraint Bill, Sister Subbalakshmi lectured against the custom and gave evidence before the Joshi Committee about the harmful effects of youthful marriage. Her activities suggest that she was idealistic yet shrewd. She was willing to compromise as long as it served her long-range goals.

Spiritually, Sister Subbalakshmi was deeply attracted to Swami Vivekananda and the Ramakrishna Mission. She regarded Ramakrishna and his disciple Vivekananda as the first religious reformers to be deeply concerned with the woman question. Although the model of the Catholic nun attracted her in her childhood, as an adult Sister Subbalakshmi drew her spiritual sustenance and philosophy of action from reformed Hinduism.

CONCLUSIONS

What these examples accentuate is the extent to which successful experiments in female education were a product of the labor of educated Indian women. Many of the schools were geographically limited, communally bound, and caste-sensitive. They were schools for females only, the teachers were females, and curricula were geared to gender-specific socialization.

Looking at female education and its products in the second decade of the twentieth century one can begin to answer the question of how far female education had achieved the results desired by the three groups who had promoted it: the British rulers, Indian male reformers, and educated Indian women.

The British wanted their civil servants to have educated wives to further ensure their loyalty. Uneducated wives (or wives who were educated only in the vernacular and traditional subjects) would split the household into two worlds. Just as the British were certain that rebellious plots were hatched and nurtured in inaccessible zenanas, they believed English-educated Indian women would raise their children to be anglophiles. Despite this dream, education did not promote loyalty among women except those married to civil servants. They became help-mates to their husbands but there were some renegades even among this group. Many women became critics of British policy in India.

Reform-minded Indian men were interested in developing a progressive society. If women were educated, Indian society could no longer be characterized as decadent and backward. On a personal level, these men yearned for companionship and the support an educated woman could give them as they advanced professionally. They wanted women to take responsibility for helping the less fortunate members of their communities. On the national level, they envisioned women in charge of social reform while men pursued politics.

Educated women accompanied their husbands to their civil service postings, joined husbands who had left their ancestral homes, opened schools, and entertained district magistrates. The two-person career was finally possible with the appearance of the carefully groomed, English-speaking wife. Women took over the task of social reform at a time when men were becoming obsessed with political action and worried that social reform might complicate the task of arousing the masses. While men feared education might cause women to "go too far," female educators promised to graduate "professionalized housewives." The educational system was overwhelmingly conservative, but the education of women had unexpected and unanticipated consequences.

The first generation of educated women found a voice: they wrote about their lives and about the conditions of women. The second generation acted. They articulated the needs of women, critiqued their society and the foreign rulers, and developed their own institutions. That these institutions were often as conservative as those designed by men should not be taken as a sign that these women wished to preserve the status quo. Rather it should be taken as evidence that they understood their subordinate position very well.

Through their efforts to develop institutions women learned the limits of their power. Deviant behavior was severely punished. Within households girls who wanted to learn were teased and ostracized. Those who attended schools were stoned in the street and marginalized in the classroom if they attended boys' schools. They were harassed when they sought to practice their professions. By straining for new lives, these "new women" learned where the boundaries were and just how far they could go. But this was a dynamic process; women were becoming educated and then becoming the educators. The boundaries of the early nineteenth century had been stretched considerably by the

5 The companionate wife, Shudha Mazumdar in riding breeches, Darjeeling, *c.* 1933

early twentieth century. What was deviant behavior for one generation was acceptable behavior for the next. What is more important, by the early years of the twentieth century Indian women were full participants in the redefinition of their futures.

CHAPTER 3

THE EMERGENCE OF WOMEN'S ORGANIZATIONS

The educational experiments of the late nineteenth and early twentieth centuries produced a "new woman" with interests that went beyond the household. Lado Rani Zutshi, the mother of Manmohini Sahgal, was educated at home by tutors. Manmohini wrote about her mother:

[she] settled in Lahore in 1917 to educate her daughters ... she joined the YWCA to continue her English and painting lessons. In the evenings she went to her class riding a bicycle. No other Indian lady of her status in Lahore had the courage to do this ... In Lahore, she started a ladies' recreation club and became its president.[1]

For the first time in India's history women began to communicate with women outside their families and local communities. On the one hand there was a small group of women who shared English as a common language. This made possible communication across language barriers. On the other hand, there were growing numbers of women literate in the vernaculars which enabled them to learn about women's issues in the new women's journals. Both groups, marginalized by more traditional society, sought the companionship of women like themselves. Encouraged by their male guardians to "move with the times" they joined the new clubs and associations formed for women. From small local clubs and women's auxiliaries of the Indian National Congress and the National Social Conference came a variety of organizations and associations that reflected women's concerns. By the eve of Independence in 1947 a coalition of national women's organizations could rightfully claim it was the second most representative body in India.

These organizations became the medium for the expression of "women's opinion." At the same time they were a training ground for women who would later take up leadership roles in politics and social institutions. Those institutions, in turn, played an important role in the construction of the Indian nation. Their model was undoubtedly

---

[1] Manmohini Zutshi Sahgal, *An Indian Freedom Fighter Recalls her Life*, ed. Geraldine Forbes (New York, M. E. Sharpe, 1994), p. 33.

6 Raja Indra Chandra Singh Ladies' Group, n.d.

Western: the view of women and of women's civic responsibility was adopted wholesale. Nevertheless, in the Indian context these organizations developed in harmony with a view of the "new woman" as a companion and help-mate to man, an ideal mother, and a credit to her country.

ASSOCIATIONS FOR WOMEN
FOUNDED BY MEN

The first organizations for women were begun by men who belonged to the new religious reform associations. In Bengal, Keshub Chandra Sen, the charismatic leader of the Brahmo Samaj, developed educational programs, a women's journal, prayer meetings, and Bharat Ashram (literally "Indian hermitage") where families lived together and emulated the lifestyle of the English middle class. Before long, other members of the Samaj argued that Keshub was too conservative and they broke with him to form the Sadharan (General) Brahmo Samaj.[2] Members of the Sadharan Brahmo Samaj, motivated by the ideal of

---

[2] Sivanath Sashtri, *History of the Brahmo Samaj*, 2nd edn. (Calcutta, Sadharan Brahmo Samaj, 1974), pp. 105–64.

male–female equality, formed new associations for women of their families.

The Prarthana Samaj did similar work in Bombay. Those men who were closely involved with the Samaj from the beginning, especially the famous Prarthana trio – G. R. Bandavarkar, Narayan Ganesh Chandavarker, and M. G. Ranade – were concerned with social reform, principally improving women's status. When Pandita Ramabai Saraswati arrived in western India in 1882, Justice Ranade and his friends helped her set up the Arya Mahila Samaj for the general uplift and enlightenment of women.[3]

Ramabai, Justice Ranade's wife, became the backbone of this organization. Ramabai wanted the Samaj to provide a support network for newly educated women through weekly lectures and "at homes" where women could meet and become friends. As these women developed self-confidence, she predicted they would begin to define the role of the educated woman. The Arya Mahila Samaj imagined the ideal woman as an efficient housewife, entering the public world to help during emergencies such as floods, famines, and plagues.[4]

Women also met in the women's auxiliaries of general reform associations. The most notable of these was the Bharata Mahila Parishad (Ladies' Social Conference) of the National Social Conference. The National Social Conference was formed at the third meeting of the Indian National Congress in 1887 to provide a forum for the discussion of social issues; the Mahila Parishad was not inaugurated until 1905. The women who took part in the general meetings of the National Social Conference doubted their male colleagues took women's problems seriously.[5]

The first meeting of the Bharata Mahila Parishad was held in a hall packed with over 200 women. Women had arranged this meeting and barred men from attending. They began with prayer, in Marathi and Gujarati, and an opening statement by the president, Lady Bhalchandra. Ramabai Ranade, newly widowed, was one of the first speakers. She encouraged women to work side by side with men for the regeneration of the nation. They could, she suggested, devote their

---

[3] "Arya Mahila Samaj," *Directory of Women's Institutions*, ed. K. J. Chitalia, vol. 1, *Bombay Presidency* (Bombay, Servants of India Society, 1936), p. 6.

[4] "Arya Mahila Samaj" (n.d.), notes by Mrs. Leela Joshi (received from the author); "Arya Mahila Samaj: An Appeal" (n.d.), cyclostyled sheet received from Sarojini Pradhar; "Pandita Ramabai Saraswati," *Women's Forum* (March–April, 1972), no page numbers.

[5] "The Indian Social Conference," *ILM,* 3 (1904), p. 225.

spare time to volunteer work: teaching orphans, inspecting schools for girls, and helping widows find respectable employment.[6] Next, Mrs. Abbas Tyabji read a paper on Muslim women's education, followed by lectures on philanthropic and charitable work. The general discussion focused on a number of issues including medical relief, domestic life, early marriage, and child welfare.[7]

At subsequent annual meetings, there were usually as many as 300 and sometimes over 700 women present. The organizers believed it was important for women to meet separately from men even if the issues and speeches were remarkably similar to those heard in the meeting of the National Social Conference. The main topics continued to be female education and the need to abolish "evil" social customs, such as child marriage, dowry, and neglect of widows. The discussions of what roles women might play in changing the situation were tentative. By and large the women who attended these meetings believed they first needed to educate themselves about the problems.[8]

Within the Parsee community the major organization for women's social work, the Stri Zarthosti Mandal (Parsee Women's Circle) emerged from plaque-relief work done by the family of Mr. Naoroji Patuck. Deeply touched by the hardships suffered by women, Mr. Patuck set up a work class in his home. By 1903 there were over fifty women enrolled and his family decided to ask other women to join them in forming an organization. Miss Serenmai M. Cursetjee became the first president and remained at the helm of the Mandal for the next thirty-six years. During this time the organization expanded its agenda to include medical care and education and successfully sought funding from the wealthy Parsee philanthropist Sir Ratan Tata.[9] Equally important, the organization served as a training ground for women who became active in a wide range of activities and organizations in the 1920s and 1930s.

As these associations received publicity, they spurred the formation of new organizations for women. Begum Jahan Ara Shah Nawaz, later a prominent and influential member of national women's organizations, explained that the first ladies' society she joined was the brain-

---

[6] "Mrs. Ranade's Address," *ILM*, 3 (1904), p. 259.
[7] "The Ladies Gathering," *ILM*, 4 (1905), pp. 219–20.
[8] "The Indian National Social Conference," *ILM*, 5 (1906), pp. 230–2; "Ladies Gathering at Surat," *ILM*, 6 (1907), p. 380; "The Ladies Social Conference," *ILM*, 8 (1908), pp. 227–8.
[9] *Golden Jubilee Stri Zarthosti Mandal, 1903–1953, and Silver Jubilee Sir Ratan Tata Industrial Institute, 1928–1953 Volume* (Bombay, 1953), pp. 5–7.

child of her uncle, Shah Din. He had read about a Sikh Conference in Lahore where 2,000 women collected enough money to set up a high school for girls. Fearful that Muslim women would fall behind, he ordered the women in his (Mian) family to meet twice a month to discuss female education and social reform. They were to write articles on these topics, present them at meetings for discussion, and begin "social work" with poor women in surrounding villages. The experience gained from working within the family led these women to initiate a larger organization and Begum Shah Nawaz's mother, Amir-un-Nisa (called the Mrs. Pankhurst of the Mian family), became a founder-member of Anjuman-e-Khawatin-e-Islam (the Muslim Women's Association) in the Punjab. By 1915, women of the Mian family were playing a leading role in the All-Indian Muslim Women's Conference.[10]

While male-inspired and male-guided organizations for women did invaluable work in educating women and providing them with their first experience with public work, they also imposed limitations. Specifically, male reformers regarded the household as the primary focus and fundamental arena of activity for women. They envisioned households run by modernized women who had imbibed scientific ideas about hygiene and child-rearing. These men wanted their wives to take part in activities outside the home: social work to help the unfortunate and relief work when disaster struck. Their wives could assist in nation-building not through political agitation but by building institutions to ameliorate the worst situations arising from social customs. Women's associations were also useful institutions to accomplish the aim of transforming young brides into companions and helpmates. When young women attended these meetings they were temporarily removed from the influence and dominance of the older women of the households to a place where they could pursue further education, develop friendships with other educated women, and work together on philanthropic schemes.

The restrictions that accompanied male support and tutelage were revealed whenever women wanted to strike out on their own. The religious-reform and communal associations dealt with women's problems

[10] Gail Minault, ed., "Sisterhood or Separation? The All-India Muslim Ladies' Conference and the Nationalist Movement," *The Extended Family* (Columbus, Mo., South Asia Books, 1981), pp. 83–108; Jahan Ara Shahnawaz, *Father and Daughter: A Political Autobiography* (Lahore, Nigarishat, 1971), pp. 13–23, 42–50.

as defined by male leaders. But these patrons would not automatically extend their support to problems identified by women on their own. When Haimabati Mitra, a child widow from Bengal, sought out leaders of the Brahmo Samaj to help her gain an education, they looked for a bridegroom. In a conversation with her friend Sarojini, Haimabati said that all she wanted to do was study. Sarojini's retort was, "You should study after you have got married." Haimabati, by now rather cynical about Brahmo promises, said, "The future depends on God's will, of course. My wishes are of little consequence."[11] In Bombay, the Parsee Panchayat (Council) welcomed the views of women on family law but soundly defeated Bai Dinhai F. S. Patuck's proposal that sex differences be eliminated from inheritance laws.[12]

British support for female education did not extend to issues of autonomy. The much publicized Rukhmabai case (actually a series of court cases between 1884 and 1888) proved that British law could be used to force women to submit to the most onerous of patriarchal customs. Rukhmabai, married at age eleven to Dadaji Bhikaji, remained in her father's home after her marriage. She continued to study and passed the matriculation exam. When Dadaji demanded she come to live with him she refused. He sued for restitution of conjugal rights. Rukhmabai won but Dadaji appealed and the court ordered her to live with her husband or go to prison.[13] Tilak, an outspoken opponent of British rule in India, approved of this decision, claiming British law was upholding the *dharmasastras* (texts on morals and law and manuals of human conduct). Ranade and other reformers formed the Rukhmabai Defense Committee to bring this case to public attention. Pandita Ramabai exploded in anger. The government advocated education and emancipation but when a woman refused to "be a slave," wrote Pandita Ramabai, the government "comes to break her spirit allowing its law to became an instrument for riveting her chains."[14] In 1888 the two parties

[11] *From Child Widow to Lady Doctor: The Intimate Memoir of Dr. Haimabati Sen*, trans. Tapan Raychaudhuri, ed. Geraldine Forbes and Tapan Raychaudhuri, in press.

[12] *Golden Jubilee Stri Zarthosti Mandal*, pp. 25–6.

[13] Meera Kosambi, "Women, Emancipation and Equality: Pandita Ramabai's Contribution to the Women's Cause," *EPW*, 23, no. 44 (October, 1988), p. ws44; C. Heimsath, *Indian Nationalism and Hindu Social Reform* (Princeton, N.J., Princeton University Press, 1964), pp. 170–1; Dagmar Engels, "The Limits of Gender Ideology," *WSIQ*, 12, no. 4 (1989), pp. 428–9; Ruth Woodsmall, Notebooks, 1916–1917, box 3, Diaries, 1913–1917, RWC.

[14] *Letters and Correspondence of Pandita Ramabai*, ed. A. B. Shah (Bombay, Maharashtra State Board of Literature and Culture, 1977), pp. 175–8.

reached a compromise and Rukhmabai was saved from imprisonment. Rukhmabai then studied medicine in England and returned to India to become the head of a Hindu hospital in Poona.[15] This case made it clear that colonial administrators could not be relied upon to protect the women they had encouraged to seek an education when those same women defied the patriarchal system.

THE FIRST WOMEN'S ORGANIZATIONS
FOUNDED BY WOMEN

Women began to define their interests, propose solutions, and take action only after they formed their own associations. Women's associations, called by various titles, sprang up all over India in the late nineteenth and early twentieth centuries. Most were geographically limited but they shared the goal of bringing women together to discuss women's issues. Saraladevi Chaudhurani, critical of the women's meetings held in conjunction with the Indian National Social Conference, called for a permanent association of Indian women. Women responded favorably and Saraladevi began planning the first meeting. When male colleagues criticized her, she charged them with patronizing women. These men, she wrote, "advertise themselves as champions of the weaker sex, equal opportunities for women, female education and female emancipation," which they make "their pet subjects of oratory at the annual show."[16] These men lived in the "shade of Manu," she charged and were unwilling to allow women independent action. Saraladevi's organization, the Bharat Stree Mahamandal (the Large Circle of Indian Women) had its first meeting in Allahabad in 1910.[17]

The Bharat Stree Mahamandal planned to open branches in all parts of India to promote female education. It developed branches in Lahore, Allahabad, Delhi, Karachi, Amritsar, Hyderabad, Kanpur, Bankura, Hazaribagh, Midnapur, and Calcutta to bring together "women of every race, creed, class and party . . . on the basis of their common interest in the moral and material progress of the women of India."[18]

The Mahamandal's leaders regarded purdah as the main stumbling

[15] Woodsmall, Notebooks, 1916–1917, RWC.
[16] Saraladevi, "A Women's Movement," *MR* (October, 1911), p. 345.   [17] *Ibid.*
[18] J. C. Bagal, "Sarala Devi Chaudhurani," *Sahitya Sadhak Charitmala*, no. 99 (Calcutta, Bangiya Sahitya Parishad, 1964), p. 24; Saraladevi, "A Women's Movement," p. 348.

block to popular acceptance of female education. To get around this practice, they would send teachers into the homes to teach reading, writing, music, sewing, and embroidery.[19] Saraladevi had written about the importance of women escaping male domination, so only women were allowed to join this organization. Most of the members had worked previously with male-dominated women's organizations and designed projects similar to those favored by male reformers.

The few surviving accounts of these early organizations give us glimpses of women articulating their needs and assuming leadership roles. They recognized their world was different from that of their mothers and grandmothers and sought the linguistic and social skills necessary for new roles. Further education was seen as essential since many of them had married young. Some of the *mahila samities* (women's associations) taught basic subjects such as mathematics and geography while others offered only English. Especially popular were lectures and classes on health, childcare, hygiene, and nutrition in a world where "science" was equivalent to "modern." The expansion of opportunities beyond the home required that women learn new social skills such as polite conversation, serving tea, and public speaking.

Women leaders were defining women's issues as female education, child marriage, the observance of purdah, and women's status in the family. Many of them believed all women shared the same problems. Clearly they spoke from a specific class orientation but they did so at a time when there was considerable prejudice against female education, child marriage was preferred, and widow remarriage was unheard of in respectable families. Female seclusion and sex segregation prevailed but strict purdah was practiced only in some parts of India. When they assumed all women experienced difficulties with in-laws they were drawing on experience; their evaluation of women's status in the family was based on their knowledge of laws and personal observation. If asked for examples to verify their perceptions, many of these women would have recounted stories of their relatives, their servants, and what they had heard from a vast network of informants. In a limited way they understood many of the problems shared by all women. What

---

[19] "An Account of the Work Among Women in Calcutta," *ILM*, 8 (May–June, 1935), p. 176; "The Bharat Stree Mahamandal," *MR* (September, 1912), p. 312; Saraladevi, *Jibaner Jharapata* (Kalikata, Sahitya Samsad, 1958), pp. 196–7; Saraladevi, "A Women's Movement," p. 348; Latika Ghose, "Social and Educational Movements for Women by Women, 1820–1950," *Bethune School and College Centenary Volume, 1949–1959*, ed. Dr. Kalidas Nag (Calcutta, S. N. Guha Ray, 1950), pp. 150–1.

they did not share was the same economic base as the women they claimed to represent. Hence their perception of the viability of certain options was limited to women like themselves. They set up girls' schools, widows' shelters, and handicraft training centers to help only women from their own class. The rural poor would not have been able to send their daughters to school even if they favored female education. Widows' homes were suitable for women from respectable families who needed to earn some money but often these homes were restricted to brahmin widows. Handicraft production – particularly sewing and embroidery – enabled only some high-caste women to earn a living because they had access to a clientele, homes they could live in, and space to work. Jaijee Lam, widowed in 1898 at age twenty-eight with two children, earned a living embroidering saris. She was famous for her skill in Chinese embroidery, then the rage in women's fashion, and was able to support herself and her children in a respectable manner. But the family's standard of living was not due to her earnings alone; her husband left her some property. In defining women's problems and suggesting suitable remedies, the founders of these early women's organizations tended to look at women like Jaijee Lam as models. Consequently, their institutions were able to serve some of the unfortunate women of their own class but few others.

NATIONAL WOMEN'S ORGANIZATIONS

After World War I national women's organizations were created. Three major organizations: the Women's Indian Association (WIA), the National Council of Women in India (NCWI), and the All-India Women's Conference (AIWC) emerged between 1917 and 1927.

The Women's Indian Association

The Women's Indian Association had humble beginnings. Margaret Cousins, an Irish feminist, theosophist, and musician, arrived in India in 1915. Soon after, an officer of the Theosophical Society in Adyar invited a number of women to meet with her. After this meeting Cousins spoke with Dorothy Jinarajadasa (an Irish feminist married to the highly respected Singalese theosophist C. Jinarajadasa) about forming a women's organization. Many of the Indian women already belonged to the Tamil Madar Sangam (Tamil Ladies' Association) and had joined with British women in forming the National Indian

Association to promote female education, particularly English language instruction, and the teaching of crafts.[20] As the two groups began to mix more freely, they decided to form the Ladies' Recreational Club to sponsor tea parties, badminton, and tennis. Cousins and Jinarajadasa were proposing a new organization that would combine education, crafts, and sports.[21]

Once the WIA was formed, Jinarajadasa was anxious to encourage the formation of branch organizations. She wrote to Theosophical Lodge secretaries throughout Madras Presidency explaining that a local branch of the Women's Indian Association could play a key role in effecting the regeneration of India.[22] The response to these letters was so positive Jinarajadasa was inspired to write: "there is practically no opposition from the Hindu man to anything that woman really wishes to do."[23]

The women who formed this organization decided to call it the Women's Indian Association because membership was open to both Indians and Europeans. Annie Besant became the first president with Margaret Cousins, Dorothy Jinarajadasa, Mrs. Malati Patwardhan, Mrs. Ammu Swaminathan, Mrs. Dadhabhoy, and Mrs. Ambujammal as honorary secretaries. By the end of the first year there were thirty-three branches; within five years, forty-three branches, twenty centers and 2,300 members. Each branch accepted the main aims of the association but remained self-governing. This made it possible to mobilize the branches to express women's opinion.[24]

Despite this organization's obvious connection with and dependence on the Theosophical Society, it defined itself as an association that included and represented women of all races, cultures, and religions. Each branch was to chart its own course of work in four main areas: religion, education, politics, and philanthropy. The organization defined women as religious "by nature" and encouraged non-sectarian religious activity. But the most important work was educational and the branches were encouraged to set up adult classes for literacy, sewing,

[20] Kamala Bai L. Rau, *Smrutika: The Story of My Mother as Told by Herself,* trans. Indirabai M. Rau (Pune, Dr. Krishnabai Nimbkar, 1988), pp. 26–32.
[21] "Report of the Madanapalli Branch of the WIA, 1916–1937," WIA Papers.
[22] "A New Society for Indian Ladies," *New India* (May 10, 1917), p. 9.
[23] Mrs. D. Jinarajadasa, "The Emancipation of Indian Women," *Transactions of the Eighth Congress of the Federation of European National Societies of the Theosophical Society,* held in Vienna, July 21–26, 1923, ed. C. W. Dijkgraat (Amsterdam, 1923), p. 86.
[24] Women's Indian Association, *Quinquennial Report, 1917–1922,* WIA Papers.

and first aid. The WIA had been politically active from the beginning when they sent a delegation to meet with Secretary of State Montagu in 1917 to request the franchise for women. The fourth area of work – philanthropy – involved feeding the poor, setting up shelters for widows, and providing relief for disaster victims.[25] The WIA's monthly journal, *Stri Dharma,* published in English but including articles in both Hindi and Tamil, carried news of events of interest to women, reports from the branches, and articles on women's condition.

The early organizers of the WIA found it very difficult to bring women together to form local branches. The branch officer from Salem complained, "It is actual bull-work to drag our reluctant sisters from their kitchens and to persuade them to spend a few minutes at the meeting periodically."[26] Where the branches were successful it was frequently due to the determination of one or two women. In Surat, Kanuben C. Mehta asked her husband to write (in English) to Dorothy Jinarajadasa saying his wife wanted to form a branch.[27] Kanuben's first group had thirty members and they collected enough money to begin a craft class. Further efforts resulted in classes in English and drawing (each attended by fifteen girls) and weekly meetings at which adult women read and discussed books. Whenever attendance fell off, Kanuben would visit the homes of the members and urge them back to the meetings. This became a tightly knit group that responded quickly to the central office's requests for "women's opinion." Kanuben soon learned English and began to correspond directly with the center; by the end of 1921 she had organized lectures on franchise, hygiene, and child welfare.[28]

Born and nurtured in Madras, the WIA competed for women's attention with the self-respect movement. The self-respect movement had a larger agenda than women's rights; its goal was to establish a society free from the domination of the priestly caste, with justice and equality for all human beings. Ideologically more radical in its critique of existing gender relations and particularly of the role of religion in

[25] WIA, *Quinquennial Report, 1917–1922.*
[26] S. Kamakshi to Dear Sister (August 10, 1924), file no. 3, DRP.
[27] From Chhanganram Mehta to D. Jinarajadasa (March 27, 1918), DRP.
[28] Chhanganram Mehta to D. Jinarajadasa (May 2, 1918); C. Mehta to M. Cousins (June 17, 1991); C. Mehta to Dear Sister (September 12, 1919, July 28, 1920, April 10, 1921); Kanuben Mehta to Dear Sister (April 10, 1921, December 1, 1921); K. Mehta to Jinarajadasa (February 9, 1922); K. Mehta to M. Cousins (March 23, 1922, April 11, 1922); DRP.

assigning women a subordinate position, the self-respect movement found it difficult to fight issues of property ownership, caste privilege, and gender discrimination all at the same time. In the final analysis, the self-respect movement rejected brahmanical symbols while it retained the same limited definition of women's roles.[29] The presence of the self-respect movement helped limit the appeal of the WIA to high-caste women.

The National Council of Women in India

The National Council of Women in India (NCWI) was the next all-India women's organization established. By 1925 women of Bombay, Calcutta, and Madras had utilized the networks developed doing war work to link their various clubs and associations into a new council.[30] The International Council of Women convened its first meeting in Washington D.C. in 1888 to advance women's social, economic, and political rights.[31] The Marchioness of Aberdeen, president of the International Council from 1922 to 1936, learned of the Indian council and invited them to join the International Council.[32] In 1925 the NCWI was established as a national branch of the International Council of Women.

Mehribai Tata (wife of Sir Dorab Tata), chair of the Executive Committee of the Bombay Council in its first year, played a key role in its advancement. Mehribai was a member of the small Parsee community of Bangalore. Her father, H. J. Bhabba, a well-known educationalist, supervised his daughter's education and introduced her to his European friends. Accustomed to socializing with both Europeans and Indians, Mehribai was well suited to marry the eldest son of Mr. Jamsetjee Tata, the founder of Tata Industries. The couple married in 1898 and Mehribai became a member of India's most important industrial family.

During a trip to Europe in 1904, Lady Tata began to admire the commitment of English women to civic issues. In India, she had

[29] Prabha Rani, "Women's Indian Association and the Self-Respect Movement in Madras, 1925–1936: Perceptions on Women," paper delivered at the Women's Studies Conference, Chandigarh (October, 1985); C. S. Lakshmi, "Mother, Mother-Community and Mother-Politics in Tamil Nadu," *EPW*, 25, nos. 42 and 43 (October 20–27, 1990), pp. ws72–ws83.
[30] BPWC, *First Annual Report*, BPWC Papers, BPWC Library, Bombay; "History of the Council Movement," *Bulletin* (January, 1932), p. 4, Premchand Papers.
[31] Veronica Strong-Boag, *The Parliament of Women* (Ottawa, National Museum of Canada, 1976), pp. 72–3.
[32] BPWC, *Fifth Report*, p. 4, BPWC, *Sixth Report*, p. 8, BPWC Papers.

been critical of English women for doing so little to help their Indian sisters.[33] Opposed to passive charity, for example giving money to set up an orphanage, Mehribai urged middle-class women to visit the slums and talk with people about the "disgrace of living on charity" and the "necessity of self-respecting honest work."[34]

In her view, purdah, caste differences, and lack of education prevented women from working to change social conditions. As a necessary first step, she urged men to support female education and freedom of movement for women.[35] That her voice was heard, both nationally and internationally, was quite natural given her wealth, social position, and poise. Whenever she spoke in Europe or the United States she was noticed for she always appeared in "native dress" adorned with "ropes of wonderful pearls" and occasionally wearing the largest privately owned diamond in the world.

In adopting a philanthropic style modeled on that of upper-class English women, those women who joined Lady Tata were also participating in a strategy followed by their menfolk. Many of these women, particularly in Bombay Presidency, were married to wealthy men involved in industry and banking. Just as these men supported charities and made donations that would please their rulers, so these newly emancipated women engaged in public activities that would be seen as "enlightened" by British officials in India and policy-makers in England.[36]

Despite the influence of women like Lady Tata in establishing the ideology of the Council, the interests of individual members determined its work. Standing sectional committees were formed to deal with art, labor, legislation, and the press. Generally, the committees collected information, prepared memoranda, and presented these to the proper authorities.[37] The committee on legislation to improve women's status was the most active. This was partly because of the leadership of Mithan Tata Lam, the first Indian woman to pass the bar exam and

[33] Lady Tata, *A Book of Remembrance* (Bombay, J. B. Dubash, 1933), pp. 12–13.
[34] Lady Tata to Miss Serenbai Maneckjee Cursetjee (March 3, 1931), *A Book of Remembrance*, pp. 138–9.
[35] Lady Tata, "An Address Delivered by Lady Tata to the Battle Creek College, USA" (November 29, 1927), *A Book of Remembrance*, pp. 100–3.
[36] Douglas E. Haynes, "From Tribute to Philanthropy: The Politics of Gift Giving in a Western Indian City," *JAS*, 46, no. 2 (May 1987), p. 341.
[37] NCWI, *Third Biennial Report*, 1930–2, NMML.

practice law in India, and partly because this was the kind of "social work" that could be carried out without fear of losing status. Charitable schemes continued although the idea of visiting the slums and chawls (workers' quarters) never appealed to the members of the Council. The new arena of activity that interested these women was petition politics.

Because of its elitist nature, the Council failed to grow and become a vital national organization. The annual membership fee was Rs 15; it took Rs 500 to become a life member and Rs 1,000 to become a patron. When it was first organized the National Council had three life patrons: the Dowager Begum Saheb of Bhopal, Maharani Saheb of Baroda, and Lady Dorab Tata. The president was H. H. the Maharani of Baroda. The Maharani continued to serve the organization as president in 1928, 1930–4, and 1936–7; from 1938 to 1944 the Maharani Setu Parvati Bayi of Travancore was president. Other women who held important positions on the executive committee included Lady Dorab Tata; Miss Cornelia Sorabji, India's first lady barrister;[38] Mrs. Tarabai Premchand, the wife of a wealthy banker; Mrs. Shaffi Tyabji, a member of one of Bombay's leading Muslim families; and Maharani Sucharu Devi of Mourbhanj, a daughter of Keshub Chandra Sen. These were all women of wealth and position, capable of affording the expensive travel expected of the Council's leaders and with enough space to house the Council "office." Many women simply could not afford to join this organization nor did they feel comfortable in the presence of these affluent and titled women. But this was not the only reason the association did not "take," as Tarabai Premchand put it. The councils were politically and socially conservative. Because of the connection with the British and the wealth and status of the leading members, the NCWI remained aloof from the struggle for independence. Socially they opted for the status quo. As late as 1928 the Bengal Council of the NCWI passed a resolution asking for a female probation officer for Calcutta and then recommended the appointee be a British woman. They argued that having an Indian woman do this type of work was too "progressive" and should be avoided for some time.[39] They found village work difficult and unhealthy; the villagers distrustful and

[38] Antoinette Burton, "Empire, Oxford, and Imperial Culture: Cornelia Sorabji at Somerville College, 1889–1892," *At the Heart of the Empire: Indians and the Colonial Encounter in Late-Victorian Britain* (in progress).
[39] Bengal Provincial Council Report, *NCWI Report*, 1928–9.

hostile.[40] Instead of re-evaluating their techniques and perhaps modifying their style, members of the NCWI demanded that conditions for village work be improved.

The members of the NCWI looked to government for the improvements they desired. Shut off from actual work among the people whose condition they wished to improve, yet completely confident that they understood both the problems of Indian women and the solutions to these problems, they advised the government on welfare issues. They found this work congenial and their contacts, established through family, marriage, and social interaction, gave them a credibility that exceeded their experience or numbers. Their main concern was that India "measure up," in international terms, to minimum standards for health and welfare found elsewhere. And both British men and Indian men in power had a vested interest in insuring the same.

Members of the NCWI had not followed Lady Tata's advice to visit the slums but there were a few women who had. One of these was Maniben Kara (1905–79), a social worker who became a leading trade unionist.[41] As a child Maniben had secretly visited the chawls with some foreign friends. She recalled she had been shocked and ashamed: shocked because she had known nothing of this other world and ashamed because she had lived very close to it. She went on to study social work in England and returned to India in 1929. Back in Bombay, she organized the Seva Mandir (Service Organization) to work among the poor. She recalled that while Communists accused her of sabotaging a revolution, women from the slums asked if she had nothing better to do with her time.[42] Chided by those she wanted to help, Maniben became a member of M. N. Roy's group of radical humanists and redirected her energies towards organizing workers. She was unable to do much to bring women into the labor unions because of their household work and notions of female propriety. She had no interest in the work of the NCWI and they considered her work "radical."

The All-India Women's Conference

The most important of the women's organizations and the most truly Indian of the three was the last to be formed. The All-India Women's

[40] NCWI, *Biennial Report*, 1938–40, p. 7.
[41] "Life Sketch of Maniben Kara" (unpublished), received from Western Railway Employees Union (Bombay, 1979).
[42] Interview with Maniben Kara (Bombay, April 24, 1976); "Maniben Kara," s-14 (September 17, 1969), South Asian Archive, Centre for South Asian Studies, Cambridge.

Conference (AIWC)[43] first met in Poona in January of 1927, following more than six months of serious work on the part of Margaret Cousins and other women belonging to the WIA. Mr. Oaten, director of Public Instruction in Bengal, urged women to decide what kind of education was suitable for Indian girls and then tell the government "with one voice what they want, and keep on telling us till they get it." A reply to his challenge was published in *Stri Dharma* and this eventually led to plans for a Conference.[44]

Margaret Cousins sent circular letters to women leaders throughout India suggesting they organize local conferences to discuss educational issues. Each conference would prepare a memorandum on female education for presentation at an all-India Conference to be held at Poona.

At the first meeting of the Conference there were eighty-seven members from the local reception committee, fifty-eight delegates from local conferences and over 2,000 observers (men and women). The Rani Saheb of Sangli delivered the opening address and introduced the first president, the Maharani Chimnabai Saheb Gaekwad of Baroda. In her opening remarks the Rani insisted women needed a special type of education, not feminist in nature for that would imply antagonism between men and women, but an education to help them understand their position as "supplemental" to that of men. The Maharani of Baroda focused on social customs – especially purdah and child marriage – which hampered the growth of female literacy. This was a time of women's awakening, she said, noting women's new interest in politics, but she too called for education compatible with "women's nature."

Delegates to the Conference included a large number of professional educationalists as well as social reformers, women associated with the nationalist movement, and the wealthy and titled. The general resolutions outlining the best type of education for females included basic assumptions about women's place in society. The delegates favored, they said, an educational system that would allow for the fullest development of the individual's latent capacities. But at the same time they wanted to teach all girls the ideals of motherhood, how to make the home attractive, and how to help others. Their more specific resolu-

---

[43] Aparna Basu and Bharati Ray, *Women's Struggle: A History of the All India Women's Conference 1927–1990* (New Delhi, Manohar, 1990).
[44] M. Cousins, "How the Conference Began," *Roshni*, special number (1946), p. 14.

tions stressed the importance of moral and physical education, deplored child marriage, and urged special arrangements for educating purdah women.[45]

The AIWC did not advocate mass education for all women nor did they envision a world where all middle-class and upper-class women would receive the same education as men.[46] The majority of the women at the Conference agreed that the educational system should concentrate on producing educated wives and mothers but they also wanted women doctors, professors, and lawyers. Regardless of whether the curriculum stressed home science or natural science, there was general agreement that education should complement gender roles.

In their discussion of female education, delegates to the Conference commented on women's role historically. They maintained that in ancient India women had equal access to education, political power, and wealth. Social customs – particularly child marriage and purdah – resulted from foreign invasions and prevented women from receiving instruction. This interpretation of history – past greatness followed by a dark age – legitimized the organization and the thrust of its programs. But this historical interpretation also limited their appeal since the foreigners blamed for a fall in women's status were Muslims. Acceptance of the "golden age" theory both limited their potential for attracting women from other communities and classes and inhibited a radical feminist critique of their society.

By 1928 the All-India Women's Conference on Educational Reform decided there could be little progress in educational matters unless harmful social customs were eradicated. The next year the AIWC widened its scope to include all questions of social welfare and declared their main activity to be organizing public opinion on these issues. With the 1930s came the civil disobedience movement and the organization's decision to remain apolitical. In making this choice the AIWC opted to preserve its identity as a petitioning organization.

The organization faced a similar decision as the number and range of social issues grew. Beginning with education, then adding social customs which restricted female education, notably child marriage and purdah, the AIWC continued to enlarge its purview. By the mid-1930s the list of sub-committees included labor, rural reconstruction, indigenous industries, textbooks, opium, and the Sarda Act. At the same time

---

[45] AIWC on Educational Reform, Poona (January 1927), pp. 28–32, AIWC Library, New Delhi.   [46] *Ibid.* pp. 32–42.

their resolutions ranged from advocating film censorship to urging widespread instruction in birth control. The leaders were aware their work was taking them in two directions: one that would benefit women specifically and one aimed at helping the entire nation. Their work on behalf of women was increasingly focused on legal disabilities while concern with the welfare of the nation led them toward Gandhi's program of reconstruction and social action. Their interest in women's status in law propelled them towards collaboration with British officials and members of the legislature while the Gandhian emphasis on village uplift and untouchables involved work at the grass-roots level as well as a totally different interpretation of the dynamics of social change.

By 1936 the contradictions were apparent. In her presidential address that year, Margaret Cousins reviewed the progress of the AIWC since its inception. She recalled the first Conference as representing the intelligentsia whereas, in 1936, the AIWC included a "solidarity of sisters" ranging from maharanis to harijans. Their work had "raised the prestige, dignity, influence, power and capacity of our united womanhood and gained from the public a new and deep appreciation of women's ability and their rights of citizenship." Speaking of future directions, Cousins urged her sisters to pay close attention to Nehru's critique of their program as "superficial" because it did not inquire into "root causes." Their research and study of social questions must be rigorous and their efforts for reform must be defined as part of a larger plan for a regenerated India. Yet in her final statements Cousins encouraged AIWC members to continue their work on all fronts: "Work first for political liberty, for liberation from subjection both internal and external, and side by side with that supreme task work for all our already expressed ideals and reforms."[47]

Margaret Cousins' optimism about the solidarity of the sisterhood masked deep-seated problems within the organization. Even Cousins' elevation to this honorary position was debated at length in the back-rooms of the AIWC. Everyone knew that she had helped found the association but a number of women did not want an English woman as president.[48]

At the end of the 1930s and in the early 1940s the AIWC faced a series of challenges to its claim that it represented and could speak for

[47] AIWC, Eleventh Session, Ahmedabad (December 23–27, 1936), pp. 23–5.
[48] From Hilla Rustomji Faridoonji to Mrs. S. C. Mukherjee (April 4, 1936), AIWC Files.

7 Renuka Ray as president of the All-India Women's Conference with two
of her officers, 1952

all women. Amrit Kaur, one of Gandhi's devoted followers, wanted the
organization to emerge as a political force for women. This proposal
was voted down. The AIWC was committed to a comprehensive legal
bill for women. This project was not popular with Muslim women,
many of whom believed Muslim law came from the Quran and could
not be tampered with. Efforts to bring lower-class rural and urban
women into the organization centered on dropping membership dues
to 4 annas rather than developing programs of interest to these women.
None of these problems was solved at the national level.

By the 1940s the AIWC was establishing itself as the premier
organization representing women. In 1939 the old system of presenting
resolutions from the floor ended; thereafter resolutions were submitted
by the branches before the meeting. In 1941 the AIWC established its
quarterly journal, *Roshni*, and in 1946 set up a central office with a
permanent staff. With the organizational details complete they could
devote their energies to two major tasks: publicity and propaganda on
women's issues, and research to provide a data base on women in India.

The provincial branches took on new life during the war years. Some
of these organizations took up local issues, sometimes with a

vengeance, supporting peasant movements, teaching untouchables, encouraging political involvement. They reached out to women the central body had ignored. But this was hard work. In a report to the honorary general secretary Kulsum Sayani, Mrs. Dina Asana confessed her failure in educating adult women:

In some quarters – where women are willing to learn, they are so abjectly poor that they have neither the time nor the means to get out of their grinding poverty and sufferings. In other localities – [where] women have time and are willing to learn, their menfolk discourage them . . . actually prevent them from going to classes. Some of us have been successful in teaching our servants.[49]

At the same time, other branches of the AIWC became prestige organizations, places where women played out games of status and influence while accomplishing little for either the women of their own class or for the downtrodden.[50]

THE CHILD MARRIAGE REFORM ISSUE

The development of the various Indian women's national organizations, their efforts to cooperate with one another, and their relationships with Indian males, British officials, and British women can be viewed through the issue of child marriage in the second half of the 1920s. A focus on this issue is particularly significant because it is the first social reform issue in which organized women played a major role in both the development of arguments, in this case against child marriage, and the work of political petitioning. Efforts to secure passage of the Child Marriage Restraint Act taught these women lessons about competing agendas and the difficulties of collaborating with their apparent well-wishers. At the same time they learned to distinguish between effective petitioning and effective action. In many ways their work on child marriage was a rite of passage into a world where every act had political meaning.

Child marriage had long been a thorny topic in British India.[51] British missionaries and officials expressed their horror of pre-puberty

---

[49] Letter from Mrs. Dina Asana to the honorary general secretary (November 11, 1944), AIWC Files, no. 326.
[50] AIWC Files, no. 374; Kolaba Women's Association, AIWC Konkan Constituency half-yearly report for January–June 1936, AIWC Files, no. 136; AIWC Circular no. 6 (May 8, 1939), AIWC Files, no. 203.
[51] Geraldine Forbes, "Women and Modernity: The Issue of Child Marriage in India," *WSIQ*, 2, no. 4 (1979), pp. 407–19.

8 Wedding portrait, Sahayram Basu (age twenty) and his bride Ranu (age
eight), 1907

marriage which many Indians explained as only the first marriage to be followed by the *garbhadhan* (consummation) ceremony immediately on the attainment of puberty. In 1860 the criminal code set the age of consent for both married and unmarried girls at ten years. The issue reappeared in the 1880s and in 1891 the criminal code was amended to raise the age of consent to twelve years.[52] The age of the female when the marriage was consummated could now be publicly questioned, proof positive that the British were carrying out their "civilizing mission" in India. However, there were no convictions under the Act until thirty years later. By then there were new reasons to re-examine the age of marriage in India.

A revival of interest in the age of marriage and age of consent can be traced to discussions in the League of Nations. Concern with traffic in women and girls led to consideration of the age of consent and ulti-mately to proposals in the Indian Assembly.[53] Various bills addressing these questions were introduced and defeated until 1927 when Rai Sahib Harbilas Sarda introduced his Hindu Child Marriage Bill. Only a few months later a muck-raking American journalist, Katherine Mayo,[54] published *Mother India*, a devastating attack on Indians and Indian customs.[55] Using hospital records, official accounts, and per-sonal interviews, Mayo wrote a "pot-boiler" that both shocked and tit-illated the American and British reading public. Mayo berated Indians for their treatment of women of all ages, focusing particularly on sexual behavior and lingering on accounts of child brides "raped" by their older husbands. She concluded that social customs accounted for the weakness of the Indian race and made it clear that these people were not ready to "hold the reins of Government."[56] Some Indian men called the attack scurrilous; others argued that British officials had prevented them from eradicating these social evils.[57] Eager to escape blame,

---

[52] Tanika Sarkar, "Rhetoric against Age of Consent, Resisting Colonial Reason and Death of a Child-Wife," *EPW*, 28, no. 36 (September 4, 1993), p. ws1870.

[53] Barbara N. Ramusack, 'Women's Organizations and Social Change: The Age-of-Marriage Issue in India," *Women and World Change: Equity Issues in Development,* ed. Naomi Black and Ann Baker Cottrell (Beverly Hills, Sage Publications, 1981), p. 201.

[54] For an insightful review of Mayo in her pre-India days see Gerda W. Ray, "Colonialism, Race, and Masculinity: Katherine Mayo and the Campaign for State Police" (unpublished paper, 1992).

[55] Mrinalini Sinha, "Reading *Mother India*: Empire, Nation, and the Female Voice," *JWH*, 6, no. 2 (1994), pp. 6–44.

[56] Katherine Mayo, *Mother India* (New York, Harcourt Brace, 1927), p. 32.

[57] J. T. Sunderland, "Miss Katherine Mayo's 'Mother India' Weighed in the Balance, What is the Verdict?" *MR*, 16 (1929), pp. 1–6.

9 Wedding portrait, Ronen and Padmini Sen Gupta, 1938

government officials began telling the Assembly and "the world at large" that they supported beneficent social legislation.[58]

The Assembly referred Sarda's bill to a select committee of ten chaired by Sir Morophant Visavanath Joshi. The committee included only one Indian woman, Mrs. Rameshwari Nehru, recommended by the WIA.[59] Once appointed, the committee moved quickly to assess public attitudes; they sent out 8,000 questionnaires and announced a tour to hear testimony from a wide range of witnesses.[60]

The women's organizations promoted this legislation at every stage. They generated propaganda against child marriage, commented on proposed bills, petitioned, met with the Joshi Committee, lobbied to secure passage of the Child Marriage Restraint Act, and worked, after its passage, for registration of births and marriages and other legislation to make it a meaningful Act.

Throughout the country AIWC branches organized meetings at which women's opinions could be expressed. In their speeches women refused to confine their remarks to child marriage. This was only one of many customs that "crushed their individuality and denied them opportunities for education and development of mind and body."[61] Sharifah Hamid Ali organized a special campaign to support the Sarda Act. Addressing Muslim women in Sind, she told them she was the mother of seven daughters, two of whom had been "victim to this custom." This personal experience made her postpone the marriages of her other daughters until they were mature and educated. Begum Hamid Ali, who was not married until she was twenty-five years of age, believed the minimum age for females should be eighteen.[62] Another woman, Mrs. Diwan, spoke at a woman's meeting in Gujarat about the need to change consciousness among women:

It is very essential that the outlook of women should undergo a radical change. To-day women themselves believe that it is proper for them to do certain work and improper to do others . . . [and] that it is dangerous to remain unmarried. This inferiority complex must be got rid of.[63]

Women agitating against the custom of child marriage had begun to fault the whole system including their socialization into it. However,

---

[58] GOI, Home Dept., Judicial (July 11, 1927), file no. 382/27, p. 8.   [59] Ibid.
[60] Report of the Age of Consent Committee, 1928–1929 (Calcutta, 1929), p. 3.
[61] Speech by Smt. Akilabai, "Child Marriage Bill," The Hindu (clipping, n.d.), DRP.
[62] Ibid.
[63] The Indian Quarterly Register, 2, nos. 3 and 4 (July–December, 1929), (Calcutta, n.d.), pp. 395–6.

the radical statements of the platform rarely made their way into the more carefully considered petitions and resolutions delivered to government officials.

When they met with the Joshi Committee, AIWC members sought to destroy the arguments made by the opposition. They denied that women favored youthful marriage, that later marriages would lead to immorality, that all men supported child marriage, and that child marriage was a part of Vedic religion.[64] At no time did they argue that the decision of whether or not to marry, whom to marry, and when to marry should be a matter of individual right. Rather, they couched their support of a later age of marriage in terms of preparing women to fit biologically determined roles.

The Joshi Committee recommended fifteen as the minimum age of marriage with twenty-one the age of consent. There can be no doubt of the influence of world opinion on both Indian and British legislators. In America and Britain the proceedings of the legislature were followed as if the outcome would prove or disprove Mayo's conclusions.[65] In their private correspondence, British officials make it clear they felt they had no option but to support this measure. Had they not supported it, the charge of reformers and nationalists – that foreign rule inhibited social reform – would gain credence. But the final measure was a compromise, the minimum age of marriage for females was set at fourteen, for males eighteen, and the age of consent was not mentioned. Passed at the beginning of October 1929, the Act took effect in April 1930.

The women's organizations rejoiced when the Sarda Act was passed. The NCWI was the most cautious in its praise saying this was the first campaign in the battle against social evils, but not a victory.[66] The WIA was less hesitant and immediately called a meeting to congratulate Rai Sahib Harbilas Sarda. The Sarda Act, in their view, was the major achievement of 1929.[67] The AIWC reacted the most positively, calling the Sarda Act a "great achievement" and a "personal triumph."[68]

The euphoria was short-lived. Government commitment to rigid enforcement diminished from the time officials began to assess the

---

[64] AIWC, 1929, p. 95.
[65] *Legislative Assembly Debates*, January 29, 1929, vol. I, p. 197; September 10, 1929, vols. IV and V, pp. 679–80; September 19, 1929, vols. IV and V, p. 1110.
[66] NCWI, 1928–9, p. 20.
[67] WIA, *Golden Jubilee Celebration Volume* (Madras, 1967), p. 5.
[68] AIWC, 1930, pp. 12, 24.

opposition and conclude it came primarily from the Muslim community. Muslim leaders had threatened "formidable agitation" even before the Act was passed.[69] Following its approval they threatened to break the Sarda Act "and other laws" by joining with Gandhi and Congress in their anti-government campaign.[70] The British were not about to test the practicality of this threat.

Muslim leaders asked that the Act be amended to exclude Muslims.[71] The women's organizations tried to combat this move in a number of ways. The AIWC claimed they spoke for all women in India[72] and Muslim women members presented a memorial in support of the Sarda Act. In it they told the Viceroy:

We, speaking also on behalf of the Muslim women of India, assert that it is only a small section of Mussalman men who have been approaching your excellency and demanding exemption from the Act. This Act affects girls and women far more than it affects men and we deny their right to speak on our behalf.[73]

That the government did not amend or repeal the Act had less to do with the watchful eye of the women's organizations than with world opinion and the importance of political consistency. British officials were aware an amendment would suggest weakness. Moreover, the subject was one that excited "the interest and attention of the League of Nations." The best tack was to simply leave it alone since there was general agreement that the Sarda Act was a dead letter.[74]

Enforcement of the Act was practically non-existent. It was difficult to make a charge and difficult to obtain a guilty verdict. Moreover, many of those found guilty were pardoned. The number of child marriages increased as there was a rush to celebrate marriages before the Act came into effect.[75] The government blamed reform-minded Indians for not personally supporting the Act and not doing more to educate the masses about the evils of child marriage.[76] Indian reformers blamed the government.

The Child Marriage Restraint Act had a profound effect on the women's organizations. It was a consensus issue and this made it easy

---

[69] GOI, Home Dept., Judicial 1929, file no. 561/29.
[70] "Civil Disobedience Movement in Delhi," GOI, Home Dept., Political, file no. 256/I/1930.   [71] GOI, Home Dept., Judicial, file nos. 272/31, F73/31, 793/32, 76/32.
[72] AIWC, 1931, p. 43.
[73] WIA Appendix D, "Muslim Ladies Defend Sarda Act," Report, 1930–1.
[74] GOI, Home Dept., Judicial, file nos. 269/31, 65/30.
[75] GOI, Home Dept., Judicial, file nos. 818/33, 65/30.
[76] Samuel Hoare to E. Rathbone (November 7, 1933), RP, folder no. 6.

for women from different regions and communities to work together and for the three national organizations to coordinate their activities. As the Joshi Committee traveled throughout India it heard arguments against child marriage presented by numerous women. These women created the impression that India had its fair share of educated, articulate women who understood the problems of their country and had formulated answers.

Support for the women's position created the illusion that women's issues and the women who presented them were being taken seriously. Because a law prohibiting child marriage had been passed, many people considered the child marriage problem solved. Only the women's organizations and a few male reformers continued to fret about enforcement. In the long run, this experience helped women engaged in this campaign appreciate the weakness of their position.

CONCLUSIONS

During World War II the women's organizations emerged as fully mature entities able to respond to the most important national and international issues of the day. Their hegemony was short-lived but in the meantime they participated in almost every major committee or planning group meeting to discuss India's future. They took a stand on the war and worked to improve conditions in famine-stricken Bengal and other regions of the country that were suffering. They decided not to form a separate women's party but continued to work for a new civil code that would recognize women's rights.

One might look at the changes these groups went through and ask what progress, if any, they made. Their numbers had grown but they had not, except in a very few cases, reached beyond the urban middle class for members. They had gained the right to speak for India's women but they were still addressing issues of propriety and pursuing legislation they knew would not be enforced.

Both their successes and failures can be attributed to social feminism which served as the ideological basis for their demands. Although many of the participants in these women's organizations decried the term "feminism," equating it with man-hating and suffragette violence, they sought greater autonomy for women. When they petitioned for education, the vote, and amelioration of social evils it was to enable women to fulfill their social obligations to the family and nation. They sought a family order in which women would be respected and honored. A few women in these organizations questioned the double standard and demanded complete autonomy for women. But their views were subordinated to those of the majority. It is easy to understand why they did not adopt a radical ideology. These women's organizations matured with male support and flourished in partnership with male-dominated nationalist parties. To put the needs of women first would have been antithetical to their construction of the Indian woman as nurturing and self-sacrificing. Moreover, it would have forced them to choose between nationalism and feminism. The development of a social feminist ideology made possible the peaceful coexistence of feminism and nationalism in a new construct that Margot Badran has called "feminist nationalism."[77]

Who benefited from the existence of these women's organizations? The answer is the large numbers of middle-class women who gained experience in working with organizational structures. They learned first-hand the dynamics of the political world and learned them, in part, from other women. As the organizations centralized, many women became frustrated with their aims and left to work with more marginal groups. Those who stayed with the organizations put their new-found wisdom about petition politics to good use as they fought for women's franchise and women's legal rights. What always needs to be recalled is that their attempts to change the social reality for women were played out in an environment that could be especially cruel to women who did not conform. Women like Maniben Kara paid a heavy price for choosing labor union work when she became discouraged with social work. Not a small part of the price for Maniben was her realization that as a labor union leader she was not able to change the patriarchal order and bring women into the unions. Hence the history of these social organizations is one of notable accomplishments and severe limitations.

[77] Margot Badran, "Dual Liberation: Feminism and Nationalism in Egypt, 1870s–1925," *Feminist Issues*, 8, no. 1 (1988), pp. 15–34.

CHAPTER 4

THE MOVEMENT FOR WOMEN'S RIGHTS

In 1917 Secretary of State for India Edwin Montagu announced the British government's intention of including more Indians in the governing process. To learn more about Indian and European opinion, Montagu and Lord Chelmsford, the Viceroy, planned a tour of India to listen to the views of individuals and groups. Hearing of the proposed tour, Saraladevi Chaudhurani applied for an appointment for members of the Bharat Stri Mahamandal to discuss women's educational needs.[1] Members of the newly formed Women's Indian Association in Madras also requested an audience. Officials informed both groups that only deputations on political subjects were welcome so Mrs. Margaret Cousins sent a new application. She requested an audience for women to present their political demands. On December 15, 1917, Sarojini Naidu (1879–1949), an Indian poetess and long-time Congress worker, led an all-India delegation of prominent women to meet with Montagu and Chelmsford. Members of this delegation presented an address documenting the awakening of Indian women to their civic responsibilities. They wanted women to have the status of "people" in a self-governing nation within the Empire.[2] With this deputation, Indian women began their struggle to secure for themselves political and civil rights.

When these women asked for the vote, they claimed they spoke for all women. In the nineteenth century, British officials expressed their concern for "Indian women" and in that earlier time would have been delighted with such a claim. But the British now defined their "civilizing mission" differently. After World War I British

---

[1] "Ladies' Deputation," *ISR*, 28 (November 11, 1917), p. 121.

[2] "A Ladies' Deputation to Mr. Montagu," *NI* (October 25, 1917), p. 5; "Women's Deputation to Mr. Montagu," *NI* (December 13, 1917), p. 5; Dr. (Mrs.) Muthulakshmi Reddi, *Mrs. Cousins and her Work in India* (Madras, Women's Indian Association, 1956), pp. 1–5; J. H. and Mrs. Cousins, *We Two Together*, (Madras, Ganesh and Co., n.d.), p. 310; "A Copy of the Address Presented by the All-India Women's Deputation to Lord Chelmsford (Viceroy) and Rt. Hon'ble E. S. Montagu (Secretary of State)," pamphlet, Suffrage-India, FC.

critics of Indian society complained that middle-class Indians had no sympathy for the customs and traditions of the rural masses.[3] Previously it was "Indian women" who needed protecting, now it was "poor women."[4] Women who expected the British to welcome their petitions and memorials, were now criticized for ignoring the masses of Indian women.

Prominent nationalists were equally suspicious of women's demands, although for different reasons. Indian men who encouraged female education and the formation of social organizations did not relish hearing women speak about the evils of patriarchy. By remaining silent these women fed the stereotype of themselves as ignorant and subordinate. If they spoke bluntly about the sufferings of Indian women, they were labeled disloyal to their culture. Franchise and civil rights were ideal issues for women to pursue since discussions of them could take place without reference to sensitive social or cultural matters. Nevertheless, women who threw themselves into this work learned the difficulties inherent in the pursuit of women's rights within a colonial framework.

THE FIRST DEMAND FOR
WOMEN'S FRANCHISE

The Indian women who formed a deputation to Lord Chelmsford and Mr. Montagu asked for the franchise on the same terms as men. They organized women's meetings to support their request and appealed for help from the Indian National Congress and other political organizations. In 1918 the Provincial Conferences of Bombay and Madras passed resolutions to remove sex disqualification from the reform bill. Similar resolutions were approved by the Andhra Provincial Conference, the Bombay Special National Congress, the India Home Rule League, and the Muslim League.

In August of 1918 Sarojini Naidu spoke on behalf of women's suffrage at the special session of Congress held in Bombay. Mrs. Naidu persuaded her audience that extending the franchise to women was rational, scientifically and politically sound, compatible with tradi-

[3] Report on Indian Constitutional Reform, *Parliamentary Papers*, vol. VIII (Cmd. 91091), p. 116.
[4] *Ibid.*, pp. 116, 151; Judith M. Brown, *Modern India* (Delhi, Oxford University Press, 1985), p. 152.

tion, and consistent with human rights. Referring to the objection that politics would make women less feminine, she promised her audience:

Never, never, for we realize that men and women have their separate goals, separate destinies and that just as man can never fulfill the responsibility or the destiny of a woman, a woman cannot fulfill the responsibility of man . . . We ask for the vote, not that we might interfere with you in your official functions, your civic duties, your public place and power, but rather that we might lay the foundation of national character in the souls of the children that we hold upon our laps, and instill into them the ideals of national life.[5]

Five thousand delegates attended this special session; the resolution passed by a 75 percent majority.

When the Thirty-Third Session of the Indian National Congress met in Delhi in December of 1918, Saraladevi Chaudhurani presented the resolution supporting the vote for women. Saraladevi told her audience that women had as much right to chart their own destinies as men for this was the age of human rights, justice, freedom, and self-determination. The world has outgrown certain ideas, she said, particularly the "fanciful division of intellect and emotion being the respective spheres of men and women." Going beyond the assertions of Sarojini Naidu, Saraladevi contended that the "sphere of women" included "comradeship with men in the rough and tumble of life and to being the fellow-workers of men in politics and other spheres."[6]

These meetings were followed by gatherings all over India – of provincial and district Congress conferences and of women's organizations – to express support for women's franchise. Behind the scenes Indian women and a few British women, especially Dorothy Jinarajadasa and Margaret Cousins, worked conscientiously to make their case. At this time petition politics seemed the only way to make an impression on government. Moreover, British suffragists had advised them that these tactics would be effective. Montagu himself told Millicent Fawcett, a long-standing member of British female suffrage organizations, that it would be up to Indian women to make a strong case for the Franchise Committee. Mrs. Fawcett communicated this message to her friends in India, and it was cited in letters sent to WIA branches. Her letter said

---

[5] *Report of the Special Session of the Indian National Congress*, Bombay, August 19–31 and September 1, 1918 (Bombay, 1918), pp. 109–10.
[6] *Report of the Thirty-Third Session of the Indian National Congress,* Delhi, December 26–31, 1918 (Delhi, 1918) pp. 118–21.

concerned women should write to the chair of the Franchise Committee and request an interview.[7]

The Southborough Franchise Committee toured India in 1918 to gather information. They accepted women's petitions but interviewed women from only two provinces: Bengal and Punjab.[8] In their final report they concluded that granting the franchise would be premature. Lord Southborough decided Indian women did not want the vote and even if they did, social customs would impede its implementation.[9]

Indian women who had worked for the franchise were furious. The Southborough Committee had ignored their resolutions and petitions and overlooked the fact that women were already serving on municipal councils and other local bodies. The WIA swung into action. Annie Besant and Sarojini Naidu went to England to present evidence before the Joint Select Committee while local branches of the WIA held meetings, passed resolutions, and forwarded their comments to London.[10] In Bombay, women held a protest meeting and sent letters and telegrams to the members of parliament. Mrs. Jaiji Jehangir Petit, chair of the Bombay Women's Committee for Women's Suffrage, sent this cable to London: "Women ask no favor but claim right and justice. If the vote is denied it will mean serious check to women's advancement in India."[11]

Two members of the Southborough Committee had been in favor of extending the franchise to Indian women: Mr. Hogg and Sir C. Sankaran Nair, the only Indian member of the Viceroy's Executive Council. After the committee published its report, Sir Sankaran Nair met with the Bombay Committee and advised them to send a delegation to give evidence before the Joint Select Committee. The Bombay Committee on Women's Suffrage decided to send Mrs. Herabai A. Tata and her daughter Mithan (after marriage Mithan Lam) to England with Sir Sankaran Nair.[12]

---

[7] Letter from D. Jinarajadasa and Meenakshi Ammal Mahadeva Sastri to "Dear Madam" (November 14, 1918), box 70, FC.

[8] Letter from M. Cousins to A. Besant (June 4, 1919), Theosophical Society Archives, Madras.

[9] Mrs. Herabai Tata, "A Short Sketch of Indian Women's Franchise Work," pamphlet (n.d.), Suffrage-India, FC.

[10] Letter from M. Cousins to "My Dear Sisters" (May 28, 1919), AIWC Files.

[11] Tata, "A Short Sketch."

[12] Mithan Lam, "Autumn Leaves: Some Memoirs of Yesteryear," an unpublished memoir, p. 7; correspondence of Mrs. Herabai A. Tata to Mrs. Jaiji J. Petit, chairman (sic) of the Bombay Women's Committee for Women's Suffrage. For work done in England by Mrs. Tata at the time of the first Indian Reform Act, December, 1919, see account no. 612, AIWC Files.

10 Herabai and Mithan Tata in London, 1919

Herabai's budding feminism was encouraged by Princess Sophie Duleepsingh, granddaughter of the famous Ranjit Singh who had ruled the Punjab from 1799 until his death in 1839. Princess Sophie lived in England but she often vacationed in Kashmir and it was here they met. Sophie, who wore a "votes for women" badge, explained the suffrage movement to Herabai. Under her tutelage Herabai became "a firm believer and worker for the cause of women's suffrage." When the Bombay Committee decided to send a representative to England, Herabai expressed her willingness to go. Herabai's husband approved of this plan and agreed to support the venture. Their unmarried daughter, Mithan, also keenly interested in women's rights, accompanied her mother to London.[13]

Herabai wrote a detailed account of her efforts on behalf of women's suffrage. Even though the WIA sent Annie Besant and Sarojini Naidu as representatives, Herabai was the real soldier in this campaign. She wrote letters and sent memoranda to influential individuals, asked for support from a wide range of organizations, and addressed every group that invited her to speak. Herabai and Mithan researched all topics associated with women's franchise and prepared substantial reports to argue their case. Tata Ltd. sponsored their work through a contribution made to the Bombay Suffrage Committee. This was sufficient to pay for Herabai's voyage and most of her expenses; the remainder of their expenses were borne by her husband.[14]

Annie Besant warned the Joint Select Committee that they were making a mistake by ignoring women's demands. According to Besant, Indian political councils included women until the British imposed their notions of women's proper place. If the British continued to exclude them, Besant predicted Indian women would join political protests. This would have serious consequences. Any attempt to suppress their agitation would fail because Indian men "would not tolerate police interference where women are concerned."[15] Besant was raising the specter of a revolt from within the zenana, a dangerous space because it was unexplored and uncolonized.

When Sarojini Naidu spoke to the Joint Select Committee she said she represented all Indian women, even orthodox Hindu and Muslim women. Enfranchised women would be a powerful force for progress,

[13] Lam, "Autumn Leaves," pp. 4–12.   [14] See correspondence from H. Tata to J. J. Petit.
[15] Joint Select Committee on Government of India Bill, *Parliamentary Papers*, 1919, vol. II, Minutes of Evidence (Cmd. 203), p. 75.

Naidu maintained. She brushed aside all objections about the difficulties of voting while observing purdah. Only a few "upper-class" women veiled, she told the committee, and she had never known "purdah to come in the way of anything a woman ever wanted to do."[16] Unfortunately the committee did not have enough time to interview Herabai Tata and instead asked her to submit a statement. All three women, Besant, Naidu, and Tata, argued that recent educational and social opportunities had restored Indian women to their former power and influence. Indian women, they asserted, are strong and united and ready to reform society.

Most British men were skeptical. They believed the majority of Indian women were uneducated and living in seclusion and many of the Indians they listened to reinforced their stereotypes. Cornelia Sorabji (1866–1954), who studied law at Oxford and returned to India in 1894 to act as a pleader for women, opposed the work of both male and female nationalist reformers. Cornelia's father, Reverend Sorabji Karsedji had converted to Christianity from Zoroastrianism and married Francina who was a convert from Hinduism. The family was well known in Poona for their dedicated work in the fields of education and social reform. Denied admittance to the British bar,[17] the only route to practicing law in India, Cornelia represented women under *sanads* (special permission to plead) and later as an official appointed to the Court of Wards to deal with the cases of *purdahnashin* (secluded women).[18] She had an extraordinary career and became known around the world as a professional who broke with all traditions to help women. Her rejection of both nationalism and feminism has caused historians to neglect the important role she played in giving credibility to the British critique of those educated Indian women who were now part of the political landscape.

Miss Sorabji moved in influential circles and had numerous opportunities to present her British friends with the "Indian" point of view.[19]

---

[16] *Ibid.*, pp. 131–2.

[17] Cornelia Sorabji finally qualified for the bar in 1919 but until that time all women in Britain were barred by statutory law from qualifying. See Antoinette Burton, "Empire, Oxford and Imperial Culture: Cornelia Sorabji at Somerville College, 1889–1892," *At the Heart of Empire: Indians and the Colonial Encounter in Late-Victorian Britain* (in progress).

[18] Cornelia Sorabji, "Some Experiences" (March 1, 1931), newspaper clipping, Gham-Khwar-i-Hind of Lahore writes (n.d.), CS Papers, Eur. Mss., F/165/5, IOOLC.

[19] Letters from Sir Campbell Rhodes to Lady Malcolm (March 13, 1929) and C. Sorabji to Lady Stanfordham (March 13, 1929), Social Service File; Cornelia Sorabji Diaries, CS Papers, Eur. Mss., F/165/5, IOOLC.

Indian women, she asserted, fitted into two groups. She called one group "the Progressives" and defined them as a small group of educated women, perhaps 10 percent of the female population, who were largely independent of ancient customs. The other 90 percent were illiterate and lived in seclusion. All the schemes for ameliorating the hardships of women had benefited "the progressives" but left the masses of women virtually untouched.[20] Moreover, the progressives made no effort to comprehend the facts of existence for the masses of women.

In a confidential memorandum to the government regarding the proposed Montagu–Chelmsford reforms, Cornelia warned that Western ideals of government would not fit a fatalistic and superstitious society. Parliamentary democracy could only be successful in a country where the nuclear family, educational institutions, and government all encouraged social mobility, individual rights, and action. Indian ethics and institutions were the exact opposite. Until education had changed Indian institutions and attitudes, Western political institutions would be useless.[21] For the present, the government had a duty to continue its protection of the masses.

On the topic of female franchise, Cornelia wrote, "We (Indian women) cannot yet make our demands for equal citizenship and equal opportunities – our history forbids this." Progressive women had reached a high state of civilization, but the majority of women were still illiterate and ignorant. It would be "dangerous" she argued, to extend the vote to these "left-behinds." Until all women were educated, political reform could not be of "any real and lasting value" to the country.[22]

There is no conclusive evidence that Cornelia Sorabji's advice carried any weight, but members of the House of Commons ignored the profranchise memoranda presented by Indian women's organizations, the Indian National Congress, the Home Rule League, the Muslim League, and British women's organizations. Montagu observed that conservative opposition to female franchise was almost a "religious feeling." Because it would be dangerous to provoke religious men, he urged the House to pass the India Bill as it existed. A proviso could be added

---

[20] C. Sorabji, "Note on a Social Settlement for the Service of Women" (n.d.) and "Note on the Possibility Appertaining to a Social Service Institute" (n.d.), CS Papers, Eur. Mss., F/165/5, IOOLC.

[21] Confidential memorandum, "The Montagu–Chelmsford Reforms," CS Papers, Eur. Mss., F/165/13, IOOLC.

[22] From an Indian correspondent, "The Position of Women II," *Common Cause* (May 9, 1919), pp. 36–7.

allowing provincial legislative councils to add women to the list of registered voters.[23]

Indian women activists felt betrayed. They had not asked for anything extraordinary – only that the franchise be extended to women who met the qualifying standards set for men. Excluding females from the India Act seemed to be *de facto* recognition of male authority over women.[24] Their opponents had used purdah as "the chief weapon in the armory of opposition against Franchise for Indian women." Obviously, the British promise to safeguard the rights of minorities meant only male minorities. In the case of women, the majority were denied rights because the minority lived in seclusion. This paradoxical situation led Sarojini Naidu to inquire why the British did not extend the franchise to women and then make special provisions for the *purdahnashin* to protect the rights of this minority.[25]

THE NATIONALIST AGENDA AND WOMEN'S RIGHTS

Nationalist leaders also challenged women's rights activists. In 1920 Herabai and Mithan, the latter now studying at the London School of Economics and registered at the Inns of Court, traveled to Paris and met with Madame Cama. Madame Bhikaji Cama (1861–1936) was born and educated in Bombay, married in 1885 to a rather conservative gentleman, and by the 1920s was living in Europe. She traveled to London in 1902 for medical treatment, met a group of expatriate revolutionaries, joined their circle, and moved to Paris where she lived for thirty years.[26] When she met Herabai and Mithan she "shook her head rather sadly and stated: 'Work for Indian's freedom and Independence. When India is independent women will get not only the Vote, but all other rights.'"[27] Gandhi reacted in much the same way. In his first article on women in *Young India*, Gandhi stated he wanted women to take their proper place by the side of men but he would not support a "votes for women" campaign. The timing was wrong. Indians needed to struggle against the British and the franchise cam-

---

[23] H. Tata to J. J. Petit (December 7, 1919), AIWC Files; Joint Select Committee on Government of India Bill, vol. 1, Report and Proceedings of the Committee, *Parliamentary Papers* 1919, vol. IV, Part 1 of the Preamble (Cmd. 203).
[24] Letter from M. Cousins to Mrs. Fawcett (October 30, 1918), box 90, FC.
[25] "Franchise for Indian Women," *MR*, 26 (1919), p. 549.
[26] "Madam Bhikaji Cama," *DNB*, vol. 1, pp. 240–2.   [27] Lam, "Autumn Leaves", p. 12.

paign would waste their energy. Women should use their energies "helping their men against the common foe." Gandhi advised women to liberate themselves and their menfolk "from the death-grip of the existing government which is the greatest of all social evils with which society is cursed."[28]

PROVINCIAL LEGISLATURES AND WOMEN'S VOTE

This advice from nationalist leaders did not prevent pro-franchise women from continuing their fight. Bombay and Madras were the first provinces to extend the franchise to women in 1921; the United Provinces followed in 1923; Punjab and Bengal in 1926; and finally Assam, the Central Provinces, and Bihar and Orissa in 1930.

Detailed accounts of how the vote was won are not available for every province. In Bengal, women argued in favor of women's "special" contribution to politics. Men who favored the vote for women called this a natural extension of democratic rights while opponents talked of women's inferiority and incompetence in public affairs. Others lamented the neglect of husbands and children that was sure to follow the vote. One gentleman even argued that political activity rendered women incapable of breast feeding. The measure passed in 1926, not because support for female enfranchisement had increased but because the composition of the legislative body had changed when the Swaraj Party agreed to re-enter politics and came to dominate the legislature. This party united Hindus and Muslims to work for immediate independence; consequently "the woman suffrage resolution rode to victory on a wave of nationalist enthusiasm."[29]

The number of women qualified to vote was never large enough to be a matter of concern. Throughout India the numbers enfranchised were small: in Madras women were 8.46 percent of the total voters; 5.03 percent in Bombay; 3.0 percent in the United Province and Bengal; and only 2.5 percent in the Punjab. In the Central Legislative Assembly women comprised 4.36 percent of the total electorate.[30] It obviously

---

[28] M. K. Gandhi, "Women and the Vote," *Young India* (November 24, 1920), p. 2. In 1921 Gandhi expressed support for the idea of female suffrage.

[29] Barbara Southard, "Colonial Politics and Women's Rights: Woman Suffrage Campaigns in Bengal, British India in the 1920s," *Modern Asian Studies*, 27, no. 2 (1993), pp. 397–439.

[30] "Number of Women Voters in India," GOI, Public Home Dept., file no. 25/3/1929.

was the principle that counted, not the possibility that women could dominate the assemblies. Next, women demanded the right to be elected to the legislatures. The same arguments for and against their participation were repeated until finally all the provinces granted women this right.

The opponents of women's political participation voiced a number of objections. They warned of traditional gender roles breaking down and the possibility of role reversal. Not unlike their Victorian counterparts they worried about the adverse effects of this activity on women's mental and physical health. But their main fear was that Indian women would imitate Western women whose shameless behavior they deplored.[31] Voting might well play havoc with women's natural roles of wife and mother, sanctioned by tradition and revered and respected throughout time.

Male supporters of female franchise countered these arguments by highlighting women's special contribution to politics. "What Will Indian Women Do with the Vote?" asked the pro-women's franchise *Modern Review* of Calcutta. They will use the three Ws – Wisdom, Wellness and Wealth to destroy India's three Is – Ignorance, Illness and Indigence came the answer.[32] Others claimed this as India's opportunity to prove it was as advanced as Western nations. Speaking in the Legislative Assembly, Mr. N. M. Dumasia, a member from Bombay, boasted:

It is gratifying to find that in a country where men are accused of treating women as chattel the political progress of women has been more rapid than in England and free from the war of the sexes and the smashing of heads and windows which preceded the enfranchisement of women in England.[33]

Many women also wrote and spoke about the distinct contribution made by women, while others challenged the power structure. V. Kamalabai Ammal wrote a petition to the Governor-General protesting the delay in removing sex disqualification from the statutes of Bihar and Orissa. She reminded him that women were "as much children of India as males." To even allow the legislatures to vote on this issue "implies the monopoly of the male sex not only to enjoy the priv-

---

[31] For further discussion of these attitudes see Dipesh Chakrabarty, "The Difference – Deferral of (A) Colonial Modernity: Public Debates on Domesticity in British Bengal," *History Workshop Journal*, 36 (autumn, 1993), pp. 9–13.
[32] "What Will Women Do with the Vote?" *MR*, 30 (1921), p. 493.
[33] GOI, Public Home Dept., 1926, file no. 28.

ilege but to confer [it] upon others – women – as a matter of charity."[34] Mrinalini Sen, a Bengali suffragette, complained that the government was treating women in an arbitrary fashion. In a polemical article reminiscent of those written by British suffragists, Mrinalini wrote that although women were subject "to all the laws and rules of the land exercised by the British Government" and had to pay taxes if they owned property, they could not vote. It was as if the British were telling women not to go to the courts for justice but rather seek it at home.[35] Sen's comment had a special resonance on the eve of the non-cooperation movement which would urge women, and men, to no longer "go to the courts" but instead join the fight for freedom.

THE FIRST WOMAN LEGISLATOR

Muthulakshmi Reddy,[36] the first woman legislator, was appointed to the Madras Legislative Council in 1927. As she remembered, this nomination marked the beginning of her life-long effort to "correct the balance" for women by removing social abuses and working for equality in moral standards.[37]

Muthulakshmi was born in the princely state of Pudukottah in 1886. Her father was S. Narayanasami, a brahmin and the principal of Maharaja's College; her mother was Chandrammal, born to the isai velala caste, a caste whose women danced and sang in temples.[38] S. Narayanasami broke with tradition and sent Muthulakshmi to school. The child's enthusiasm for learning was so great that Muthulakshmi's teachers decided to instruct her in subjects beyond those approved by her father. At the onset of puberty she was obliged to leave school, but tutoring continued at home. Chandrammal wanted to search for a

---

[34] GOI, Home Dept., file no. 212/1929.

[35] Mrinalini Sen, "Indian Reform Bill and Women of India" (first published in *Africa and the Orient Reviews*, 1920), *Knocking at the Door* (Calcutta, Samir Dutt, 1954), pp. 68–9.

[36] Muthulakshmi has written her name Reddi and Reddy at different times. I have used "Reddy" in the text but kept the original spelling on her letters and writings in the footnotes.

[37] Muthulakshmi Reddi, "Dear Friends" speech (n.d.), file no. 11, DRP; information on Muthulakshmi Reddi comes primarily from *Autobiography of Dr. (Mrs.) Muthulakshmi Reddy* (Madras, M. Reddi, 1964) – for quote see p. 18; Dr. (Mrs.) S. Muthulakshmi Reddy, *My Experiences As a Legislator* (Madras, Current Thought Press, 1930); and interview, Dr. (Mrs.) Muthulakashami (*sic*) Reddi, Layman's Foreign Mission Inquiry, 1928–30, box 28, RWC.

[38] C. S. Lakshmi, *The Face Behind the Mask: Women in Tamil Literature* (Delhi, Vikas Publishing House, 1984), pp. 16–17.

bridegroom but Muthulakshmi had different aspirations. "I had even then set my heart upon something high and I wanted to be a different woman from the common lot," she wrote in her memoirs. She pitied women for their subordination to men and inwardly rebelled whenever she heard people say that only boys needed education.

When Muthulakshmi passed the matriculation exam she applied for admission to Maharaja's College but her application was not welcomed by the principal at the time or the parents of other students. Her gender was a factor but so was her background: the principal thought she might "demoralize" the male students. The somewhat enlightened Maharaja of Pudukottah ignored these objections, admitted her to the college, and gave her a scholarship.[39] Her father suggested she become a school teacher but she had higher aspirations. Muthulakshmi had never met an educated woman in person but she had read in magazines about women receiving BAs and MAs.

When one of her father's former students suggested she study medicine, Muthulakshmi and her father gave his proposal serious consideration. She had always been a sickly child, rarely helped by traditional medical practices and herbal remedies, and her mother's bout with typhoid provided personal motivation. Moreover, she wanted to leave home to be free of her mother's obsession with marriage. She entered Madras Medical College, completed her studies in 1912, and became house surgeon in the Government Hospital for Women and Children in Madras.[40]

During her college years, Muthulakshmi met Sarojini Naidu and began to attend women's meetings. She found women who shared her personal concerns and addressed them in terms of women's rights.

Muthulakshmi refused to listen to discussions about marriage until she graduated. Magazines and newspapers carried articles about her awards and degrees and this notoriety brought offers of marriage from reform-minded young men. The suitor who attracted her father's attention was Dr. D. T. Sandara Reddy who read about Muthulakshmi in one of these magazines. Muthulakshmi reluctantly agreed to consider his proposal although she did not want to be "saddled with marriage and become subordinate to a man whoever he might be."[41] Finally, after checking out Dr. Reddy's "attainments and conduct" and listening to her father's positive assessment, Muthulakshmi agreed to marry on the

---

[39] *Ibid.*   [40] *Autobiography*, pp. 1–17.   [41] *Ibid.*, p. 18.

condition the proposed bridegroom would promise to "always respect me as an equal and never cross my wishes." In 1914, when she was twenty-eight years of age, they married in accordance with the 1872 Native Marriage Act.[42]

As a married woman Muthulakshmi practiced medicine while she raised a family. She found it difficult and warned other aspiring women doctors: "Medical women, if they really love the profession and wish to practice should not think of marriage, because they cannot perform two functions at one and the same time."[43] But she somehow managed to juggle her career and marriage, go to England for further study, and work with women's organizations. At this time she believed British rule was beneficial to the downtrodden, especially women and the depressed classes. She thought women belonged in the political arena because of their special interests and special abilities.

Muthulakshmi's name was on a list of well-known social workers submitted to the Legislative Council by the WIA. At first she deferred, citing the demands of her medical practice and lack of experience. "I was," she wrote, "neither a politician nor was I interested in politics except what directly concerned women's life." When nominated to the Madras Legislative Council in 1926, Muthulakshmi accepted to represent "my sisters' cause in the Council."[44] Her colleagues in the Council applauded her medical and educational work but opposed her efforts on behalf of *devadasis*[45] and untouchables as well as her campaigns to obtain legal rights for women.[46] Muthulakshmi took her concerns to the public – she wrote pamphlets and letters-to-the-editor and called women's meetings. Disregarding personal criticism, she saw it her duty, as an educated woman, to speak "on behalf of our sex."

---

[42] The Native Marriage Act III of 1872 was passed on March 19, 1872. It had previously been presented as the Civil Marriage Act and the Brahmo Marriage Act. This form of marriage was available only to persons who were not Hindus or members of other established religions. It set the minimum age for marriage at fourteen for females and eighteen for males, made provision for divorce, and abandoned Hindu rituals. This Marriage Act legitimized unions between couples from different communities such as Muthulakshmi and Dr. Reddy.

[43] *Autobiography*, p. 22.   [44] *My Experiences*, p. 4.

[45] *Devadasis* were women attached to temples where they sang and danced for the gods and in return were given the right to land. The British and some reformers regarded them as little more than temple prostitutes. Daughters of *devadasis* were considered *devadasis* whether or not they performed in the temple.

[46] *My Experiences*, p. 58.

THE SECOND CAMPAIGN FOR FEMALE
FRANCHISE

The Simon Commission, appointed in 1927, was the first step towards the formulation of a new India Act. This initiated the second round in the fight for female enfranchisement. The India Act passed in 1935 increased representation but not to the extent expected by organized women. The process of delivering this second franchise decision exposed both the limits of collaboration with the British and the problems inherent in attaching women's rights to the nationalist movement.

When the Simon Commission was first announced, the WIA, then the only national women's organization committed to women's franchise, was willing to cooperate and asked that a woman be included. However, by the time the "white seven" men who composed the Commission arrived in India in February of 1929, the WIA had joined the nationalist boycott against them. The AIWC then decided to form a franchise sub-committee and by the 1930s concluded that political emancipation was the first step towards releasing women from their "shackles."[47] They also boycotted the Simon Commission. But there were other educated women, acting without the imprimatur of the major organizations, who met with the Commission and suggested giving the vote to literate women or reserving seats.[48]

At the end of October 1929 the Viceroy, Lord Irwin, announced that the British government would call for a Round Table Conference to discuss the next step towards dominion status. The WIA immediately submitted the names of three women to be included: Sarojini Naidu, Muthulakshmi Reddy, and Rameshwari Nehru.[49] Because Irwin's declaration read "discuss" not "implement" the Indian National Congress decided to boycott the conference. The WIA, solidly behind the nationalist agenda, also withdrew their cooperation. This was a difficult decision for members of the WIA. They had worked long and hard on the franchise issue and now they were walking out on an opportunity to influence the next constitutional measure.[50]

The London Conference began its meetings in November of 1930 and Indian women were represented, but not by women chosen by the

[47] *Annual Report*, AIWC, Seventh Session, 1933, p. 30.
[48] "Indian Statutory Commission," *IAR*, 1, nos. 1 and 2 (January–June, 1929), pp. 54–6.
[49] Reddi, *Mrs. Cousins and her Work in India*, p. 79.
[50] WIA Report, 1931–2, pp. 3–4.

leading women's organizations. Begum Jahan Ara Shah Nawaz was included because she was attending this conference as her father's (Sir Muhammad Shafi's) private secretary. Mrs. Radhabai Subbarayan, the other representative, had attended Somerville College, Oxford and was well known by British women suffragists. Both Begum Shah Nawaz and Mrs. Subbarayan were long-standing members of women's organizations but the British had appointed them without consulting these organizations.

At the Round Table Conference Begum Shah Nawaz and Mrs. Subbarayan spoke about the "awakening" of women and their leadership in promoting social change. Noting the British obsession with purdah, they claimed this custom would decline if women gained the vote. The ideal was adult franchise, but they were willing to accept special reservations as an interim measure.[51]

Organized women in India disagreed. Margaret Cousins and Muthulakshmi Reddy from the WIA, Mrs. Hamid Ali and Rani Rajwade from the AIWC, and Tarabai Premchand from the NCWI, together with Sarojini Naidu, issued a joint memorandum in support of universal adult franchise. One by one women who had previously supported nomination and reserved seats added their voices to the demand for "equality and no privileges" and "a fair field and no favor."[52] They had not changed their views on the importance of women voting, but they had altered their priorities. They decided to place the nationalist position – no cooperation without a firm commitment to ending British rule – above their desire for wider female enfranchisement.[53]

With the Gandhi–Irwin Pact of March 1931, Congress agreed to participate in the second Round Table Conference to draw up a plan for federation and responsible government with the reservation of certain powers. The women's organizations followed the Congress lead, agreed to participate, and sent Sarojini Naidu as their representative. Gandhi was the sole representative of the Indian National Congress,

---

[51] Mrs. P. Subbarayan, *The Political Status of Women Under the New Constitution* (Madras, n.p., n.d.), pp. 2–3; Indian Round Table Conference, November 12, 1930–January 19, 1931, *Parliamentary Papers*, 1930–1, vol. XII (Cmd. 3772), pp. 113–16; IRTC (Sub-Committee Reports), *Parliamentary Papers*, 1930–1, vol. XII (Cmd. 3772), p. 47.

[52] "Reservations of Seats for Women," *The Hindu* (November 17, 1931), p. 5.

[53] Letters from Mrs. P. N. Sirur to R. Subbarayan (April 22, 1931), R. Subbarayan to E. Rathbone (May 1, 1931), folder no. 5, RP; letters from E. Rathbone to M. Reddi (March 12, 1931), M. Reddi to E. Rathbone (March 9, 1931), E. Rathbone to M. Reddi (May 1, 1931), M. Reddi to E. Rathbone (May 6, 1931), folder no. 1, RP.

and Begum Shah Nawaz and Mrs. Subbarayan were again nominated by the British. By this time Begum Shah Nawaz had had a change of heart and firmly supported the Congress demand for universal adult franchise. But Radhabai Subbarayan withstood pressure from her friends in the WIA and continued her support for reserved seats.[54]

At the close of the second RTC a White Paper, recommending an increase in enfranchised women, was presented to both houses of parliament. Lord Lothian was named to chair the Franchise Committee to work out the details. His committee planned to tour India in 1932, collect evidence and opinions, and submit concrete proposals for the next India Act. Radhabai Subbarayan and the Honorable Mary Ada Pickford, the Oxford-educated daughter of Lord Sterndale and MP from Lancashire, were the two women appointed to the Lothian Committee. Eleanor Rathbone, a member of the House of Commons for the Combined English Universities since 1929, had long been interested in women's causes and discovered India when she read Katherine Mayo's *Mother India*. Her own book, *Child Marriage: The Indian Minotaur*, exposed the Sarda Act as "ornamental legislation" and won the praise of some Indian women. Rathbone was miffed when she was not appointed to the Lothian Committee. Undaunted by this official slight, she decided to tour India and meet with Indian women. Her object was not to elicit their opinions but rather to advise them how to fight for the vote.[55]

The Lothian Committee met with very few women in India but accepted a 1932 memorandum from the all-India women's organizations. In this document women vented their criticism of all the formulas under consideration: nomination, enfranchising educated women, and the franchise for a percentage of urban women.[56] This was their official stance, though actually there was a great deal of support for special electorates and nominated seats. Amrit Kaur, chairperson of the AIWC in 1932, had to scold Miss Dass, a member from Bihar and Orissa, for organizing women's support for a separate electorate. "Standing Committee members must be loyal," Kaur admonished.[57]

---

[54] Subbarayan, *Political Status,* p. 16; letter from M. Reddi to "Dear Madam" (November 16, 1936), AIWC Files, no. 135.

[55] Barbara N. Ramusack, "Cultural Missionaries, Maternal Imperialists, Feminist Allies: British Women Activists in India, 1865–1945," *Western Women and Imperialism: Complicity and Resistance,* ed. Nupur Chaudhuri and Margaret Strobel (Bloomington, Indiana University Press, 1992), pp. 126–8.

[56] "Memorandum of the All-India Women's Conference," 1932, AIWC Files, no. 95.

[57] Letter from Amrit Kaur to Miss Dass (January 23, 1932), AIWC Files, no. 95.

While in India Miss Pickford wrote letters to her sister in England describing the work of the committee. Pickford had no love for Indian women: Radhabai Subbarayan was "dull and unimaginative" and the debates of Madras women "cat fights." Occasionally her committee hired cars and visited villages to interview "ordinary people." As she traveled throughout the country Pickford made snap judgments, most of them negative, without a trace of self-consciousness about the spectacle she and other members of the committee created when their ten motorcars roared into villages. In the villages the committee's interpreters ordered people to appear for questioning. Often the women ran away but on one occasion an elderly widow with inherited property told them she always asked her son how to vote. This confirmed Pickford's opinion of villagers as backward and "quite unfit for any form of direct franchise."[58] In their final report the Lothian Committee rejected adult franchise because of the country's size, large population, and high rate of adult illiteracy. They agreed more women should be enfranchised, to facilitate social reform, and recommended increasing the ratio of female to male voters from 1:20 to 1:5.[59]

Before Indian women could react to these recommendations, they were faced with the communal award that confirmed reserved seats for Muslims and extended them to the depressed classes. Gandhi maintained that the lower castes, the "untouchables" or "harijans" (children of God), were Hindus and should not be treated as a separate group. He began a fast in opposition to the award. The Poona Pact of September 1932, a compromise measure, granted reserved seats to the depressed classes within the total Hindu constituency. When Congress leaders, including Gandhi, accepted this agreement it was clear they had abandoned universal franchise. But the women's organizations denounced the Poona Pact and other communal awards as divisive for women.[60] Begum Shah Nawaz and a number of other Muslim women disagreed. Since their menfolk supported this formula, they advised women's organizations to accept this decision because it would promote religious harmony.[61]

The White Paper of 1933, recommending the voting strength of

---

[58] Letters to Dorothy (January 19–April 12, 1932), Pickford Papers, Eur. Mss., D. 1013, IOOLC.
[59] Report of the Indian Franchise Committee, 1932, *Parliamentary Papers*, 1931–1932, vol. VIII (1) (Cmd. 4086), pp. 16, 82–7.   [60] WIA, 1932; AIWC Files, no. 20.
[61] "Women and the Communal Decision," *ILM*, 5 (September–October, 1932), p. 510.

women to men be increased to 1:10, was the final blow to the demand for universal franchise. Some of the women who had defended universal franchise advocated a women's non-cooperation movement. The pragmatists disagreed and urged women to redefine themselves as a minority community in order to enter the competition for political representation. Muthulakshmi Reddy advised:

We cannot but accept the qualifications decided on by our men and accepted by them. As Gandhiji himself is justifying his cooperation with the government for the sake of removing the evil of untouchability, the women social workers and educationalists are eager to get the maximum for themselves, and they rightly feel that in the present backward condition of the county they cannot think of non-cooperation.[62]

Early in 1933 women leaders decided to work for a franchise ratio of 1:5. British women supported this work and urged them to collect evidence about the numbers of educated women who wanted the vote. Radhabai Subbarayan, Dorothy Jinarajadasa, Begum Shah Nawaz, and Sarala Ray asked individuals and organizations to voice their support. But there were still women demanding adult franchise[63] and Muslim women who stood behind the communal award. By and large, AIWC leaders omitted difference of opinion from their reports.[64] After much debate the three women's organizations produced a joint memorandum reiterating their demand for adult franchise and objecting to the various schemes for separate electorates and reservation of seats. As a temporary and short-term measure they agreed to accept the enfranchisement of literate women and urban women.[65]

Eleanor Rathbone cautioned the women's organizations that another request for adult franchise coupled with refusal of the wifehood qualification might kill all schemes to increase the ranks of the enfranchised. Rathbone and her British friends held two assumptions not shared by their Indian counterparts. They believed any plan to increase women's representation was desirable because more women in the legislatures

---

[62] Letter from Dr. Reddi (February 13, 1933), AIWC Files, no. 95.
[63] Rameshwari Nehru to M. Reddi (March 1933), AIWC Files, no. 95.
[64] Letter from Mrs. Huidekoper to Rani Rajwade (May 20, 1933), AIWC Files, no. 37; letter from A. Kemcharar to Hon'ble Organizing Secretary of the AIWC (May 31, 1933), AIWC Files, no. 34.
[65] *Stri Dharma*, 16 (September 1933) p. 549; "Memorandum II on the Status of Women in the Proposed New Constitution of India," addressed to the members of the Joint Select Committee, June 1933, pamphlet, Suffrage, FC; Minutes of Evidence given before the Joint Select Committee on Indian Constitutional Reform, 1934, *Parliamentary Papers*, 1932–3, vol. VIII (IIc), pp. 1617–22.

would lead to social reform. Second, they assumed universal adult franchise was only a few years away.[66] These British women advised their Indian "sisters" to drop the demand for universal franchise and accept reservations and other special schemes.

Muthulakshmi Reddy and her colleagues thought through their position very carefully. Muthulakshmi knew adult franchise was doomed from the beginning, but she no longer had illusions about the benevolence of the British. She based her demand for adult franchise not on political expediency but morality; "our cause is righteous," Muthulakshmi wrote, and "in the end it will prevail."[67] She informed Rathbone the wifehood vote was not the answer because Indian wives were not like English wives. English wives had more education, but also, "your marriage laws never allowed polygamy nor gave unlimited power to the husband over the body and soul of the wife." Muthulakshmi believed the net effect of enfranchising wives of property owners would be to double the vote of conservative, orthodox men "generally opposed to all reforms in society." She found reserved seats equally unattractive as a scheme for bringing women into the political picture. At one time Muthulakshmi approved of this idea – after all, she was nominated, not elected, to the Madras Council – but she was appalled by the appointment of undeserving women. She came to the painful conclusion that just having "a woman" in a powerful position was not the answer and she would far rather have "one or two good women . . . in each council or assembly to represent women's point of view." Muthulakshmi concluded: "Women are still new to the public work here and unless we have chosen women of character, grit, and courage to occupy places of honor and responsibility, women cannot help to achieve much."[68] In the final analysis, she preferred to rely on petition politics and the expression of public opinion rather than fight for a few more women legislators.

When they were in the last stages of preparing the India Act, the Linlithgow Committee decided to examine witnesses from Indian women's organizations. Rajkumari Amrit Kaur, Muthulakshmi Reddy, and Begum Hamid Ali spoke for the AIWC, WIA, and NCWI. Mrs.

---

[66] Press Agency (April 22, 1933), RP, folder 8; British Committee for Indian Women's Franchise Press Correspondence, House of Commons (May 5, 1933), RP, file no. 311; Rathbone to Reddi (February 9, 1933), RP, file no. 11.

[67] "Women and Reform," *The Hindu* (February 23, 1932), p. 9.

[68] M. Reddi to E. Rathbone (March 31, 1933), RP, file no. 1.

Sushama Sen and Mrs. L. Mukherjee spoke on behalf of the Calcutta Mahila Samiti and presented a memorandum from 450 women members of municipalities, District Boards and Taluk Boards in Madras (prepared by Radhabai Subbarayan), and another memorandum from 100 prominent women of Mangalore (prepared by Mrs. N. L. Subba Rao, Mrs. Subbarayan's sister).[69] Lady Layton, Sir Philip Hartog, and Mrs. O. Strachey presented the position of the British Committee for Indian Women's Franchise. They all insisted on the importance of increasing the number of enfranchised women.[70]

The Secretary of State agreed the evidence was compelling. The Linlithgow Committee commented: "India cannot reach the position to which it aspires in the world until its women play their due part as educated citizens." But they declined, ostensibly for administrative reasons, to give women that opportunity. Provincial administrations complained that too many voters, particularly women voters, would unnecessarily complicate the procedure. Moreover, they labeled the schemes to increase the number of women voters cumbersome and difficult to implement. The final plan placated the bureaucrats. The committee approved of a number of different programs to increase the number of women voters: wives could vote in some provinces, literate women in others, and the wives of military officers in still others. The Act also introduced special electorates for women.[71] The India Act of 1935 fixed the ratio of voters at 1:5 yet there were few women who regarded this as a significant victory.

To many women it seemed as if all their allies had betrayed them. The British officials and administrators were interested in managing the woman question without challenging the status quo. British women tried to be helpful, but they were condescending and convinced of the efficacy of British rule. Indian males who led Congress agreed to compromises without consulting the women's organizations.

WOMEN'S LEGAL DISABILITIES

As organized women gained experience in the public arena, they became more aware of their dependent status. When they sought leg-

[69] E. Rathbone to R. Subbarayan (May 27, 1933 and June 23, 1933), RP, file no. 5; Mrs. P. K. Sen, "Supplementary Memorandum on the Franchise of Women," pamphlet, Suffrage, FC.
[70] Minutes of Evidence.
[71] Joint Committee on Indian Constitutional Reform (Session 1933–4), vol. I, Report 1934, *Parliamentary Papers,* 1933–4, vol. VI.

islative change, they became conscious of their subject status. They were excluded from new representative structures because they did not own property or were not married to men with property. Their education, experience with social work, agitation for the franchise, and involvement with the struggle for independence gave them a sense of a mission and confidence in their abilities. To be denied the same civil rights as men because of gender seemed unfair. Even worse, they realized that without these rights they would find it difficult to secure reform measures in the future. In 1934 the AIWC, disappointed with the Sarda Act and the proposed India Act, asked the government to appoint an all-India commission to consider the legal disabilities of women. The issues they specified for study were inheritance, marriage, and the guardianship of children. Their ultimate goal was new law.[72] The appeal came from ideas contained in a pamphlet: *Legal Disabilities of Indian Women: A Plea for a Commission of Enquiry*, authored by Renuka Ray, legal secretary of the AIWC.[73] Renuka Ray argued in favor of new laws for all women, regardless of community. The legal position of Indian women was "one of the most inequitable in the world today," she wrote. Legal change would both alleviate the suffering of individual women and allow India to join the modern and progressive states of the world. Ray wanted new personal and family law that would make women independent and fully equipped to participate in public life. The AIWC said boldly: "we want no sex war"; they were demanding equality to allow women to play a role in the affairs of the country, not equality of the "Western variety."[74]

Assembly bills introduced in the 1930s suggested a piecemeal approach to improving women's status. Among the measures introduced between 1937 and 1938 were the Hindu Woman's Right to Property Bill, an amendment to the Child Marriage Restraint Act, a bill to allow intercaste marriage, the Hindu Woman's Right to Divorce Act, the Muslim Personal Law Bill, the Prevention of Polygamy Bill, and the Muslim Women's Right to Divorce Bill. In the provincial legislatures anti-dowry bills, marriage laws, and bills to allow women to inherit were introduced.

The new legislatures formed after the elections of 1937 included a

---

[72] *Annual Report*, AIWC Ninth Session, 1934, Karachi, pp. 17–31, 70–1.
[73] Renuka Ray, "Legal Disabilities of Indian Women," reprint from *MR* (November 1934); "Women's Movement in India," *Manchester Guardian*, (August 15, 1935), AIWC Files, no. 84. [74] *Annual Report*, AIWC, Tenth Session, 1935.

number of progressive men who recognized women's contribution to the nationalist movement and were aware of women's issues. At the same time India's visibility in international organizations increased. Reformers in the legislatures wanted progress at home, but they were equally concerned with India's image in the League of Nations and International Labor Organization.

When these bills were discussed it became apparent that male reformers and the women's organizations had different concepts of women's legal needs. G. V. Deshmukh introduced the Hindu Woman's Right to Property Bill to remove "the existing disabilities from which Hindu women suffer." Actually, all he proposed was an equal share for wives and daughters with male heirs if the head of the family died intestate.[75] Women's organizations agreed to support this bill despite their reservations. Members of the Bhagini Samaj, a Bombay women's organization, wrote a memo to the government suggesting a new law of succession "where the female heirs will come as heirs according to modern notions."[76] Muthulakshmi Reddy commented that a more pressing problem than inheritance was intolerance of independent women. She advocated a return to the morality of the past where both men and women exercised self-control. In her utopia mature females lived alone, supported themselves, and made their own decisions about marriage.[77] Commenting on a divorce bill, Mrs. Damle of Yeotmal said this would not help women. Women did not need divorce, they needed economic independence and more power so they could prevent their husbands from taking second wives.[78] These reform-minded women were not satisfied with piecemeal acts; they wanted comprehensive legislation accompanied by social and economic change.

Male opposition to even moderate reform remained strong. Some men based their disapproval on the sanctity of religious beliefs and practices: customs and behaviors supported by Hindu law were unalterable. Others raised the fear that legislation would bring chaos. What sensible governing body would want to create "havoc in the household," they asked. Still others focused on women's nature and said Hindu women were not suited for public life. Some men decided

[75] "The Hindu Woman's Right to Property Act, 1937," GOI, Home Dept. Judicial 1938, file no. 28/25/38.
[76] Letter to Secretary/Govt. of Bombay/Home Dept. from Bhagini Samaj (July 3, 1936), Hansa Mehta Papers, folder no. 119, file no. 2, NMML.
[77] M. Reddi, "A Plea for Marriage Reform," *ISR*, 46 (August, 1936), p. 790.
[78] GOI, Home Department, Judicial and K.W. 1938, file no. 28/9/38, p. 16.

to speak for women, declaring how happy the women they knew were with the current situation.

We do not know what the majority of women wanted and neither the reformers nor their opponents tried to find out. Instead, each argument was advanced as the view of "thousands," "the majority of educated people," "the multitude," or "99 percent of the people." Government files are equally uninformative since they include only solicited opinions from male-dominated associations and organizations with conservative social and political agendas.

Women who advocated equal rights decided to support every law that seemed progressive. Gandhi, although he wanted to improve women's status, disagreed with these tactics. Instead of supporting each and every measure for reform, Gandhi urged women activists to spend their time in the villages learning about local customs. In doing so they would understand that legal changes were irrelevant for most rural women.

The Indian National Congress proved an equally difficult ally. Only a few Congress members agreed that women's legal rights deserved the highest priority. Women reminded their male colleagues they had marched, demonstrated and gone to jail for the country. Now, they asserted, "It is our birthright to demand equitable adjustment of Hindu law regarding women's rights according to the requirements of present conditions of our society."[79] Jawaharlal Nehru supported women's participation in public life but privileged agrarian reform over family law reform and was completely against collaborating with the British to gain women's rights legislation.[80] His comments and those of other Congressmen did not deter women; rather women regarded these comments as evidence that some of their so-called "friends" were intractably opposed to any changes in women's status.

It was in this context that Sri Jinaraja Hedge, a member of the Central Assembly, moved the resolution to set up a committee on the legal disabilities of women. The Muslim League replied they had no objection as long as the committee confined its enquiry to Hindu law. Congress members approved of a committee but warned against changes that might "upset the framework on which the Hindu social system was based." The law member, N. N. Sircar, sensing the mood of the

[79] AIWC Files, no. 64 (215).
[80] Harold Levy, "Indian Modernization by Legislation: The Hindu Code Bill," Ph.D. thesis, University of Chicago (1973) p. 220.

Legislature suggested the enquiry be limited to residence and mainte-nance.[81] The women supporting legal change decided to throw their weight behind N. N. Sircar and take what they could get.[82]

Meanwhile, bills introduced earlier were defeated one by one. The debates shocked women leaders who were unaware of the opposition's intractability. Begum Hamid Ali deplored the "utterly unsympathetic attitude" of the men in the assembly and concluded they were "afraid" they might lose half of their land, power, and money. Legal reform would not solve all women's problems, but it would give financial security to some women who could live their own lives and care for their children.[83] Increasingly women couched their pleas in terms of human rights and spoke less often about the special contribution of women to politics. Women, Begum Hamid Ali said, "are asking for nothing more than just and humane treatment and to be liberated from their disabilities."[84]

The government agreed to appoint a committee of eminent lawyers to study Hindu law and make recommendations but the war and polit-ical disturbances caused them to delay until 1941. In January Sir B. N. Rau was appointed chair of the committee and asked to look carefully at the various bills on the Hindu woman's right to property. When the women's organizations protested, the committee received instructions to examine all questions of women's property rights. But the request to add a woman to the committee was ignored.[85]

Never before had all the women's organizations worked so hard to support a measure. Other issues, particularly women's franchise, had stimulated debate within the women's organizations. Now they worked cooperatively to gather information for the Rau Committee. Questionnaires sent to the women's organizations by the Rau Committee were distributed to their various branches and local leaders were asked to return them as quickly as possible.[86] Their efforts were rewarded by members of the Rau Committee who read this evidence

---

[81] *Annual Report,* AIWC, Fourteenth Session, 1940, pp. 106–7; WIA, Twenty-Third Annual Report, 1939–49, p. 12, WIA Papers; half-yearly report of the member in charge of legisla-tion (February 3, 1939), AIWC Files, no. 214.

[82] Letter from Delhi Women's League to Mrs. Sukthankar (April 14, 1939), AIWC Files, no. 215.

[83] Begum Hamid Ali, presidential speech, *Annual Report,* AIWC, Fourteenth Session, 1940, pp. 20–1.   [84] *Annual Report,* AIWC, Fourteenth Session, 1940, p. 80.

[85] *Annual Report,* AIWC, Sixteenth Session, 1942, pp. 36–7.

[86] *Ibid.*; NCWI, *Eighth Biennial Report,* 1940–2, Bombay, p. 9.

with special care. The final report, submitted in June of 1941, recommended two substantial innovations: codification of the law and "comprehensive, fundamental and substantial modification" of the law.[87]

By 1941 the Indian National Congress was boycotting the legislatures. At first only Congress leaders were arrested and sent to jail, but by spring thousands were involved in civil disobedience. This presented a dilemma for women who were both nationalists and feminists: should they cooperate with the Rau Committee to secure rights for women or join the Congress boycott? Congress had by this time established a National Planning Committee sub-committee composed of women and asked them to submit proposals regarding women's place in a planned economy. And Congress had taken the first steps towards setting up a Women's Department.[88]

One of the women caught in the middle was Radhabai Subbarayan, a Congress member, a member of the Central Legislative Assembly, and a long-standing feminist. Subbarayan was invited to work with the Rau Committee, but Congress asked her to refuse. Gandhi dismissed the Rau Committee as a government ploy to divert attention from real issues, but he did not ask women to boycott the committee. He suggested a compromise solution: women who wanted to work with the Rau Committee could do so as individuals but not as spokespersons for any group.[89] Mridula Sarabhai disagreed and insisted women put nationalist issues first. She admitted this proposed reform was the "equivalent to what a Temple Entry Bill would mean to Harijan workers" but urged women to stand solidly behind the non-cooperation movement.[90] Other Congress stalwarts, notably Sarojini Naidu, Vijayalakshmi Pandit, and Amrit Kaur continued to call for legal reform. Congress women in the Central Legislative Assembly, Mrs. Renuka Ray and Mrs. Radhabai Subbarayan, spoke in favor of the committee's work.

When the Rau Committee's report was released in 1941, the AIWC sent copies to its branches with instructions to hold meetings and for-

---

[87] Levy, "Indian Modernization," p. 20.
[88] National Planning Sub-Committee of Women's Role in the Planned Economy, All-India Congress Committee Files, no. G-23/1640; "Scheme of the Work of the Women's Department," All-India Congress Committee Files, no. Wd-2, 1940–2; Sucheta Devi, secretary, Women's Department, All-India Congress Committee, "The Aims of the Women's Department of the AICC," All-India Congress Committee Files, no. Wd-9, NMML.
[89] AIWC, 1941, file no. 265.
[90] Mridula Sarabhai to S. Kripalani, honorary general secretary, AICC (March 14, 1941), AICC Files, no. P-9/1941, NMML.

mulate supportive recommendations.[91] In May of 1942 the government published two bills framed by Rau on succession and circulated them for opinions. They were referred to the Legislature, considered, modified, and again circulated. Two bills emerged in 1943: one on marriage and one on succession. Throughout the entire process women who were concerned with the issue of women's rights remained supportive.[92]

In January of 1944 a committee was appointed to formulate a code of Hindu law. They were to begin work in February and prepare a draft code by August of the same year. The Rau Committee was resuscitated with the addition of three new members including one woman, Mrs. Tarabai Premchand, a long-time member of the Bhagini Samaj and officer of the NCWI. Between January and March the committee visited eight provinces where they examined 121 individuals and representatives of 102 associations.[93]

At the outset the committee said it intended to speak primarily with lawyers but would make special efforts to interview women and representatives of orthodox Hinduism. In fact, approximately 25 percent of the witnesses were women. But more significant than the number of women interviewed was the interpretation placed on their evidence. Unlike previous committees that dismissed women's testimony as representative of the educated elite, this committee tended to dismiss the views of orthodox Hindus. In Bengal, where they met only women who opposed legal reform, they concluded that women favoring reform had been prevented from meeting them. Women who opposed reform were disregarded as parroting the views of their husbands.[94] To underscore women's sentiment in favor of reform, the committee sprinkled women's views liberally throughout the report. This created the impression that Indian women were well informed about legal changes and supportive of them.

The Rau Committee's final report masterfully blended two views of Hindu society. This document nationalized the women's rights movement, claiming that it would be possible to combine the best elements

[91] *Annual Report*, AIWC, Sixteenth Session, 1942, pp. 37–9.
[92] *Annual Report*, AIWC, Seventeenth Session, 1944; "A Note on the Hindu Law Code," AIWC Files, no. 369; "All-India Women's Conference Evidence Before the Hindu Law Committee," 1943, AIWC Files, no. 314; NCWI, "A Brief Report on the Law Committee" (November 15, 1943), T. Premchand Papers; Mr. D. G. Dalvi, "Note on the Bill for the Enactment of the Hindu Code," pamphlet (n.d.), Hansa Mehta Papers, file no. 32, NMML.
[93] Dalvi, "Note."
[94] Report of the Hindu Law Committee, B. N. Rau Papers, file 11, pp. 7–9, NMML.

from the ancient Hindu texts with legal principles suitable for contemporary society. In short, the committee was offering to rationalize Hindu law without claiming an intention to modernize Hindu society.[95]

The report was published in 1946, but not re-introduced for consideration until the Constituent Assembly had become the Dominion Parliament. Those women who worked to present women's opinions did not regard this as a victory. They had compromised on a number of issues and realized they would be asked for more compromises before the legislation was passed.

CONCLUSIONS

There are some studies that portray the women who fought for civil rights as puppets of the nationalist project and others that paint them as anglophiles with no understanding of their own society. Did these women exercise agency in choosing their issues and tactics? And if so, what motivated them?

These women were educated and mentored by men but there were vast differences between the Mahakali Pathshala and Bethune College in Calcutta, and Karve's school and Pandita Ramabai's in Poona. Similarly, the social organizations educated women joined differed in ideology and activities. Bombay's Bhagini Samaj, patronized by Gujarati women who spoke Gujarati at their meetings, had a different character from the NCWI with its wealthy and titled clientele, conducting their business in English. And the products of these experiences differed in temperament and commitment. It takes only a brief look at the correspondence of any of the women's organizations to sense the strong personalities of the women leaders. They held their opinions firmly and changed them, not out of weakness, but because it was strategically necessary.

In their effort to gain civil rights for women – the vote and legal changes in particular – these women became petitioners to the British rulers. The rights they sought could not be granted by their menfolk. Nor could British women, only recently enfranchised and inadequately represented in parliament, grant them rights.

British women took up the cause of Indian women as part of their

---

[95] Levy, "Indian Modernization," pp. 272, 335.

own feminist agenda but with a firm belief in the efficacy and value of British rule. They too were petitioners on behalf of Indian women. They genuinely wanted rights for Indian women but they also wanted credit for extending Britain's civilizing mission. When all was said and done, they believed British rule served the interests of Indian women.

The Indian National Congress was inconsistent in its support for women's political and civil rights. At the time of the first franchise discussion, the INC supported women's demands. When the decision was thrown into the provincial legislatures, women continued to enjoy the support of Congress. At the time of the second franchise discussion, the INC expected women's organizations to follow their lead. They left women out of the major discussions, yet counted on complete solidarity. When the women's organizations emerged as a force to be reckoned with, the INC took steps to keep them in check. Women complied but grumbled behind their public documents.

These campaigns – for the franchise and for legal rights – show women in an activist stance. They may have been misguided, acting out of their own narrow caste and class view of the world, but they were not puppets. They made choices in the final analysis to support the nationalist project, but they were conscious of what they were doing. The distinction is important because the historical record illuminates the complicated motivations that underlay women's decisions.

Experience taught women that the battle for rights would not be easy. Time and again they were forced to work for and accept whatever modicum of justice they could get. The franchise compromise and the Rau Committee's report did not adequately reflect the views of organized women. These women, naively, strove to achieve what they regarded as equitable and suitable for Indian society. But women's goals were not salient in this tumultuous political environment. The members of the women's organizations gained less than they had hoped for. Increasingly they began to define themselves as a minority community with unique problems that could not be addressed through political channels alone.

CHAPTER 5

WOMEN IN THE NATIONALIST MOVEMENT

Helena Dutt, a Bengali revolutionary, said "[we] were like caged tigers" in explaining how she and other girls her age leapt into education and politics.[1] Women more conservative than Helena and her friends were told "the house is on fire" and they should come out of the burning house and help put out the fire.[2] From liberal homes and conservative families, urban centers and rural districts, women – single and married, young and old – came forward and joined the struggle against colonial rule. Though their total numbers were small, their involvement was extremely important. Women's participation called into question the British right to rule, legitimized the Indian nationalist movement and won for activist women, at least for a time, the approval of Indian men.

Politics completely altered the goals and activities of organized women. Education, social reform and women's rights appealed to some progressive women, but the movement to rid the country of its foreign rulers attracted people from all classes, communities, and ideological persuasions. Nationalist leaders deliberately cultivated linkages with peasants, workers, and women's organizations to demonstrate mass support for their position. Women were amazed to find political participation approved of by men who wanted their wives to behave in the home like the perfect wives in religious texts. Manmohini Zutshi Sahgal, a freedom fighter jailed in Lahore in 1930, wrote about a woman who joined a demonstration and was arrested while her husband was at work. He sent word to the jail that she could not return home after her release. Manmohini's mother, Lado Rani Zutshi, intervened on behalf of the woman. The husband said it was a great honor to have his wife arrested, but she had not asked his permission to leave the house.[3] In the end, he accepted her back but the lesson was not lost on Congress

---

[1] Helena Dutt, interview (Calcutta, September 25, 1975).
[2] Latika Ghosh, interview (Calcutta, February 29, 1978).
[3] Manmohini Zutshi Sahgal, *An Indian Freedom Fighter Recalls her Life*, ed. Geraldine Forbes (New York, M. E. Sharpe, 1994), p. 78.

workers: women's political work had to be conducted without a hint of social rebellion.

The story of women's role in the nationalist struggle is not simply one of marionettes who were told when to march and where to picket. First, the numbers of women who played some role in this movement, however small, far exceeded expectations. The nature of their work influenced how women saw themselves and how others saw their potential contribution to national development. At the same time their involvement helped to shape women's view of themselves and of their mission.

WOMEN'S EARLY CONTRIBUTIONS TO THE NATIONALIST MOVEMENT

Bankim Chandra Chattopadhyaya (1838–94) wrote the novel *Anandamath* (published in 1882) that portrayed revolutionaries sacrificing their lives for the Motherland. Bankim's emotional hymn, "Bande Mataram" ("Hail to the Mother") became famous throughout India. This call to save the Motherland was not a call to women to join the political movement but rather a linking of idealized womanhood with nationalism. In fact, a new journal for women, begun in 1875, stated: "We will not discuss political events and controversies because politics would not be interesting or intelligible to women in this country at present."[4] The situation began to change after a number of Bengali women wrote to the Viceroy in support of the Ilbert bill that would allow Indian judges to try cases involving Europeans. In 1889, four years after the Indian National Congress (INC) was founded, ten women attended its annual meeting. In 1890, Swarnakumari Ghosal, a woman novelist, and Kadambini Ganguly, the first woman in the British Empire to receive a BA and one of the India's first female medical doctors, attended as delegates. From this time on, women attended every meeting of the INC, sometimes as delegates, but more often as observers. Attending with their fathers and husbands, their contribution was both decorative and symbolic. A chorus of fifty-six girls from all regions of India performed the song "Hindustan" in 1901. The next year two Gujarati sisters sang a translation of this song at the opening session. These educated and politically knowledgeable girls

---

[4] From *Banga Mahila*, 1 (May, 1875), quoted in Meredith Borthwick, *The Changing Role of Women*, p. 337.

and their mothers informed the world that India was as advanced as any Western country in its vision of women's public roles.[5]

In 1905 the British partitioned the province of Bengal. Women joined men in protesting this division by boycotting foreign goods and buying only *swadeshi* goods, that is, goods produced in the province of Bengal. Nirad Chaudhuri has recalled how his parents decided to put away the children's foreign-made clothes and buy Indian-made outfits. Later, in 1909, his mother took a sudden and violent dislike to a glass water pitcher that survived the *swadeshi* movement and ordered one of her sons to smash it.[6] Other women took a vow to devote themselves to the Motherland and observed it by every day setting aside a handful of rice for the cause.[7] Still other women gave their support to the revolutionary organizations. Nanibala Devi (1888–1967) was married at age eleven, widowed at fifteen, received some education at a Christian mission, and was finally forced to take shelter with her nephew Amarendranath Chattopadhyay. He was the leader of the new Jugantar (New Age) Party dedicated to violent defeat of the foreign rulers. Nanibala joined the party and acted as their housekeeper, occasionally posing as the wife of one of the revolutionaries.[8] In this context, where public and private roles were sharply divided by both ideology and physical arrangements, women's political acts were hidden from the British authorities. Women hid weapons, sheltered fugitives, and encouraged the men, their domestic roles providing cover for these subversive and revolutionary acts. The activities of these Bengali women sympathetic to the *swadeshi* movement were quite different from their representative roles in the INC. There the delegates appeared as the equals of men, but their true significance was symbolic. They sang in praise of Mother India and posed as regenerated Indian womanhood. In the protest movement against the partition of Bengal, women did not do the same things as men. Instead, they used their traditional roles to mask a range of political activities. While the public and the private continued to exist as distinct categories, usual defini-

---

[5] Aparna Basu, "The Role of Women in the Indian Struggle for Freedom," *Indian Women: From Purdah to Modernity*, ed. B. R. Nanda (New Delhi, Vikas, 1976), p. 17; Bimanbehari Majumdar and B. P. Majumdar, *Congress and Congressmen in the Pre-Gandhian Era, 1885–1917* (Calcutta, Firma K.L. Mukhopadhyay, 1967), pp. 128–9.

[6] Nirad C. Chaudhuri, *The Autobiography of an Unknown Indian* (Berkeley, University of California Press, 1968), pp. 224–5.

[7] J. C. Bagal, *Jattiya Bangla Nari* (Calcutta, Vishva-Bharati, Bhadra 1361 [1954]), p. 15.

[8] "Nanibala Devi," *DNB*, vol. I, p. 446.

tions of appropriate behavior in each sphere were redefined and given political meaning.

ENTER MOHANDAS K. GANDHI

Mohandas K. Gandhi (1869–1948) returned to India in 1915 as the hero of the South African struggle. Soon after his introduction to Bombay society, he met women who belonged to women's social reform organizations. He was invited to talk to one of these groups, composed of middle-class women, about the poverty of the masses. He told his audience India needed women leaders who were "pure, firm and self-controlled" like the ancient heroines: Sita, Damayanti, and Draupadi. Sita, the heroine of the great legend the *Ramayana*, followed her husband into exile, suffered abduction, and underwent an ordeal of fire to proof her fidelity. Damayanti, the faithful and long-suffering wife of Nala, was able to recognize her husband in any guise. Draupadi, wife of the five Pandava brothers in the *Mahabharata*, India's other great legend, was wagered and lost in a dice game. When her new master ordered her stripped, the god Krishna recognized her chastity and innocence and intervened. These were heroines who had suffered at the hands of men but survived with dignity. It was these heroines Gandhi recalled when he told women to wake up and recognize their essential equality with men. Only when they appreciated the strength of their ancestresses, would women comprehend their right to freedom and liberty.[9]

With the end of World War I and renewed demands for self-rule, the government passed the Rowlatt Acts at the beginning of 1919 prohibiting public protest and suspending civil liberties. This was when Gandhi began to develop a program for women. On April 6, the day marked for a general strike throughout India, he addressed a meeting of "ladies of all classes and communities," and asked them to join the *satyagraha* (peaceful resistance) movement to facilitate the total involvement of men.[10] Within a week, hundreds of peaceful protesters were massacred in a walled garden in the city of Amritsar. Men, women, and children were killed in this brutal massacre, unmasking forever

[9] M. K. Gandhi, *Women and Social Injustice*, 4th edn. (Ahmedabad, Navajivan Publishing House, 1954), pp. 4–5; Jaisree Raiji, interview (Bombay, May 2, 1976).
[10] M. K. Gandhi, "Speech at Ladies Protest Meeting," *Collected Works of Mahatma Gandhi*, 90 vols. (Delhi, Publications Division, Ministry of Information and Broadcasting, 1958–84), vol. xv, p. 89.

Britain's "civilizing mission." Gandhi called off the campaign but it was already clear that women had joined the fight against the British. Gandhi urged them to take the *swadeshi* vow to give up foreign goods and spin every day. India's poverty, he explained, was caused by ignoring indigenous crafts and purchasing foreign-made goods.[11]

Gandhi evoked India's sacred legends, especially the *Ramayana*, when he asked Hindu women to join the political movement. In a series of articles and speeches on British atrocities in the Punjab, Gandhi compared the British rulers to the demon Ravana who abducted Sita, wife of the righteous King Ram. Under colonialism the enslaved people were losing all sense of *dharma* (righteousness). Restoration of the rule of Ram would come only when women, emulating the faithful and brave Sita, united with men against this immoral ruler.[12]

Appearing with the Muslim leader Maulana Shaukat Ali at a meeting in Patna, Gandhi modified his message to appeal to Muslim women. Gone were references to the *Ramayana* and the *Mahabharata*; now Gandhi asked women to spin and encourage their husbands to join the movement.[13] On other occasions Gandhi told Muslim women that British rule was the rule of Satan and exhorted them to renounce foreign cloth to save Islam.[14]

Shrimati Ambujammal, one of Gandhi's loyal followers from Madras, outlined how Gandhi touched the hearts of both Hindu and Muslim women. First, he explained to women there was a place for them in the movement, then he expressed his faith in their courage. It was possible to help the movement without leaving home or neglecting the family. "Do what you can," Gandhi advised women, convincing them that every act counted.[15] At the same time, he reassured families their women would not sacrifice family honor or prestige. Sucheta Kripalani credited Gandhi for his special attention to male attitudes: "Gandhi's personality was such that it inspired confidence not only in women but in guardians of women, their husbands, fathers and brothers." Since his moral stature was high, "when women came out and

---

[11] Gandhi, " Speech at Women's Meeting Bombay," *CWMG*, vol. xv, pp. 290–2; "Speech at Women's Meeting, Surat," *CWMG*, vol. xv, pp. 322–6; "Speech at Women's Meeting Dohad," *CWMG*, vol. xvi, pp. 79–80; "Speech at Women's Meeting, Godhra," *CWMG*, vol. xvi, p. 168.

[12] Gandhi, "Duty of Women," *CWMG*, vol. xviii, pp. 57–8; "Speech at Women's Meeting at Dakor," *CWMG*, vol. xviii pp. 391–5.

[13] Gandhi, "Speech at Women's Meeting Patna," *CWMG*, vol. xix, pp. 67–8.

[14] Gandhi, "Speech at Meeting of Muslim Women," *CWMG*, vol. xx, p. 397.

[15] S. Ambujammal, interview (Madras, January 19, 1976).

worked in the political field, their family members knew that they were quite secure, they were protected."[16]

The non-cooperation movement began with members of the reformed councils withdrawing from these councils. The next step was to boycott the law courts and schools. Congress accepted this program at a special session held on August 20, 1920. It was a victory for Mohandas K. Gandhi and promised a more active role for women than that offered by the *swadeshi* vow. Congress declared April 6–13, 1921 *satyagraha* week, and women interested in politics held meetings to show their support. At one of the several meetings which Sarojini Naidu addressed, women decided to form their own political organization. Rashtriya Stree Sangha (RSS), an independent women's organization, required its members to join the District Congress Committee. Speaking to this group in August, Urmila Devi, the widowed sister of the Bengali Congress leader C. R. Das, urged women to be ready to leave their homes to serve the country. By November, 1,000 Bombay women were demonstrating against the Prince of Wales' visit to India.[17]

In Bengal, events took an even more dramatic turn. C. R. Das, the most important Congress leader in eastern India, decided Congress volunteers should sell *khaddar* (homespun cloth) on the streets of Calcutta to test the government's ban on political demonstrations. The first batch of volunteers, including C. R. Das's son, was arrested. Then his wife, Basanti Devi, his sister, Urmila Devi, and his niece, Miss Suniti Devi, took to the streets and were arrested. When word of their arrest spread, the power of this tactic was clear: a huge crowd of "Marwaris, Muslims, Bhattias, Sikhs, coolies, mill-hands and school boys" milled around until the police released the women. One man said he felt women from his own household had been arrested. The next day, December 8, 1921, the whole city was in commotion. As for the women from the Das family:

they resumed picketing cloth shops and selling *khaddar* joined by numerous lady volunteers, especially Sikh ladies. Calcutta students came out in hundreds, joined

[16] Smt. Sucheta Kripalani, Oral History Transcripts, NMML.
[17] Gail O. Pearson, "Women in Public Life in Bombay City with Special Reference to the Civil Disobedience Movement," Ph.D. thesis, Jawaharlal Nehru University (1979), pp. 175–84.

the prohibited volunteer corps and marched out with *khaddar* on, seeking imprisonment.[18]

On that day alone, 170 protesters were arrested. Gandhi immediately recognized the value of having women form picket lines. Writing in *Young India* he urged women from other parts of the country to follow the brave example of Bengali women. The arrest of respectable women was viewed as an appropriate tactic to shame men into joining the protests. Less predictable, and certainly not an intended outcome, was the way these arrests affected other women. At the All-Indian Ladies Conference in Ahmedabad, 6,000 women listened to Bi Amma, the mother of Shaukat Ali and Muhammad Ali, leaders of the All-India Khilafat Committee. These were Gandhi's allies. Bi Amma urged women to enlist as Congress volunteers and, if their menfolk were arrested, to join the picket lines and keep "the flag flying."[19]

Times were changing. Women from all provinces of British India stepped forward in response to Gandhi's call. In East Godavari District, Madras, a group of women gathered to meet and listen to Gandhi. Smt. Duvvuri Subbamam, a woman attending this assembly, "jumped into the freedom struggle" at this time and resolved to form a women-only cadre of *devasevikas* (god-devoted servants).[20]

Gandhi's appeal went beyond "respectable" women to women marginalized by middle-class society. He had a reputation as a political leader who believed women counted and had faith in their capacity to help the nation and themselves. Learning that he would visit Kakinada, also in East Godavari District, in April of 1921, a twelve-year-old girl, Durgabai (later Durgabai Deshmukh), wanted local *devadasis* to meet him. Durgabai was an unusually head-strong young woman. Married at age eight, she refused to live with her husband when she reached maturity. Her father and mother, both dedicated to social reform, supported this decision and Durgabai gave her husband permission to marry a second wife.[21]

---

[18] *IAR*, 2 (1922), p. 320.

[19] Gail Minault, "Purdah Politics: The Role of Muslim Women in Indian Nationalism, 1911–1924," *Separate Worlds*, ed. Hannah Papanek and G. Minault (Delhi, Chanakya Publications, 1982), pp. 245–61; *IAR*, 1 (1922), p. 454.

[20] K. Sreeranhani Subba Rao, "Women and Indian Nationalism: A Case Study of Prominent Women Freedom Fighters of the East Godavari District of Andhra Pradesh," paper given at the Third National Conference of Women's Studies, Chandigarh (1985), pp. 6–7.

[21] *We Greet You Brother*, Andhra Mahila Sabha souvenir commemorating the Shasthi Abdi Poorthi [Completion of the Sixtieth Year] of Sri V. V. D. Narayana Rao, July 2, 1972 (Hyderabad, Andhra Mahila Sabha, 1972), p. 3.

In preparation for Gandhi's' visit, Durgabai visited the *devadasis* to tell them about Gandhi and then asked the organizers if a separate meeting could be arranged. Congress officials jokingly replied it could be arranged if she raised Rs 5,000 for the Mahatma. The *devadasis* collected the money and Durgabai obtained permission to hold the meeting in a school compound. When Gandhi arrived, there were at least 1,000 women waiting to meet him. He talked to them, with Durgabai translating, for over an hour. The women listening took off their jewelry and added another Rs 20,000 to the purse.

"Morally indecent" Bengali women were also touched by Gandhi's message. Manada Devi Mukhopadhyay tells in *Sikshita Patitat Atmarcharit* ("Autobiography of an Educated Fallen Woman," 1929), of how she and other prostitutes joined in collecting funds for Congress in 1922 and in 1924 participated in C. R. Das' *satyagraha* against the lascivious and corrupt Mahant of Tarakeswar temple.[22]

As Gandhi traveled and spoke, he urged women to boycott foreign cloth, spin, and join in public defiance of British laws. At the same time, women's organizations were petitioning the British government for the franchise. Gandhi responded that he knew all about the disadvantages of Indian women but the problem was not with law or religion but with man's lust. Real change would come when both men and women began to view their relationships differently.[23] He advocated celibacy instead of legal change.

Saraladevi Chaudhurani, Muthulakshmi Reddy, Amrit Kaur, and many other women who followed Gandhi did not abandon the franchise issue. They were impressed with his empathy for women, personally committed to his vision, but unwilling to give up their work on behalf of civil rights. Gandhi was able to live with their ambiguity. He wrote lengthy letters to Saraladevi urging her to study Hindi and prepare herself for a leadership role.[24] That she ignored much of his advice did not seem to bother Gandhi who found other women willing to listen to his lectures.

Between the suspension of non-cooperation in 1922 and his resumption of a leadership role in 1928, Gandhi devoted himself to reconstruc-

[22] Sandip Bandhyopadhyay, "The 'Fallen' and Non-Cooperation," *Manushi*, 53 (July–August, 1989), pp. 18–21. The author notes controversy surrounding the authorship of this book. Some argue Manada Devi was a real person, others believe this was the work of a male author.
[23] Gandhi, "The Position of Women," *Young India* (July 21, 1921), pp. 228–9.
[24] Letters from Gandhi to Saraladevi, from Deepak Chaudhury, Saraladevi's son.

tion. During these six years he spoke to women's groups about constructive work, continuously reiterating that Sita was the ideal role model and spinning could solve India's and women's problems.[25] One of his goals was to persuade well-to-do women to learn about the conditions of rural and poor women. But he cautioned them not to neglect their own families in the process.

Women followed Gandhi for different reasons. Rajkumari Amrit Kaur (1889–1964), a member of the Ahluwalia royal family of Kapurthala state, served as Gandhi's secretary for sixteen years. She admired Gandhi for his fight for justice.[26] Sushila Nayar (b. 1914), Gandhi's medical doctor in his later years, said she became a Gandhian in 1919. Sushila's mother called him "Mahatma" (Great Soul) and told her young children about him. Sushila said, "I learned about Gandhi from the time I was a small child. Not having a father, he was something like a father to me."[27] These were women who had exercised personal choice in choosing to follow Gandhi and they accepted his ideas judiciously.

Other women followed Gandhi because their menfolk accepted his leadership. The women from Motilal Nehru's family fitted this pattern; they became supporters of Gandhi when Jawaharlal and his father Motilal recognized his leadership. We do not know if Swarup Rani, Motilal's wife, had any interest in politics but she welcomed Gandhi into their family and joined public demonstrations. Lado Rani Zutshi, the wife of Motilal's nephew, jumped at the opportunity to play a role in Congress activities.[28] With so few personal accounts available, it is difficult to guess at what motivated all the women who declared themselves Gandhians and stepped forward to play a public role.

THE CIVIL DISOBEDIENCE CAMPAIGN

Gandhi returned to politics in 1928 and launched a civil disobedience campaign that brought large numbers of women into public life. Women's participation in the civil disobedience movement of 1930–32 differed qualitatively and quantitatively from the early 1920s and won them a place in history.

---

[25] Gandhi, "Untouchability, Women and Swaraj," *ISR*, 37 (March 26, 1927), p. 465; Gandhi, "Speech at Women's Meeting," Coimbatore, October 16, 1927, *CWMG*, vol. xxv, p. 148.
[26] Amrit Kaur in foreword to Gandhi's *Women and Social Injustice*, p. iii.
[27] Dr. Sushila Nayar, interview (New Delhi, April 6, 1976).
[28] Sahgal, *An Indian Freedom Fighter*, p. 15.

11 In training to join Gandhi: Bharat scouts, Allahabad, 1929

Bombay

Bombay women's picketing and demonstrations from 1930 to 1932 received more press attention than women's activities in any other part of the country. The numbers of women marching were in the thousands and their pickets were organized and effective. That Bombay's women took the lead seemed natural given the cosmopolitan nature of the city, its transportation system, and the presence of Parsees and Christians, both communities supportive of female education. The large Gujarati population found the message of their fellow Gujarati, Gandhi, especially appealing.

The women's political organization, the Rashtriya Stree Sangha, had remained under the presidency of Sarojini Naidu with Goshiben Naoroji Captain and Avantikabai Gokhale as vice-presidents. It stated its goals as *swaraj* and women's emancipation. By 1930, the leadership and structure of the RSS were sufficiently developed for it to spawn a new, smaller organization, the Desh Sevika Sangha (Women Serving the County) (DSS) whose members were ready for action.[29]

[29] *BC* (July 23, 1930), p. 4; booklet from Gandhi Seva Sena (Bombay, n.p., n.d.), pp. 1–3.

12   Portrait of Sarojini Naidu, *c.* 1930

Gandhi began the civil disobedience campaign in March of 1930 with his 240-mile march from Ahmedabad to Dandi to make salt in defiance of the British monopoly. The WIA specifically asked him to include women but he refused because he feared the British would call Indian men cowards who hid behind women.[30] Nevertheless, women were very much involved and gathered at every stop to hear the Mahatma speak. The police reported meetings where there were thousands of women; in one case they estimated there were 10,000 women in the crowd. Gandhi talked to these village women about their patriotic duties: picketing liquor and toddy shops, boycotting taxed salt, and spinning and wearing *khaddar*.[31] He noted that women's patience and antipathy to violence made them particularly well suited for constructive work.

Gandhi was constructing a new ideal for Indian woman that rewrote passivity and self-suffering as strength. Gujarati women living in Bombay responded to this message by forming an organization to plan and direct efforts to close shops selling foreign cloth.[32]

April 6, the anniversary of the Amritsar massacre, was chosen for the formal breaking of the salt laws. A front line of seven people, including two women, Kamaladevi Chattopadhyay and Avantikabai Gokhale, were the first to step onto the beach, light fires, and boil sea water. Kamaladevi remembered that day:

this was their [women's] first appearance in any modern militant political campaign and I could hardly suppress my excitement at the enormity of the occasion and my own good fortune to be amongst the first ... It seemed such a stupendous moment in my life, in the life of the women of my country.[33]

The crowds that appeared were larger than anyone had expected. The *Bombay Chronicle* reported "thousands of Gujarati women" marshaled at the Chowpatty Sea Face, collecting sea water in their brass and copper jugs.[34] In the heart of the city, women volunteers picketed toddy shops and asked owners to close their doors and patrons to leave the premises. Other women sold salt on the streets, while still others went house to house urging housewives to buy only *swadeshi* products.[35]

---

[30] *BC* (March 11, 1930), p. 1; *BC* (November 31, 1930), p. 1; Vijay Agnew, *Elite Women in Indian Politics* (New Delhi, Vikas, 1979), p. 39.

[31] GOI, Home Dept., Political, file no. 247/II/1930.

[32] "Speech at Gujarat Women's Conference, Dandi," *CWMG*, vol. XLIII, pp. 251–2; "Special Task Before Women," *CWMG*, vol. XLIII, pp. 271–5.

[33] Kamaladevi Chattopadhyay, *Inner Recesses/Outer Spaces: Memoirs* (New Delhi, Navrang, 1986), pp. 152–3.   [34] *BC* (April 14, 1930), p. 1.

[35] *BC* (April 16, 1930), p. 1, (April 17, 1930), p. 1, (April 18, 1930), p. 1, (April 30, 1930), p. 1.

13 Women brining brine to salt pans in Vile Parle Camp, Bombay during civil disobedience movement, 1930

The DSS had designed and supervised this campaign. In the early excitement of activity, women flocked to join this organization that soon had 560 members. It was apparent many of these were "ornamental *sevikas*," for when pressed into service they lost interest. The number of active DSS members dropped to about 300.[36]

"Ornamental *sevikas*" were a nuisance, but the "wrong kind" of woman posed a serious problem. DSS leaders admitted being approached by "undesirable women," but were clear they only wanted to recruit from the "good classes." Goshiben Captain (1884–1970), one of the Oxford-educated granddaughters of Dadabhai Naoroji who was a founding member and leader of Congress, insisted that members should have impeccable credentials. She believed women of high status would elicit respect from the public. Goshiben warned women demonstrators to only perform actions that preserved their dignity and "innate modesty." This would preclude marching side by side with women of "undesirable" character. She also vetoed "leftist" suggestions

---

[36] *BC* (July 23, 1930), p. 5; Report of the Desh Sevika Sangha, Bombay, 1930–1, p. 5. This report was given to the author by Miss N. J. Dastur, Bombay.

that women lie in the doorways of foreign cloth shops to deter customers.[37]

Goshiben's concerns were valid; there was a real danger that women demonstrators would be equated with women of the streets and harassed as they picketed shops. Cornelia Sorabji wrote an article for the *National Review* charging the Indian National Congress with turning women out of rescue homes (shelters for women "rescued" from brothels) to join the civil disobedience movement. She claimed that 90 percent of the women political demonstrators arrested in the Punjab were prostitutes.[38] For women new to political roles performed in public spaces, these allegations were threatening. Women joined the political movement with the approval of their families, not as an act of rebellion against the predominant gender ideology. In the final analysis most politically active women chose respectability over solidarity with their fallen sisters.

In May, with the *sevikas* already picketing, Sarojini Naidu was nominated to lead the raid on the Dharasana salt works. Sarojini directed the protest that began on May 15, 1930, was arrested the same day, and released. Her presence was symbolic both for Indian nationalists and British authorities. Many of her Indian supporters feared for her safety, but she told them: "I am here not as a woman but as a General."[39] Meanwhile, the local authorities knew everyone regarded her as a woman and were in a quandary about how to treat her and other women demonstrators.[40] On May 21, Sarojini led the second batch of raiders, was again arrested, and this time sentenced to a year in prison. Her leadership inspired hundreds of women to emulate her bravery by marching in the streets.

Demonstrations and picketing continued in Bombay until 1931 when Gandhi was released from jail. During this time women proved their effectiveness in agitational politics. Merchants, faced with women picketing their shops, signed the pledge not to sell foreign cloth until an honorable peace had been arranged for the country.[41] On the streets women joined men for flag-raisings and demonstrations. On June 23,

---

[37] Appendix 6, The Constitution of the Desh Sevika Sangha as amended May, 1931, AICC Files, no. G-8/1929; Goshiben Captain, interview (May 16, 1970), s-22, South Asian Archive, Centre for South Asian Studies, Cambridge.

[38] C. Sorabji, "Prison Detenus and Terrorists in India," *National Review*, 102, no 6 (January 11, 1934), CS Papers, Eur. Mss., F165/11, IOOLC.   [39] *BC* (May 19, 1920), p. 3.

[40] Dagmar Engels, "The Limits of Gender Ideology," *WSIQ*, 12, no. 4 (1989), pp. 425–37.

[41] Report of the Desh Sevika Sangh, 1930–1 (n.d.), p. 7.

1930, the police ordered Congress volunteers to leave the Esplanade. The volunteers refused. As the police advanced, the women moved forward to shield the men and were injured when the police charged the crowds. At the center of the demonstration was a seventeen-year-old school girl clinging to the national flag. When the police tried to pry her away from the flag pole, she shouted "I shall die first."[42]

The Desh Sevikas organized a number of demonstrations that grabbed headlines and inspired women all over India. Processions of one to two thousand women, accompanied by their children, were not unusual at this time. Even larger numbers came to listen to speeches about *swadeshi* and freedom. The largest crowd celebrated Gandhi's birthday and the release from prison of three of the most important women leaders: Lilavati Munshi, Perin Captain, and Mrs. Lukanji. A mile-long chain of women, led by *sevikas* dressed in orange saris and carrying placards, numbered more than 5,000. Crowds of 10,000 assembled at both ends of this parade.[43] These numbers could not be matched in other areas of India, but patriotic women everywhere emulated the spirit.

Bengal

Women of Bengal came forward at this time but their demonstrations were smaller and their activities more radical than those of Bombay women. Calcutta women made and sold salt, picketed cloth and liquor shops, preached the value of *khaddar*, and took processions into the streets. The capital city was also the heart of revolutionary struggle and women's colleges became centers for recruiting new members. In district towns and villages women joined processions, wore *khaddar*, and hid fleeing revolutionaries. In this setting Gandhi's influence was no greater than that of prominent local leaders. Bengali nationalism had always valorized violence and this ethos profoundly influenced the participation of Bengali women in the freedom struggle.

The Mahila Rashtriya Sangha (MRS), begun in 1928, was the first formal organization to mobilize women for political work. Latika Ghosh, an Oxford-educated teacher, founded this organization because Subhas Chandra Bose had asked her to. Subhas, an extremely popular leader, was impressed with Latika's ability to successfully field a women's demonstration against the Simon Commission and insisted

[42] *BC* (June 23, 1930), p. 1.   [43] *BC* (October 4, 1930), p. 1.

she develop a women's organization connected with Congress. The MRS had goals similar to the RSS in Bombay; they wanted to achieve *swaraj* and improve women's status. MRS leaders argued that these goals were inseparable: until women's lives improved the nation could never be free; and until the nation were free women's condition would not improve. The first step to *swaraj* was the education of women to their double oppression as colonial subjects and inferior sex.

MRS espoused a radical ideology but followed a mobilization strategy that constructed women as innately religious. Latika Ghosh wrote articles calling on women to wake up and take a good look at their country. India had been rich, now it was dominated by a foreign country, infamous for its poverty, and led by weaklings. "Recall the tales of our grandmothers," she instructed her readers, and asked them to think back to the battles between the *devis* (goddesses) and *asuras* (demons). They should remember that just as the *devis* were losing, the fearsome goddess Durga appeared as *shakti* (divine energy) and the *asuras* were defeated. Then there were the examples set by Rajput queens who first sent their husbands and sons into battle and then prepared for their own death. Latika told her readers they were the *shaktis* of the nation and she issued this directive: "Every one of you must be like a spark which will burn down all selfishness, all petty dreams – purified by fire, only the bright, golden love of the Motherland will remain."[44]

In 1928 Subhas Bose decided to have uniformed women volunteers march with men in the procession to inaugurate the annual Congress meetings in Calcutta. He made Latika Ghosh a colonel and charged her with recruiting her own company for the parade. Latika enlisted 300 women: students from Bethune College and Victoria Institution, two of the most important institutions of higher education for women, and teachers employed by Calcutta Corporation. Their uniforms consisted of dark green saris with red borders worn over white blouses – the colors of the Congress flag. A number of sensitive issues arose during the training period: would women march with men? should the young women wear trousers? would they stay in camp at night? Colonel Latika argued for the trappings of modesty, saris instead of trousers and no females in camp at night, but she stood her ground on the issue of

[44] Latika Bose (following her divorce Latika resumed use of her maiden name Ghosh and she preferred to be known as Latika Ghosh), "Mahila Rashtriya Sangha," *Banglar Katha* (Ashwin, 1335 [1928]), p. 5; *Banglar Katha* (Jaistha, 1335 [1929]), p. 7.

women marching in the regular procession. She confessed she made a poor colonel, unable to stay in step or salute properly, but she wanted her female volunteers to appear as the equals of men in the struggle for freedom.[45] She achieved her goal; observers reported seeing women in a new light:

As the ladies clad in their saris marched past to the sound of the bugle and the beating of the drum, there could be traced not a touch of all the frailties that are so commonly attributed to them. No faltering, no hesitancy, no softness associated in popular minds with the womanhood of Bengal but chivalry written on every face and manifest in every movement.[46]

Calcutta women formed the Nari Satyagraha Samiti (NSS) in 1929 in response to the Congress call for women to be ready to serve the nation. Urmila Devi, one of the first women arrested for political activity, was named president; Jyotimoyee Ganguli vice-president; Santi Das and Bimal Protiba Devi joint secretaries. This group had a core of fifteen to twenty women who were willing to picket and risk arrest. They were all Bengali women belonging to the three highest castes: brahmins, kayasthas, and vaidyas. They were educated, from professional families, and had all observed some form of purdah. They chose white *khaddar* saris as their uniform.[47]

Santi Das was a teacher who had set up her own school and she recruited her students and Calcutta Corporation teachers to NSS. Usually 15–20 women took part in NSS activities although occasionally 200–300 women marched in a procession. These numbers are not a good indicator of the impact of women's political activities. Middle-class women, rarely seen outside their own homes, astounded and thrilled the general public when they appeared as *satyagrahis*. When twenty-two women were arrested for picketing in July of 1930, Burrabazar shopkeepers immediately closed their doors in fear of crowd violence. A few days later four women sat on bales of foreign cloth and prevented coolies from moving the merchandise. Had the police dared touch these women, the watching crowds would have exploded in violence. Instead, the police responded with gentlemanly tactics such as cutting off the water supply to the picket lines.[48]

At the same time as these women were picketing and joining pro-

[45] L. Ghosh, interview (Calcutta, February 29, 1976).
[46] "Rally of Lady Volunteers," *Forward* (December 20, 1928), p. 7.
[47] Santi Das Kabir, interview (New Delhi, March 25, 1976).
[48] *ABP* (July 24, 1930), p. 3, (July 26, 1930), p. 5.

cessions, other women were recruited by revolutionary organizations. In some cases women, initially attracted to Gandhi, joined the revolutionaries because they craved action or were appalled by police violence. Kamala Das Gupta (b. 1907) wanted to join Gandhi's ashram in 1929 but he told her she must first obtain her parents' permission. Her parents would not allow her to go. By her account, she became depressed and in this mood read Sarat Chandra Chatterjee's novel *Pather Dabi* ("The Right of the Way").[49] Attracted by his world of romance and heroism, Kamala spoke to her *lathi*-fighting instructor,[50] Dinesh Mazumdar, who was a member of the revolutionary group Jugantar. She met his senior colleague and was given books to read. At last Kamala found what she had been yearning for, a way to sacrifice herself for India. She joined Jugantar.[51]

Most of the women who became involved with revolutionary groups at this time were students. Revolutionary ideals have a natural appeal to the young but these young women had very little physical autonomy and were socialized to behave modestly. It is important to note that revolutionary activity was seldom their first political experience. Most of them joined secret societies after they had worked with women's organizations and with Congress.

Bina Das, the young college student who fired a pistol at Governor Jackson, is the most famous of the revolutionary women. Bina, her elder sister Kalyani, Surama Mitra, and Kamala Das Gupta first decided to form a student organization for the discussion of political matters.[52] The Chattri Sangha (Association for Female Students) organized study classes, athletic centers, swimming clubs, cooperative stores, libraries, and a youth hostel. Because these girls were already accustomed to public life, Congress looked to the Chattri Sangha for recruits.

When Gandhi called for civil disobedience in 1930, Kalyani led the Chattri Sangha girls in a demonstration outside Bethune College. When Nehru was arrested, these young women demanded the college be closed. Mrs. Das, the principal, ignored their demands so they went on

---

[49] *Pather Dabi*, published serially between 1923 and 1926, was the first popular novel in Bengali on revolutionary activities.
[50] A lathi is a staff, often tipped with metal, used as a weapon.
[51] Transcript of interview with Kamala Das Gupta, Oral History Project, NMML; Kamala Das Gupta, interview (Calcutta, July 12, 1973).
[52] Kamala Das Gupta, *Swadinata Sangrame Banglar Nari* ["Bengali Women in the Freedom Movement"], (Calcutta, Basudhara Prakashani, 1970), pp. 36–44.

strike.[53] She summoned the police but they only ordered the young women to disperse. Later, at Presidency College, the police decided to teach these young women a lesson. Female students who threw themselves in front of their male colleagues during a police charge were put in prison vans, taken to distant suburbs, and abandoned. The long walk home was meant to cool their fondness for demonstrations but private motor cars and taxis followed the police vans and brought the abducted girls back to Calcutta.[54] Finally, the British Commissioner, fed up with police ineptitude, ordered the imprisonment of women leading these demonstrations.[55]

"The time was ripe for the movement," Kalyani wrote about the appeal of revolutionary ideology for women. At this time, older revolutionary leaders were losing control of their organizations. Formerly a few top leaders made all the decisions and members took vows of obedience and celibacy. Now younger members were unwilling to wait for orders from above; they formed new organizations, recruited women, and planned daring attacks.[56]

On April 18, 1930, the Indian Republican Army, a revolutionary organization led by Surya Sen, attacked the city of Chittagong. The police successfully counter-attacked within a few hours but this daring strike, as the Intelligence Bureau noted, had an electric effect on young people:

Recruits poured into the various groups in a steady stream, and the romantic appeal of the raid attracted into the fold of the terrorist party women and young girls, who from this time onwards are found assisting the terrorists as housekeepers, messengers, custodians of arms and sometimes as comrades.[57]

In October of 1930 the British decided to apply special ordinances allowing them to search and detain individuals without proving reasonable suspicion. Rigorous application of these ordinances made it dangerous to join even peaceful demonstrations. In September of 1931 the police fired on unarmed detainees held at Hijli detention center in Midnapur. Kalyani personally experienced police brutality when

[53] Kalyani Das Bhattacharjee, "A Short Life Sketch of Kalyani Bhattacharjee," unpublished; *ABP* (April 17, 1930), p. 6.
[54] K. Bhattacharjee, "A Short Life Sketch,"; Kalyani Bhattacharjee, interview (Calcutta, March 14, 1976); Smt. Kalyani Bhattacharjee, transcript of taped interview, from K. Bhattacharjee; *ABP* (July 17, 1930), p. 3, (July 19, 1930), p. 3, (July 23, 1930), p. 3.
[55] Engels, "The Limits of Gender Ideology," pp. 433–5.
[56] Ishanee Mukherjee, "Women and Armed Revolution in Late Colonial Bengal," National Conference of Women's Studies, Chandigarh (1985), p. 8.
[57] *Terrorism in India, 1917–1936*, compiled in the Intelligence Bureau (GOI, Home Dept., 1936, reprinted Delhi, 1974), p. 34.

arrested for addressing a meeting in Hazra Park. She was "locked in an underground cell without saris, bedding, or a mosquito net, and given only three mugs of water per week."[58] These experiences underscored the futility of non-violent protest.

Whereas previously women had supported revolutionaries by keeping house for them, spreading propaganda, collecting funds, hiding and transporting weapons, and even making explosives, now they were directly involved in revolutionary acts. Santi and Suniti, two schoolgirls from Comilla, shot Magistrate Stevens to death on December 14, 1931. They had presented him with a petition to allow a swimming competition and when he went to sign it, they both pulled revolvers from beneath their shawls and fired directly into his body.[59] Stevens died on the spot and Santi and Suniti were taken to Comilla District jail where they signed a statement admitting their guilt. Santi and Suniti wanted to become the first women martyrs and were angry to hear they would not be hanged but would instead go to prison.[60]

In February of the next year, Bina Das attempted to shoot the Governor of Bengal at the Calcutta University Convocation ceremonies. This well-educated Brahmo girl from a respectable middle-class family seemed an unlikely recruit to revolutionary operations.[61] She also read *Pather Dabi* and admired Doctor Babu, the character who never lost his faith in revolution and insisted the old order must go even though pain and suffering would accompany its demise. In 1928, while marching with Latika Ghosh's volunteers, Bina was approached by members of a secret society. She decided to join them and immediately began recruiting students for the movement. She decided to shoot Governor Jackson after a number of her colleagues were arrested. At her trial Bina spoke of the depressing effect of the accounts of murder and indiscriminate beatings in Chittagong, Midnapur, and Hijli detention center. "I felt," she said in court, "I would go mad if I could not find relief in death. I only sought the way to death by offering myself at the feet of the country."[62]

In September Pritilata Waddedar, a Chittagong school teacher, led

---

[58] Bhattacharjee, "A Short Life Sketch."
[59] Akhil Chandra Nandy, "Girls in India's Freedom Struggle," *The Patrika Sunday Magazine* (Calcutta, September 2, 1973), pp. 1–2.
[60] Santi Das Ghosh, interview (Calcutta, February 24, 1976); Tirtha Mandal, *Women Revolutionaries of Bengal, 1905–1939* (Calcutta, Minerva, 1991).
[61] "The Case of Bina Das," *ISR*, 42 (February 20, 1932), p. 387.
[62] Bina Das, "Confession," in the possession of the author.

fifteen men in a raid on the Chittagong Club. The revolutionaries entered the club and began shooting, injuring ten or twelve persons and killing one elderly European woman. When the lights went out, the attackers fled. During the escape Pritilata swallowed poison and died about 100 yards from the club.[63] She left a testament:

I wonder why there should be any distinction between males and females in a fight for the cause of the country's freedom? If our brothers can join a fight for the cause of the motherland why can't the sisters? Instances are not rare that the Rajput ladies of hallowed memory fought bravely in the battlefields and did not hesitate to kill their country's enemies. The pages of history are replete with high admiration for the historic exploits of these distinguished ladies. Then why should we, the modern Indian women, be deprived of joining this noble fight to redeem our country from foreign domination? If sisters can stand side by side with the brothers in a Satyagraha movement, why are they not so entitled in a revolutionary movement?[64]

By 1933 most of the women revolutionaries were in prison. There had been between sixty and seventy women who had aided the revolutionary groups, and of those approximately forty were imprisoned.[65] They were patriotic young women and their aim had been to arouse the masses to action. Educated, knowledgeable about political issues, they also wanted to prove that women could be as brave as men.[66] In the rural districts of Midnapur, 24-Parganas, Khulna, Bakhergunge, Noakhali, and Chittagong women responded to the call to break the salt laws. There are many accounts of their bravery. Jyotimoyee Ganguli, a Congress organizer, traveled to the village of Narghat near Tamluk, and found about 300 women and 700 men waiting to hear a woman preach about "the great Ahimsa [non-violent] war waged by their Gandhiji against the Government." The police warned her against speaking, but she turned to the audience and asked them what she should do. They asked her to stay and the police turned on the crowd. The women, who had been sitting on a bank behind the men, rushed forward in an attempt to shield the men. These men and women managed to hold the police away from Jyotimoyee who delivered her speech.[67]

---

[63] *Terrorism in India, 1917–1936*, p. 50; Kali Charan Ghosh, *The Roll of Honour, Anecdotes of Indian Martyrs* (Calcutta, Vidya Bharati, 1965), pp. 483–4.
[64] Quoted in Mandal, *Women Revolutionaries*, p. 4.
[65] The numbers are not precise because of the secret nature of their activities. Some revolutionaries have never been identified as such.
[66] Geraldine H. Forbes, "Goddesses or Rebels? The Women Revolutionaries of Bengal," *The Oracle*, 2, no. 2 (April 1980), pp. 1–15.
[67] Miss J. Ganguli, "The Day of Crucifixion," *MR*, 47 (May, 1930), pp. 621–2.

If the police hesitated to manhandle the students at Bethune College, they made up for their restraint when they faced rural women. Police violence against demonstrating women in Contai was so severe that Congress called for an enquiry. The findings were serious enough to merit special government instructions to the Bengal police to deal gently with women protesters.[68] But police "gentleness" was usually reserved for middle-class women and tales of rape and mistreatment of lower-class women continued to pour in. The police were particularly vicious in Chittagong where the armory raid and the proclamation of a Free India by Surya Sen's group had posed a clear threat. Because village people aided the fleeing revolutionaries, all villagers were regarded as potential enemies. According to one non-official report, Gurkha guards searched the home of Bipen Behari Sen after midnight, arrested his two sons and took them away for questioning, and then returned to gang-rape his daughter.[69]

In this tumultuous environment, it was difficult to generate interest in women's rights. Just as Congress had expected rewards for their loyal service during the First World War, women activists expected their male colleagues to turn their attention to women's issues. When it became apparent that Bengal Congress was not particularly interested in these topics, women leaders called for a meeting to form a separate women's Congress. In the first week of May 1931, Santi Das wrote letters to women members of District Congresses asking each to elect ten delegates. These women organized meetings, elected their delegates, and held discussions about social reform issues.[70]

When they arrived at the conference headquarters in Calcutta, the delegates were met by young volunteers wearing crimson *khaddar* saris, ushered to their seats, and treated to a speech by the grandmother of politics and feminism, Saraladevi Chaudhurani. In comparison with the district speeches, full of platitudes about Indian womanhood and their awakening during the civil disobedience movement, Saraladevi's speech hit hard.

Saraladevi explained why they needed a separate Congress for women. Women were treated, from their earliest childhood, as separate and inferior. As girls they were denied sweets while their brothers ate their fill; as adults they were exploited by men for their own pur-

---

[68] Engels, "The Limits of Gender Ideology, p. 434.
[69] *Legislative Assembly Debates*, vol. VII (GOI, 1932), p. 3107.
[70] "Future of Indian Womanhood," *ABP* (April 29, 1931), p. 6.

poses. Women's needs, feelings, and point of view had never been identical to men's but men had shown no interest in understanding women. Now was the time to speak publicly about their status and join the world-wide women's movement.[71]

Saraladevi acknowledged men's role in bringing women into the freedom movement, but she doubted they really cared about improving the lives of women. Women were rewarded with flowery speeches but not appointed to sub-committees and councils. Summing up women's experiences with politics she said Congress "assigned to women the position of law-breakers only and not law-makers." Women must demand equal treatment and equal status. United they would impress Congress leaders and perhaps even Jawaharlal Nehru would be moved to give the same attention to "teeming womenfolk" he accorded the "teeming masses." Saraladevi asked why Congress had never conceived of an anti-brothel campaign, since prostitution was as harmful to women as alcoholism was to men. She concluded what was certainly the most forceful feminist speech of the 1930s with a call for legal, economic, social, and educational equality. She spoke to an audience more conservative than herself and in their final session they reiterated the usual demands, rejected resolutions favoring birth control and equal treatment for women, and decided not to form a separate women's Congress.[72]

Madras

Women's political demonstrations in Madras were less dramatic than those in either Bombay or Bengal. Women picketed and marched in processions but it was always difficult to mobilize large numbers of women for action. Support for the *swadeshi* pledge and for spinning, wearing, and selling *khaddar* could be mustered, but there were no dramatic demonstrations of the kind found in Calcutta and Bombay. Madras women never joined the revolutionary movement, nor were they subjects of extreme police violence.

The explanation for this rests with the nature of politics in Madras as well as the tactics of the nationalist movement in this province. First, there had been considerable debate within the Madras Congress as to whether or not to accept Gandhi's leadership. There were many leaders

[71] "Srimati Saraladevi Chaudhurani's Speech at the Bengal Women's Congress," *Stri Dharma*, 14, (August 1931), pp. 506–10; "Women's Congress," *ABP* (May 3, 1931), p. 7.
[72] "Bengal Women's Conference," *The Hindu* (May 3, 1931), p. 9.

who did not support his plan. Second, Congress was seen as a party of the brahmin elite. Third, in other parts of the country women were especially successful in enforcing the boycott of foreign-made cloth. In Madras, C. Rajagopalachariar, a leading member of Congress, was more concerned with prohibition than with foreign cloth. Secretary of the Prohibition League of India and member in charge of the anti-drink campaign of the Indian National Congress, he regarded this as an issue that transcended caste and community and had the potential to unite people in a struggle against the government. Unfortunately, picketing liquor shops was one of the most dangerous forms of protest in Madras and deemed inappropriate for women.

Smt. S. Ambujammal (b. 1899) was the only daughter of S. Srinivasa Iyengar, a brilliant lawyer and Congress leader. She was raised on stories about Gandhi in South Africa. Because S. S. Iyengar held traditional views on sex segregation, Ambujammal met Gandhi's wife, Kasturbai, but not Gandhi when this famous couple came to stay in their house. She joined the non-cooperation movement in 1920, began to wear *khaddar* and spin, but rarely left the house. Ambujammal's dedication to the freedom movement was fueled more by personal issues than political interests. She was married as a child to a man who, by her own account, "had something wrong with him." Ambujammal never went to her father-in-law's home; instead, her husband came to live in her father's home where he was supported and cared for by her parents. She dated her real entry into the movement from 1928 when she decided to form the Women's Swadeshi League.[73]

Members of the League took the *swadeshi* vow, spun a certain amount of thread each month, and spread the word about the value of homespun cloth. Ambujammal became president of this organization with Mrs. Jamammal (S. S. Iyengar's widowed sister) as treasurer. Krishnabai Rau organized the Desh Sevikas (Women Serving the Country), women willing to picket, and Indirabai Rau (Krishnabai's sister) took over propaganda. In the beginning this organization consisted of the officers and a few other women who met daily to spin and discuss the progress of the protest movement. When the call came for women to join the movement they went door to door preaching the value of *swadeshi*, organized *swadeshi* exhibitions, sold *khaddar* in the

[73] Transcript of interview with Mrs. S. Ambujammal, Oral History Project, NMML; Smt. S. Ambujammal, interviews (Madras, January 19, 1976, January 25, 1976); S. Ambujammal, "Face to Face," lecture delivered at Max Mueller Bhavan, Madras (January 22, 1976).

streets, and joined men in picketing.[74] Women especially enjoyed joining *prabhat pheries* or morning walks when they sang freedom songs. In the early morning hours women, sometimes numbering in the hundreds, would walk through the streets singing songs of *swadeshi* and *swaraj*.

Krishnabai Rau (b. 1906), a loyal Gandhian since childhood, responded to Gandhi's call for civil disobedience by resigning her position as lecturer in Crosthwaite Girls' College, Allahabad, and returning to Madras. Well known for her leadership skills and ability to speak publicly (as a student Krishnabai had organized the Madras Youth League and given evidence before the Joshi Commission), she organized the Desh Sevika Sangha under the aegis of the Swadeshi League. Dressed in orange saris and blouses, DSS women picketed foreign cloth shops with men volunteers. Standing at the entrance of shops, they stopped customers and pleaded with them: "India is already downtrodden. Please do not help in its further degradation by buying foreign made goods."[75]

When the police first moved against the demonstrators, they attacked the men but not the women. This only strengthened women's resolve to join the movement against the British. A woman magistrate recalled:

I thought to myself 'What kind of justice . . . could I render if the cases were brought to me by the police who themselves were so cruel and corrupt?' My mind began to revolt and so I resigned my honorary assignment . . . and joined the Desh Sevikas in the service of my motherland.[76]

It was not long before the police began to treat women protesters the same as men. Madras women were among the first arrested in the country. Rukmani Lakshmipathy (1891–1951), accompanying C. Rajagopalachariar in his march to Vedaranyam to break the salt laws in 1931, was arrested and became the first female political prisoner in Vellore women's jail.[77] At first no salt *satyagraha* had been planned for Madras but Durgabai saw this as essential for arousing support for the civil disobedience movement. She first wrote to Gandhi and then persuaded Shri T. Prakasam to lead the volunteers. Knowing he would be

---

[74] "Independence Day," *The Hindu* (January 27, 1931), p. 2.
[75] *Smrutika: The Story of My Mother as Told By Herself,* the story of Shrimati Kamala Bai L. Rau, trans. from Tamil by Indirabai Rau (Pune, Dr. Krishnabai Nimbkar, 1988), p. 47.
[76] *Smrutika,* p. 48.   [77] "Rukmini Ammal Lakshmipathi," *DNB*, vol. II, p. 401.

arrested, T. Prakasam designated Durgabai "dictator" of the movement. Then it was her turn to be arrested.[78]

At a meeting held to protest the brutal treatment of the *satyagrahis*, 5,000 mill-hands began to stone the watching police. The police retaliated by *lathi*-charging the group, killing three people and wounding five.[79] This event frightened both Congress leaders and women *satyagrahis* neither of whom wished to incite mob violence and/or provoke police retaliation. It had the effect of dampening the enthusiasm of women for mass demonstrations.

North India

In North India women from Allahabad, Lucknow, Delhi, and Lahore joined public demonstrations and shocked a public unused to seeing respectable women in the streets without veils. In these northern cities demonstrations occasionally attracted as many as 1,000 women, but most of them were much smaller. They were dramatic events because of their unusual quality rather than their size. Leadership came from a few families, for example the Nehrus and the Zutshis, and most demonstrators came from schools and colleges. Unlike other parts of the country, women's organizations were neither the training ground nor recruiting stations for politically active women.

In Allahabad women from the Nehru family were important leaders. They made public speeches and went door to door urging women to join the movement. Swarup Rani Nehru, Jawaharlal Nehru's old and frail mother, emerged from a lifetime in the zenana to walk through the streets in *khaddar*. Her messages to women were simple and clear: if you love the Motherland, you will join; if you love my son Jawaharlal, you will join. One of the popular songs of the time for women was entitled: "Song of Jawaharlal Nehru's Mother Calling for Participation in the Holy War." Kamala, Jawaharlal's wife, was constantly on the move at this time, demonstrating in Allahabad, speaking in Lucknow, traveling to Bombay, and taking a more active role than her health had previously allowed. Her message was also direct: all must join, take the

---

[78] Durgabai Deshmukh, *Chintaman and I* (New Delhi, Allied, 1980), p. 10; "Lady Satyagrahis Welcomed," *The Hindu* (March 11, 1931), p. 5; "Ladies Conference," *The Hindu* (June 9, 1931), p. 9; transcript of an interview with Smt. Durgabai Deshmukh, Oral History Project, NMML.

[79] David Arnold, *The Congress in Tamilnadu* (New Delhi, Manohar, 1977), p. 125.

vow of *swadeshi*, and wear *khaddar*. If women united, the rebellion could never be crushed.[80]

In Lahore demonstrations against the Simon Commission were marked by violence. The police *lathi*-charged the demonstrators and struck Lal Lajpat Rai, the great patriot of the Punjab, who died a few months later from his injuries. When Congress met in Lahore in 1929, Sardar Bhagat Singh (later hanged for revolutionary activities) organized the Lahore Students' Union.

Lado Rani Zutshi, the wife of Motilal Nehru's nephew, and three of her daughters, Manmohini, Shyama, and Janak, led the movement in Lahore. Manmohini (b. 1909) was raised on politics. In 1929, as a student at Government College (for men), Manmohini chaired the student reception committee welcoming Subhas Bose to preside over the second All-Punjab Student Conference. The same year she became the first woman president of the Lahore Student Union and served as a volunteer at the Lahore Congress.[81]

The atmosphere was already charged with patriotic fervor when the announcement of civil disobedience gave these young people a focus. Speaking to students Jawaharlal suggested they go to the banks of the Ravi river and symbolically "make salt" and then concentrate on picketing foreign cloth and liquor shops. Bimla Luthra recalled her reaction and that of her friends when they listened to Jawaharlal:

We girls were completely bowled over by him, not only because he was so handsome, but also because he appeared to us to symbolize the spirit of rebellion against foreign domination at the political level and . . . the stifling conservatism and orthodoxy which made us feel continually that we were an inferior class of people, good only for the home and kitchen.[82]

When Bhagat Singh and his comrades were sentenced to death, Manmohini decided to post women pickets at three colleges in Lahore: Government College, Law College, and Forman Christian College. It was a wildly successful demonstration as men students absented themselves from classes to cheer the young women. As the excitement mounted, so did police tempers. By 2.30 in the afternoon sixteen

---

[80] Geeta Anand, "Appeal of the Indian Nationalist Movement to Women," senior thesis, Dartmouth College (1989); *ABP* (April 20, 1930), p. 6, (November 7, 1930), p. 4, (November 23, 1930), p. 5; *BC* (July 14, 1930), p. 4, (November 7, 1930), p. 1, (December 1, 1930), p. 1, (January 3, 1931), p. 1; *The Tribune* (August 7, 1930), p. 9.

[81] Sahgal, *An Indian Freedom Fighter*, ch. 5.

[82] Bimla Luthra, "Nehru's Vision of Indian Society and the Place of Women in it," unpublished paper (n.d.), NMML.

women and thirty-five men were arrested. Manmohini wrote of her experience:

We were excited and enthusiastic about being taken to prison. We felt as if a great honor had been conferred on us. We shouted slogans and sang national songs while waiting for the formalities to be completed. In fact, the three of us, my sisters and I, dearly hoped to be imprisoned three times so we would be termed "habitual offenders."[83]

She was sentenced to six months imprisonment and served the first of her three incarcerations.

In Delhi, Satyavati Devi, the granddaughter of Swami Shraddhanand, became one of the leaders. The Swami, or Munshi Ram as he was known in his earlier years, was deeply influenced by Swami Dayananda, converted to the Arya Samaj, and worked with his brother-in-law Lala Devraj of Jullundar to promote female education. It was after he moved to Delhi in 1918 that he joined the political movement and won fame for his leadership of non-violent demonstrations.[84] When Satyavati Devi spoke to women, she reminded them of her lineage and urged them to join her in making personal sacrifices for the nation. She explained her commitment:

I am Swami Shardhanand's [sic] granddaughter and Dhani Ram advocate's daughter and I have two little children. Ordinarily my place was in my home. But at a time when my motherland is passing through [a] life and death struggle, I am one of millions of India's women and only one of thousands of Delhi's women who have left their hearth and home and their traditional seclusion [to] muster under Mahatma Gandhi's standard to fight.[85]

Take to the field, Satyavati Devi told women, because foreign domination is unbearable. Judging her impassioned speeches inflammatory, the authorities moved quickly: they arrested and imprisoned Satyavati Devi, released her, re-arrested her, and finally sentenced her to two years imprisonment in 1932. From prison came songs such as "Satyavati's Message from Jail" urging women forward:

> Jump into the burning fire,
> And stand firm in the holy war,
> Do not retreat from the battle,
> So says Sister Satyavatiji.
> In the battle you must die before men

---

[83] Sahgal, *An Indian Freedom Fighter*, ch. 6, p. 73.
[84] "Munshi Ram Shraddhanand," *DNB*, vol. IV, pp. 185–7.
[85] *BC* (May 28, 1930), p. 7.

Don't be afraid of bullets or sticks,
Move your head forward first
So says sister Satyavatiji.[86]

In prison she contracted pleurisy and then tuberculosis but continued to work with Congress throughout the 1930s.[87]

Women's demonstrations in Delhi had a great impact on the men who witnessed them. The government's confidential records include detailed reports of how women's activities brought men into the movement. On one occasion Delhi women, dressed in red saris, blocked access to the courts. They were surrounded by male supporters who acted as a protective shield. On another occasion a crowd of Sikhs gathered at a Gurudwara in Delhi to watch a women's protest. When news spread that one of the women had been killed by a policeman, the people rioted.[88]

The women were steadfast in the face of police attacks and astounded everyone with their bravery. Issues of women's rights received little attention even though many of their leaders were committed to feminist issues. Kamala Nehru wrote and spoke about the "degraded plight of women," and women's rights; Vijayalakshmi Pandit worked for many years with women's organizations; and the female students were inspired by an ideal of male–female equality. But these feminist ideas only permeated elite circles and when these leaders began organizing women's processions, they became acutely aware of the strength of conservative attitudes.

In the north, the political movement engaged elite women and women without any education. They belonged to two different worlds but they shared the burden of social norms that inhibited their autonomy. Women leaders wanted to mobilize their less sophisticated sisters for political action and they knew this would be impossible without the permission of husbands and fathers. Therefore, it was expedient to concentrate on nationalist issues and leave feminist issues out of their speeches. In prison, the practice of separating women depending on class background, and placing them in different sections of the prison with different food and amenities, mitigated against uneducated lower- and middle-class women learning the ideology of the elites.

[86] Anand, "Appeal of the Indian Nationalist Movement," p. 41.
[87] M. Kaur, The *Role of Women in the Freedom Movement (1857–1947)*, (New Delhi, Sterling, 1968), p. 196.
[88] "Civil Disobedience in Delhi," GOI, Home Dept. Political, file no. 256/I/1930.

POLICE VIOLENCE AND THE BRITISH AS THE DEMON RAVANA

The role of women in the non-cooperation movement of the 1920s and the civil disobedience movement of the 1930s called into question Britain's civilizing mission in India. Beginning in the nineteenth century, British rulers justified their rule by calling attention to the degraded status of India's women. They regarded their efforts to provide education and medical care and pass laws to protect women as proof of their moral purpose. The involvement of women in the nationalist struggle severely challenged the notion that the British were the legitimate rulers of India, and at the same time lent full support to the Congress as the rightful heirs to political power.

The construction of the British as moral rulers was called into question by widely publicized accounts of their violent attacks on peaceful demonstrators. British mistreatment of women clashed with prevailing gender ideology and seriously undermined their self-proclaimed role of protector. The scriptures of both Hinduism and Islam praise modest and chaste women. The ideal woman, valorized in law, legend, and folklore, was faithful to her husband and untouched, sometimes unseen, by other men. Men who protected women were honorable.

When Gandhi asked women to take part in the political movement, he instructed them to be like Sita. The British were the equivalent of Ravana (the demon abductor of Sita) and the world would not be set right until the moral rule of Ram (Sita's husband) was re-established. These ideas resonated with his female audience for whom Sita was a living legend. Although not many girls went to school they were taught these legends in the home and even low-caste people learned them through folk theater and stories.[89]

From the earliest days of women's protests the British were charged with brutal treatment of women demonstrators. In 1920 Sarojini Naidu accused the Martial Law Administration in the Punjab of grossly mistreating women. The British expressed shock; the Secretary of State for India Edwin Montagu had his secretary reply: "Mr. Montagu finds it difficult to believe that anybody could for one moment have thought that such occurrences were possible." In reply, Mrs. Naidu quoted details from the Report of the Enquiry Committee of the Indian

---

[89] Ambujammal, interview (Madras, January 19, 1976).

National Congress. She reminded Montagu's secretary that "pardah [*sic*] is as sacred to the Indian women as is her veil to the Catholic Nun and forcibly to unveil an Indian woman constitutes in itself a gross outrage."[90]

During the civil disobedience movement accounts of police brutality against women were epidemic. In Bardoli District, Gujarat, the peasants of the village of Badmani stopped paying taxes. The police, in their efforts to intimidate the villagers, beat many people. They locked one elderly woman in a house without food or water.[91] In Bombay, three young women complained that the officer arresting them, Sergeant Mackenzie, and another police constable visited their cells after midnight and made indecent gestures.[92] Lilavati Munshi, a leader of the Desh Sevikas, made this incident the subject of a rousing speech she delivered to a crowd collected to congratulate Jawaharlal on his jail sentence. Lilavati challenged the assumption that Indian women had ever been the objects of British chivalry. They protect their own women, Lilavati reminded her audience, referring to a recent case where the government had spent several thousands of rupees rescuing a woman abducted by Pathans. But Indian women were not safe in their own country. This was not an issue for Indian men, Lilavati continued, it was a women's issue, and when Indian women joined the fight for freedom, they must always remember they were fighting a government that accorded them no respect.[93]

A huge rally was held in Bombay to protest the police decision to pick up women demonstrators, transport them out of the city, and abandon them in a jungle at night. Lady Jagmohandas called this action tantamount to rape: "No system of Government that insulted the womanhood of the country had ever succeeded and no people however meek and down-trodden would tolerate [it] for a long time." Mrs. Annapurnabai G. V. Deshmukh spoke about Sita and Draupadi and the "religious belief of the Hindus that whenever a Hindu woman was harassed or insulted, the Lord came to her rescue and saved her honor." Even the gods would recognize the moral bankruptcy of this government![94]

The heavy hand of the police was felt in the rural areas. Newspaper accounts and Congress reports seldom mentioned these women by

[90] M. Kaur, *The Role of Women*, Appendix G, pp. 259–62.
[91] *BC* (October 29, 1930), p. 1. [92] *BC* (October 30, 1930), p. 7.
[93] *BC* (October 31, 1930), p. 1. [94] *BC* (November 4, 1930), p. 4.

name, but reported their mistreatment as symbolic of British disregard for Mother India and Indian womanhood. For example, it was reported that in January of 1931 the police beat "women of Borsad" unconscious when they participated in demonstrations. Kasturbai Gandhi communicated she had seen police grab women by the hair, hit their breasts, and utter indecent insults.[95] The British authorities denied these charges, but occasionally the assaulted women pressed charges and the courts heard their cases. Following their arrest and detention for picketing a cloth shop in Benares, a group of women complained they had been stripped and beaten. The police denied the allegations and claimed this was a Congress plot; the judge agreed it was a phony charge. During the course of the trial, each woman who presented evidence was discredited in moral terms. Kulda Devi was revealed as an "unattached" woman, a maidservant by trade, and the "kept woman" of a Bengali. She was also characterized as a professional Congress volunteer. Munni, a widow, was described by the police as a woman who lived from the proceeds of a brothel. Charubala had left her husband and was living with Umesh Chandra; in the police records she was "a woman of loose character." Khanto was a widow who lived in a house of women, Manorama was a widow, Shybolini was a widow, Gauri was a child widow who had drifted to Benares, and Bagola Devi did not have any fixed address. Dismissing the charges, the judge declared that these were the "flotsam thrown up on the streets, hardly the respectable women of India."[96] Moral character, as defined by the British, was the touch-stone for judging the truth or falsity of the accusations. The British, like many of their Indian subjects, did not regard Indian women without male guardians worthy of protection from physical and sexual harassment.

A more sensational event, although it involved only one woman, became known as the "*thali*-snatching case." The *thali*, a gold chain worn around the neck, indicates that a South Indian woman is married. It is removed only after the death of her husband. Mrs. L. S. Prabhu was arrested for picketing in Tellicherry and sentenced to six months imprisonment and a fine of Rs 1,000. She refused to pay the fine so the sub-divisional magistrate, Mr. Dodwell, ordered her to hand over her

[95] *BC* (January 26, 1931), p. 7, (February 3, 1931), p. 7.
[96] "Allegations that the police at Andra, Madras stripped and flogged women arrestees. Enquires into ill-treatment of women volunteers by the police of Dasaswamedh [*sic*], Benares," GOI, Home Dept., Political, file no. IV/1932.

jewelry. She refused and Dodwell, even though he had been warned the *thali* was sacred to a married woman, ordered a policeman to remove it from her neck. Mrs. Prabhu could not possibly allow a strange man to touch her so she asked her female co-defendants to remove it. The *"thali*-snatching" incident caused such a commotion that British officials had to admit their blunder and restore Mrs. Prabhu's *thali*.[97] Official documents instructing police and magistrates how to deal with women had warned against the use of force and improper behavior. The chief commissioner of Delhi, John Thompson, acknowledged "an Indian government would be much better qualified to deal with it [a women's demonstration] than we are, as they would be free from the odium which attaches to a 'foreign government' when it employs what is called repression."[98]

In 1932 the Indian National Congress invited the India League of London to investigate charges of police brutality. The League accepted and their delegation, composed of two British women, one British man, and one Indian man, traveled to India to see conditions first-hand. In India they requested permission to see the jails and speak with political prisoners. Eager to discredit this delegation before its work began, British officials charged that it was dominated by "suffragettes" and denied it interviews with political prisoners. The delegation found substantial evidence of violence, both in the enforcement of ordinances and in lock-ups. After citing reliable information that women had been sexually threatened, sexually abused, beaten, and raped, the delegation, in a masterful example of understatement, concluded: "Nor has womanhood been respected as it ought to have been by the agents of a so-called civilized Government."[99] The report of this delegation made it clear, to the British public as well as Indians, that the British rulers were not protectors of women but rather perpetrators of violence against women.

CONCLUSIONS

By 1934 the civil disobedience movement that began with the salt march was over. Women's participation in agitational politics must be viewed, first, in terms of what it meant for the nationalist movement and, second, how these actions shaped the women's movement.

[97] "Thali Snatching in Court," *ISR*, 42 (February 6, 1932), p. 363.
[98] GOI, Home Dept., Political, file no. 14/4/1932.
[99] GOI, Home Dept., Political, file no. 40/XII, 1932.

The participation of women legitimized the Indian National Congress. Women's activities validated Indian unity and *satyagraha*. The techniques of *satyagrahis* were designed to wrest moral authority from the Raj and return it to the unarmed, non-violent subjects. Even the British understood that this method had a special appeal for women. One official wrote:

> there is no doubt that but for them [women] the movement would never have gained the force it has had. It is due to them that the sympathy of many not otherwise likely to have been in sympathy has been evoked.[100]

The participation of women in the freedom movement also shaped the movement for women's rights. Most important, it legitimized their claim to a place in the governance of India. Saraladevi Chaudhurani posed the question: "How can we attain rights?" and answered: "By the strength of our agitation. We must force menfolk to concede to our demands and at the same time carry on propaganda among ourselves."[101]

Women won great respect for their political work and social benefits followed. In the years following the civil disobedience movement more and more women entered the professions, and some men learned to work side by side with them as colleagues. The legal structure for family law was reviewed, and efforts to modify it were undertaken.

And there were psychological gains. The stories of what participation meant can best be told by individuals. Ambabai, a woman of Karnataka had been married at age twelve. Widowed at age sixteen, Ambabai joined in picketing foreign cloth and toddy shops in Udipi. She was arrested and sentenced to four months in prison, released, and re-arrested. Between these prison terms, she made speeches, taught spinning, and organized *prabhat pheries.* Ambabai regards these as the happiest days of her life.[102] Although British officials dismissed the protests of widows, Ambabai's story points out how the Congress program transformed her life from one of purposelessness and boredom to one of vital engagement and commitment.

At the same time, the participation of women had some clear drawbacks. Those demonstrating claimed to represent all Indian women, but the number of groups involved, other than upper- and middle-class Hindu women, was never large. A few Muslim women were steadfast

---

[100] GOI, Home Dept., Political, file no. 253/30/1930.
[101] Tamil Nad Women's Conference, Erode, *Stri Dharma*, 14, no. 12 (October 1931), p. 563.
[102] Ambabai, interview (Udipi, May 24, 1976).

followers of Gandhi; many more either found it difficult to accept the overtly Hindu ideological basis of his ideas or were neglected by the Congress organizers.

There were distinct regional differences in the number of women who joined, in their relationship with Congress leaders, and the extent to which they synthesized women's interests with nationalist issues. Bombay women were the best organized, the most independent, and fielded the largest demonstrations. Most of their leaders also belonged to women's organizations and they articulated a clearly "feminist nationalism." In Bengal women attracted a great deal of attention because of their militancy. Marching alongside men in the Congress parade and later joining the revolutionary parties, they became the subjects of folksongs and legends. Their peaceful demonstrations were fewer but they too attracted a great deal of attention in a society where purdah was widely practiced. These women espoused a feminist ideology but time and again put it aside in favor of the broader struggle. In Madras, where leaders were unwilling to use women's talents, fewer women joined the movement. In North India, the Nehru and the Zutshi families provided strong women leaders who put the nationalist agenda first. One cannot doubt their grasp of the importance of feminist issues but their immediate concern was mobilizing women for political demonstrations. They did not think it possible to raise women's consciousness about both politics and women's rights at the same time.

Most women leaders were unable to get beyond their own sense of respectability when they sought recruits. An exception to this of course were the women who joined the revolutionary movement. They worked closely with men, wore disguises, traveled alone or in the company of strangers, and learned how to shoot, drive cars, and make bombs. Even though they were valorized they were not regarded by all as "respectable" women. Gandhi called them "unsexed" and Rabindranath Tagore wrote a novel in which the sexual allure of the revolutionary heroine was used to recruit young men to the cause.[103] The revolutionary women have described themselves as sacrificing all the things a woman wants – marriage, children, a home – for the country. No one, including the revolutionary women themselves, considered revolutionaries representative of Indian womanhood.

[103] Rabindranath Tagore, *Four Chapters*, translation of *Char Adhyaya* (1934) by Surendranath Tagore (Calcutta, Visva-Bharati, 1950), p. 13.

The demonstrations organized by the women in cities did little to generate a feminist consciousness. They marched and picketed in sex-segregated groups, usually wearing distinctive orange or white saris to emphasize their purity and sacrifice. Their directives came from the Congress Committees. Rural women, unless they were widows, protested with their families. Male guardianship prevailed even though the Indian freedom movement was not characterized by "patriarchal nationalism." Women could "come out" because the house was on fire. The expectation was that once the fire was out, women would go back inside the house.

CHAPTER 6

WOMEN'S WORK IN COLONIAL INDIA

Dr. Haimabati Sen, a medical doctor in charge of the women's hospital in Chinsurah, described her daily routine in 1895:

I would get up every day at four in the morning, prepare a breakfast for my husband and the children, and go downstairs with hot water and edibles for the patients. I would first help the patients wash . . . I would finish this chore of helping them wash and give them a piece of *batasa* or candied sugar as their snack . . . Where there were children staying with the mother I would make some *halua* [semolina sweet] and give them small quantities of it. It would take me a little over an hour to attend to the patients and come back. I would go back home, have a wash, wake up the children, dress them, give them breakfast, arrange for my husband's meal, get dressed, have something to eat and then go back to the hospital. This was my daily routine.[1]

The labor of women like Dr. Haimabati Sen, as a medical professional and wife and mother, has largely been hidden from history. Memoirs rarely offer such rich detail about women's work. Unfortunately, our sources on women's work in the nineteenth and even much of the twentieth century are vague and unanalytical. The dearth of reliable data presents a serious challenge for historians attempting to probe the consequences of colonial rule for laboring women.

In 1921, the year the non-cooperation movement began, over thirty-nine million women or one-third of the female population were in the workforce. Very few of these were professionals: there were 68,000 medical professionals, 30,000 women employed in educational and scientific fields, and 6,000 women in law and business. By far the largest employer of women was the manufacturing sector, both in established mills and factories and in minor manufacturing such as vegetable oil production and tailoring. Domestic workers numbered 737,000.[2] In 1928 about 250,000 women worked in factories, about 58,000 of them

---

[1] "The Memoirs of Dr. Haimavati Sen," trans. Tapan Raychaudhuri, ed. Geraldine Forbes and Tapan Raychaudhuri, unpublished ms., p. 220.

[2] Jaipal P. Ambannavar, "Changes in Economic Activity of Males and Females in India: 1911–1961", *Demography India*, 4, no. 2 (1975), pp. 362–4. There are small differences in other sources which also claim to use the Indian census. I assume the differences are a result of giving approximate figures.

in cotton mills and 55,000 in jute mills. Another 250,000 women worked in tea gardens, where they were 27 percent of the workforce. Seventy-eight thousand women worked in the mines.[3] The number of women employed in sex work must be have been significant if we accept the estimate of Bombay city's prostitutes as between 30,000 and 40,000 in 1921.[4] The women who worked in agriculture and domestic production outnumbered all these categories but their labor was not recorded in the census.

Significant numbers of women were in the workforce by the 1920s but work did not become a women's issue until the 1930s. In 1929 *Women in Modern India,* edited by Evelyn C. Gedge and Mithan Choksi, was published with a foreword by the doyen of women's organizations and the nationalist movement, Sarojini Naidu.

Sarojini Naidu called this book the "authentic voice of modern Indian womanhood."[5] It included fifteen articles, three on medical work, one on social work and one on women and the law. There were no articles on the conditions or demands of women working in the factories, mines, or plantations. Kamaladevi Chattopadhyay, in the introductory chapter on "The Status of Women in India," wrote:

Man has not questioned the woman's right to enter any field of activity or any profession although he held complete sway everywhere for many years now, keeping the women out and restricting their influence and scope of work by rigid rules and customs."[6]

Time and again, women leaders commented favorably on the absence of economic competition between men and women. Sarojini Naidu expressed this in her "I am not a feminist" speech as president of the AIWC in 1930. A feminist, she declared, is one who admits "her inferiority and there has been no need for such a thing in India as the women have always been by the side of men both in councils and the fields of battle." Women's work, Sarojini told her audience, is spiritual reform of the world.[7] She wanted women to be politically active because they were psychologically and spiritually different from men. While Sarojini Naidu denied she was a feminist, I would call her ideology social feminism. By linking social feminism with nationalism, she

---

[3] A. R. Caton, ed., *The Key of Progress* (London, Humphrey Milford, 1930), pp. 155–7.
[4] "Bombay Prostitution Committee's Report," *ISR* (August 27, 1922), p. 2.
[5] Evelyn C. Gedge and Mithan Choksi, eds., *Women in Modern India* (Bombay, D. B. Taraporewala Sons and Co., 1929), foreword.
[6] Gedge and Choksi, *Women In Modern India,* p. 4.
[7] AIWC, Fourth Session, Bombay, 1930, p. 21.

and her colleagues hindered the development of a radical feminist critique of women's work.

THE COLONIAL ECONOMY AND WOMEN'S WORK

Women's new professional opportunities as well as their employment in urban brothels were a consequence of British domination. Colonial rule transformed the traditional economic system and in the process fundamentally dislocated the non-agricultural, village-based economy. The decline of the local economy and with it the demise of local small-scale services and industries left many women unemployed. Women had formerly participated in a wide range of small-scale enterprises; they processed food grains and oil seeds, made bread, shoes, pottery, nets, and ropes, raised cattle, and repaired various things. All these activities declined. In Bengal the female-dominated household industry of rice-husking was replaced by mechanized threshing machines placed in mills. When machines were introduced, men replaced women as rice-huskers. The new mills allocated menial jobs to women but norms of female seclusion precluded Bengali Hindu and Muslim women from accepting this employment.[8]

The modern sector – the economic sector that emerged with colonial rule – provided women with new opportunities for employment. For example, the professions of teaching and medicine were now open to a few women. Factories, mines, and plantations employed significant numbers of women but under such harsh conditions it is difficult to view this employment in a positive light.

Poor women often found employment in exploitative industries. Women leaders ignored this reality, focusing instead on education, the franchise, and legal rights. They regarded women from the higher castes who sought employment as victims of unfortunate circumstances. The work of lower-caste women was taken for granted. Women leaders could afford their excursions into social work and politics because they had supportive fathers and/or husbands. But they lacked the economic wherewithal to make independent decisions and were locked, often unconsciously, in behaviors and attitudes that maintained class status.

[8] Mukul Mukherjee, "Impact of Modernization on Women's Occupations," *IESHR*, 20, 1 (1983), pp. 27–45.

14 Women weavers in Assam, *c.* 1900

The members of the women's organizations wrote and spoke of women's and men's roles as complementary. Gandhi's references to Sita and Draupadi linked living legends with the social feminism of the women's organizations. He did not want women to "go against their natures," Ambujammal said, nor did he want them to blindly follow bad husbands. Gandhi urged women to emulate ancient heroines in their work for the country's freedom. *Satyagraha* could also be utilized to reform bad husbands.[9] Neither Gandhi nor women leaders envisioned women as productive, salaried workers.

There is another side to this story. Conditions of female employment were of special interest to international organizations at this time. The League of Nations and the International Labour Organization sought to create standards that all modern, progressive nations would accept. Indian women, long affiliated with organizations such as the International Council of Women and the International Women's Suffrage Alliance, were eager to play a role in these particular international bodies.

[9] Ambujammal, interview (Madras, January 19, 1976).

The women's organizations claimed they represented all Indian women; consequently they received requests from these international bodies for data about working women. To reply, they set up committees to study the conditions of employment for women in factories, mines, and prisons. At the same time they were developing programs and institutions to improve the lives of working women. Inexperienced in this world of work, they taught crafts to destitute women and lectured laboring women on the importance of housework and family relations. India's "new" women were learning about the plight of working-class women, trying to ameliorate their situation, vying for acceptance from international organizations, entering the professions, and establishing themselves as patriotic citizens all at the same time. Successfully balancing this agenda proved impossible within the framework of social feminism.

PROFESSIONAL POSITIONS

In the 1920s and 1930s women's organizations demanded educational and medical services for females. Separate institutions were required to deliver these services because sex-segregation norms prevented women from using institutions designed for men. Women leaders insisted new institutions be staffed by female professionals. The jobs created were for women much like themselves: educated, able to move about freely, and comfortable interacting with both men and women.

Medicine was one of the new careers opened to Indian women in the late nineteenth century. Western medical training had long been available to Indian males but it was not until 1885 that Lady Dufferin, wife of the Viceroy, established the National Association for Supplying Female Medical Aid to the Women of India or the Dufferin Fund. This association provided financial assistance to women willing to be trained as doctors, hospital assistants, nurses, and midwives; aided in establishing medical training programs for women; and encouraged construction of hospitals and dispensaries. Wealthy Indians – maharajas, landowners, and industrialists – contributed to this fund and were rewarded with titles and special honors. By 1888 the government of India was supervising the work of the association and providing employment for women graduates.

Kadambini Basu, one of India's first women doctors and a beneficiary of this scheme, graduated from Bethune College in 1883 and entered Medical College the same year. Shortly after entering medical school, Kadambini married her long-time mentor and friend, Dwarkanath Ganguly. Dwarkanath was a staunch member of the Sadharan Brahmo Samaj and an advocate of male–female equality. When the government announced a scholarship of Rs 20 per month for women medical students, Kadambini applied and was granted the award. In 1886 she was awarded the GBMC (Graduate of Bengal Medical College), instead of the more prestigious MB (Bachelor of Medicine) degree, because she had failed one part of her final practical exams. She established a thriving private practice and in 1888 was appointed to the Lady Dufferin Women's Hospital with a salary of Rs 300/month.[10] Later she went to Edinburgh and Glasgow for additional degrees.

Kadambini was a successful doctor and a good wife and mother. There are accounts that attest to her personal supervision of the household and devoted attention to her five children. Her interest in political affairs was such that she served as one of the first women delegates to the Indian National Congress. Despite these accomplishments the orthodox magazine *Bangabasi* indirectly called her a whore.[11] Kadambini won a libel case against them but this attack was illustrative of the widespread antagonism towards new professional women.

Anandibai Joshi[12] (1865–87), a Marathi woman, also received her medical degree in 1886. She graduated from the Women's Medical College in Philadelphia as their first Indian student and the first Hindu woman to study medicine abroad. Anandibai was married at age nine to Gopalrao Vinyak Joshi, a man determined to educate his wife. Accounts differ regarding Anandibai's desire to study and all we know is that she advanced rapidly under her husband's tutelage. She bore and lost a son at age thirteen and within a year decided to study medicine.[13]

In 1880 Gopal wrote to an American philanthropist in India asking him to provide for Anandibai's education. This letter was forwarded to the United States and published in the *Missionary Review*. Almost

---

[10] Malavika Karlekar, "Kadambini and the Bhadralok," *EPW*, 21, no. 19 (April 26, 1986), pp. ws25–ws31; Karlekar, *Voices from Within: Early Personal Narratives of Bengali Women* (Delhi, Oxford University Press, 1991) pp. 175–82.

[11] David Kopf, *The Brahmo Samaj and the Shaping of the Modern Indian Mind* (Princeton, N.J., Princeton University Press, 1979), pp. 124–6; Karlekar, "Kadambini," p. ws27.

[12] Her name is spelled Anandabai and Anandibai and Joshi and Joshee in different accounts.

[13] Mrs. Caroline Healey Doll, *The Life of Anandabai Joshee [sic]* (Boston, Roberts Brothers, 1888). There is a fictionalized account of Anandibai's life by S. J. Joshi, *Anandi Gopal*, translated by Asha Damle (Calcutta, Stree, 1992).

immediately, Anandibai was invited to study in America and offered full financial support. Before anything was decided Gopal, a postal employee, was transferred to Calcutta. Anandibai accompanied her husband to this "foreign" province where she was harassed for not observing purdah. In Calcutta she realized she had no choice: if she wanted to pursue her studies, she would have to go abroad. Anandibai explained her decision to a mixed audience at the Baptist College Hall in Serampore, February 24, 1883, at what must have been one of the earliest public speeches made by an Indian woman. It might have been easier for her to get an education, she explained, if she were a Christian or a member of the Brahmo Samaj, but because she was Hindu she had been verbally and physically threatened when she ventured out of her house alone. She told her audience she realized she could not pursue her ambition in India.[14]

Anandibai Joshi sailed from Calcutta on April 7, 1883, arrived in New York, and was taken by her sponsors to enroll in the Women's Medical College in Pennsylvania. The climate, poor food and lodgings, and demands of her course left her ill and exhausted. At her graduation Anandibai told her cousin Pandita Ramabai that she would remain in Boston for a year to gain experience. Within six months she was seriously ill, had canceled her plans, and set sail for India. Anandibai had been appointed resident physician of the women's ward of Albert Edward Hospital at Kohlapur but never took charge of her post. She died soon after reaching India.[15]

Christian women were always more numerous in the medical profession than women from other communities. Hilda Lazarus, born in Vizagapatnam (now in Andhra Pradesh) in 1890, was one of the most successful Indian Christian doctors. Her grandparents, both from high-ranking brahmin families, had converted to Christianity long before Hilda was born.

Hilda studied first in her father's school; then at a local college for her FA (First Arts); Presidency College, Madras for her BA; and finally Medical College, Madras for her MB and BS (Bachelor of Surgery). Following graduation she was appointed assistant to the obstetrician

---

[14] *The Life of Anandabai Joshee*, pp. 85–6.

[15] *The Letters and Correspondence of Pandita Ramabai*, compiled by Sister Geraldine, ed. A. B. Shah (Bombay, Maharashtra State Board of Literature and Culture, 1977) pp. 171–5; "Dr. Anandibai Joshee," *ILM*, 7 (January 1934), pp. 315–16; Maud Diver, *The Englishwoman in India* (Edinburgh and London, William Blackwood and Sons, 1909), pp. 220–8.

and gynecologist at Lady Hardinge Medical College Hospital in Delhi. This was 1917 and Hilda Lazarus became the first Indian woman appointed to the Women's Medical Service (WMS). Dr. Lazarus spent thirty years in the WMS, retiring in 1947 as its chief medical officer. During her career, she presided over a number of hospitals and set up several programs to train female doctors, nurses, and midwives.[16]

Discussing her early life and career, Dr. Lazarus remembered her mother and father as deeply committed to female education. From childhood she wanted to be a doctor. Any plans she had to marry ended with the death of her fiancé in 1913. A member of the WMS, Dr. Lazarus served in a number of different hospitals. Quick to pick up new languages, she made a point of learning the regional language with each new posting. Dr. Lazarus wore *khaddar* saris to advertise her admiration for Gandhi and sympathy for nationalist aspirations. Her main goal was to increase the number of Indian women professionals, knowing full well that European and Eurasian women had the advantage in obtaining scholarships and employment. Dr. Lazarus was extremely critical of the insensitive and inefficient schemes supported by the British medical establishment. Although she was Christian, she did not identify with the British.[17]

In the late nineteenth century and the early decades of the twentieth century, demand for women medical professionals grew. The demand came from: middle-class Indian women who regarded Western medicine as modern and scientific; the manufacturing sector mandated to provide medical services for their employees; and the government who demonstrated their "civilizing mission" by establishing clinics, hospitals, and dispensaries. Except in the most anglicized families, upper-class and middle-class women avoided male doctors and sought the services of women. For the very poor, medical care of any type was a luxury; but for women working in the organized sector – factories, mines, and plantations – laws mandated the provision of medical services. The supply of trained medical women never equaled the demand.

Education for girls was respectable, but few parents wanted their daughters to go beyond primary school and only an infinitesimal number encouraged their daughters to become doctors. Moreover, most girls' schools omitted science courses as too rigorous for female

---

[16] *Autobiography of Hilda Lazarus* (Vizagapatnam, SFS Printing, n.d.), pp. 1–5.
[17] Hilda Lazarus, "Sphere of Indian Women in Medical Work," *Women in Modern India*; Hilda Lazarus, interview (Vizagapatnam, January 30, 1976).

minds. Miss Janau, the principal of Bethune College, observed that college girls became physically weaker with every year of study. Agreeing with her, another teacher characterized these students as inadequately prepared for their subjects. Consequently, they exhausted themselves trying to pass their exams.

Once they had passed the necessary subjects, women had to find medical colleges willing to admit them. The Lady Hardinge Medical College for women opened in Delhi in 1916.[18] After World War I, in direct response to the demand for women doctors, scientific subjects were added to the curricula in women's colleges and more medical colleges accepted women candidates. By 1929 nineteen men's medical colleges and schools admitted women, and there was one medical college and four medical schools for women only.[19]

Attending a men's medical college presented a distinct set of challenges. All the female boarders stayed together, making it impossible to observe caste rules. Even young women who considered themselves radical freethinkers had to consider the grave consequences of breaking these rules. With their degrees they might become successful professionals, but their brothers, sisters, and cousins could suffer the consequences of their acts. If they chose to live in private homes, they had to endure public taunts as they traveled to and from classes.

These young women students had to guard their reputations. This meant avoiding unnecessary travel and missing the dramas, clubs, and other entertainments available to their male colleagues. Attending classes presented yet other hurdles. Muthulakshmi Reddy, like other women of her generation, was either the lone female in her classes or in the company of one or two others. Professors usually placed women at the front of the room, off to one side, or in some other way separated them from the male students. There were a few professors who did not allow female students in their classes and assigned junior assistants to lecture them.[20]

It is no wonder so many women failed to complete medical school. Muthulakshmi Reddy's account of her years in medical college includes references to colleagues who failed their exams or dropped out. The

[18] Calcutta University Commission, 1917–1919, *Women's Education* (Calcutta, Superintendent Government Printing, 1919), p. 28.
[19] Dr. Hilda Lazarus, "Sphere of Indian Women in Medical Work," *Women in Modern India*, p. 51. Medical colleges were able to issue university degrees. Medical schools, often attached to hospitals, were regarded as training schools and could only issue certificates.
[20] *Autobiography of Dr. (Mrs.) S. Muthulakshmi Reddy* (Madras, M. Reddi, 1964), pp. 12–18.

few survivors graduated into a world that held them in high esteem and offered positions with high salaries. Although the path had been treacherous, the professional rewards were significant.

These women doctors faced a number of challenges as they embarked on their careers. First, it was difficult to combine family life with professional demands, yet society had little tolerance for single women. Second, they had to contend with sexual harassment. In Ahmedabad in the early 1930s the case of Dr. (Miss) Ahalyabai Samant, the director of the municipal dispensary of Nadiad, was reported in the newspapers. Dr. Balabahi Harishankar Bhatt, the municipal councilor, abducted and assaulted Dr. Samant. The district and sessions judge sentenced Bhatt to one year in prison hoping this would make it clear that women doctors were to be treated with respect. The chief justice of the High Court overturned this decision and simply fined Bhatt. According to the chief justice:

If women engaged in professional work come out into the open world they must adopt the standards of the ordinary men and women of the world. They cannot expect to retain the hyper-sensitive notions of modesty which their ancestors in purdah may have possessed.[21]

Third, these women worked in a profession dominated by European and Anglo-Indian women. They received less pay and had to contend with racial prejudice. Gender discrimination was evident in salaries paid to Dufferin Fund doctors who earned less than one-third the salary of British or Indian men in the Indian Medical Service. But there was also a disparity between the salaries of British women and Indian women. Theoretically, salary depended on credentials but it was extremely difficult for Indian women to obtain the same degrees as their British colleagues. In Bengal, Indian women could earn the VLMS (the Vernacular Licentiate in Medicine and Surgery), a certificate obtainable without knowledge of English, but it doomed them to a salary less than one-tenth that earned by a woman holding an MB or MD degree.

In 1907 British women doctors practicing in India formed the Association of Medical Women in India and proposed the formation of a Women's Indian Medical Service modeled on the IMS. They stressed Britain's "civilizing mission" in India, contending that Indian women, the forgotten citizens of the British Empire, wanted and needed

---

[21] "Professional Women and Professional Standards," *ISR*, 41 (August 1, 1931), p. 761.

Western medical care. Since there would never be enough Indian women to meet the demand, it was essential to improve the conditions of employment to attract well-trained foreign women. In 1914 the Women's Medical Service (WMS) became a reality. The WMS professed concern for Indian women professionals and offered to integrate them through a two-tier system of superior and inferior grades, but it was British women doctors who gained the most from this measure.[22] It was not until 1947 that an Indian woman, Dr. Lazarus, held the position of chief medical officer.

Women entering the professions of teaching and law faced similar problems to those of medical women. Obtaining requisite training was often difficult as was the problem of certification. Many women studied privately for exams. They were less likely to hold the degrees and certificates necessary for employment in formal institutions. Women like Cornelia Sorabji had attended the proper institutions and passed the required exams but could not practice law because of gender discrimination.

Women professionals faced a range of problems. Those who worked in institutions for women and children were sheltered by the workplace; employment in institutions serving both sexes was more problematic. Women generally found marital status afforded a degree of protection yet they had to balance household demands with those of their profession. Unmarried women, including widows, found it difficult to find a place to live and a way to protect themselves from sexual harassment. The higher their salaries and the more supportive their families, the easier these problems were to resolve. As a consequence, the accounts of women professionals vary markedly: some women were accorded a great deal of respect and met with few problems pursuing their professions, others complained bitterly about the hardships they endured.

FACTORY WORK

The first cotton and jute mills, established in the 1850s, employed women, but accurate records are available only after 1911. It is esti-

---

[22] David Arnold, *Colonizing the Body* (Berkeley, University of California Press, 1993), pp. 265–6; Dagmar Engels, "The Politics of Child Birth: British and Bengali Women in Contest, 1890–1930," *Society and Ideology: Essays in South Asian History Presented to Professor Kenneth Ballhatchet*, ed. P. Robb (Delhi, Oxford University Press, 1993), p. 222–46; "Rules for the Women's Medical Service for India," *Thirty-third Annual Report of the National Association for Supplying Medical Aid to the Women of India for the Year 1917*, appendix III, IOOLC.

mated that approximately 100,000 workers were employed in Bombay textile factories in the 1890s. Twenty to twenty-five percent were women, three-quarters of whom worked full-time with the remainder employed seasonally or whenever production accelerated. Women worked cleaning cotton and winding and reeling thread but never as weavers.[23] There were about 14,000 women working in the jute mills of Bengal at this time. They too performed unskilled tasks and were subject to seasonal unemployment.

During the last quarter of the nineteenth century factory legislation, designed to improve working conditions for women, received attention from many quarters. About the same time as Lord Shaftesbury was drawing attention to factory conditions in England, Major Moore wrote a report on the administration of the Bombay Cotton Department and Mr. J. A. Ballard, the Mint Master of Bombay, reported on the hardships of women and children in Indian factories. A seven-member government-appointed committee (all were men – three Englishmen and four Indians) reviewed the situation and by majority vote declared legislation unnecessary. When two of the English appointees voted in favor of regulatory reform, they were called "ignorant English philanthropists and grasping English manufacturers" and accused of trying to raise the cost of labor and thereby make Indian goods less competitive.[24] Despite local hostility to legislation, India had its first Factory Act by 1881. An 1891 amendment limited women to an eleven-hour day, and a 1911 Act prohibited women from working at night. The impetus for these changes came from England; within India there was no demand for change from philanthropists, reformers, factory owners, or workers.[25]

A series of international conferences, in Berlin in 1890, Paris in 1900, and Berne in 1905, all tried to define minimum working conditions suitable for all countries. The 1905 conference produced the first international convention and the 1919 International Labour Conference in Washington, D.C. stimulated further conventions. The International Labour Organization (ILO), composed of the eight most important industrial states in the world, was established at this meeting. Indian

[23] *Report of the Textile Factories Labour Committee* (Bombay 1907), v/26/670/4, IOOLC.
[24] Janet Harvey Kelman, *Labour in India* (London, George Allen and Unwin, 1923), pp. 219–22.
[25] J. C. Kydd, *A History of Factory Legislation in India* (Calcutta, University of Calcutta, 1920), pp. 35–64.

leaders promptly complained about India's exclusion from the newly formed League of Nations. In 1922, following a re-examination of the criteria for membership, India was granted the right to be represented at the ILO.[26] During the next decade the ILO recommended that India institute certain legislation to be eligible for a seat on the governing board. It was in line with these recommendations that Indian factory legislation was reformed.

By 1920, women's employment in Bombay cotton mills had declined from an earlier high of about 25 percent in 1911 to 20 percent. This decline parallels legislation to protect women and can be read as an employer decision to avoid costly medical benefits and restrictive regulations. There may also have been production changes that made the specific work done by women redundant. Retrenched women fought their employers with protests and strikes, but to no avail. Faced with a desperate situation some women offered to work fewer hours for lower wages so more women could keep their jobs. The trade unions vetoed this suggestion and women laborers found themselves replaced by male workers.[27]

In Calcutta the jute mills in the 1920s employed approximately 66,000 women, about 20 percent of the total number of workers. Women spun and carded jute and finished the jute sacks but they did not work on the jute presses. Hindu and Muslim Bengali women, their work performance hindered by purdah restrictions, accounted for only 10 percent of the female jute workers. Almost 80 percent of these women were classified as "dependants," that is, part-time workers. Ninety percent of the female workforce were migrant women from Bihar, the Central Provinces, Madras, and the United Provinces. They toiled in the mills for three times the wages of the Bengali women who did piecework within their homes.[28] The decline of female employment in the jute mills, related to increased mechanization and the imposition of labor legislation, was discernible from 1930.[29]

---

[26] Kelman, *Labour in India*, pp. 54, 222–3.
[27] Morris D. Morris, *The Emergence of An Industrial Labour Force in India* (Berkeley, University of California Press, 1965), pp. 53–68; Radha Kumar, "Family and Factory: Women in the Bombay Cotton Textile Industry, 1919–1939," *IESHR*, 20, no. 1 (983), pp. 81–110.
[28] Dr. A. C. Roy Choudhury, *Report on an Enquiry into the Standard of Living of Jute Mill Workers in Bengal* (Calcutta, Bengal Secretariat Books Depot, 1930), pp. 6–7.
[29] Dagmar Engels, "The Changing Role of Women in Bengal, c. 1890–c. 1930, with Special Reference to British and Bengali Discourse on Gender," Ph.D. dissertation, SOAS, University of London (1987), ch. 6; Kelman, *Labour in India*, pp. 80–9.

Women factory workers earned the best wages in the mills of Bombay, Ahmedabad, and Calcutta. In the 1920s full-time workers earned between Rs 9 and Rs 30 per month in Calcutta, and slightly higher wages, Rs 12 to Rs 34 per month, in Ahmedabad and Bombay. These were substantial wages. The lady doctor's salary at the Women's Hospital in Chinsurah was only Rs 50/month at this time. But these wages do not indicate well-being. Housing conditions, water supplies, and sanitation were notoriously poor in urban areas. On the job, the *naikins* (female overseers) supervised their work and acted as procuresses for their bosses. Most of the women workers had migrated to Calcutta as single women and the combination of sexual harassment and low wages forced many of them into liaisons with men or outright prostitution.[30]

Inquiries into working conditions and their concluding reports include only a few interviews with female laborers. One exception was the Royal Commission on Labour in India or the Whitley Commission (June 1931) that interviewed a few women working in factories, mines, and plantations. Fifty-two of their 837 witnesses (0.06 percent) were women identified only by name and place. For example, at Jalgoan they interviewed Saini, Jangli, Pathani and Italabai; at Nagpur, Radhabai Nimbalker and Bhukabai Kapuskar; in Calcutta, Halub and Tulsi's wife; and at Guhati, Sapti and Parabti. The report contains no other details about these women. The little evidence there is of these interviews does not suggest agreement on issues such as hours of work or protective legislation. Nevertheless, writers of the report concluded that women workers wanted female inspectors and medical professionals.[31]

Detailed studies of the standard of living provide a glimpse into the private lives of the women working in Calcutta's jute mills. One report claimed workers spent approximately two-thirds of their earnings on food and one-seventh, the next largest category, on miscellaneous items, including amusements, intoxicants, medical care, religious expenses, and beautification. It was in these two categories – food and miscellaneous – that workers often spent more when they earned more. Staples accounted for about 50 percent of the food expenditure but new

[30] Kelman, *Labour in India*, p. 110; B. Joardar, *Prostitution in Nineteenth and Early Twentieth Century Calcutta* (New Delhi, Inter-India Publications, 1985), p. 21.
[31] J. H. Whitley, chair, *Report of the Royal Commission on Labour in India* (Whitley Report), *Parliamentary Papers*, 1930–1, vol. XI (Cmd. 3883).

workers exchanged the villager's simple diet of coarse grain or rice for an "urban diet" that included milled rice or grain, lentils, fish and meat, milk, ghee and oil, vegetables, refined sugar, tea, snacks, and sweets. The shift to a greater variety of foods, from the unrefined to the refined, and to the consumption of snack food, helps explain the heavy expenditure on non-staple food. Women's clothes changed only slightly in this setting. All women, except those from Madras, adopted the blouse or jacket and sari for work in the factory but continued to go without shoes. In contrast, men adopted leather footwear, shed their "up-country" headgear in favor of caps, and carried umbrellas. Only the men frequented tea-shops. All workers included the barber's and washerman's fees, soap, hair-oil, tobacco, toddy, betel-leaves, and religious activities among their miscellaneous expenses. There were always new amusements and new fashions beckoning these workers. Consequently almost all of them were in debt for about three months' income at exorbitant interest rates.[32]

WOMEN'S ORGANIZATIONS AND LABOR ISSUES

Women's organizations developed their interest in women factory workers in response to the Royal Commission inquiries and ILO initiatives. Until they were stimulated by an external force, these women focused attention on issues significant to them, namely civil rights, education, and the social environment. They argued that these concerns were shared by all Indian women because they assumed that women, except for the most unfortunate, were economic dependants. Most women belonging to women's organizations seemed unaware that a significant percentage of women supported themselves and their families. Indeed, they had no direct experience with salaried work; less than 2 percent of middle-class women and virtually no aristocratic women were wage earners.[33]

The Whitley Committee, touring India in 1929, asked women's organizations to prepare memoranda describing their activities among workers. The All-India Women's Conference was a new organization and had nothing to report. The Bombay Provincial Women's Council

---

[32] Kelman, *Labour in India*, p. 136; Roy Choudhury, *Report on an Enquiry*, pp. 7–22.
[33] Miss G. Pimpalkchare, research worker with industrial department, government of Bombay, interview (n.d.), RWC, box 28.

had been interested in the welfare of women workers for some time, so they complied with the request. Preparing these reports stimulated their interest and enthusiasm for a discussion of the economic and social conditions of working women.[34]

Following publication of the Whitley Committee's report, the National Council of Women in India formed a study committee on labor and the Bombay Council scheduled a three-day conference on women and labor. In the meantime the AIWC decided to broaden its mission to include social issues and appointed a number of sub-committees. "Indigenous industries" was added in 1930. By 1931 the AIWC had instituted a sub-committee on labor, begun visiting mills, and sent out questionnaires to gather data on conditions in the factories. Both the Bombay Council and the AIWC approved of the Whitley Report's recommendations for reduced hours of work, women inspectors and medical practitioners, maternity benefits, and prohibition of women working below ground in the mines.

The women's organizations called on government to pass legislation and made efforts to "get in touch with women and child labourers." In Bombay, the Council's three-day conference was designed to enlighten their members about the labor issues and bridge the gap between themselves and women laborers. On the first day, with only middle-class women in attendance, there were lectures on the employer–employee relationship by Lady Nilkanth, on labor legislation by Mr. Deshpande, and on health services for women laborers by Dr. N. H. Vakil. Deshpande talked specifically about the Royal Commission and urged his audience to lobby legislators. On the second day, a Sunday, women workers were invited to attend lectures delivered in the vernacular. The first presentation, "Things for Women Workers to Learn," focused on nutrition, cleanliness, and education. The second lecture, on "Women Workers in America," informed the audience about health care in American factories. The third day of the conference was devoted to consciousness-raising and planning for the future. Middle-class women visited the worker's lines and learned about living conditions. At the end of the conference the attendees decided to form study circles and make efforts to improve the day-to-day lives of women laborers.[35]

The AIWC concentrated on legislation. They asked the government to appoint a female representative to the ILO and by 1935 were offi-

---

[34] BPWC, Fifteenth Report, 1933, p. 26.   [35] *Ibid.*, pp. 26–9.

cially reporting to this body. ILO interests became their interests and ILO measures galvanized their attention, making them oblivious to the real issues and concerns of women laborers.[36] The importance of the international connection becomes evident in AIWC demands for social insurance, maternity benefits, and other measures to improve working conditions. By and large they ignored Rajkumari Amrit Kaur's warning that special legislation had already caused employers to lay off women and hire men.[37]

The Bombay Council's programs touched the lives of real working women. They set up regional centers offering medical services, sewing lessons, and literacy classes. They also arranged for piecework for the wives and children of laborers. Lectures and entertainment, sometimes for audiences of 800 women, were arranged at the mills. Bombay mill owners appreciated their work, contributing 40 percent of the Council's annual budget by 1939.[38] Factory women showed up in large numbers to consult with medical personnel, listen to lectures, and attend literacy classes – adequate proof that they valued these services. On one occasion, when the Council ran short of money, the women workers collected money and paid the teacher.[39]

It is unclear what course of action would have benefited women employed in factories. Working women were not asked to define their needs and they have left neither diaries nor memoirs for posterity. The legislation introduced set maximum hours of work, prohibited women from working nights, disallowed child labor, and mandated maternity benefits. These regulations were rarely followed, but when mandated they led to the firing of women and the hiring of men in their place. Many of the women factory workers found these regulations unsuitable and developed strategies that subverted the original intention. For example, hours of work were limited to give workers adequate rest. For women struggling to survive, fewer hours meant less pay and led them to go in search of part-time employment in other factories. Maternity leave, designed to benefit the health of the mother and child, was a burden for women who needed to work. At the very same time as legislation made employment of women more cumbersome, factory owners had the option of becoming more mechanized or hiring from a large pool of male labor. Women in the jute

<hr>

[36] AIWC, Ninth Session, Karachi, 1934, p. 31.
[37] AIWC, Eleventh Session, Ahmedabad, 1936, pp. 74–8.
[38] BPWC, Twenty-second Report, 1940, p. 36. [39] *Ibid.*, p. 39.

mills, Dagmar Engels wrote, "were trapped between two worlds and got the worst of both."[40]

Most historians of the labor movement in India, faithful to what appears in documents and records, have ignored the role of women in labor unions. Nevertheless, women's presence in strikes and labor disturbances, as strike breakers and as labor leaders, was noted from the 1920s. Prominent women such as Maniben Kara, Ushabai Dange, and Parvati Bhore in Bombay and Santosh Kumari Devi and Prabhabati Debi in Calcutta, became leaders of trade unions and represented both women and men to management. Other accounts have noted women's presence at the head of demonstrations in the 1928–9 Bombay textile strike and commented on their militancy.[41] These topics have been sensitively and creatively explored in Samita Sen's dissertation, "Women Workers in the Bengal Jute Industry, 1890–1940: Migration, Motherhood and Militancy." Sen acknowledges the dedication of women leaders, characterized as "mothers" or sometimes "sisters," but notes that their presence had little impact on the recruitment of women to the jute mills. She accounts for both the marginalization of women workers and of issues salient to them as due to:

the assumption of different and complementary roles of men and women in the family [which] also laid the basis for a material division of labour by sex, and thereby defined the constraints on women's participation in wage-labour and the organized politics of the working class.[42]

The women's organizations ignored empirical evidence that new regulations were not improving the conditions of work for women and continued to support the ILO demand that international standards be extended to Indian women. If they were criticized, it was by Indian women who came to accept the ideas of Open Door International led by Mrs. Winifred Le Sveur. Open Door insisted on absolute equality between women and men workers. They opposed special regulations, for example, limitations on loads carried, as unnecessary restrictions that would lead to retrenchment. Ammu Swaminathan[43] defended the ILO and AIWC position against this line of debate. Their ideology came from Europe and India was not Europe, she argued. Indian women needed patrons:

[40] Engels, "Changing Role," p. 241.
[41] Radha Kumar, *The History of Doing: An Illustrated Account of Movements for Women's Rights and Feminism in India, 1800–1990* (New Delhi, Kali for Women, 1993), p. 69.
[42] Samita Sen, "Women Workers in the Bengal Jute Industry, 1890–1940: Migration, Motherhood and Militancy," Ph.D. dissertation, Trinity College, Cambridge (1992), p. 218.   [43] Sometimes spelled Swaminadhan.

Our working women are neither educated nor organized enough to speak for themselves and it is this helplessness due to illiteracy and harmful social customs, such as child marriage, etc. that alone makes us ask for a certain amount of protection for them.[44]

There were a few middle-class women who attempted to learn about the conditions of factory women. Maniben Kara tried to do social work among these women and concluded that her efforts were futile. She joined the labor unions but since only 1 percent of their membership was female, her work was with men. Godavari Gokhale (later Parulekar) found her consciousness raised when she worked with the employees of the Bombay mills. Godavari and her friend, Miss Bhalerao, formed the Women's Fellowship of Service as a women's wing of the Servants of India Society. From 1936 to 1939 they worked at projects approved by the Servants. Godavari focused on labor: teaching sewing, promoting labor unions, organizing domestic workers, and developing adult literacy programs. By her own account she was radicalized by the conditions she encountered and was driven toward a greater appreciation of the Communist Party. She had a special interest in women as industrial workers and believed their concerns could be integrated into organized labor's demands for justice.[45]

Legislation framed by the ILO was adopted in India during the lean years of the world-wide depression. Protective legislation cannot be blamed for increased unemployment among women factory workers because much of it was never implemented. Women as a percentage of all factory employees, not just textile factories and jute mills, had hit a high of 16.5 percent in 1927 and slipped to 15 percent in 1932.[46] Employers may have predicted women workers would be more expensive and less flexible in the long run and consciously reduced their numbers. But this is only a hypothesis; decreased demand and technological innovations are sufficient explanations for the decline in female employment. If the women's organizations and others who fought for this legislation can be faulted, it is for their failure to come to know and understand the problems of the constituency they claimed to represent. Ammu Swaminathan was quite right in arguing that the Indian situation differed from the European. However, neither she nor

---

[44] Letter from A. Swaminathan to Mrs. Winifred Le Sveur (April 1, 1936), AIWC Files, no. 10.   [45] Godavari Parulekar, interview (Bombay, February 24, 1980).
[46] Shyam Kumari Nehru, ed., *Our Cause: A Symposium of Indian Women* (Allahabad, Kitabistan, 1938), p. 138.

her co-workers took the next step of ascertaining what Indian women workers wanted. Instead, middle-class women accepted prima facie that legislation designed in Western countries would benefit Indian women.

WORK IN MINES

By the mid-1920s more than one-third (approximately 80,000) of all mine workers were women working above and below ground. In the Central Provinces women were 56.6 percent of all mine workers and 47 percent of those working underground. In Bengal 35 percent of all mine workers and 34 percent of all underground workers were women. In Bihar and Orissa women were only 30.9 percent of the total mine workforce but 39 percent of the underground workers. Although the total numbers of women employed was low in other provinces, women were a significant presence in the workforce and at least one-third of them worked underground.[47]

Despite these numbers, little was known about the conditions of women working in mines. Middle-class women in women's organizations took no notice of this work until the mid-1930s, more than ten years after the legislatures took up these questions. The explanation for this is twofold. Not only were the mines located in areas remote from the urban sites of these organizations, but they employed populations (often termed "tribals") marginal to both the traditional rural Hindu and Muslim culture and to the progressive society of the cities. Mine women were totally beyond the social purview of the modernizing woman.

The number of women employed in mines was high because of the recruiting methods used. It was difficult to procure labor so mine owners hired contractors to sign up "labor gangs" that included whole families. In eastern India the most effective way of obtaining steady labor was to purchase *zamindari* properties,[48] distribute land to tenants, and require those tenants to work in the mines in lieu of rent. About 50 percent of the labor force was recruited in this way.[49]

---

[47] "Distribution of Labour in Mines 1922" (September 10, 1928), WBA, file no. 1-M-26.
[48] *Zamindari* refers to the land under the control of a *zamindar*. *Zamindars* did not actually own the land but had the proprietary rights secured by the Permanent Settlement of 1793. They had the right to collect rent from the people settled on their *zamindari* and they, in turn, submitted revenue to the government.   [49] Engels, "Changing Role," pp. 211–40.

Regularization of mine conditions began at the turn of the century, but it was not until the 1920s that questions were raised about the employment of women below ground. When framing what was to become the 1923 Mines Act, the government asked the Mining Boards, the Mining Federation, and local governments to give their opinions on this issue. Most of the respondents opposed restrictions arguing that tribals preferred to work as families. Men cut the coal; their wives and children carried it away and loaded it. These informants agreed: "men cannot carry coal," and families needed the earnings of both men and women to survive. After making a compelling argument for family solidarity in the workplace, Mr. Swan, chairman of the Mining Board of Bengal, admitted that if only men (i.e. no women) worked underground, coal prices would be higher.[50] Other memos supporting the status quo had similar wording. The secretary of the Mining Federation used child-bearing as proof that work underground was not harmful to women. The problem, he noted, was international organizations that wanted India to fit a particular standard. Like Swan, he concluded with a warning that if only men were employed underground the price of coal would rise from 8 annas to 12 annas per ton, the demand for coal would decrease, and the laboring class would suffer.[51]

While mining officials opposed this legislation, public opinion rallied in favor of it. "The principle that women should not be allowed to work underground in mines has long been accepted in nearly all civilized countries," read a draft memo from the government of Bengal's commerce department, "and there are no sufficient reasons for continuing in India a practice generally abandoned elsewhere."[52] Once again, it appears that international standards were setting the tone for what it meant to be a modern nation.

The regulations of 1929 excluded women from working underground except in exempted areas including Bihar, Bengal, Orissa, Central Provinces, and the salt mines of the Punjab. In those areas the number of women underground would be gradually reduced over a ten-year period. By 1939 there were to be no women working underground.[53]

In 1933 the AIWC appointed a committee of three women to visit

[50] Commerce, Government of Bengal, no. 15 (July 30, 1927), WBA, file no. 1-R-5(3).
[51] Commerce, Government of Bengal, no. 14 (July 28, 1927), WBA, file no. 1-R-5(3).
[52] Commerce, Government of Bengal, no. 13 (May 20, 1927), WBA, file no. 1-R-5(1).
[53] Whitley Report, p. 127.

mines in Bengal and Bihar and suggest how to implement the Whitley Report recommendation to totally abolish female labor in mines.[54] In 1934 Mrs. A. Chatterjee, Mrs. Renuka Ray, and Miss Iris Wingate toured seven mines in Ranganj and Jharia. In their report to the AIWC, they argued forcefully for termination of underground work for women.

These women were neither naive nor insensitive. Mrs. Chatterjee had studied at Oxford, Renuka Ray was a graduate of the London School of Economics, and Iris Wingate worked with the YWCA in India. They observed women in poor health, worn out by double work, and relying on opium to keep their children quiet. Women worked in the mines because they needed money and preferred working with their husbands to being left behind in their villages. Chatterjee, Ray, and Wingate understood that these women would not appreciate their interference. They warned the AIWC that if they achieved their goal, that is, prohibition of women's work underground, they would bear the responsibility for finding alternative work.[55]

Finding alternative work for women miners was not easy. When Chatterjee, Ray and Wingate studied the rural economy, they applauded the work of Amrit Kaur and other Gandhians on the Rural Reconstruction Committee. This Committee focused on the interrelatedness of health, education, and production. Emulating their work, the AIWC instructed its branches to adopt a village and concentrate on its uplift.[56]

In 1939, just after women's work underground ended, the government used the war as an excuse to lift the ban on their employment. Women willingly returned to underground work. The women's organizations began their protest anew but looked foolish protesting on behalf of women miners who wanted the work. Renuka Ray was well aware of the irony. The problem was really one of wages, she wrote. Men were underpaid so women had to work. She dressed her plea in the cloth of social feminism, explaining the motivations of mining women in terms her middle-class readers would understand:

[54] Aparna Basu and Bharati Ray, *Women's Struggle: A History of the All-India Women's Conference 1927–1990* (New Delhi, Manohar, 1990), pp. 58–62.
[55] AIWC, Ninth Session, Karachi, 1934.
[56] AIWC, Eleventh Session, pp. 50, 74–8; AIWC, Twelfth Session, Nagpur, 1937, p. 140; AIWC, Thirteenth Session, Delhi, 1938, p. 71; letter from legal convenor, Delhi (April 21, 1936), AIWC Files, no. 139.

When driven by economic necessity there is no question of any choice. During the last famine in Bengal, respectable women brought up in middle-class homes were sometimes forced to sell their bodies so that they could feed their starving children. These women told us they would have infinitely preferred death but had to choose a life of shame for the sake of their children. Does this mean they preferred a life which they considered worse than living hell? Is it to be wondered that women readily go down into the mines when the ban has been withdrawn?[57]

Her co-workers agreed. Unfortunately, there are no accounts of interviews with the women miners. Renuka Ray was right when she focused on wages, but she constructed mining women as dependants, assuming that if their husbands received higher wages, the wives would receive their due. There is some indication that these women wanted to work next to their husbands so that they would be on the spot when their husbands were paid. After the war men replaced women in the mines and the women were neither retrained nor re-employed.

NEW JOBS IN THE CITY: MAID SERVANTS AND PROSTITUTES

The dominant gender ideology constructed women as dependent housewives; the reality was that thousands of women worked to survive. Urban areas acted as magnets, not just for men seeking jobs, but for women without guardians. Poor and uneducated, they found work as maid servants, coolies, and prostitutes. These unregulated occupations flourished in the modernizing urban sectors. No legislation limited their hours of work or improved their working conditions. Only prostitutes were discussed. Voluntary social workers labeled them a social problem and tried to rescue them from their work.

Godavari Gokhale's effort to organize domestic workers stands out as a singular event. Household servants were numerous. The 1911 census reported that domestic workers were 39 percent of all working women in Calcutta, a figure compatible with accounts from other cities, but apparently not visible.[58] Maid servants were employed in every middle-class home, yet their employers seldom thought of them as workers. Perhaps this was because the distinction between dependent relative and domestic servant was often slight. One of the

---

[57] Renuka Ray, *Women in Mines*, tract no. 2, AIWC (Arunch, India, AIWC, 1945), p. 17.
[58] The first systematic study of this topic is now being conducted by Swapna Banerjee, Temple University, Philadelphia: "Middle Class Bengal Women and Female Domestic Workers in Calcutta, 1900–1947."

15 Washermen and washerwomen, c. 1900

criticisms of Indian families was that they made drudges out of widowed female relatives. Anandibai Karve, widowed at age twelve, described her work in her deceased husband's home as taking care of the cattle, milking the cows and buffaloes, feeding the bullocks, cooking breakfast for the farm hands, getting grass for the calves, washing the clothes, and cleaning the kitchen utensils.[59]

From the employer's viewpoint it was a benevolent system. Shudha Mazumdar has warmly described the role of family servants in socializing the next generation.[60] It was not unusual for middle-class families to include photographs of their favorite servants in family albums. Whether the servants felt as integrated into the families as some of the accounts suggest cannot be ascertained. Despite the large numbers of women who have been employed in domestic work over the years, it is only very recently that they have added their voices to the historical record.[61]

---

[59] D. D. Karve, ed. and trans. *The New Brahmins: Five Maharashtrian Families*, with editorial assistance from Ellen E. McDonald (Berkeley, University of California Press, 1963), p. 65.

[60] Shudha Mazumdar, *Memoirs of an Indian Woman*, ed. Geraldine Forbes (New York, M. E. Sharpe, 1989), pp. 32–6, 81.

[61] See Malavika Karlekar, *Poverty and Women's Work: A Study of Sweeper Women in Delhi* (New Delhi, Vikas Publishing, 1982).

In contrast, there is a considerable literature on women who supported themselves and their families through prostitution. By the middle of the nineteenth century there were over 12,000 prostitutes in Calcutta (out of a total population of 400,000), approximately 90 percent of them widows.[62] In the adjacent district of the 24-Parganas, there were probably an additional 15,000 women who earned a living through prostitution. In 1911 this occupation employed about 25 percent of Calcutta's working women. At the same time the prostitute population had grown to between 30,000 and 40,000 in Bombay.[63] These figures are less than precise but they take on significance when compared to other areas of work for women. Prostitution supported more women than the new professions of teaching and medicine.

Who were the women included in the category "prostitute"? First, there were women who were born into castes that traditionally made their living by dancing and singing. They, in turn, passed on their art to their daughters. Those who did not bear daughters often purchased or adopted female children. Veena Oldenburg has argued that these women, technically entertainers, were able to exercise agency in selling their services and thereby subvert the patriarchal paradigm.[64]

Women belonging to the *baishnava* (devoted to the god Vishnu) sect were often called prostitutes. Having left their homes and families to "seek god within," they lived in groups and were labeled deviants for their unsanctioned relationships with men. In the best of circumstances, their sexual liaisons liberated them from earthly attachments; in the worst of circumstances, pimps masqueraded as holy men and treated these women like ordinary prostitutes.

Devadasis, dancers who served the gods of Hindu temples, attracted the attention of reformers starting in the 1870s. Rituals "marked and confirmed . . . [their] incorporation into temple service," committed them to training in classical dance, and advertised their availability for sexual liaisons with appropriate patrons. *Devadasis* were given land grants to meet their expenses and treated with respect in the region

---

[62] Dr. (Mrs.) Usha Chrakraborty, *Condition of Bengali Women around the Second Half of the Nineteenth Century* (Calcutta, Usha Chakraborty, 1963), pp. 25–7; Sumanta Banerjee, "Marginalization of Women's Popular Culture in Nineteenth Century Bengal," *Recasting Women*, p. 143.

[63] "Bombay Prostitutes Committee's Report," *ISR* (August 27, 1922), p. 2; B. Joardar, *Prostitution*, p. 21.

[64] Veena Talwar Oldenburg, "Lifestyle as Resistance: The Case of the Courtesans of Lucknow," *Contesting Power*, ed. Douglas Haynes and Gyan Prakash (Delhi, Oxford University Press, 1991), pp. 23–61.

served by their temple.[65] By the second decade of the twentieth century, many reformers styled them "temple prostitutes" and maintained that ordinary pimps and madams were now calling their women "*devadasis*." Many of the *devadasis*, along with entertainers, religious women, and courtesans, refused to be labeled prostitutes and resisted the reformers' overtures.[66]

The question of agency for these women is an interesting one. Female ascetics may have taken a step towards independence by leaving their families to seek god, but in their new religious families they were subordinate to men. Oldenburg contends that courtesans accepted the dominance of patriarchy but only "as a necessary compromise to escape from its stifling power."[67] *Devadasis* may well have protested legislation designed to ban their way of life, but they were not free agents. The ceremony dedicating them to the temple both advertised their availability for a sexual relationship with a patron of the temple and denied them to men of their own community for either marriage or sexual intimacy. The temple authorities dictated acceptable partners – the eldest sons of wealthy landed or business families – and gave mothers and grandmothers veto rights. Amrit Srinivasan makes it clear this was not a dismal life: "The economic and professional benefits were considerable and most importantly, not lacking in social honour."[68] Reformers were offended by the apparent independence and success of these women. These would-be saviors called *devadasis* "prostitutes" and attempted to "normalize" them by depriving them of their lands and profession.

There were large numbers of women, with no connection to religion or the arts, who were prostitutes in the conventional sense, that is, selling sexual favors for money. Most accounts agree that there were large numbers of widows among the prostitutes, which suggests that brothels were havens for women with nowhere else to go. Girls were also seduced or stolen from their homes and forced into this business. Among the ranks of prostitutes were married women who found their lives intolerable and escaped from one kind of oppression to another. Some working women turned to prostitution to make ends meet;

---

[65] Amrit Srinivasan, "Reform and Revival: The Devadasi and Her Dance," *EPW*, 20, no. 44 (November 2, 1985), p. 1869.

[66] *Ibid.*, pp. 1869–75; B. Kesavanarayana, *Political and Social Factors in Andhra, 1900–1952* (Vijayawada, Narodaya Publishers, 1976), p. 226.

[67] Oldenburg, "Lifestyle as Resistance," p. 48.

[68] Srinivasan, "Reform and Revival," pp. 1869–70.

others had drifted to the cities in times of economic hardship and were unable to find employment of any other kind. Some women provided sexual favors in exchange for protection.

Several of these women have been able to tell their stories. In 1874 the Great National Theater of Calcutta, offering Western-inspired theater, staged *Benisanhar* by Haralal Roy. Generally male actors played female roles, but in this case Binodini, a daughter of a prostitute, played the female lead. The play became an acclaimed hit and Binodini a star; she acted in over fifty plays during the next fourteen years. In 1913, her letters to her mentor, Girish Chandra Ghosh, were published as *Amar Katha* ("My Story"). In this presentation, Binodini expressed no love for her former profession, but rather stated her desire to be a wife:

We [Binodini refers to "our type"] too desire a husband's love, but where do we find it? . . . There is no shortage of men who come to us in lust, and charm us with their talk of romance; but which of them would give his heart to test whether we have hearts too?[69]

Accounts of prostitutes are also found in the records of the vigilance societies. European men and women founded these vigilance societies; Indians joined in the 1920s. As Dr. Jerbanoo E. Mistri put it, finally Indian women who had remained "silent and distant spectators" began to see that their "self-interest, self-respect, and honour" were connected with the practice of prostitution.[70] By the 1930s both the president and vice-president of the National Vigilance Association were Indians and Indians dominated the provincial branches.

Among the Vigilance Association's records are short sketches, letters, and translated statements about and from the women in rescue homes. These records must be used with caution for they were kept by people who denounced prostitution and represented women who had left this way of life. The prostitutes all told similar stories. The unmarried women reported they were seduced, abducted, or kidnapped (not always separate and distinct categories) when they were away from their traditional guardians. Young girls traveling or visiting relatives in distant places were vulnerable and gullible. Either they innocently followed an

---

[69] "Binodini Dasi," *Women Writing in India, 600 BC to the Present*, vol. 1, *600 BC to the Early Twentieth Century*, ed. Susie Tharu and K. Lalita (New York, The Feminist Press, 1991), p. 292.
[70] Dr. (Miss) Jerbanoo E. Mistri, "Economic and Basic Course of Prostitution," Bombay Social Service Conference (Second Session) Papers (Bombay, 1928), JBC, Box-Bombay, FL.

"uncle" or "friend of the family" or fell in love with a casual acquaintance. These young women were "ruined" by the men who abducted them and then sold them into brothels. Young girls and women, forced by modesty to seek medical personnel and institutions designed for women only, were deceived by procuresses disguised as women doctors or trapped when they entered brothels masquerading as hospitals for women. Many of the women, especially widows and orphans, reported they had nowhere to go and sought refuge in brothels.

In addition to abducted and seduced women and those who needed shelter, there was a third group whose mothers, brothers, husbands, and other relatives forced them into prostitution. A fourth group of women left abusive husbands and sought the protection of the brothel.[71]

The first reform legislation affecting prostitutes was the 1923 Prostitution Act which made it illegal for a male, but not a female, to manage a brothel. Concern with public health and morality, combined with an international interest in the traffic in women and girls led to further amendments of this Act, in 1926 and 1927.

The Vigilance Association wanted brothels abolished but wherever this happened, prostitutes began soliciting on the streets. Recognizing a need, women's organizations set up rescue homes to train prostitutes to earn their livelihood in some other way. The rescue homes also tried to reunite these women with their families and caste people.[72]

Regulationists or segregationists, a group dominated by government officials and the police, worried about the "disposal of the women" once the brothels were closed.[73] They argued that prostitution could not be outlawed and even if it were, there would never be enough rescue homes for all these women. Regulationists wanted brothels and prostitutes contained in designated areas to facilitate "administrative supervision, the maintenance of order, sanitation and medical supervision."[74] A number of influential educationalists and medical men supported this position, often eclipsing abolitionist aims.

Women's organizations transformed these issues to incorporate the rhetoric of "Indian womanhood" and nationalist aspirations. When the

[71] SPL, *First Annual Report* (Bombay, 1929), pp. 3–8; SPL, *Second Annual Report* (Bombay, 1930), pp. 9–12; BVA, *Annual Report*, 1930, pp. 11–13; "Cases of Prostitution in Bombay," BVA (August 9, 1926), JBC, Box-Bombay, FL.
[72] Letter from Miss Dickenson to Miss Neilans, BVA (August, 9, 1928), JBC, Box-Bombay, FL. [73] *Ibid.* [74] Supplement, *ISR* (August 22, 1922), n.p.

Bengal Legislature discussed the Suppression of Immoral Traffic Act in 1931, Mr. S. M. Bose called attention to the women's petition with 16,000 signatures. "The women of Bengal are no longer asleep," he said, and they are "keenly aware of the danger that threatens their womanhood."[75] Muthulakshmi Reddy tied the *devadasi* issue to the national project, warning:

even we women have come to realize that a foreign government has no sympathy with the legitimate aspirations of the people, and can never actively help in mending our defective social system. Unless and until full provincial autonomy and Dominion status is granted, there can be no real social and moral progress.[76]

The League of Nations took up the question of traffic in women and girls and this spurred reformers and government officials in India to take a second look at the *devadasi* practice of adopting girl children. *Devadasis* responded by forming organizations to institute reform from within and protect their way of life. They fought a losing battle. Now the stakes were high: both public morality and India's prestige in the international community were at risk as *devadasis* became the focus of discussion. Those agitating for abolition called this system masked prostitution even though they were fully aware of the difference between professional dancers attached to the temples and ordinary prostitutes. The 1947 Devadasi Act abolished dedication of girls to temple service, barred temple dancing, and declared that any bogam, kalavanthulu, sani, nagavasulu, devadasi, or kurmapuvalu woman[77] who danced was a prostitute.[78]

During these years India accepted the various measures suggested by the League of Nations to suppress immoral traffic and prevent people from living on the earnings of prostitutes. The women's organizations became more involved with the abolition of *devadasis* than with abolition of prostitution. There was a general acceptance of prostitution as a necessary evil, and many of those women who fought for abolition, for example, Charulata Mukherjee and Romola Sinha in Bengal, devoted their energies to rescue homes. Whatever reformers wanted to do – abolish or contain prostitution or ameliorate the hardships of endangered women – they continued to regard men as providers and

---

[75] GOI, Home Dept., file no. 24/XII/31.
[76] M. Reddi to E. Rathbone (February 2, 1929), RP, folder no. 1.
[77] These are all names of the different castes from which *devadasis* come. *Devadasi* refers to both a role (temple dancer) and a caste.
[78] Kesavanarayana, *Political and Social Factors*, p. 229.

women as dependants. Few of the women interested in this topic were capable of approaching prostitution as sex work and trying to determine what would be the best course of action. Instead, they "rescued" these women and provided them with an alternative shelter.

CONCLUSIONS

The lives of India's working women deteriorated under colonial rule. Jobs in the modern sector did not offset the decline of traditional industries for either men or women, but women suffered the greatest loss. Because labor was plentiful, women continued to work in the unskilled, unmechanized sector where they were poorly paid and unlikely to advance to better positions.[79]

The new professions open to women – teaching, law, and medicine – required education and family support. Even Kadambini Ganguly was called a whore; unmarried woman without impeccable credentials and respectable families were even more vulnerable to verbal and sexual harassment. Nevertheless, there were professional women who gained respect, independence, and personal satisfaction. Especially significant for the history of women in India is the fact that most of these new professional women worked with women and contributed to the development of new educational and medical institutions. These institutions have, in turn, made it possible for middle-class females to attend schools and colleges and enter a wide range of professions in contemporary India.

Entry into jobs associated with the regulated modern sector of the economy – factories, mines, and plantations – did not bring long-term positive gains. Women's work in factories was always limited to the most unskilled jobs and just as benefits were being mandated, women were replaced with machines and/or male workers. The statistical evidence points to a downward trend in women's employment in the industrial sector. This is a reflection both of the decline of small-scale industries that employed women and their redundancy in larger factories. Unfortunately, women never established a foothold in the organized labor movement.

Women easily found employment in the unregulated sector whether it was commercialized agriculture in rural areas or prostitution and

[79] D. R. Gadgil, *Women in the Working Force in India* (Bombay, Asia Publishing House, 1965), p. 27.

domestic work in urban areas. These were unrecognized areas of work without regular hours, fixed wages, and benefits. Most of the women forced into these areas of employment lived with physical and sexual violence. The radical humanist M. N. Roy observed that laboring women were not emancipated by employment but rather became "beasts of burden."[80]

Few middle-class women sought employment, but those who belonged to progressive society worked as volunteers in women's organizations. They wanted women professionals – to staff the new schools and medical centers for women and of course, to minister to their needs – but they remained ambivalent about employment outside the home. Even the concerns of women professionals received scant attention in the deliberations of these women's organizations.

Leaders of women's organizations were eager to join the modern world of international agencies. It was the universal codes of the international organizations that informed their view of India's working women. Even while these elite women joined the nationalist movement and rejected Britain's "civilizing mission," they embraced international bodies and their dictates.

They agitated for protective legislation knowing full well that women working in mines and factories could not afford to be without jobs. The alternative employment they offered was in the declining handicraft industry. There is no doubt they knew a great deal about the lives of laboring women but they regarded employment for women as unnatural. Consequently, they focused their attention on normalizing conditions for these women – teaching hygiene and nutrition, setting up crèches, working for legislation to restrict the work day. Godavari Gokhale and Maniben Kara stand out for their concern with improving laboring women's status through labor unions.

Civic-minded women wanted to close brothels and suppress temple dancing. Both efforts would force women out of employment considered morally decadent and degrading by the middle class. They made it their mission to rescue these women, provide them with some kind of shelter and training, and fight a double standard that sanctioned sexual experimentation by men and demanded purity from women.[81]

---

[80] M. N. Roy, "The Ideal of Indian Womanhood," *Fragments of a Prisoner's Diary,* 2 vols. (Calcutta, Renaissance Publishers Private Ltd., 1957), vol. I, pp. 168–71.
[81] "Suppression of Traffic in Women and Children and Bengal Discussions," *Stri Dharma,* 15, no. 12 (October 1932), p. 662.

It would be unfair to ignore the writings of women who understood the relationship between these social issues and the economic status of women. Many women, attracted by Marxism and the Communist Party, took a different approach to women's work. Lakshmi Menon, a teacher who worked diligently to improve the status of women and later represented India at the UN, went to the heart of the matter when she discussed the problem of traffic in women and children. Much of the prostitution throughout the world could be traced to poverty and lack of alternatives for women but in India particular customs – child marriage, the inauspiciousness of widowhood, arranged marriages, and "our general attitude towards girls" – made the situation worse. When laboring women turned to prostitution it was to supplement their inadequate wages, she said. In this context Menon criticized the Madras Regional Conference on Social Hygiene for its 1935 program of rescue work, propaganda, and VD clinics. They were ignoring issues of employment and wages for women, facilities for girls' education, and the "unjust laws and horrible social customs" which deprived women of options.[82] Menon admired the Soviet code which she believed struck at the root of women's inequality. Guaranteed employment, training programs, protective policies, and "a new sex code" which abolished the double standard seemed to be the answer.[83] Menon argued that women's labor could not be separated from social norms and institutions and advocated radical restructuring following the Soviet model. But this was not a widely share view. Employment for women in India continued to be viewed as an unfortunate state needing welfarist solutions rather than measures designed to give women equal education, opportunities, and wages.

[82] Lakshmi N. Menon, "Traffic in Women and Children," *Our Cause*, p. 191.
[83] *Ibid.*, pp. 197–8.

CHAPTER 7

A TIME OF TRANSITION

By the mid-1940s the all-India women's organizations had lost their hegemony. For almost two decades the women's organizations spoke for all Indian women. They demanded the trappings of "modern life": education, health care, protective legislation, and civil and political rights within the framework of a social feminist ideology that constructed women as socially and psychologically different from men. They acknowledged India's special problems, especially child marriage, purdah, and the oppression of widows, and agreed that these practices made reform doubly hard. But in their view two things gave reform its impetus. First, these customs had not existed in India's "golden age." Second, as Indian women, they were blessed with a legacy of goddesses and heroines who willingly sacrificed themselves for husbands and families. This habit of sacrifice was now valorized as worthy of extension to civil society and the nation. These organizations had been nurtured by two opposing forces: nationalist aspirations and colonial domination. Their vision of modernized women threatened neither the patriarchy of the British rulers nor the patriarchy of Indian nationalists.

The ideology of the women's organizations was too Hindu, too middle-class, and too urban to appeal to or adequately represent all Indian women. An informal survey completed in 1932 estimated that 90 percent of Indian women were wage-earners and only "married women among the well-to-do families and those of higher social standing do not work for wages."[1] Muslim women, unless they could agree to a secular–Hindu national project, were not adequately represented. Urban and rural working women took part in patriotic demonstrations but they were never fully integrated into the women's organizations. In fact, well-educated women like Latika Ghosh modified their vision of civil society to appeal to their more traditional sisters. Though it was evident women's organizations did not speak for all women, their memorials and petitions claiming this constituency went virtually unchallenged until the late 1930s.

[1] Survey of Women's Interests and Distinctive Activities, 1930–2, RWC, box 33.

189

Over the next two decades women became active in a variety of social and political movements undermining the hegemonic claims of the major women's organizations. New ideologies significantly altered the discussion of what women needed. Women jailed for their revolutionary activities read socialist literature in prison and joined Marxism's first converts. They gained a new vision of women's place in society and after being released worked side by side with men spreading the message of socialist revolution. They also formed their own women's organizations to work specifically on women's issues and to give public voice to their interpretation of women's demands.

There were other women whose rebellion against social feminism took place outside of Marxism. Violent revolution fascinated some women, while others were attracted by radical feminism, and still others were engaged in social rebellion against familial patriarchy. They joined political parties, worked with small revolutionary cells, and sometimes acted independently. It was no longer possible to field hundreds of disciplined orange-sari-clad *sevikas* to demonstrate Indian womanhood's opposition to foreign rule. This was a troubled time for India and both domestic and world-wide events demanded a new idealism and pragmatism from politically active women.

THE POLITICAL SETTING

In accordance with the India Act of 1935, one-sixth of India's adult population voted in the elections held in 1936 and 1937. The provinces gained responsible government while dyarchy remained the mode of operation for the central government. Congress swept the provincial elections and in 1937 was able to form governments in seven of eleven provinces.

In 1939 the British declared Indians at war without first consulting these newly constituted bodies. In response, Congress ministries resigned, and Gandhi called for individual *satyagraha*. Germany broke the non-aggression pact in 1941 and invaded the USSR. With the USSR now Britain's ally, members of the Communist Party of India (CPI) were released from prison and supported the British war effort. Later the same year the Japanese attack on Pearl Harbor and their menacing of the Southeast Asian region made India even more central to the war effort. Gandhi asked Congress members in 1942 to join the Quit India movement and opposition to British rule took a new turn. Some

Indians supported Gandhi's non-violent protest, others joined the underground against the British, while still others strove to mount an effective war effort. By 1943 one of the worst famines of modern times spread across Bengal.

These were years of growing communalism. The India Act of 1935 decreed that religious identity and political power would be irrevocably intertwined. Consequently, events leading up to the end of colonial domination in 1947 were fraught with religious antagonism. British India was partitioned to create India and Pakistan and the princely states were incorporated into one or the other of these new countries. In those provinces which felt the partition most drastically – Bengal and Punjab – the problems of the refugees and their resettlement presented extraordinary challenges. India had seen war, famine, partition, and the establishment of two new states in less than a decade. In this turbulent climate, radical movements fueled by Communist ideology began to challenge long-tolerated forms of exploitation.

From the end of the 1930s to the early 1950s women participated in a wide range of social and political movements. The process by which the hegemonic discourse of women's organizations was replaced by a number of competing discourses can be charted by looking at women's role in the elections of 1937; the development of communalism and the pro-Pakistan movement; the Quit India movement of 1942 and the anti-British movement during the war years; and the radical movements for socio-economic justice. What changed significantly was the presence of women in all major events of the times. Their involvement helped shatter the essentialist construction of the "Indian woman" that helped some women but hindered others in their quest for equality.

THE ELECTIONS OF 1937

The Government of India Act of 1935 granted the vote to women over twenty-one years of age who qualified because they owned property or had attained a certain level of education. Now six million Indian women could vote and stand either for election to general seats or seats reserved for women only. Earlier, Indian women's associations asked for "a fair field and no favor." This was an idealistic position. Faced with the reality of financing campaigns and establishing connections with powerful groups, many of these women now wanted "safe" seats.

Congress was reluctant to back aspiring women politicians as candidates. With the 1935 Act in place, Congress began its transition from an anti-imperialist movement to a political party. In doing so it showed a "clear preference for propertied men." Sumit Sarkar has commented:

Despite its national and multi-class ideals, the Congress as a ruling party found it almost impossible to go on pleasing Hindus and Muslims, landlords and peasants, or businessmen and workers at the same time. A steady shift to the Right, occasionally veiled by 'Left' rhetoric increasingly characterized the functioning of the Congress ministries as well as of the party High Command between 1937 and 1939.[2]

"Women's organizations" should be added to the list of groups Congress could not go on pleasing with its shift to the right, for it made no special effort to enlist and support women candidates for the 1937 election.

Even Jawaharlal Nehru and Mahatma Gandhi, great supporters of women's political activism, were lukewarm in their support of women's involvement in political affairs. Before the election Ammu Swaminathan wrote Nehru about issues raised by members of the AIWC. She included a copy of the AIWC manifesto to "Candidates for the Coming Election," issued from Vizagapatnam on July 26, 1936. Women make a special contribution to the general welfare and progress of the country, the document declared. It outlined the social and educational reforms needed: equal opportunity for women and untouchables; free and compulsory education; rural reconstruction; an end to purdah, child marriage, and immoral traffic in women; communal unity; social insurance and public health clinics; measures to help the unemployed; and protection of civil liberties.[3] The AIWC asked for a list of INC candidates and wanted to know who among them accepted the terms of the manifesto. They lamented the absence of women on the Congress Working Committee and asked Nehru to appoint a woman. Ammu Swaminathan concluded: "we want the premier national organization of the country to be in full sympathy with the viewpoint of women and all that connotes."[4]

Nehru replied that Congress planned to set up women candidates for reserved seats in the provincial legislatures. The issue of women in general seats was in the hands of the All-India Parliamentary Board and

---

[2] Sumit Sarkar, *Modern India, 1885–1947* (New Delhi, Macmillan India, 1983), pp. 350–1.
[3] Manifesto issued on behalf of the AIWC to "Candidates for the Coming Election" (Waltair [Vizagapatnam], July 26, 1936), JN, file no. G48, 1936.
[4] A. Swaminadhan to J. Nehru (August 22, 1936), AIWC Files, no. 130.

the provincial boards. As for the manifesto, Congress was in total agreement with its principles. He scolded her and her AIWC colleagues for ignoring the role of political freedom in achieving social transformation. Finally, he faulted their ideology:

many items in your programme are, if I may say so, superficial in the same sense that they do not enquire into the root causes of the evils which we want to get rid of. Partly no doubt these evils are due to our own customs but largely they are the result of political subjection and a thoroughly bad economic system.[5]

The Working Committee was another issue. Prior to this formal complaint from the AIWC, old friends and supporters approached Nehru about the omission of a woman from this important body. He responded by publicly chiding women for their meek protest: "Women of India have not yet learned to demand their rights boldly." Nehru urged women to organize, vocalize their demands, and prepare to fight reactionary forces. The private letters exchanged between Gandhi and Nehru on this subject sheds light on their attitudes towards women's role in the party. At first Gandhi did not take women's reproach seriously. When he learned some people were blaming him, he reminded Nehru that it was Nehru who wanted Sarojini Naidu off the Working Committee. No one else objected to having a woman on the committee but, Gandhi recalled, "You even went so far as to say that you did not believe in the tradition or convention of always having a woman and a certain number of Mussalmans in the cabinet."[6] Nehru claimed he was the injured one. He wanted more women in positions of power but had to contend with men more traditional than himself. His advice to women was patronizing. Nehru told women they had a duty to help "men in the struggle for political freedom," but the fight for women's emancipation was their own. They would have to force men to grant their demands.[7] It was clear that the promises of the civil disobedience campaign had been set aside in favor of *realpolitik*.

As Nehru had promised, the Congress Party supported women running for reserved seats. Seasoned women's rights advocates like Dr. Muthulakshmi Reddy questioned separate seats for women,[8] but few women relished the idea of a political campaign. Most women inter-

---

[5] J. Nehru to A. Swaminadhan (September 2, 1936), JN, G 48, 1936.
[6] M. K. Gandhi to J. Nehru (May 29, 1936), JN, G 48, 1936.
[7] J. Nehru, "Women and the Freedom Movement," *The Hindu* (October 6, 1936), *Selected Works*, 15 vols. (New Delhi, Orient Longman, 1972–82), vol. VII, pp. 482–3.
[8] "Against Separate Electorates," speech by M. Reddy, DRP, file no. 11.

ested in politics hoped for an uncontested seat. Begum Shah Nawaz wrote that Muslim women in Lahore were trying to guard against more than one woman candidate standing for each seat. They hoped to save women from the odious task of campaigning and, at the same time, "set an example of unity and agreement before the men."[9]

Radhabai Subbarayan, one of the few women who stepped forward to run for a general seat in Madras, felt betrayed by Congress. The chairman of the Madras Provincial Congress Reception Committee offered her Congress support until a man decided to run for the same seat. Almost immediately, Congress deserted her to support her rival. Mrs. Subbarayan asked C. Rajagopalachariar for an explanation and he told her it was because she refused to sign the Congress pledge. The male candidate was a party man so the issue was not gender discrimination but party solidarity. Rajagopalachariar told her Congress could not relinquish a seat "merely because it was a woman candidate that was seeking to be elected." He concluded, "I do not believe that [the] advanced type of women politicians want political favors because they are women." Radhabai Subbarayan withdrew but not without some parting shots at Congress. Recalling Gandhi's comments at the Round Table Conference, she pointed out the absence of women candidates in Madras and other provinces. The *Madras Mail* commented that this incident:

demonstrates the insincerity of much of Congress sympathy with the aspirations of women, and proves that the Congress party is no better than others in its treatment of women candidates. Women are useful to head disobedience processions but scarcely good enough to sit with the Party in the Assembly.[10]

Apparently all parties behaved the same way because the percentage of women candidates never exceeded the percentage of seats reserved for women. In Bihar and the Central Provinces even though 3 percent of the total seats were reserved for women, women comprised only 1 percent of the total candidates.[11]

Many women were uncomfortable with election politics and argued for a political role outside the legislatures. Petition politics was a comfortable realm and there was much to be done. The AIWC asked

9 "Moslem Women's League," clipping from Shah Nawaz (June 19, 1936), RP, file no. 10.
10 "Congress and its Sense of Chivalry," *Justice* (October 19, 1934); "Mr. Rajagopalachariar Explains," *Justice* (October 19, 1934); "Mrs. Subbarayan's Reply to Mr. C. R. Chariar," *The Hindu* (n.d.); "Why She Withdrew," *Justice* (n.d.); "Mrs. Subbarayan Withdraws," *Madras Mail* (n.d.), RP, file no. 5.
11 Jana M. Everett, *Women and Social Change in India* (New Delhi, Heritage, 1979), p. 136.

educated women to present women's demands to candidates, enroll women voters, disseminate information about the candidates, and prepare lists of potential women candidates for the political parties.[12] When they realized that no one was listening and no one cared, these women concluded they too were the victims of broken promises.[13]

The same women who were annoyed with the political parties during the campaigns were pleased with the final results. The total number of seats in all the provincial legislatures was approximately 1,500 and 56 were now held by women. Forty-one were returned from reserved constituencies, ten from general constituencies, and five were nominated to provincial legislative councils. The majority of these women, thirty-six, were Congress candidates, eleven were independents, three belonged to the Muslim League and one was an Unionist.[14] An additional thirty women were elected to the Central Assembly. Radhabai Subbarayan was nominated to this Assembly. Their numbers were small but women were finally visible in positions of power and authority: Vijayalakshmi Pandit (Nehru's sister) was appointed to the United Provinces' cabinet as Minister for Local Self-Government and Public Health; Anasuyabai Kale, of Central Provinces, Sippi Milani of Sind, and Qudsia Aizaz Rasul of United Provinces became deputy speakers; and Hansa Mehta, Bombay, and Begum Shah Nawaz, Punjab, became parliamentary secretaries. Hailing this as a victory for women's cause, the women's organizations urged the nomination of women to commissions, boards, and councils. Women, they argued, were the only ones qualified to solve the many problems that affected women and children.[15]

Nationalist politics had been feminized but election politics remained male-dominated. Women had hoped their consistent support of Congress in the non-cooperation movement of 1920–1 and the civil

---

[12] "Report of the Franchise Sub-Committee for the Period Ending July, 1936," AIWC Files, no. 118; M. Kamalamma to secretary, Madras Parliamentary Committee (September 14, 1936), AIWC Files, no. 130; M. Reddi to Mrs. Y. Hasan, Mrs. P. Iyer, and Mrs. Chabra, AIWC Files. no. 135; "An Appeal to Women who are Qualified to Vote" (WIA flier), AIWC Files, no. 135.

[13] M. Reddi to "Dear Friend" (n.d.) and M. Reddi, "Women and Congress" (n.d.), RP, file no. 11; M. Kamadami to Mrs. S. C. Mukherjee (n.d.), AIWC, Files, no. 119; S. M. Reddi to Madam (November 16, 1936), AIWC Files, no. 135.

[14] Everett, *Women and Social Change*, p. 138.

[15] WIA Report, 1936–8, p. 27; "Women's Franchise in the New Constitution," *ISR*, 47 (April 24, 1937), p. 529; Kaur, *The Role of Women in the Freedom Movement (1857–1947)*, (New Delhi, Sterling, 1968), pp. 204–5.

disobedience movement of 1930–2 would earn them political rewards. This did not happen but women with political aspirations continued to believe in their male colleagues. They accepted their small victory and listened to the men they trusted most, Nehru and Gandhi, and resolved to work even harder to achieve their goals.

MUSLIM WOMEN AND ELECTION POLITICS

This environment was particularly challenging for Muslim women. Activists who belonged to the AIWC and other women's organizations lent credence to an ideology that claimed women were united despite class, caste, and religious differences. In the new world of communal politics, even the semblance of unity was difficult to maintain.

The AIWC characterized itself as apolitical even though its leading members belonged to Congress, passed resolutions to support Gandhi's constructive program, and frequently praised Gandhi and Nehru for supporting women's issues. When Muslim members tried to influence the wording and substance of memorials and petitions they were ignored and treated, according to their accounts, like younger sisters. Nevertheless, there were a number of prominent and capable Muslim women, notably Hajrah Ahmed, Sharifah Hamid Ali, and Kulsum Sayani, whose commitment to nationalism and feminism kept them connected with the women's organizations and supportive of secular policies.

Jahan Ara Shah Nawaz wrote to Eleanor Rathbone about the diffi-culties she faced at this time. As early as 1934 she was approached regarding the Assembly seat for Lahore–Amritsar. A member of both the All-Parties Muslim Conference and the All-India Muslim League, Begum Shah Nawaz knew she would be a strong candidate, but declined to run. Muslim leaders in the Punjab were already angry that of the few seats for Muslims, one was reserved for a woman. She did not want to incur their wrath.

When these same leaders accepted reserved seats for women as a fact of life, they asked Begum Shah Nawaz to organize a communal women's organization. Some of her friends and associates, Mrs. Mukherjee, Mrs. Rustamji, Rani Rajwade, and Mrs. Hamid Ali, warned her this would hurt the work of the AIWC. They told her that by mobi-lizing Muslim women she was abandoning her former assertion that women were the champions of unity. But if she supported the AIWC position against reserved seats for women, she would gain enemies within her own community. There were rivals as well as friends within the AIWC who, Begum Shah Nawaz believed, were eagerly waiting for an opportunity to denounce her. Under pressure from both sides, she decided her principal loyalty was to her fellow Muslims. Begum Shah Nawaz argued that support for the Muslim men's political aspirations was the only road to harmonious relations between Hindus and Muslims.[16]

As identity became a key element in power politics, mobilizing women became crucial to the Muslim League. For many years Begum Shah Nawaz had worked closely with the AIWC and she and her colleagues had reached a consensus about key issues. Now communal politics forced them into new antagonistic relationships. Writing about the further alienation of Muslim women from the major women's organizations following the victory of the Hindu Code Bill, the author Shahida Lateef says:

the Indian women's movement lost its momentum and leadership. This affected Muslim women adversely since the feminist platform had groomed their leadership and provided an ideology which could unite all women. And worse, the memory of the solidarity forged and nurtured by the women's movement was forgotten.[17]

Begum Shah Nawaz agreed to organize a separate political league for Muslim women and by June of 1936 a meeting of the General Council of the Punjab Provincial Moslem Women's League was announced in a newspaper as meeting in her home.[18] The newspaper article invited Muslim women to establish an All-India Moslem Women's League. Once organized, the League became a sub-committee of the All-India Muslim League with Begum Modh Ali as president and Begum Hafiz-ud-din as secretary. The League's declared goal was to stimulate the political consciousness of Muslim women.[19] Muhammad Ali Jinnah, the leader of the Muslim League, had not wanted a separate organization for women but the League Council and Begum Shah Nawaz con-

[16] Shah Nawaz to E. Rathbone (September 17, 1934), RP, folder no. 10.
[17] Shahida Lateef, *Muslim Women in India: Political and Private Realities, 1890–1980s* (London, Zed Books, 1990), p. 94.
[18] Begum Shah Nawaz, "Women's Movement in India," Indian paper no. 5 at the Eighth Conference of Pacific Relations (New York, International Secretariat, Institute of Pacific Relations, 1942), pp. 1–12; Jahan Ara Shahnawaz, *Father and Daughter: A Political Autobiography* (Lahore, Nigarishat, 1971), p. 94.
[19] Shah Nawaz, "Women's Movement," p. 6; "Punjab Assembly Electoral Machinery" (June 19, 1936), "Moslem Women's League" (June 19, 1936), clippings sent to E. Rathbone, RP, folder no. 10.

vinced him purdah restrictions and the habit of sex segregation made this necessary.[20] In the 1937 election Begum Shah Nawaz won a seat in the Punjab as a Unionist.

Jahan Ara Shah Nawaz's move in the direction of the Muslim League strained her relationships with her old AIWC colleagues. When they opposed separate electorates, she scolded them for their political naiveté. She ignored Begum Hamid Ali, her Muslim colleague who was totally committed to joint electorates, and argued that Muslim women wanted separate seats. When partition became an issue she joined demonstrations, faced tear gas and *lathi* attacks, and was eventually imprisoned.[21] Following partition she became a member of the Pakistani Constituent Assembly in Karachi and was elected vice-president.[22]

Begum Qudsia Aizaz Rasul, the daughter of Sir Zulfiqar Ali Khan, descendant of the ruling family of the tiny state of Malerktola in the Punjab, became an outspoken opponent of communal politics. Her father ignored the advice of his contemporaries and sent her to Jesus and Mary Convent in Simla. Even his own family objected and the *ulama* issued a *fatwah*[23] condemning convent education as anti-Islamic. Zulfiqar Ali Khan stood his ground and Qudsia went from Jesus and Mary Convent to Queen Mary's College in Lahore. But Zulfiqar Ali Khan also had a traditional streak and insisted his daughter observe purdah and continue to wear the *burqah*.[24]

In 1929 Qudsia married Nawab Syed Aizaz Rasul, a *taluqdar* (member of the landed gentry) of Avadh. Her mother-in-law was very traditional but her husband opposed purdah. Begum Qudsia seized the opportunity, discarded her veil (except in the presence of her mother-in-law), and began to speak publicly against purdah. In 1936 she decided to contest a general (Muslim) seat for the United Provinces' Legislative Council instead of a seat reserved for women. Once again the *ulema* issued a *fatwah*. They warned the electorate about this scandalous woman who denounced purdah and competed with men. The *fatwah* had little effect. Qudsia Begum recalled "I was elected by a thumping majority which only showed that Muslims were not really

---

[20] Shahnawaz, *Father and Daughter*, p. 165.   [21] *Ibid.*, pp. 150–3, 165, 185–8.

[22] "Notes on Jahanara Shah Nawaz," RWC, box 69.

[23] An *ulama* is a body of Muslim religious scholars whose task it is to keep society moving in the right direction. A *fatwah* is a religious edict.

[24] "Begum Aizaz Rasul," RWC, box 68, pp. 1–3.

as orthodox as they were made out to be." In the Legislature she earned additional reproaches when she spoke in favor of birth control and asked for women police officers. While serving as secretary to the Muslim League, Begum Qudsia won election to the Constituent Assembly. In this new role, she asked Muslims to voluntarily give up reserved seats. Qudsia Rasul and her husband decided to stay in India after partition, testimony to her faith that Muslims would be accorded full citizenship.[25]

Begum Sharifah Hamid Ali, a tireless worker for women's rights, stood firm with the women's organizations. Her father, Abbas Tyabji, was the grandson of the merchant-prince Bhai Mian Tyabji. Abbas Tyabji, a Bohra Muslim, was educated and lived in England for eleven years. After his return to India he married Ameena, his uncle Badruddin Tyabji's daughter. Both Sharifah's parents supported women's education and social reform and broke with tradition by disregarding purdah restrictions and sending their daughters to school. Begum Sharifah lived with her husband, a member of the Indian civil service, in the districts of Bombay Presidency where she began her social work.[26] Shahida Lateef contends that Muslim women's participation in the women's movement was "always overshadowed by Muslim separatist politics."[27] This was not the case with Mrs. Sharifah Hamid Ali who rejected all politics that would divide the people of India. It was not separatist politics that made her cooperation with AIWC members difficult, but rather their arrogance about Islam and Muslims.

Sharifah Hamid Ali was appointed to the women's sub-committee of the National Planning Committee. The sub-committee, established in 1939, was charged with reviewing the social, economic, and legal status of women and suggesting measures to make equality of status and opportunity a possibility in the planned economy of free India.[28] Two other Muslim women appointed to the committee, Begum Amiruddin from Madras and Mrs. Zarina E. Currimbhoy from Bombay, stopped cooperating because meeting dates were changed at whim and no one listened to them. Begum Hamid Ali was the only Muslim woman working with the committee; she wrote memoranda, urged the Committee to consult an authority on Muslim law, and argued for a

---

[25] *Ibid.*, pp. 3–9.   [26] "Mrs. Sharifah Hamid Ali (1884)," AIWC Files (unnumbered).
[27] Lateef, *Muslim Women in India*, p. 94.
[28] National Planning Committee, sub-committee on women's role in the planned economy, AICC, file no. G-23 (1940).

different point of view. But she found that when she explained Muslim law to her co-workers, they either did not listen or could not understand her point. Reading a draft report, she found, "[it] showed such ignorance of Islam – its laws and practice (in spite of my having sent a very clear and detailed report in my evidence on these matters) that I had to protest very strongly against its inclusion."[29] Begum Hamid Ali signed the final report only after Nehru intervened, granted the sub-committee an extension, and personally asked for her signature.[30] Rani Rajwade, chair of the sub-committee, was not at all sympathetic. She feared, she wrote to Jawaharlal Nehru, "Begum Hamid Ali is thinking on communal lines."[31]

Kulsum Sayani, the daughter of Dr. Rajabally Patel (a Khoja Muslim and Gandhi's first physician upon his return to India from South Africa), grew up calling Gandhi *"Kaka"* (Uncle). Her mother was the first Muslim girl to attend school in Bombay and her aunt the first to matriculate. Kulsum was educated at home by a governess and, at age eighteen, married Dr. Janmohamed Sayani, the first physician in charge of a new Congress hospital in Bombay. Both were devoted to Mahatma Gandhi and wanted to serve their country, Dr. Sayani through his medical work, and Kulsum through social service.[32]

Kulsum Sayani had joined a number of women's organizations in search of a meaningful project when Miss Godavari Gokhale drew up guidelines for Bombay's first literacy campaign. Launched in 1938, it was so successful the government took charge. To oversee the program they created the Bombay City Adult Education Committee and appointed Kulsum Sayani to its membership.

Kulsum Sayani traveled to England that year and upon her return decided she wanted to teach purdah women. She thought a home-class scheme would cause the least inconvenience to her target population of lower middle-class women and submitted a plan to the Committee. They advanced her Rs 100 and she set up daily classes in six buildings. Kulsum Sayani found educating these women an uphill battle: her poorly paid teachers were indifferent and the pupils soon lost interest.

[29] Begum Hamid Ali to Jawaharlal Nehru (April 1, 1940), JN, part 1, vol. xxxi, 1937.
[30] Series of letters between Begum Hamid Ali and Jawaharlal Nehru and from Nehru to Rani Rajwade, JN, part 1, vol. cxxxvi, 1940.
[31] Rani Rajwade to J. Nehru (March 31, 1940), JN, part 1, vol. cxxxvi, no. 5006.
[32] Interview with Kulsum Sayani (January 4, 1957), RWC, box 68, pp. 1–2.

She decided to personally supervise the program and began to spend her days going "from lane to lane, house to house and floor to floor talking, enthusing and persuading women to learn to read and write."[33] When the Committee's money ran out the Bombay branch of the AIWC provided enough money to support eleven classes enrolling 420 women. The Bombay Committee then decided to finance fifty educational centers for purdah women. To provide reading material for newly literate women, Kulsum Sayani set up and financed the monthly newspaper *Rahber* ("Guide"). Her "post-literacy paper" carried stories and articles in Urdu, Nagri, and Gujarati script with translations into simple Hindustani. This was her personal effort to effect national integration.[34]

During the war and the agitation for partition, Kulsum Sayani remained a staunch Gandhian. Sarojini Naidu and Rameshwari Nehru were her mentors; "Rameshwari was my ideal of Indian womanhood," she wrote.[35] She deplored the effect of the "Jinnah movement" on poor Muslims. Crying "Islam in danger" only inflamed the people and turned them against programs that were helping them. Kulsum Sayani's loyalty to Gandhi and Congress earned her the taunts and threats of Muslims who called her educational endeavors destructive to religion.[36]

Hajrah Ahmed joined the Communist Party in 1937 after years of working with the AIWC. A new awareness of the conditions of working-class women led Hajrah Begum to the party. Still working with the AIWC, she unsuccessfully attempted to raise her co-workers' consciousness about the conditions of working women. However much she tried, she could not change their mission.

In 1940 the AIWC began hounding Hajrah Begum about her "political" work (she had apparently refused to attend a reception at the Governor's house) while serving as organizing secretary of the Allahabad branch. Hajrah Begum did not see this as "political" in the usual sense of the term but conceded, "I have been associated in the past with the Congress and am Socialist by conviction and I simply cannot become non-political."[37] Less than a month later when her husband,

---

[33] Kulsum Sayani, "My Experiences and Experiments in Adult Education," unpublished paper, p. 2.   [34] Sayani, "My Experiences," pp. 1–4.
[35] Interview with Kulsum Sayani (July 30, 1970), p. 16, South Asian Archive, Centre for South Asian Studies, Cambridge.
[36] Interview with Sayani (RWC), pp. 2–3; interview with Sayani (Cambridge), pp. 17-18.
[37] Hajrah Begum to Lakshmi Menon (July 26, 1940), AIWC Files (unnumbered).

Dr. Z. A. Ahmed, went to prison for political activities, she voluntarily resigned as organizing secretary "for Baby's sake."[38]

Later Hajrah Begum resumed her efforts to try to bring Congress and AIWC women to see the value of the Communist Party's goals. Once again she became an organizing secretary and following Independence became an editor of *Roshni*, the AIWC journal.[39] Although critical of the bourgeois mentality of the AIWC, Hajrah Begum regarded it as an organization committed to keeping Hindu and Muslim women together. It was the Muslim League that fomented communalism by insisting Muslim women leave the AIWC. Communal electorates made it almost impossible to ignore this demand.[40]

These five were representative of elitist Muslim women. They all enjoyed formal education and were the beneficiaries of the attitudes of progressive fathers and husbands. They were among the privileged few who traveled and had some autonomy in decision making. Jahan Ara Shah Nawaz, Qudsia Rasul, Sharifah Hamid Ali, Kulsum Sayani, and Hajra Ahmed worked with women's organizations until the 1940s. Separate electorates for Muslim women and the consequence of the Communal Award presented each with a special challenge. Jahan Ara Shah Nawaz and Qudsia Rasul made decisions about their relationship with the Muslim League, one supporting from the margins, the other defying from within. Sharifah Hamid Ali and Kulsum Sayani were social reformers forced to deal with political issues. They both chose Congress and women's organizations but not without soul-searching in Sharifah's case, and the pain of public harassment for Kulsum. Hajrah Begum had the fewest doubts. She chose the Communist Party which denounced all religions and her work, with both Congress and AIWC women, was inspired by a party decree.

The all-India women's organizations had recruited Muslim women and made efforts to represent their interests. Worried that condemnation of purdah might be seen as cultural imperialism, the women's organizations adjusted to it as a fact of life and only vaguely condemned it in resolutions.[41] Female seclusion and sex segregation were observed

---

[38] Hajrah Begum to Lakshmi Menon (August 15, 1940), AIWC Files (unnumbered).
[39] Hajrah Begum, "Women in the Party in the Early Years," *New Age* (December 14, 1975), pp. 11–12.   [40] Hajrah Begum, interview (New Delhi, April 2, 1976).
[41] Geraldine Forbes, "From Purdah to Politics," *Separate Worlds*, ed. Hannah Papanek and Gail Minault (Delhi, Chanakya Publications, 1982), pp. 236–8.

by both Hindus and Muslims but the two communities differed when they remembered the "golden age." Hindu women harked back to a time when women were active participants in the life of the community; Muslims to the veiling of the Prophet's wives. To the extent the leaders in women's organizations conceived of purdah as a problem, they labeled it a Muslim problem. When it came to politics, the women's organizations talked as if all women were equal and threw their support behind universal franchise. Faced with the reality of communal elections, they had no answer. The Congress claimed it could speak for all Indians and the women's organizations echoed this statement. The Muslim League objected and asked Muslim women to be loyal to their own people.

These women, except for Begum Shah Nawaz, blamed the Muslim League for driving a wedge between Hindu and Muslim women. The blame must be shared by the Indian National Congress and the women's organizations. The insensitivity of Rani Rajwade is a case in point. Sharifah Hamid Ali was not a traditionalist, she had worked long and hard with the AIWC on a wide range of issues. All she wanted was to have her colleagues understand Islamic law before they made their recommendations. But no one was ready to listen.

THE QUIT INDIA MOVEMENT

In September of 1939 the British government announced India's entry into the war. Congress offered full cooperation in return for a truly responsible government and the promise of independence at the conclusion of the war. There was no satisfactory reply. In November Congress ministries resigned and planned their protest.

By this time women were members and sometimes even leaders of student associations, peasant movements, and labor unions. The presence of women in the various movements of the day was as significant for the anti-British movement during the war years as was their election to legislative seats and their appointment to positions of power and authority.

Gandhi sanctioned civil disobedience at the beginning of October 1940. Individual *satyagrahis*, in the beginning people personally chosen by him, made public anti-war speeches in defiance of emergency orders. One by one Congress leaders declared themselves opposed to the government, were arrested and imprisoned. Altogether four hundred Congress men and women were jailed in 1940. By June of 1941 almost 20,000 had gone to jail but the movement declined after that. Congress leaders were not very happy with this campaign, termed by Sumit Sarkar "far and away the weakest and least effective of all the Gandhian national campaigns."[42] But Gandhi was pleased and Congress leaders were reluctant to lose his leadership. At the beginning of December the government decided to release *satyagraha* prisoners creating high hopes for détente. On December 7, the Japanese attacked Pearl Harbor and the next day the USA entered the war.

On August 8, 1942, the All-India Congress Committee met in Bombay and passed a resolution calling for British withdrawal from India. Until this occurred Congress sanctioned non-violent mass struggle and instructed the people that in the event there were no orders from Congress, "every man and woman . . . must function for himself or herself within the four corners of the general instructions issued."[43] The Quit India resolution spoke directly to women "as disciplined soldiers of Indian freedom" and attracted them to the movement.[44]

Gandhi asked the Indian people to conduct a non-violent campaign using previously sanctioned techniques: salt-making, boycotts of courts and schools, picketing cloth and liquor shops, and non-payment of taxes. The British reacted by arresting Congress leaders. Mass protests followed and when the authorities responded to these with force, they provoked a massive and violent attack on the symbols of state authority.[45] The movement began in the cities with strikes, demonstrations, and clashes with the police and moved to the countryside where peasants rebelled against landowners and the agents of British authority. Women participated in the initial strikes and demonstrations in cities, were among the radical students who organized peasant movements, and, when protest was suppressed, joined the secret underground.

Usha Mehta operated a clandestine radio transmitter in Bombay. A child during the civil disobedience movement of 1930–2, she joined the "monkey army" of children who ran errands and carried messages for adults. When Congress leaders called for volunteers to join the Quit India movement, Usha Mehta looked for a way to help. The government

---

[42] S. Sarkar, *Modern India*, pp. 381–3.
[43] Aruna Asaf Ali, *The Resurgence of Indian Women* (New Delhi, Radiant Publishers, 1991), pp. 136–7; S. Sarkar, *Modern India*, p. 388.
[44] Aruna Asaf Ali, *The Resurgence*, p. 136.   [45] S. Sarkar, *Modern India*, pp. 389–91.

were blacking out news of the rebellion so Usha decided to set up a radio transmitter. The "Voice of Freedom" began broadcasting news of resistance and arrests, profiles of patriotic young people, and Gandhi's famous "Do or Die" speech launching the Quit India movement. Usha and her brother continued broadcasting until their arrest on November 12, 1942. Following extensive interrogation, Usha was sentenced to four years' imprisonment. In prison she found many people who, like herself, had joined the movement out of conviction, patriotism, and regard for Congress leaders, especially Mahatma Gandhi.[46]

When the movement spread to the countryside, large numbers of peasant women joined men in protesting against taxes, land tenure, and landholder's rights. At the end of September 1942, peasants attacked police stations and destroyed telegraph lines in four sub-divisions of Midnapur District. The British responded with repressive measures and a new round of violence began. On September 29 the people of Tamluk sub-division marched on the town with the intention of capturing the court and the police station. Face to face with the soldiers guarding the court, they hesitated. Matangini Hazra, a seventy-three-year-old widow, stepped forward, lifted the Congress flag, and gave her first public speech.

Matangini Hazra (b. 1870) had been the child bride of Trilochan Hazra, a sixty-year-old widower. By age eighteen she was a widow. At age sixty-two she took the Congress pledge and ten years later, in 1942, she asked to lead a battalion. On September 29 she urged the crowd onward in the name of Gandhiji and refused to stop when challenged. She was shot first in the hand holding the flag and then in the head. The authorities were clearly determined to squash this rebellion. Equally determined, the people of Midnapur District continued their resistance and were brutally repressed.[47]

Aruna Asaf Ali (b. 1909) became a leader of the underground movement in 1942 and was forced to remain in hiding until 1946. *Roshni*, the AIWC journal, called her the "direct successor" to the fictional character Devi Chaudharani, the dacoit queen who robbed from the rich and gave to the poor, and the historical Rani of Jhansi, the warrior queen who fought the British in 1857.[48] Aruna Ganguli was born in

---

[46] Kaur, *The Role of Women*, pp. 228–9; Dr. (Miss) Usha Mehta, Oral History Transcripts, NMML.

[47] Kaur, *The Role of Women*, p. 215; "Matangini Hazra," *DNB*, vol. II, pp. 159–61; Sarkar, *Modern India*, pp. 401–2.   [48] "Aruna Asaf Ali," *Roshni*, 1, no. 1 (February, 1946).

Bengal, raised as a child in the hill station, Nainital, and attended the Convent of the Sacred Heart in Lahore. She refused to consider an arranged marriage and left home to accept a teaching job at the Gokhale Memorial School for Girls in Calcutta. She met Asaf Ali, a Muslim barrister from Delhi, while vacationing in Allahabad and after some time he proposed. She defied her father's objection to her marriage with a Muslim more than twenty years her senior and married Asaf Ali in 1927. They moved to Delhi where Rameshwari Nehru introduced Aruna to the Delhi Women's League and Satyavati Devi brought her into the civil disobedience movement. Aruna broke the salt law, was arrested, sentenced, and imprisoned in Lucknow.

In 1941 Aruna Asaf Ali courted arrest by offering individual *satyagraha* and was sent to prison but she was soon released.[49] Within hours of the AICC Quit India resolution, top-ranking Congress leaders, including her husband, were arrested. In their absence, Aruna went to preside over a flag-raising ceremony and announced the arrests. As she unfurled the flag, the police threw tear gas into the crowd. "The experience of that morning," she remembered, "made me decide that I would not again tamely enter jail by offering Satyagraha."[50]

Aruna Asaf Ali met with other delegates to the Congress session and they decided to return to Delhi. They traveled by train to Agra, and then by automobile to the capital. Aruna Asaf Ali, together with Congress socialists J. P. Narayan, Rammanohar Lohia and Achyut Patwardhan, and Gandhians Sucheta Kripalani and R. R. Diwakar, decided to go underground to try to coordinate and channel the anger of undisciplined mobs. Their aim was to organize resistance and hinder the war effort. During her three and a half years in hiding, Aruna was constantly in motion, urging people to "liberate" the land from foreign rule.[51]

Gandhi was critical of Aruna who, he said, "would rather unite Hindus and Muslims at the barricades than on the Constitutional front."[52] Sucheta Kripalani criticized Aruna and her associates for sabotaging the war effort. In her defense, Aruna claimed she advocated planned dislocation of the war effort but not wanton destruction. She quoted their pamphlet on the "A.B.C. of dislocation":

[49] Dhan, *Aruna Asaf Ali* (Lahore, New Indian Publications, 1947), pp. 1–8; "Aruna Asaf Ali," *DNB*, vol. I, pp. 70–1.   [50] Aruna Asaf Ali, *The Resurgence*, p. 138.
[51] *Ibid.*, p. 140.   [52] "Aruna Asaf Ali," *DNB*, vol. I, p. 70.

Dislocation is a common and effective method used by enslaved and oppressed peoples against their rulers ... Thus, if telegraph wires are cut, fishplates on railway lines are removed, bridges are dynamited, industrial plants put out of order, petrol tanks set on fire, police stations burnt down, official records destroyed – they are all acts of dislocation. But a bomb thrown at a market place or a school or a *dharmashala* [a shelter for pilgrims] is not dislocation. It is either the work of agents provocateurs or misdirected energy.[53]

While some historians have characterized her as the most important leader of the resistance, Aruna characterized herself as "a splinter of the lava thrown up by the volcanic eruption of the people's indignation."[54]

Following the release of Congress leaders in 1945, the Working Committee met and condemned the violence that had occurred. Aruna Asaf Ali and Mr. Achyut Patwardhan wrote the Congress president that they would not recant for their actions because they acted with noble intentions. Furthermore, they claimed their authority derived from the All-India Congress Committee.[55] Gandhi disagreed with Aruna's tactics but he did not denounce her. Instead, he praised her bravery and agreed to meet her while she was still in hiding from the police. When Nehru was released from prison he made special mention of Aruna Asaf Ali as "one of India's brave women."[56]

The historian R. P. Dutt argued that the mass protests and sporadic destruction of property did not constitute an organized struggle.[57] Other historians disagreed and maintained there were two centers directing activities, both underground, both led by women. Aruna Asaf Ali, capable of endorsing revolutionary tactics, was one; Sucheta Kripalani, pledged to non-violence, the other.[58]

Sucheta Mazumdar Kripalani (1908–74), was born in Ambala where her father, Dr. S. N. Mazumdar, was a medical officer in the Punjab Medical Service. She attended a number of schools, her final degree being an MA in history and political science from St. Stephen's College, Delhi. She taught school in Lahore and then became a lecturer at Benares Hindu University. A long-time follower of Gandhi, Sucheta married another Gandhian, Acharya Kripalani, in 1936, in a well-publicized celibate marriage. They moved to Allahabad in 1939 where

[53] Aruna Asaf Ali, *The Resurgence*, pp. 141–2.   [54] *Ibid.*, p. 140.
[55] Dhan, *Aruna Asaf Ali*, p. 27.   [56] Aruna Asaf Ali, *The Resurgence*, pp. 142–3.
[57] R. Palme Dutt, *India Today*, 2nd edn. (Calcutta, Manisha, 1946), reprinted 1970, pp. 572–3.
[58] G. Ramachandra, "Her Memory Will Live," an obituary, in *Sucheta: An Unfinished Autobiography*, ed. K. N. Vasvani (Ahmedabad, Navajivan Publishing House, 1978), pp. 238–9.

Sucheta began working in the Congress office. In 1940 she was chosen to organize a women's department of the Indian National Congress.[59]

The women's department was charged with finding the best ways to utilize "women's genius and peculiar gifts for the revolutionary purposes of achieving independence and then making a contribution in national life."[60] The document stating the aims of the new department said that women's first duty was to the nation: "only thus can they progress and bring about their emancipation from the age long slavery to habit and custom."[61] This document made it crystal clear that service to the nation was the only way to win rights. The tasks of the department were to study the disabilities of Indian women, recruit women to Congress, coordinate and guide the activities of Congress women, and maintain contact with other women's organizations.[62] The women's department wanted to raise the political consciousness of women and identify Congress with social change that benefited women.[63] Clearly this new department intended to co-opt the functions of the national women's organizations and place women under the control of the Indian National Congress.

The women's department had hardly begun its work when Sucheta offered individual *satyagraha* and was imprisoned for two years. She was out of prison when Congress leaders were arrested in 1942 and, hearing the news, decided to go into hiding. Sucheta's first job was to establish contact with groups still active throughout India and encourage them to continue non-violent activity. The aim, she wrote, "was to bring the Government to a stand-still by any method, excluding violence against individuals."[64] Wearing a variety of disguises, Sucheta traveled from province to province to keep leaders in touch with one another and help them plan activities. In 1944 she was captured and lodged in Lucknow jail as a "dangerous prisoner."[65]

After her release in 1945 Sucheta tried to revive the women's department. She wanted to enroll women as party members and organize them to carry out social and political programs. Within a year she realized that Provincial Congress Committees were uninterested in her scheme and switched her attention to mobilizing the women's vote.[66]

---

[59] "Sucheta Kripalani," *DNB*, vol. II, pp. 364–5.
[60] "The Aims of the Women's Department of the AICC," AICC, file no. WD-7, p. 1.
[61] *Ibid.*   [62] *Ibid.*
[63] "Scheme of the Work of the Women's Department," AICC, file no. WD-2, p. 1.
[64] Ramachandra, *Sucheta*, p. 32.   [65] *Ibid.*, pp. 32–7.
[66] Circular no. 1 (November 17, 1945), AICC, file no. WD-9; Sucheta Devi to secretaries, Provincial Congress Committees (February 5, 1946), AICC, file no. 6-22.

In 1946 she became a member of the Constituent Assembly, positioned to take part in the earliest actions of independent India. Communal violence claimed her attention in 1947 and she joined Gandhi in the riot-stricken areas of eastern Bengal where he hoped to stop the killing. Always loyal to Congress she maintained that women had done their duty to the country and been rewarded with "emancipation."[67]

In contrast to 1930, when women were asked to wait until men completed the march to Dandi and then assigned special duties, in 1942 women fought alongside men and suffered the same consequences. Activist women were so caught up in the struggle, they ignored gender issues or, like Sucheta Kripalani, put them aside until independence had been achieved. Only women who held themselves aloof from the conflict could put all their energies into calling for a feminist agenda. This meant the feminist movement, as defined by the women's organizations, continued to espouse social feminism and work for legal change while many from their ranks had left and were engaged in more dangerous and compelling activities.

THE BENGAL FAMINE

The Bengal famine of 1943–4, understood by historians as a man-made disaster, caused the death of at least 3.5 million people and the impoverishment and dislocation of millions more.[68] Agricultural laborers, fishermen, and those engaged in rural transport were the first to suffer the consequences of drought and poor harvests. The urban areas, particularly Calcutta, experienced the famine primarily through the influx of starving people. Throughout the countryside men went in search of work leaving women and children to fend for themselves. Women who previously earned a living by husking paddy or trading in the local market were deprived of their incomes.[69] In addition to food shortages, women faced sexual harassment when they sought employment or help from relief centers.

During the famine years women were visible both as victims and activists. Starving women begged for food in public places and door to

---

[67] Sucheta Devi, "Women and Satyagraha," AICC, file no. 9.
[68] See Paul R. Greenough, *Prosperity and Misery in Modern Bengal* (Oxford, Oxford University Press, 1982); Amartya Sen, *Poverty and Famines* (Delhi, Oxford University Press, 1981).
[69] Sen, *Poverty and Famines*, p. 72; Renu Chakravartty, *Communists in the Indian Women's Movement, 1940–1950* (New Delhi, People's Publishing House, 1980), p. 32.

door in the suburbs. They flocked to the red-light districts, doubling the number of women in Calcutta's brothels.[70] Middle-class women came forward to provide relief and women in Mahila Atmaraksha Samiti (Women's Self-Defense League) (MARS) organized and led women's demonstrations calling on the government to take action.

In Calcutta, women's organizations banded together in 1939 to demand the release of political prisoners. One of the groups involved in these protests was the Congress Mahila Sangha (Women's Association) begun as an "AIWC with politics." Their concern was teaching women how to protect themselves in the event of a Japanese invasion. After 1941 this organization grew as Communist women, newly released from prison, joined its ranks. Renu Chakravartty wrote about public reaction to the boldness of her and her colleagues:

they thought us to be a peculiar type of women, going all over the area from house to house, shamelessly talking to everybody . . . Many [women] became members of our area samities. Others shooed us away. Menfolk made sarcastic remarks and asked their wives to stay away from us.[71]

It was not easy to hold the attention of the women who attended their meetings. Women brought their children, talked among themselves, and left when they were bored. The organizers experimented with plays, songs, and stories to hold their audience. As the meetings became more interesting and accessible, the movement grew and in 1942 was renamed Mahila Atmaraksha Samiti. In addition to calling for the release of Gandhi and other nationalist leaders, MARS taught women about the evils of fascism and instructed them in self-defense.[72]

On March 17, 1943, a procession of 5,000 women from Calcutta and its suburbs marched to the Legislative Assembly protesting against rising prices and demanding food. Hunger marches by women followed in Bankura, Pabna, Madaripur, Badarganj, Dinajpur, and Chittagong.[73] MARS members were prominent in all these demonstrations and there is no doubt they gave local women courage. In Midnapur 200 women went to the rice mill demanding lower prices. They stood their ground when threatened with police action and were finally allowed to buy rice at their price.[74]

In April 1943, 500 women attended the first MARS conference. Mohini Devi, an elderly freedom fighter, presided and Ela Reid, an

[70] Renu Chakravartty, *Communists in the Indian Women's Movement*, p. 28.
[71] *Ibid.*, p. 18.   [72] *Ibid.*, pp. 20–9.   [73] *Ibid.*, pp. 34–5.   [74] *Ibid.*, p. 39.

American follower of M. N. Roy, became organizing secretary. At this meeting Renu Chakravartty, Kamala Chatterjee, and Manikuntala Sen, all members of the Communist Party, spoke about women's primary interests: food and self-defense.[75] By this time MARS branches were in twenty-one districts with over 22,000 women as members.

Famine work attracted a number of women who had belonged to the revolutionary movement in the early 1930s. Experienced in organizing, toughened by jail experience, and deeply moved by the suffering they witnessed, these women stepped forward to lead the movement. Kalyani Das Bhattacharjee, the organizer of Chattri Sangha, toured the famine-stricken regions of the province and set up 200 medical relief centers run by women.[76]

The AIWC set up food kitchens in Bankura District which fed about 50,000 people daily and established relief centers in Bhola, Rajbari, Tamluk, Comilla, and Mymemsingh Districts. Foodgrains were supplied to the city of Calcutta and Vijayalakshmi Pandit, after touring the province, devised a plan for children's homes. All over India AIWC branches raised money for famine relief.[77] Their work was impressive and they saved many lives, but unlike MARS they did not encourage political activism.

Leftist women like Renu Chakravartty and Manikuntala Sen were becoming increasingly critical of the AIWC. They had worked in the organization and acknowledged its good work, but found AIWC resistance to mass membership frustrating. When the question of including poor women in the AIWC was broached in 1942, some of the older members called this a Communist plot.[78] Younger women maintained that by ignoring political aspects of oppression the AIWC did nothing to help women fight continued exploitation.[79]

---

[75] *Ibid.*, pp. 36–7.
[76] Kalyani Das Bhattacharjee, "A Short Life Sketch of Kalyani Bhattacharjee," unpublished, p. 5.
[77] Aparna Basu and Bharati Ray, *Women's Struggle: A History of the All India Women's Conference 1927–1990* (New Delhi, Manomar, 1990), pp. 74–5.
[78] AIWC, minutes of the half-yearly meeting of the standing committee (June 1942), p. 6; Renu Chakraborty, "New Perspectives for Women's Movement after Twenty-Five Years of Drift," *Link* (August 15, 1972), pp. 177–81.
[79] Renu Chakravartty, interviews (Calcutta, July 23, 1972, August 15, 1972).

INDIAN NATIONAL ARMY

Outside the country, Indian women joined Subhas Chandra Bose's Indian National Army.[80] Bose,[81] a disaffected Congress leader, escaped from Calcutta in January 1941, and made his way to Berlin to strike a deal with Hitler. Almost a year and a half later he traveled by submarine to Tokyo where he took charge of Indian prisoners of war. These prisoners were taken to Singapore to be transformed into an army of liberation.

On July 9, 1943, the Indian Independence League of Singapore made Subhas Bose their president and promised him the funds and personnel necessary to fulfill his dream. He called for total mobilization: 300,000 soldiers, Rs 30,000,000, and "a unit of brave Indian women."[82]

A few days later Bose addressed the women's section of the League and asked them to join the Rani of Jhansi brigade. Bose wanted women to be full partners in the freedom struggle; now he was proposing a women's regiment to fight with Indian men.[83] He had discussed the women's regiment with his secretary during their submarine journey to Japan and composed this speech long before he reached Singapore.[84]

Subhas Bose also added a Department of Women's Affairs to the League and appointed Dr. Lakshmi Swaminathan[85] as head. Lakshmi Swaminathan (b. 1914) was born in Madras, trained as a medical doctor, and practiced medicine in Singapore. She recalled her impression of Subhas Bose after their first meeting: "His utter, absolute sincerity struck me most and I felt this man would never take a wrong step and that one could trust him completely and have the utmost confidence in him."[86] The first goal of the department was to recruit women for the INA, but its long-range goal was equality for women.[87]

Subhas Bose told Dr. Lakshmi and the women of Singapore he wanted them to follow the brave example of women freedom fighters in India. Women had demonstrated their fearlessness through

[80] On the Indian National Army see, Peter Ward Fay, *The Forgotten Army* (New Delhi, Rupa and Co., 1994).
[81] The most exhaustive work on Subhas Bose is Leonard A. Gordon's *Brothers Against the Raj* (New York, Columbia University Press, 1990).
[82] M. Gopal, ed. *The Life and Times of Subhas Chandra Bose* (Delhi, Vikas, 1978), p. 280.
[83] Gordon, *Brothers against the Raj*, p. 496.
[84] Krishna Bose, "Women's Role in the Azad Hind Movement," unpublished paper, p. 4.
[85] Also written Swaminadhan, she was the daughter of Ammu Swaminathan.
[86] Quoted in Gordon, *Brothers against the Raj*, p. 497.
[87] Lakshmi Swaminathan Sahgal, interviews (Kanpur, March 19, 20, and 21, 1976).

Gandhian protests and revolutionary acts, he told them. To continue this tradition and link it with India's historical fight for freedom, the regiment was named after the Rani of Jhansi, the heroine of 1857.[88]

The first Rani of Jhansi training camp opened near Singapore on October 22, 1943, with Subhas Bose presiding. Dr. Lakshmi Swaminathan, now Captain Lakshmi, took charge of the regiment's fighting and nursing units. Janaki Davar, one of the young women who volunteered to become a rani, first read about the regiment in the newspaper. When Subhas Bose came to Kuala Lumpur, she went to hear his speech and offered her earrings for his war chest. Her parents were furious but she persuaded them to invite Captain Lakshmi for tea. Janaki recalled that afternoon:

I had got hold of an application form for the regiment and filled it out, and after father had met Captain Lakshmi I asked him to sign it; I had to have a parent's signature; and he signed it. Before he could change his mind I turned it in at the League. After several weeks, instructions came to go down to Singapore.[89]

At age seventeen, Janaki became a rani. Japanese military leaders scoffed at the idea of a women's regiment but the Japanese press and Indians found it inspiring. It dramatically underscored the concept of total mobilization and made it clear the INA was not just a prisoner-of-war army.

The three camps – at Singapore, Rangoon, and Bangkok – soon had about 1,000 women recruits. Only a minority received nurse's training, the rest were instructed as soldiers. Their preparation was essentially the same as that for men and they even wore a uniform of caps, shirts, jodhpurs, breeches, and boots. Some leaders had suggested sari uniforms, but Subhas Bose and Captain Lakshmi agreed the ranis must dress as soldiers if they were to be taken seriously. Bose wanted them to have short hair but decided to leave it up to the young women; about 90 percent had their hair cut.[90]

With their training completed, the young ranis begged to see action at the front. The evidence suggests Subhas Bose intended employing them in combat, but subsequent events made that impossible. A contingent of women was moved to Burma just as the Japanese were being pushed back from Imphal. It was clear then the only fighting the ranis would do would be as a retreating army. By June of 1945 they had

---

[88] Arun, ed., *Testament of Subhas Bose* (Delhi, Rajkamal Publications, 1946), pp. 193–4.
[89] Quoted in Peter Ward Fay, *The Forgotten Army*, p. 220.   [90] Sahgal, interviews.

returned to Singapore while Captain Lakshmi stayed behind in the jungles of Burma to carry on rescue work. The ranis saw their commander, Subhas Bose, for last time on August 14 when they staged a drama on the life of the Rani of Jhansi.[91]

When the British returned to Burma and Malaya, they first interrogated the men who had joined the INA and then the women. Expecting shy and helpless women coerced into joining this army, the British were shocked when these young women appeared in full uniform, saluted smartly, and declared themselves members of the Rani of Jhansi regiment. Only a few of these women returned to India after the war, but their "story" demonstrated that women were willing to take up arms to free India from its foreign rulers.

The real impact of Subhas Bose's INA was not in military terms, but in its psychological effect. Tales of the brave ranis were memorialized in popular publications such as *Jai-Hind: The Diary of a Rebel Daughter of India with the Rani of Jhansi Regiment* masquerading as Captain Lakshmi's diary. But as important as the legend of the intrepid ranis, was the impact of this experience on the women themselves. Several of these women, especially Captain Lakshmi, went on to what Leonard Gordon has called "exceptional careers of service." Long after the war, they recalled Subhas Bose's faith in their ability to sacrifice for the good of the nation.[92]

MOVEMENTS FOR SOCIAL AND ECONOMIC EQUALITY

In the post-war period a number of educated young women joined peasant movements. Jail-going for their political work in the Quit India movement had radicalized them, just as it had radicalized another generation a decade earlier.[93] When they joined these peasant movements they were fighting for a vision of India that promised social and economic justice for men and women and rich and poor. It was a revolutionary vision that anticipated change far beyond that contemplated by either the Indian National Congress or the women's organizations.

---

[91] K. Bose, *Women's Role*, p. 7; Geraldine Forbes, "Mothers and Sisters: Feminism and Nationalism in the Thought of Subhas Chandra Bose," *Asian Studies*, 2, no. 1 (1984), pp. 23–30. [92] Gordon, *Brothers against the Raj*, p. 497.
[93] Geeta Anand, "The Feminist Movement in India: Legacy of the Quit India Movement of 1942," senior thesis, Dartmouth College (1989), pp. 8–15.

The tebhaga movement

In September of 1946 the Bengal Provincial Kisan Sabha (Peasant's Organization) called for a mass struggle among sharecroppers to keep *tebhaga* (two-thirds) of the harvest. Young Communists went out to the countryside to organize peasants to take the harvested crop to their own threshing floor and make the two-thirds share a reality. The movement began in North Bengal and gradually spread throughout the rest of the province.[94]

Rani Mitra Dasgupta, Manikuntala Sen, Renu Chakravartty and other women who had worked with MARS during the famine years wanted to bring rural women into this movement. Although the party was lukewarm in its support for this idea and the male peasants suspicious, they found rural women ready to work with them. At first women played a subsidiary role, helping harvest the crops, cooking food for the leaders, acting as lookouts, and sounding the alarm to alert their colleagues to danger. As police repression became more brutal and the Communist Party, unprepared for armed struggle, withdrew from active leadership, women formed their own militia, the *naribahini*.[95]

Manikuntala Sen and Renu Chakravartty told their leaders women's problems had to be addressed along with problems of economic exploitation and political oppression. First and foremost, meeting times had to be convenient for women. Second, if women were going to play a prominent role in the movement, something had to be done to free them from household work.[96] Third, something had to be done about the women's complaints that their husbands beat them, drank too much, and took away the money they earned through petty trade. But male CPI leaders wanted peasant women to be "good comrades" and put the struggle above personal concerns. CPI women argued unsuccessfully for a program that would encourage peasant women to defy their husbands.[97]

Bimala Maji, a widow of Midnapur District, became a successful organizer of women. She had worked with Manikuntala Sen during the famine to encourage destitute women to form self-help committees. These women's committees obtained paddy, on trust, from landlords;

---

[94] S. Sarkar, *Modern India*, pp. 439–41.
[95] Peter Custers, "Women's Role in the Tebhaga Movement," *EPW*, 21, no. 43 (October 25, 1986), pp. ws97–ws104.   [96] Renu Chakravartty, interviews.
[97] Manikuntala Sen, interview (Calcutta, February 21, 1976).

husked, sold it, and kept the profits after repaying the landlords. During the *tebhaga* campaign the Communist Party sent Bimala to Nandigram to recruit women for the movement. At first women were reluctant to join but before long Bimala had mobilized women to demand *tebhaga* and collect the harvest. Pursued by the police, Bimala went underground. As the police arrested Communist Party and Kisan Sabha leaders, Bimala had to assume more and more responsibility. It was she who made the decision and led peasants to destroy the threshing floors of the *jotedars* (rich peasants) and sell the landlords' share of the harvest. After an extensive search, the police captured her and kept her in a cage for a month until she was tried for 140 offenses. She was detained in prison for two and a half years.[98]

There were many women like Bimala Maji and the history of the *tebhaga* movement is especially important for a history of women in India. The Communist cadres and Kisan Sabha were content to have women play a secondary role in the movement. Women helped harvest the paddy, carried it to the threshing floor, and sounded the alarm when enemies approached. As the movement became more militant and police repression more violent, the leaders of the movement lagged behind their followers. This was when peasant women stepped forward to play a significant role and formed the *naribahini*. The origin of these women's units is unclear; most likely they grew out of experiences when women successfully repulsed the police. Peter Custers accounts for their appearance in terms of the lack of central control. There was, he asserts, "a connection between the increasingly spontaneous character of the uprising and the more and more prominent role played by women."[99] Custers argues it was the withdrawal of the Communist Party with its "patriarchal prejudices" that allowed women leaders to emerge.[100]

Warli movement

Godavari Parulekar worked among the Warlis, *adivasis* (sometimes referred to as tribal or aboriginal peoples) in western India, between 1945 and 1947 to help them obtain social and economic justice. The daughter of a Poona advocate, Godavari Gokhale received an excellent formal education and was encouraged by her father to think and act independently. After studying law, she passed the bar exam and then

---

[98] Custers, "Women's Role," p. ws100.   [99] *Ibid.*, p. ws101.   [100] *Ibid.*, p. ws102.

requested admission to the Servants of India Society.[101] Working among women in Bombay tenements she became friends with young Communists. It was at this time she met and married the labor leader Shamrao Parulekar. During the war years she was frequently arrested, detained, and imprisoned for her work with labor unions. At the conclusion of the war she joined the Warli peasants as they struggled to escape their status as bonded labor.

The primitive Warlis had once owned much of the land in Thana District, about sixty miles from Bombay. Under colonial rule, speculators from all over India came into the region and appropriated their land. These outsiders became powerful landlords and the Warlis their captive labor force. The Warlis were now allocated land as sharecroppers and required to pay the landlords one-third to one-half of their harvest as rent. Moreover, they were required to work without remuneration.

After attending a *kisan* (peasant) conference in 1945 Warli leaders were inspired to take up a red flag and defy their landlords. The landlords counter-attacked, badly beating the Warlis. When the Maharashtra Kisan Sabha (Maharashtran Peasants' Association) heard about the battle they sent Godavari Parulekar as their representative to live with the Warlis.[102]

Godavari soon learned that Warli women were triply oppressed. Victims of rape by landlords, Warli women were considered less "pure" than Warli men, and not infrequently accused of witchcraft and killed. Godavari understood the nature and seriousness of female oppression but could do little about it. Her first concern was imparting a rudimentary political education to a people engaged in revolutionary struggle.

During the time Godavari was allied with the Warlis they suffered vicious attacks from both the police and army. In 1946 she was forbidden to enter the Warli areas but continued to do so in secret. She stayed in hiding for nearly three years but was caught in 1950 and spent the next three years in prison.[103] Finally the Warlis won the right to be paid for their work and some of the worst forms of exploitation were abolished.

---

[101] See chapter 6.
[102] Sources for information on Godavari Parulekar's work with the Warlis include, Godavari Parulekar, *Adivasis Revolt* (Calcutta, National Book Agency Private Ltd., 1975); Godavari Parulekar, interview (Bombay, February 24, 1980); Renu Chakravartty, *Communists*, pp. 162–9.   [103] Godavari Parulekar, interview.

Godavari Parulekar had always worked for women's rights and economic justice at the same time. In Bombay her efforts on behalf of both causes – for example, the literacy campaign, encouraging labor unions, the domestic workers' union, and sewing classes – were significant. But when she worked with the Warlis, she was unable to focus on the specific problems of women. Warli women gained the same freedom as their men but this movement had done nothing to liberate them from the gender oppression endemic to their society.

Telangana struggle

The "Telangana people's struggle," lasting from 1946 to 1951, was the armed uprising of men and women against the Nizam of Hyderabad. Hyderabad was India's largest princely state with a population of over seventeen million. About 40 percent of the people lived on feudal estates where powerful owners had their own courts and jails. The feudal system allowed these owners to demand manual labor from both men and women. It was the landlord's privilege to sleep with a new bride on the marriage night. The custom of *adi bapa* required a bonded female servant to accompany her master's daughter to the girl's marriage home. Once there, she had to serve the new bride and provide sex for the groom. In addition, landlords endured no censure for raping and making concubines of women who took their fancy.[104] The other 60 percent of the population were settled on lands held by the Nizam. They were ruled by *deshmukhs* (overseers) who forced them to labor and beat them at will.[105]

Upper- and middle-class women, both Hindu and Muslim, escaped the oppression experienced by peasant women, but were controlled by purdah. Under the Nizam, Hyderabad was one of the most backward of the princely states. Social reforms and institutions for female education, measures that had begun to transform the lives of some women in British India and other princely states, were unknown in Hyderabad.[106]

By the 1930s women's organizations had survived strong opposition and established branches in Hyderabad. At first the meetings were places for upper- and middle-class women to socialize but they soon became forums for the discussion of women's issues. Their work on behalf of education and social reform nurtured women leaders who

[104] Vasantha Kannabiran and K. Lalita, "That Magic Time: Women in the Telangana People's Struggle," *Recasting Women*, p. 182.　[105] Renu Chakravartty, *Communists*, pp. 121–2.
[106] Kannabiran and Lalita, "That Magic Time," pp. 182–3.

increasingly became aware of larger political and economic issues. When it was clear India would become independent, the Nizam began to negotiate with the British regarding his future. The Communist Party saw his regime crumbling and called on the All-India Trade Union Congress, the All-Hyderabad Student's Union, and the women's organizations to join it and the Andhra Mahasabha against the Nizam. At its height the Telangana movement included 3,000 villages and over three million people.

Women played an important role in this struggle. There were deliberate attempts to mobilize women and in doing so the issues especially important to them – wages, wife-beating, childcare, hygiene, the right to breast-feed infants during work, food, and even lavatories – were discussed. This was an organizing tactic, not a challenge to fundamental ideology and strategies. In the final analysis, the very fact that these issues were raised was enough to gain the "loyalty and support [of women] without leading to an increased awareness of the nature or source of that subordination."[107] Women fought, side by side with men, for land, better wages, an end to forced labor, and against exorbitant interest rates. And they were the victims of some of the worst atrocities.

"We Were Making History": *Life Stories of Women in the Telangana People's Struggle,* a collection of life stories of women who took part in the Telangana struggle, allows us to hear the voices of women who would never have written their memoirs. Among the many memories recorded is the disjointed narrative of Golla Mallamma about the Razakars (a private militia of the Majlis, a fundamentalist Islamic sect) coming to her village:

As they came to our well, they lit a match. They set fire to a cattle shed and killed people. As we beat our breasts and wept, they stripped us . . . We began to run. We kept saluting them and running . . . Rajakka why don't you tell them? It was near their well. Rajakka will tell you . . . They burnt the ones they killed . . . They killed the ones they burnt . . . They burnt our houses too . . . They burnt and killed everyone in our village.[108]

In the liberated areas peasants seized and redistributed land and put an end to bonded and forced labor. In 1948 Hyderabad state was incorporated into India by a "police action" and the Indian army moved to

---

[107] *Ibid.,* p. 187.
[108] Stree Shakti Sanghatana, *"We Were Making History"*: *Life Stories of Women in the Telangana People's Struggle* (New Delhi, Kali For Women, 1989), p. 63.

suppress this uprising. By 1950 the Communists decided to follow the Chinese model and designated Telangana the "Yenan of India." In response, the army intensified its efforts causing moderate sympathizers to withdraw their support. In 1951 it was obvious there was little chance of victory and the movement was called off.

The Telangana movement had brought substantial gains for the peasantry. Many were able to retain the land they had acquired and forced labor ended. Peasant women benefited by the end of forced labor, *adi bapa*, and concubinage. But women did not receive land unless they were widows. The party had not developed a policy for women and party leaders were unable to see them as equals in the struggle.[109]

CONCLUSIONS

The period between the campaign for the 1937 legislatures and the first election in free India saw women come alive politically. In the early years of the twentieth century a few women began participating in political meetings and expressing their opinions. These were such rare occurrences that the presence of women in political arenas seemed to evoke even greater reference for Mother India. In the 1920s, women joined public demonstrations and brought hundreds of new recruits into the freedom movement. By the 1930s they marched, protested, picketed, and courted arrest endorsed by Gandhi's leadership and tactics. By World War II the situation had changed dramatically.

While Congress called for a Quit India campaign, the Communists worked to build a strong base in the countryside. Some Congressites went to jail, others worked underground. Subhas Bose escaped to Singapore to build an Indian National Army to liberate India with the help of the Japanese. And throughout the country, groups long held in check – peasants, sharecroppers, laborers, *adivasis* – vented their grievances.

A new generation of young women – educated, unmarried, willing to undertake dangerous and difficult tasks – joined these movements. No longer were their activities confined to "women-only" groups. In acting these women often incurred the enmity of their families and neighbors and the hostility of those they wanted to help.

They were building the first bridges between urban middle-class

---

[109] *"We Were Making History"*, pp. 15–17.

women and the rural masses. That most of them were feminists seems evident from their writings, that most found their feminism largely irrelevant in the countryside is not surprising. Issues of social reformers – purdah, the legal status of women, and female education – paled in comparison with the brutality of forced labor and sanctioned rape. These educated women brought with them ideological tools that gave them a way of thinking and speaking about the conditions they witnessed. Learning about women's problems first-hand, gaining the trust and acceptance of the women they sought to help, and working to accomplish real change was an entirely different proposition.

Manikuntala Sen has written about trying to teach impoverished peasant women, during the *tebhaga* movement, about Marxism. The women were suffering from encounters with drunken and abusive husbands. Instead of tackling these problems or trying to teach about modes of production and the evils of capitalism, Manikuntala Sen confessed she talked about a future where children would be healthy and well fed. When Godavari Parulekar first traveled to Warli villages she discovered only Warli men could cook for guests while "impure" women were ordered to pound grain and grind spices. She was unable to do anything to change the situation. Those who tried to work with factory women learned that these women worked ten-hour shifts and then went home to cook and perform household tasks. Women involved in famine relief became sadly aware of starving women prostituting themselves to feed their children or capitulating to the desires of male relief workers. By listening to the women they met in the cities and countryside, activist women became aware of the extent to which women were oppressed by poverty, household work, and a patriarchal system which failed to value women.

Between the Quit India movement and Independence in 1947 Indians faced a devastating famine and the threat of invasion. British officials were bewildered by a naval mutiny, peasant movements, and industrial strikes. For women it was difficult to maintain ideological purity. Some women held fast to a vision of "universal womanhood" untouched by the divisions of caste, class, party, and religion. But most women found they owed their loyalties to groups with ideologies more compelling than the social feminism espoused by the women's organizations.

The women activists of the 1940s challenged the norms of respectability that obsessed an earlier generation of women leaders. In the 1930s *sevikas* dressed in orange or white saris to signal their purity and devotion to the nation. They wanted to be recognized as different from ordinary women and courted a symbolic identification with Bharat Mataram (Mother India). This style was anathema to the needs of the 1940s. Women who could work with angry mobs, peasants, "tribals," factory workers, famine victims, and revolutionaries were required. The work was dangerous and exhausting and a number of middle-class women experienced first-hand the brutality usually reserved for their poorer sisters. Yet it seems that, for the first time, women of different classes were linked in a common struggle.

As women broadened their scope two things happened. First, they lost their identification with the goddess and became "enemies" who could be beaten or killed without a moment's notice. The other significant change was the decline in their influence. Saraladevi Chaudhurani, Sarojini Naidu, Latika Ghosh, Lilavati Munshi, Manmohini Zutshi, and Satyavati Devi were all listened to with rapt attention. Their speeches to crowds or political assemblies were reported in newspapers and acclaimed by leaders. Women lost their privileged position when their numbers in political parties and movements increased.

It is interesting to speculate why women's concerns and ideas were not incorporated into the various struggles, either against the Raj or for social and economic justice. It was certainly not because women stood aloof from the battles or failed to do their part. Manikuntala Sen, for example, knew a lot about women's condition and wanted to make their emancipation an integral part of the movement for economic justice. Her superiors in the party were not interested in tying gender oppression to the demand for a fair share of the harvest. Most women leaders objected to partition, but their views played no part in the final decisions. Yet it was women who were charged with keeping families together and making households run. When the division was made final, many found their lives shattered.

As women had become more active and their contribution real, as opposed to symbolic, they undermined the hegemony of the women's organizations and the myth that women spoke with one voice. Social feminism had nothing to offer the women of Telangana or the refugees after partition. Women had begun working with a wide range of parties and organizations, but none of these were seriously interested in gender justice. Unfortunately, the ideologies which replaced social feminism for activist women did not advocate emancipation from patriarchy.

CHAPTER 8

WOMEN IN INDEPENDENT INDIA

On August 14, 1947, India and Pakistan gained independence from British rule. Dhanvanthi Rama Rau, president of the All-India Women's Organization in 1946, remembered that time:

All Indians lived through terrible, dark months after Independence. With the Partition of the country and the unexpected, cruel, and unhappy exchanges of populations between Pakistan and India forced on the peoples of both countries, tragedies of a magnitude and intensity beyond the grimmest imagination of any leader were enacted . . . The rejoicing of our nation on its liberation from nearly two hundred years of colonial rule was turned to mourning at the suffering of our people who were driven from their homes in Pakistan.[1]

On January 30, 1948, Mahatma Gandhi died from an assassin's bullet. Within a year women active in the major women's organizations had lost their dream of a unified country and their beloved leader.

India and Pakistan constructed themselves differently, India as a secular, democratic nation and Pakistan as a religious, authoritarian nation. This chapter will focus only on India and will attempt to draw out the historical roots of problems and issues of Indian women in the period following Independence. Specifically, it will consider women's political role, the relationship of women to the modern economy, and the new women's movement.

WOMEN'S STATUS IN
POST-INDEPENDENCE INDIA

The Indian Constitution declared equality a fundamental right. This document also guaranteed equal protection of the law, equal opportunities in public employment, and prohibited discrimination in public places. The Hindu Code, passed as separate Acts between 1955 and 1956, rewrote for Hindus the laws of marriage and divorce, adoption, and inheritance. Adult suffrage added women to the electoral roles and political parties pledged their commitment to women's issues. The new

---

[1] *An Inheritance: the Memoirs of Dhanvanthi Rama Rau* (Bombay, Allied Publishers Private Limited, 1978), pp. 227–8.

state developed a bureaucratic structure designed to meet the specific needs of women. This included creating the National Social Welfare Board, assigning special duties to block development officers, and asking the Department of Health and Welfare to prepare a specific plan with women in mind. In the documents of the new Indian state the past had been undone, modernity was triumphant, and women were no longer subordinate to men.

The immediate concerns of people were not constitutional rights but political reality. The partition of British India into India and Pakistan affected millions of women and men as populations fled both countries. When the migrations were over more than eight million people had moved from Pakistan to India or from India to Pakistan. Ritu Menon and Kamla Bhasin have argued that the story of 1947 is:

> a gendered narrative of displacement and dispossession, of large-scale and wide-spread communal violence, and of the realignment of family, community and national identities as people were forced to accommodate the dramatically altered reality that now prevailed.[2]

Many women – estimates range from 80,000 to 150,000 – were abducted during this time. Because they were seen as dependants of patriarchal households, India and Pakistan agreed on procedures for recovery and restoration.[3]

Over 30,000 women were "recovered" by 1957, the last year the Abducted Act was renewed. Their stories were not all alike. Some faced horrible brutality and were grateful to be rescued. Others had made peace with their new surroundings by the time they were discovered and saw "recovery" as a second abduction. The state, assuming the mantle of "father-patriarch," was enforcing the concept of the legitimate family.[4] It is only now that this policy is being questioned by scholars applying a feminist perspective.[5]

Many of the women who participated in the social reform and political activities of the 1920s, 1930s, and 1940s were pleased with the constitutional provisions and legal reform. Belonging to the upper and

---

[2] Ritu Menon and Kamla Bhasin, "Recovery, Rupture, Resistance: Indian State and Abduction of Women During Partition," *EPW*, 28, no. 17 (April 24, 1993), p. ws2.
[3] *Ibid.*, pp. ws3–ws4.   [4] *Ibid.*, pp. ws2–ws11.
[5] The Review of Women's Studies section in the April, 1993 issue of *EPW*, 28, no. 17 (April 24, 1993), was devoted to this topic. It included the following articles: Ritu Menon and Kamla Bhasin, "Recovery, Rupture, Resistance," pp. ws2–ws11; Urvashi Butalia, "Community, State and Gender," pp. ws12–ws24; Karuna Chanana, "Partition and Family Strategies," pp. ws25–ws34; Ratna Kapur and Brenda Crossman, "Communalising Gender/Engendering Community," pp. ws35–ws44.

middle classes of society, they were poised to become the beneficiaries of new opportunities. The government asked prominent women's organizations to assist them in developing five-year plans. These women agreed with government that economic growth was the most salient issue and shared the assumption that women would gain from expected prosperity.

The best-known of the women's organizations became institutionalized as they secured permanent buildings, well-staffed offices, libraries, and bureaucracies of their own. They set up and continue to administer programs designed to serve women, especially day-care centers, hostels for working women, educational centers, and medical dispensaries. Like the government with which they have been closely allied, their approach has been "welfarist."[6] Prominent women's organizations have been criticized for this and faulted for not preparing women for new responsibilities.[7] Pat Caplan, in her research on Madras women's organizations, observed women blocking change and perpetuating the traditional socialization of women as dependants.[8]

The Communist women were the most vocal in expressing their dissatisfaction with constitutional provisions, five-year plans, and government and party promises. In 1954 Vibhla Farooqui and her female colleagues in the CPI organized a national conference to address women's issues. At this conference they founded the National Federation of Indian Women (NFIW) to focus attention on "[women's] struggle for equal rights and responsibilities in all spheres of life and for improvement in their living conditions."[9] They viewed prevailing political forces as trying to "reduce the role of women's organizations to charitable work combined with, off and on, passing resolutions"[10] and pleaded for a new orientation. At the same time they found their male colleagues in the CPI indifferent to women's issues and reluctant to include women on working committees. Vimal Ranadive, secretary of the Communist Party of Bombay from 1951 to 1962 and a trade union worker from 1962 to 1972 recalled another dif-

---

[6] M. Mathew and M. S. Nair, *Women's Organizations and Women's Interests* (New Delhi, Ashish Publishing House, 1986), pp. 35–7.
[7] From Sulabha Brahme, quoted by Neera Desai in "From Articulation to Accommodation: Women's Movement in India," *Visibility and Power*, ed. Leela Dube, Eleanor Leacock and Shirley Ardener (Delhi, Oxford University Press, 1986), p. 294.
[8] See Patricia Caplan, *Class and Gender in India* (London, Tavistock Publications, 1985).
[9] *Tenth Congress of the National Federation of Indian Women*, Trivandrum, December, 1980 (Delhi, NFIW, 1980), p. 3.   [10] *Ibid.*, p. 3.

ficulty – that of attracting working women to trade union meetings.[11] Leftist women found themselves fighting "feudal ideas" on two fronts: within their parties and in society.[12]

There were other women, close followers of Gandhi, who saw economic and social change as more important than legal and constitutional rights. They too were dissatisfied. But many of these individuals also believed in voluntarism and focused their attention on grass-roots projects. Krishnabai Nimbkar, the former Krishnabai Rau who led demonstrations in Madras during the civil disobedience movement and went to jail for her actions, never lost her attachment to Gandhian principles. Antipathetic to bureaucracies and centralized government planning, she and others like her made small inroads into the system but could not change the direction of major programs.[13]

There are three major observations that can be made about the period immediately following Independence. First, the celebration of victory was shunted aside by the refugee issue. Second, even without this tragedy, there would have been disgruntlement among women over issues of institutionalization and bureaucratization. And third, during the struggle for independence some women accepted the domination of Congress but others did not. Many of these women worked with the revolutionary fringe and these tendencies carried on after Independence.

Despite sporadic criticism, the Indian government's commitment to equality was not seriously challenged until 1974 when *Toward Equality*, a report on the status of women, was published. In 1971 the Ministry of Education and Social Welfare appointed a committee "to examine the constitutional, legal and administrative provisions that have a bearing on the social status of women, their education and employment" and to assess the impact of these provisions.[14] There had been an internal demand for such a document but the actual timing was in response to a United Nations request to all countries to prepare reports on the status of women for International Women's Year scheduled for 1975.

[11] Geeta Anand, "The Feminist Movement in India: Legacy of the Quit India Movement of 1942," senior thesis, Dartmouth College (1989), p. 21.
[12] Neera Desai and Vibhuti Patel, *Change and Challenge in the International Decade, 1975–1985* (Bombay, Popular Prakashan, 1985), pp. 68–9.
[13] Letter from Dr. (Mrs.) Krishnabai Nimbkar to G. Forbes (August 12, 1992).
[14] *Toward Equality*, report of the Committee on the Status of Women in India (New Delhi, Government of India Ministry of Education and Social Welfare, 1974). p. xii.

Dr. Phulrenu Guha, Union Minister for Social Welfare, chaired this committee with Dr. Vina Mazumdar, appointed in 1972, as member-secretary. The remaining nine members of the committee represented a wide spectrum of interests and experience. Only two of the members, Maniben Kara and Dr. Phulrenu Guha, had directly experienced the struggle for independence. Other members had worked closely with women's organizations, were well-known academicians, or were involved in politics. The committee was asked to suggest ways to make women full members of the Indian state. In order to write this report, the committee commissioned a number of studies and interviewed about 500 women from each state. By 1973 they had concluded their proceedings. These studies and the report issued in 1974 were the first major effort to understand the extent to which constitutional guarantees of equality and justice had not been met for women. Authors of this report charged that women's status had not improved but had, in fact, declined since Independence:

The review of the disabilities and constraints on women, which stem from socio-cultural institutions, indicates that the majority of women are still very far from enjoying the rights and opportunities guaranteed to them by the Constitution . . . The social laws, that sought to mitigate the problems of women in their family life, have remained unknown to a large mass of women in this country, who are as ignorant of their legal rights today as they were before Independence.[15]

This declaration, that social change and development in India had adversely affected women, shocked many Indians. Mrs. Indira Gandhi was Prime Minister and India was one of the few countries in the world that regularly sent women abroad as ambassadors, representatives to the United Nations, and delegates to international conferences. To celebrate International Women's Year, organizations all over the country were programming special sessions to publicize women's achievements. Only one year before *Toward Equality* was released, Femina, a popular magazine for "modern women," published a special Independence Day issue with a cover portraying *Indira Gandhi* as the Goddess Durga. The brief note explaining the cover gloated:

To be a woman – a wife, a mother, an individual – in India means many things. It means that you are the store-house of tradition and culture and, in contrast a volcano of seething energy, of strength and power that can motivate a whole generation to change its values, its aspirations, its very concept of civilized life.[16]

---

[15] *Toward Equality*, p. 359.   [16] *Femina*, 14, no. 17 (August 17, 1973), p. 5.

The feature story, "Shakti in Modern India," credited Mahatma Gandhi with bringing women into politics and thereby:

setting into motion the process of liberation of Indian women. Once out of the home . . . the Indian woman has been quick to seize every opportunity to free herself from male domination.[17]

These contrasting images are startling now and were startling at the time.

Toward Equality's impact on programs and policies for women in India as well as our reading of the history of women in India from Independence until 1970 has been momentous. Following publication of the report the Indian Council of Social Science Research (ICSSR) established an advisory committee on women's studies headed by Dr. Vina Mazumdar. This supported further research into questions raised in the report. Almost all of the research carried out under the direction of this advisory committee attempted to discover the conditions under which women lived and worked in contemporary India. In 1980 the Center for Women's Development Studies, an autonomous research institute, was founded, with Vina Mazumdar as director. This center has carried forward the work of studying the status of women and making recommendations to the government regarding policies. The Research Center for Women's Studies at SNDT Women's University began its work in 1974 as a research unit. Under the able directorship of Neera Desai, it was accorded the status of Center for Advanced Research in Women's Studies by the University Grants Commission in 1980.

The over-all picture of Indian women presented in *Toward Equality* and the studies carried out by these and other research institutes is depressing. Much of this literature has focused on the failure of programs and policies. Nevertheless, the advances made by some Indian women have been and continue to be awe-inspiring. Further, institutional changes have made a difference, as is evidenced by the leading roles Indian women continue to play in India and on the world stage. They have been strong enough to mount a challenge to ultra-conservative forces that would have them return to "traditional roles" that were fictionalized ideals even in the nineteenth century. But the main point of the report, that millions of Indian women have not benefited

---

[17] Shanta Serbjeet Singh, "Shakti in Modern India," *Femina*, 14, no. 17 (August 17, 1973), p. 47.

from "modernity" whether it be economic, technological, political, or social, remains true even today.

WOMEN AND POLITICS

The record of Indian women in politics is often cited in rebuttal to accounts and reports that dwell on the subordination of women. Indian women can vote and stand for election to all provincial and central bodies. Women have been ministers, ambassadors and, most notably, the Prime Minister. While the extent of their involvement falls far short of the equality promised by the Constitution it is significant in comparison with other countries of the world.

Women vote in approximately the same proportion as men. Analysts argue that most women follow the lead of male family members, but a few surveys and anecdotal accounts suggest that women are increasingly interested in political power and vote independently. However, it does not appear that women vote for women's issues or necessarily for women candidates.

The number of women elected to the assemblies often seems larger than it is because of the personalities involved. The first assembly had very few women, about 2 percent, but included Masuma Begum who later became the Minister of Social Welfare and deputy leader of the Congress Party; Renuka Ray, a veteran social worker; Durgabai (later Durgabai Deshmukh), a well-known Gandhian and, after Independence, chair of the Central Social Welfare Board; and Radhabai Subbarayan, appointed delegate to the first Round Table Conference. Accounts from the time suggest that men in the assembly listened carefully to their speeches.

In the following elections, the return was somewhat better and women consistently held 4–5 percent of the seats in the Lok Sabha (the lower house of India's parliament) until the 1980s when their numbers increased to 7–8 percent. In the less powerful Rajya Sabha (the upper house of parliament), where members are elected by their state assemblies and nominated by the President of India, women have held between 7 percent and 10 percent of the places.[18]

The number of elected women compares favorably with other coun-

---

[18] Wendy Singer, Department of Political Science, Kenyon College, Ohio, is now engaged in a study entitled "'Women' and Elections in India: 1936–1996." This will be the first study of women as voters, candidates, and audience for campaign rhetoric.

tries. Historically women's representation has reached 30–40 percent only in Scandinavian countries, the former Soviet Union, and those countries until recently referred to as the "Eastern bloc." As of June 1991, India's percentage of women in parliament, 7.1 percent, compared favorably with the USA's 6.4 percent, the United Kingdom's 6.3 percent and France's 5.7 percent.[19]

Examined next to other nations, India's record of women in politics is impressive. However, it is not remarkable from a historical perspective. The politics of agitation brought women into all facets of the freedom movement where they demonstrated their bravery. Following Independence these women found it difficult to make the transition from agitational politics to electoral politics.

First, there has been the problem of party backing. The political parties all give lip service to the ideal of women in politics but have been reluctant to gamble with seats.

Second, woman candidates have disliked the rough and tumble of political life. While many expressed a willingness to put up with the hardships of a political campaign, they have not been able to change social attitudes about women's proper place. Those women who accepted the challenge have had to endure sexual harassment and sordid gossip. Many women found themselves agreeing with Anutayi Limayi, former member of the Executive Board of the Prajya Socialist Party, who expressed her dislike for the political process and preference for the gentler arena of social welfare work.[20] Ela Bhatt, a trade unionist and the founder of the Self-Employed Women's Association (SEWA), remembered her early years in trade union work:

there were no other women . . . I was very shy. Also, our people are not so kind, so they make up all kinds of stories. I had to travel . . . I had to go by car, and with men. Then you also stay overnight when you go. So it was not much approved. So I had to fight a lot and I used to feel, What am I doing? Am I doing the right thing?[21]

These statements have led some social scientists to suggest the legacy of the freedom movement is the problem. Wendy Singer observed women avoiding the political arena for the security of "behind-the-scenes"

---

[19] Marie-Jose Ragab, "Women in Parliaments," *National NOW*[National Organization of Women] *Times* (June, 1991), p. 8.   [20] Anand, "The Feminist Movement," p. 31.
[21] Quoted in Elisabeth Bumiller, *May You Be the Mother of a Hundred Sons* (New York, Random House, 1990), p. 137.

petitioning. In Singer's view, the method that gave women power in the 1930s, marginalized their influence in 1989.[22]

The third problem women in politics face is related to their representation as both "feminine" and "unfeminine" (or unsexed).[23] Indian news media never fail to notice a woman politician, but much of the attention focuses on either their performance of traditional roles and dress, appearance, and style or on their masculine traits. In some instances – and Mrs. Gandhi is a case in point – political women become icons – dressed in the garb of a powerful goddess or the heroic Rani of Jhansi. But there is little room for either goddesses or warrior queens in day-to-day political life and women politicians must perform like their male colleagues. Like men, women must do battle for the bills they want passed and the constituencies they serve. In short, they must learn the games of power.

What is worthy of attention is the striking number of women who have held responsible positions. For example, Rajkumari Amrit Kaur became Union Health Minister in 1947; Renuka Ray was West Bengal's Minister for Relief and Rehabilitation; and Sucheta Kripalani was general secretary of the Congress in 1959, Labor Minister in the Uttar Pradesh cabinet in 1962, and Chief Minister of United Province from 1963 to 1967. Vijayalakshmi Pandit was appointed Uttar Pradesh's Minister for Health and Local Self-Government in 1937 and following Independence was selected as a delegate to the United Nations. In 1947 she was appointed ambassador to the USSR and in 1949 ambassador to the USA. In 1953 she was elected president of the United Nations General Assembly. This is only a short list of the women who have wielded power and influence in post-Independence India.

The most important political woman in India was Mrs. Indira Gandhi (1917–84), India's only woman Prime Minister and the second woman to head a state in the twentieth century.[24] Mrs. Gandhi's long tenure in office, from 1966 to 1977 and 1980 to 1984, ended with her assassination on October 31, 1984. Her one political defeat was in 1977

[22] Wendy Singer, "Women's Politics and Land Control in an Indian Election: Lasting Influences of the Freedom Movement in North Bihar," in Harold Gould and Sumit Ganguly, eds., *India Votes* (Boulder, Westview Press, 1993), p. 182.
[23] Rajeswari Sunder Rajan, *Real and Imagined Women* (London and New York, Routledge, 1993), p. 115.
[24] Mrs. Sirimavo Bandaranaike was Prime Minister of Sri Lanka (then called Ceylon) from 1960 to 1965.

following her declaration of an "emergency" in India and the suspension of a number of constitutionally guaranteed civil liberties.

Indira was the only child of Jawaharlal Nehru, India's "Father of the Country," and Kamala, a Gandhian and leader of women's demonstrations in northern India. Indira was raised on politics. Her grandfather Motilal, a leading member of the Indian National Congress since the turn of the century, was proud to have three generations of his family in prison at the same time. Kamala (1899–1936), Indira's mother, was unprepared by her traditional family for the sophisticated atmosphere of the Nehru household, but later took part in demonstrations and delivered forceful feminist speeches. Indira was nineteen years old when her mother died of tuberculosis. Six years later Indira married Feroz Gandhi, her mother's devoted friend and confidant. They had two sons, Rajiv and Sanjay, but began to live apart as Feroz's political career became more demanding and Indira was increasingly occupied with the needs of her father the Prime Minister.

As her father's companion, Indira organized his domestic affairs, accompanied him on his many trips abroad, and played the role of official hostess. Older Congress bosses considered her malleable and since they thought they had nothing to fear, made Indira president of the Indian National Congress Party in 1959. Nehru died in 1964. Lal Bahadur Sastri succeeded him but died unexpectedly in 1966 leaving the country without a leader. Indira's candidacy was supported by Congress Party leaders who wanted "a Nehru" in office and believed she would be easy to control.

In office, Indira demonstrated more strength than predicted. By 1972 she was victorious at home, with Congress in power both at the center and in many of the states; and triumphant abroad having supported Bangladesh in its war of independence against Pakistan. Three years later the high court at Allahabad overturned her election. Mrs. Gandhi refused to accept their decision, declared a state of emergency, and temporarily saved her own power. In the process she sanctioned measures that brought about the Congress Party's first defeat at the center since Independence. Mrs. Gandhi was in opposition between 1977 and 1980 when she was returned to power. That year her favored younger son, Sanjay, was killed when the plane he was flying crashed.

Back in office, Indira Gandhi responded in a patterned fashion to threats to her power. She proclaimed dissident states ungovernable, declared President's Rule, and used the central police and intelligence

forces to suppress regional opposition.[25] In 1984 Indira was assassinated by two Sikhs from her own guards. They were enraged by
Operation Bluestar, the invasion of the Golden Temple of Amritsar,
Sikhism's holiest shrine. This assault was designed to capture Sant
Bhindravale, the leader spearheading a violent movement for an independent Sikh state. Rajiv Gandhi, Indira's eldest son, won the following election and remained Prime Minister until his defeat in 1989. He
was assassinated in 1991 while campaigning to return to office.

Indira Gandhi consistently denied she was a feminist. Speaking at a
New Delhi college, she said, "I am not a feminist and I do not believe
that anybody should get a preferential treatment merely because she
happens to be a woman."[26] But at the same time she referred to women
as "the biggest oppressed minority in the world," and said Indian
women were handicapped from birth.[27] But in talking about herself,
she denied gender had played a role in either her socialization or her
political success.[28] When *McCall's*, a US publication designed for
women, purchased a full-page advertisement in the *New York Times* to
promote a feature story on her elevation to head of state in India, Indira
was not pleased. She told reporters, "I do not regard myself as a
woman. I am a person with a job to do."[29]

Mrs. Gandhi frequently talked about the importance of women as
mothers and homemakers and extolled women's traditional roles.[30]
Interviewed by Meher Pestomji of *Eve's Weekly,* Mrs. Gandhi said her
greatest fulfillment came from motherhood.[31] Indira said that the
emancipation she wanted for the average woman in India, was "an
honourable status, in life, and that she should be able to exert her influence for the good and benefit of the community."[32]

When asked about the role of women in politics, Mrs. Gandhi replied

[25] Paul R. Brass, *The Politics of India Since Independence* (Cambridge, Cambridge
University Press, 1990), p. 321.
[26] Indira Gandhi, "What Does 'Modern' Mean?" New Delhi, Miranda House (March, 1993),
Great Women of Modern India, vol. VII, *Indira Gandhi*, ed. Verinder Grover and Ranjana
Arora (New Delhi, Deep and Deep Publications, 1993), p. 169.
[27] Indira Gandhi, "India's Programme for International Women's Year," Lok Sabha (April,
1975), *Indira Gandhi*, p. 137.
[28] Indira Gandhi, "Equality – An Indian Tradition," interview (March 1968), *Indira Gandhi*,
p. 142.   [29] *The Asian Student* (November 23, 1974), p. 5.
[30] Indira Gandhi, "Women's Power," speech, YWCA, Bombay (February 1975), *Indira
Gandhi*, p. 153.
[31] Meher Pestonji, "All Eyes on Mrs. G!" *Eve's Weekly* (October 27–November 2, 1979), p.
12.
[32] Indira Gandhi, "All Women are Teachers," speech, Lady Irwin College, New Delhi
(November 1967), *Indira Gandhi*, p. 141.

that Indian men, beginning with Mahatma Gandhi, welcomed women to share power. Moreover, men fought for women's rights in the past and they could be trusted to do so in the future. The Prime Minister did not think having more women in parliament would affect the political scene.[33] Female emancipation would come when women, and men like her father, worked to make the Constitution a reality.[34]

Asked about *Toward Equality*'s conclusion, that the position of women had not improved since Independence, Indira answered: "the people who sit on these committees look at us from Western standards. Very few of them have their feet firmly on Indian soil." Indians, she declared, were not sexists and were barely cognizant of the fact that the country was led by a woman.[35]

Regrettably, feminist scholars, with the exception of Rajeswari Ranjan who has looked at issues associated with representation,[36] have not yet tackled questions associated with the Prime Minister's gender, what this meant to the country, and the extent to which her policies were relevant for women. Recent books on women in contemporary India have either ignored the fact that India had a woman holding the most important political office,[37] or claimed that reverence for the goddess operates in daily life to assist certain women in attaining political power.[38]

It is interesting that in *Toward Equality* the only reference to the Prime Minister's gender was included in two general sentences about women in politics:

Though only a very few women were able to reach the highest level of power and authority, those who did so were recognized for their administrative skills and capacity to manage their affairs. Since 1952 there have been 13 women ministers in the Union Government – 6 of them Deputy Ministers, 5 became Ministers of State, 1 attained Cabinet rank and the other Prime Minister – a position which she has retained since 1966.[39]

How should one understand the elevation of a number of Indian women to prominent positions and what does this mean for women in

---

[33] "All Eyes on Mrs. G!" p. 15.
[34] Indira Gandhi, "Tasks Before Indian Women," speech, SNDT Women's University, Bombay (June 1968), *Indira Gandhi*, pp. 162–83.
[35] "All Eyes on Mrs. G!" p. 15.
[36] Rajeswari Ranjan, "Gender, Leadership and Representation," *Real and Imagined Women*, pp. 103–28.
[37] Joanna Liddle and Rama Joshi, *Daughters of Independence* (London, Zed Books, 1986).
[38] Sara S. Mitter, *Dharma's Daughters* (New Brunswick, N.J., Rutgers University Press, 1991), p. 80. [39] *Toward Equality*, p. 297.

India? Ashis Nandy has termed this apparent inconsistency between highly placed political women and the status of the masses of Indian women "[the] commonplace paradox of every social interpretation of the Indian woman."[40] He explains women's political (and scientific) success in terms of the culture's non-gendering of aggressive and activist traits. This hypothesis, with its focus on culture, is akin to those which articulate the cultural/symbolic linkage between *shakti* (power) and the feminine.[41] Taking a slightly different tack in his discussion of the relationship between cultural values and social structure, Gerald D. Berreman recognizes that women's roles are subordinate to those of men, but argues that women are taken seriously as human beings. Women's activities may be circumscribed but women themselves are never trivialized.[42]

Other scholars have focused on the elite status of women in prominent positions. While it is true that most of the women who attained positions of power belonged to "political families," they did not all belong to an elite in the sense of a wealthy and powerful minority. There was a vast difference between Amrit Kaur and Durgabai Deshmukh and between Vijayalakshmi Pandit and Krishnabai Rau. To label them elites and suggest they were the beneficiaries of dynastic politics, fails to recognize the differences in actual status and the value of the tutelage these women received. It also overlooks their personal political savvy.[43] To understand the elevation to power of certain women I think it is far more useful to look at family culture, opportunities, and individual personality.

The political scientist Mary Katzenstein has summed up the prominence of Indian women in politics as "the Mrs. Gandhi anomaly." According to Katzenstein, political factors, especially the mobilization of women during the struggle for independence and Gandhian ideology, as well as the importance of kinship, have combined to

---

[40] Ashis Nandy, "Woman Versus Womanliness: An Essay in Speculative Psychology," *Indian Women: From Purdah to Modernity*, ed. B. R. Nanda (New Delhi, Vikas Publishing, 1976), p. 158.
[41] See Susan S. Wadley, "Introduction," *The Powers of Tamil Women*, ed. Susan S. Wadley (Syracuse, N.Y., Maxwell School, 1980), pp. ix–xv.
[42] Gerald D. Berreman, "Women's Roles and Politics: India and the United States," in Robert W. O'Brien, *et. al.*, eds., *Readings in General Sociology*, 4th edn. (Boston, Houghton Mifflin Co., 1969), pp. 68–71; Gerald D. Berreman, "Race, Caste and Other Invidious Distinctions in Social Stratification," *Race*, 13 (July, 1971–April, 1972), pp. 386–414.
[43] Imtiaz Ahmed, "Women in Politics," in Devika Jain, ed., *Indian Women* (New Delhi, Government of India, Ministry of Information and Broadcasting, 1975), pp. 301–12.

create opportunities for women to move into leadership positions.[44]

Have the women in positions of political power been effective? As far as solving the problems of India's women, the answer is no. In India women vote in substantial numbers and hold high political office yet rarely have they used their vote or office to consistently advance women's cause. Many of the women in power have referenced their gender in political campaigns, referring to themselves as mothers, wives or dutiful daughters, but they have not gendered their political roles. Only a few women have focused specifically on women's problems. For example, Mrinal Gore, a member of the Legislative Assembly of Maharashtra in the 1970s and member of the Lok Sabha in 1980, was fondly called "Paaniwalibai" (the water-woman advocate) for organizing women against price rises and chronic water problems. Time and again, Mrinal Gore returned to what she argued were fundamental problems for women: "In so many villages today, I think half the life of a woman is spent in fetching water."[45] Extraordinary women like Mrinal Gore, Phulrenu Guha, and Renuka Ray, to name only a few, have made their mark but they have not had the political clout to improve the lot of women as a whole.

The exigencies of political life preclude concentrating only on issues of interest to women or approaching all issues from a feminist perspective. Nevertheless, women in political positions are highly visual and may serve as models of empowered women. Ela Bhatt, a member of the Rajya Sabha, said that having a woman as Prime Minister made all women more aware of their rights.[46]

If the question is whether or not women can be effective politicians the answer is yes and the degree of success would be ascertained by examining individual careers. Indira Gandhi may have owed her ascent to power to dynastic politics but she was certainly an effective politician. But the fact remains, political participation has not benefited Indian women to the extent envisioned in the 1920s and 1930s by those working for female enfranchisement.

[44] Mary Fainsod Katzenstein, "Toward Equality? Cause and Consequence of the Political Prominence of Women in India," *Asian Survey*, 18, no. 5 (May, 1978), p. 483.
[45] Binoy Thomas, "Mrinal Gore: 'Paaniwalibai,' Watered Down," *Society* (March, 1980), pp. 20–7; Mrinal Gore, interview (Bombay, March 18, 1980).
[46] Bumiller, *May You Be the Mother*, p. 151.

ECONOMIC ISSUES

There are many who would argue that the key to women's status is their economic position. Regardless of the indices consulted – ownership of property, control of resources, wages earned, food consumed, access to medical care, or sex ratio – Indian women are not the equals of Indian men.

Questions about the extent to which women's lives may have improved over time are difficult to answer because historians have paid so little attention to this topic. Prior to Independence, work loads, life conditions, even the views of working women were of little concern. Only rarely did the committees and commissions set up to study specific questions regarding labor include interviews with the workers themselves, and when they did it was generally the men they asked. Occasionally members of the women's organizations spoke on behalf of their "less fortunate" sisters. This has changed in the sense that we now have studies of female workers in a range of industries from construction[47] to milk production.[48]

Moreover, recent scholarship challenges both the modernization paradigm and its assumptions regarding women. Champions of modernization have claimed that technology, industrialization, and capitalism improve living conditions for the entire population and that women experience economic change in the same way as men. The early leaders of independent India shared some of the assumptions about the benefits of technology and industrialization and hoped to alleviate or correct the worst abuses of capitalism through long-range planning and continued state involvement. While there were a number of Marxist scholars ready to challenge the benefits of this planned change, the second assumption, viewing women as natural beneficiaries, went unchallenged until the advent of feminist scholarship.

The most disturbing comment on contemporary Indian society has been made by those economists and demographers who have noted India's differential sex ratio.[49] At the beginning of the century there

---

[47] Leela Gulati, "Devaki, the Construction Worker," chapter 5 of *Profiles in Female Poverty* (Delhi, Hindustan Publishing, 1981).

[48] Devaki Jain, "Milk Producers of Kaira," *Women's Quest for Power* (Sahibabad, U.P., Vikas Publishing, 1980).

[49] Barbara D. Miller, *The Endangered Sex* (Ithaca, N.Y., Cornell University Press, 1981); Amartya Sen, "More Than 100 Million Women Are Missing," *The New York Review* (December 20, 1990), pp. 61–6.

were 972 females per 1,000 males, by 1941 the ratio had fallen to 945 females per 1,000 males and it fell even further, to 933 females per 1,000 males, by 1981.[50] The economist Amartya Sen wrote: "We confront here what is clearly one of the most momentous, and neglected, problems facing the world today."[51]

It is important to note that there are variations in sex ratios in different regions of India. In 1981 Kerala reported a female to male sex ratio of 1,032: 1,000, while Haryana and Punjab, two of India's more prosperous states, reported sex ratios of 870:1,000 and 879:1,000 respectively. Most researchers agree that female survival chances are lower than those for males because of differential feeding and health care. Jocelyn Kynch and Amartya Sen have drawn our attention to the combination of the lowness of the female–male ratio with the declining trend of this ratio. They comment:

Indeed, with economic and social progress, as the *absolute* position of both men and women has improved, the *relative* position of women seems to have fallen behind. If we judge well-being in a poor country like India by the capability to live long, women's well-being has fallen vis-à-vis men's, even though absolutely both have increased substantially.[52]

Why this happens cannot be adequately explained by turning to cultural values or poverty and underdevelopment. The most compelling explanations for this pattern look at women's low rate of participation in the market economy and the low valuation placed on them as human beings.

Toward Equality blames women's low economic status on public policies that view women's work as supplemental to family incomes and to the economy generally. Statistical evidence from the census showed a decline in women's participation in the formal economic sector, both as a percentage of the total female population and as a percentage of the total population. Members of the committee explained this decline, first, as part of the process of the "transformation of the role of the household and small-scale industry in the national economy."[53] As production moved from the household to the organized sector of the economy, women were the biggest losers. They were

[50] Bina Agarwal, "Rural Women, Poverty and Natural Resources: Sustenance, Sustainability and Struggle for Change," *EPW*, 24, no. 43 (October 28, 1989), p. ws47.
[51] Amartya Sen, "More Than 100 Million Women Are Missing," p. 66.
[52] Jocelyn Kynch and Amartya Sen, "Indian Women: Well-being and Survival," *Cambridge Journal of Economics*, 7, no. 3/4 (September/December, 1983), p. 371.
[53] *Toward Equality*, p. 153.

not able to compete for jobs in the new industries that relied more heavily on technology and called for skills and education women did not have. Second, their presence in the modernized workforce was not viewed as desirable. The authors of *Toward Equality* commented: "opposition to increasing opportunities for women's participation in economic activities springs . . . from a conservative view regarding women's 'proper' role in society." This has led to economic marginal-ization of women in the unorganized sector where they are especially vulnerable to discrimination and exploitation.[54]

At the same time, women have made substantial gains in the profes-sions and in certain sections of the service industries. To conclude that these gains have been neutralized by women's disappearance from other areas of the economy is valid only in the statistical sense. However, women's growing importance in the service industries and professions focuses new attention on the problems associated with housing, transportation, sexual harassment, and conservative atti-tudes.[55]

The available data on the lives of working women challenges the assumption that women's position will automatically improve as the economy modernizes.[56] The very opposite seems to have happened; when work moves from the household to the factory or mill, it is women who lose. For example, the *beedi* (traditional cigarette) indus-try, infamous for its exploitation of women, is being mechanized. Instead of benefiting from higher wages and improved working condi-tions, women who work in this industry are losing their meager incomes.[57]

Recent data also calls into question assumptions about the benefits to women of family prosperity. Most social scientists interested in India's economic development have assumed that richer families would provide better food, clothing, and medical care for their daughters as well as their sons. Not so. In studies of child nutrition in rural areas, it

[54] *Ibid.*, pp. 149–50.
[55] Madhu Kishwar, "Sex Harassment and Slander as Weapons of Subjugation," *Manushi*, 68 (January–February, 1992), pp. 2–15.
[56] For example, see the articles in a special issue of *EPW*, 24, no. 17 (April 29, 1989), pp. ws1–ws44: C. Sridevi, "The Fisherwoman Financier"; Nirmala Banerjee, "Trends in Women's Employment, 1971–1981"; Jeemoi Unni, "Changes in Women's Employment in Rural Areas, 1961–1983"; Roger Jeffrey, Patricia Jeffrey and Andrew Lyon, "Taking Dung-Work Seriously"; and Miriam Sharma, "Women's Work is Never Done."
[57] Prayag Mehta, "We Are Made to Mortgage Our Children – Interviews With Women Workers of Vellore," *Manushi*, 22 (1985), pp. 14–17.

16 Entertainer, Rajasthan

17 Indian women police, n.d.

appears that well-off peasant families continue to spend on sons and deprive daughters. In other words, son preference persists even in prosperous families.[58]

"Female feticide," that is, the practice of aborting the female fetus after sex-determination tests, offers another challenge to the view that prosperity will benefit females. Mostly it is the middle class who condone this practice that makes possible both small families and sons.[59]

The third assumption challenged by recent studies is that employed women will demand changes in the system. In India there are organizations that strive for better working conditions for women, encourage labor unions to take the demands of women seriously, and publicize sexual harassment in the workplace. But they have not been able to change public policy. In those areas where women have organized they have had some impact on the system and been able to garner for them-

---

[58] Amartya Sen, *Commodities and Capabilities* (Amsterdam, North Holland, 1985), pp. 88–95.

[59] Uma Arora and Amrapali Desai, "Sex Determination Tests in Surat," *Manushi*, 60 (September–October, 1990), pp. 37–8; Manju Parikh, "Sex-Selective Abortion in India: Parental Choice or Sexist Discrimination," *Feminist Issues* (fall, 1990), pp. 19–32; Vibhuti Patel, "Sex-Determination and Sex Preselection Tests in India: Recent Techniques in Femicide," *Reproductive and Genetic Engineering*, 2, no. 2 (1989), pp. 111–19.

selves a greater share of the resources available. For example, SEWA of Ahmedabad has been successful in helping women obtain small loans to build their businesses. But improved economic status does not guarantee these women will become rebels against a system that oppresses them. Far more common is a tendency to seek status in the existing system and that may mean using hard-earned money for a daughter's dowry rather than her education.

THE CONTEMPORARY WOMEN'S MOVEMENT

The first women's movement, dubbed in retrospect "first-wave feminism,"[60] condemned tradition and religion for women's suffering and sought redress in education and legal change. It was feminist in the sense that leaders of the organizations forming this movement recognized women as oppressed because of their sex. They constructed women as biologically, psychologically, and spiritually different from men and based their claim for representation in public life on the complimentarity of this difference. Women, social feminists had argued, could bring a special knowledge of the household and family matters to forums where public policy was debated and formulated. This ideology fitted well with Gandhi's view of women and the nationalists' desire to bring women into the freedom movement. With the British gone, social feminism was incapable of either explaining women's subordination to men or providing a blueprint for change.

Beginning in the 1930s some feminists critiqued the patriarchal state and family system but they were unable to forcefully challenge social feminism. In the 1960s, women dissatisfied with the status quo joined struggles of the rural poor and industrial working class. Neera Desai has catalogued this activity and given it a place in the development of the contemporary women's movement:

Participation of women in the Naxalbari movement, anti-price rise demonstrations, Navnirman Youth Movement in Gujarat and Bihar, rural revolt in Dhule District in Maharashtra and Chipko Movement provided a backdrop for the ensuing struggles on women's issues.[61]

[60] Geraldine Forbes, "Caged Tigers: First Wave Feminists in India," *WSIQ*, 5, no. 6 (1979), pp. 525–36.
[61] Neera Desai, ed., *A Decade of Women's Movement in India* (Bombay, Himalaya Publishing House, 1988), p. vii.

Gail Omvedt has traced the origins of the contemporary women's movement to the early 1970s when rural and working women were first trained as leaders.[62] But there were few linkages at that time to the urban, intellectual women who could articulate the oppression of rural and working women in feminist terms. Most well-educated women would agree with Vina Mazumdar who recalled those years and said about herself and her academic associates: "We hadn't a clue."[63]

The UN declaration of International Women's Year and the International Women's Decade led to the appointment of the Guha Committee and its subsequent report. These two events coincided with a new spirit among individuals, groups, grass-roots activists, and researchers that made them search for ways to prevent "the oppression and exploitation, sexual harassment and domestic violence" they were now experiencing and which they knew were equally a fact of life for the agrarian poor, artisans, and tribal populations.[64]

Vina Mazumdar remembered her shock when she first read the data being assembled by the Guha Committee. Her second reaction was anger and the feeling that "something has to be done."[65] The heat and energy generated by *Toward Equality* and the emerging research data provided the intellectual foundation for a new women's movement.

The contemporary feminist movement emerged in the late 1970s and early 1980s. Replacing the all-India women's organizations were a large number of autonomous groups, joined not through the structure of a formal association, but through the connections of their leaders, an emerging feminist press, the general media's coverage of women's issues, and periodic large-scale meetings or conventions. Mary Katzenstein has defined the contemporary women's movement in India as similar to the women's movement in Europe in that feminist groups are dispersed, without one centralized organization, and with "political commitments and language . . . more leftist than liberal."[66] In Katzenstein's words this movement is made up of "a panoply of organizations" from all castes and classes, rural and urban areas, and involving both activist and academic women.[67] Autonomous organiza-

[62] Gail Omvedt, *Reinventing Revolution* (Armonk, N.Y., M. E. Sharpe, 1993), pp. 76–7.
[63] Quoted in Bumiller, *May You Be the Mother*, p. 124.
[64] A. R. Desai, "Women's Movement in India: An Assessment," *EPW*, 20, no. 23 (June 8, 1985), p. 992.   [65] Quoted in Bumiller, *May You Be the Mother*, p. 126.
[66] Mary Fainsod Katzenstein, "Organizing Against Violence: Strategies of the Indian Women's Movement," *Pacific Affairs*, 62, no. 1 (spring, 1989), p. 54.
[67] *Ibid.*, p. 54.

tions played a major role in awakening a new consciousness about women's problems. In October 1975 a coalition of activist women organized the United Women's Liberation Struggle Conference in Pune. Over 700 women, including agricultural laborers and professors, coolies and bank employees, teachers and students, met for two days to discuss a range of women's issues from dowry to clean drinking water.[68] This conference was followed by others in different regions of India. What is especially significant about these conferences is the class diversity and the breadth of issues under discussion. This diversity was only possible in what Omvedt has characterized as "a new atmosphere of cultural radicalism" that made possible a critique of the Ram–Sita paradigm.[69]

This women's movement continued to focus on traditional practices, beliefs, and institutions as the source of oppression. It also attended to violence against women, the institutional framework for the maintenance of gender differences, and the impact of the economic situation on the day-to-day lives of women.

One of the first steps taken by the leaders of this movement was to break the silence: to expose the "various categories of humiliation, atrocities, tortures and individual and mass assault to which they [women] were subjected."[70] This meant breaking through the image of the ideal Indian woman as accommodating, self-sacrificing, and devoted to serving her family. It also necessitated an attack on the family. At the same time, newly vocal activist-scholars stepped up their criticism of the growing powers of the central state. The women committed to fomenting change were now critiquing the family, the government, and the larger society.

Exposing gendered violence began in the mid-1970s but escalated toward the end of the decade. In 1979 a small group of women in New Delhi began to publish *Manushi, A Journal about Women and Society* in Hindi and English. This has now become India's premier feminist journal, treating specifically women's issues, such as sexual harassment or the adjustment expected of a new bride; violence against women, in the home and as a weapon of political and social control; history and literature on, about, and by women; and social/political/economic issues such as communalism and public health policy.

In 1980 the Mathura case shocked middle-class women into demon-

---

[68] Omvedt, *Reinventing Revolution*, p. 82.   [69] *Ibid.*, p. 83.
[70] A. R. Desai, "Women's Movement," p. 992.

strating against police brutality and government complacency. Mathura, a low-caste girl of between fourteen and sixteen years of age, was detained by the police for questioning and raped in the police station. Released, Mathura complained about the rape but the policemen claimed she had consented to sexual relations. The sessions judge believed the policemen, but the Nagpur branch of the Bombay High Court found them guilty of rape and imposed prison sentences. The incident happened in 1972. Six years late the Supreme Court reversed this judgment since there was no evidence Mathura had resisted.

Professor Upendra Baxi of Delhi University Law School noticed this case in a law journal and together with three colleagues, Raghunath Kelkar and Lotika Sarkar of Delhi University and Vasudha Dhagamwar of Pune University, wrote an open letter to the Chief Justice urging him to review the case.[71] Women's organizations demanded the case be reopened. When the Supreme Court dismissed these petitions on technical grounds, women in New Delhi and Bombay demonstrated in the streets shouting: "Supreme Court, Supreme Court. Against you, where can we report?"[72]

The government appointed a Law Commission to study the problem and suggest amendments to the existing law and in 1980 a criminal law amendment bill was introduced. This was deemed unsatisfactory. When the Supreme Court reviewed the issue, it concluded: "the uncorroborated testimony of a rape victim should not be ordinarily doubted."[73] Women activists had wanted rape recognized as a violent crime but knew this legislation would not protect women from rape.[74]

Rape was only one issue that galvanized the contemporary women's movement. "Dowry murders," the term used to refer to the deaths by burning of young married women by their in-laws, emerged as a new phenomenon in the late 1970s. One of the first protests against these incidents occurred in July of 1979 when 200 angry demonstrators shouted slogans in front of a house in a prosperous New Delhi suburb. A young wife of twenty-four years had burned to death in her father-in-law's home and the crowd were demanding a police investigation of this "accident." Earlier that evening the woman had

---

[71] Subhadra Butalia, "The Rape of Mathura," *Eve's Weekly* (March 8–14, 1980), pp. 10–13.
[72] "The Rape Rap," *India Today* (June 30, 1983), p. 44.   [73] *Ibid.*, p. 44.
[74] "The Raped Still Tremble," *Probe India* (March 1983), p. 53; Vibhuti Patel, "Recent Communal Carnage and Violence Against Women in Connivance with the State Machinery," presented to the House of Commons, UK (February 2, 1993).

gone to her parent's home and told them her husband wanted a scooter. She also told them her in-laws were mistreating her. When her husband came to take her home, she resisted and he beat her in the presence of her brother. Her brother called the police but they would not interfere. Hours later she burned to death in a kitchen fire. Many of the neighbors refused to believe this was an accident and those protesting accused the dead woman's in-laws of committing a "dowry murder."[75]

In the following months women activists began to pay particular attention to the deaths of young, newly married women. The number of deaths attributed to accidental fires was extraordinary. There were 358 such death in Delhi in 1979, less than fifty were suicides, twenty-three were labeled "dowry burnings," and the remainder were classified as "accidental." Everyone who investigated these deaths heard from grieving families and shocked neighbors eager to expose these accidents as grisly murders. Families produced evidence in the form of letters from their daughters about continuous harassment and demands for additional dowry. Neighbors had their own stories to tell: of wife abuse, of seeing young women with their saris on fire run into courtyards screaming for help, and of hasty funeral services. Only rarely were the police involved and on most of those occasions they seemed to concur that the deaths had been suicides or accidents.[76]

The number of accidental deaths that fitted this pattern increased to 466 in Delhi by 1981 and 537 by 1982.[77] In 1982 a group of women activists in New Delhi set up Saheli, a small-scale women's center, in a garage in a south Delhi residential colony. None of the volunteers who staffed this space believed they would be able to stop dowry murders but they hoped to provide counsel and shelter for endangered women. Saheli volunteers began to keep records on the deaths of women and

---

[75] Suaina Low, "The Gentle Stirrings of their Discontent," *Imprint* (May 1983), p. 38.
[76] The literature on "dowry deaths" is extensive. For example, see Chairanya Kalbag, "Until Death Do Us Part," *India Today* (July 15, 1982), pp. 52–3; *Saheli Newsletter*, 1, no. 2 (June, 1984); Lotika Sarkar, "Feeble Laws Against Dowry," *Facets*, 3, no. 3 (May–June, 1984), pp. 2–5; Sevanti Ninan, "At the Crossroads of the Courts," *Express Magazine* (November 27, 1983); Vimla Farooqui, "Dowry as a Means of Acquiring Wealth and Status," *HOW* (May, 1983), pp. 11–12, 16; "Daughters, Dowry and Deaths," *Newsletter, Research Unit on Women's Studies*, SNDT Women's University, 4, no. 4 (November, 1983), pp. 1–2; Law Commission of India, *Ninety-first Report on Dowry Deaths and Law Reform* (August 10, 1983). There have also been numerous articles in *Manushi*.
[77] These numbers were obtained from Saheli, a New Delhi organization. They cite their source as police records.

whenever possible intervened with the police to demand more thorough investigations.[78]

Saheli was the first of many small centers established to address issues of domestic violence and harassment. "Dowry murders" were reported daily in the capital's newspapers, discussed in all the established women's organizations, and addressed by the editors of important feminist publications.

Outside Delhi, cities and towns all over India began to report unusually high numbers of young newly married women dying following domestic fires. The numbers never approached those in Delhi but they pointed to a widespread pattern of violence against women. For those who have studied dowry murders two conclusions seem apparent: these deaths are related to the larger issue of the low valuation of women, and consumerism has brought about a new way of exploiting women's dependency. In other words, dowry deaths are about both tradition and modernity.

As the campaign against these deaths escalated, politicians hastened to condemn the practice and blame it on non-compliance with the Dowry Prohibition Act of 1961. Pramila Dandavate introduced a private member's bill in 1980 to amend the laws against dowry. Activists agreed that additional legislation was in order.

By August of 1982 the Joint Committee of the Houses (chaired by Shrimati Krishna Sahi), appointed to examine the question of the working of the Dowry Prohibition Act, presented their report to the Lok Sabha.[79] During subsequent hearings the Law Commission of India presented a report titled "Dowry Deaths and Law Reform." These hearings produced a bill in 1984 that was then amended, and passed, in 1986. This legislation increased the punishment for accepting dowry and decreed that in cases where a woman died an unnatural death, her property would devolve on her children or be returned to her parents. The campaign was over, new legislation had been passed, but dowry deaths continue.[80]

In September of 1987 the death of Roop Kanwar, an eighteen-year-

---

[78] *Saheli Newsletter*, 1, no. 2 (June, 1984); *Saheli Report* (November 25, 1983). Both were privately circulated.

[79] Report of the Joint Committee of the Houses to Examine the Question of the Working of the Dowry Prohibition Act, 1961, C.B. (II), no. 333 (New Delhi, Lok Sabha Secretariat, 1982).

[80] Flavia Agnes, "Protecting Women Against Violence? Review of a Decade of Legislation, 1980–1989," *EPW*, 27, no. 17 (April 5, 1992), pp. ws19–ws33.

old woman burned to death with her husband's corpse in the village of Deorala in Rajasthan, claimed the attention of feminists. Roop Kanwar was hailed as a sati, that is, a virtuous women who had chosen death instead of widowhood. Sati was abolished in 1829 and as Veena Oldenburg has written:

With the law in place and enforced, the act of committing sati – whether the widow's participation was voluntary or coerced –was shorn of all mystification, glory, glamour, and ritual significance, and adjudged to be simply a crime.[81]

Nevertheless, hundreds attended this sati-style death and cheered as Roop Kanwar burned to death. On September 16 the *chunari mahotsava*, a ceremony that commemorates a recent sati and consecrates the ground where it took place, was performed with an estimated 500,000 people in attendance. While Rajasthani men guarded the site of the pyre, enterprising businessmen sold photographs and souvenirs, and clever politicians reverentially visited the spot.[82]

Roop Kanwar's death mobilized feminists and liberals to protest this so-called sati as a crime of violence, called "cold-blooded murder" by some. They condemned society for neglecting and mistreating widows, thereby forcing some women to prefer death to the living hell of widowhood.[83] For the first time in history Indian feminists made the burning of women their issue and declared they would not stand by while their sisters were murdered in the name of some distant and purportedly hallowed tradition. The government reacted with legislation. Parliament passed a Sati Prevention Bill, a repeat of the 1829 legislation, and outlawed its glorification. According to Veena Oldenburg this law obfuscates the difference between voluntary and coerced sati, defines sati as a women's crime, and makes the other people involved in the sati guilty only of abetting the woman's act.[84]

There was a sensational aspect to the Mathura case, "dowry deaths," and the Deorala sati that attracted both Indian media and foreign attention. Young single women at colleges and universities and working at jobs in cities read about these incidents, met and talked about them, and decided to take action. In major Indian cities street theater, demonstra-

---

[81] Veena Talwar Oldenburg, "The Roop Kanwar Case: Feminist Responses," *Sati, the Blessing and the Curse,* ed. John S. Hawley (New York, Oxford University Press, 1994), p. 102.   [82] "A Pagan Sacrifice," *India Today* (October 15, 1987), pp. 58–63.   [83] "Sati – Cold Blooded Murder," *Research Center Women's Studies Newsletter,* 8, nos. 3 and 4 (December 1987), pp. 1–14.   [84] Oldenburg, "The Roop Kanwar Case," p. 126.

tions, documentation centers, and new organizations emerged.[85] And in the rural areas new groups and coalitions formed to protest exploitative work and issues of violence.

The government responded to the urban campaigns about rape, dowry deaths, and sati murders with legislation. Flavia Agnes commented on the startling number and extent of the enactments:

> If oppression could be tackled by passing laws, then this decade would be adjudged a golden period for Indian women . . . Almost every single campaign against violence on women resulted in new legislation.[86]

Unfortunately, hard questions about the deeper causes of this violence and the ability of the law to remedy the situation were rarely asked. The result has been a decade of extraordinary legislation and subsequent despair because these laws have meant so little in practice. Once passed this legislation depended for enforcement on men whose view of women and their place in the world had not changed. In the process of "breaking the silence" feminists had turned to the government for help. The government responded and assured women it could and would be their protector. Now it appears the "protector" has used women's issues for its own ends. Real issues have not been addressed but the central state has emerged with more control of people's private lives.[87]

Even as questions of violence against women have brought a new and significant focus to the women's movement other issues have fragmented this new solidarity. The gravest challenges have come from a revitalized and gendered communalism as illustrated by the Shah Bano case and the dispute over the mosque at Ayodhya.

In April of 1985, the Supreme Court granted Shah Bano, a divorced Muslim woman, the right to financial support from her former husband. The Muslim community protested. This was the final decision in a long series of suits and appeals in which her ex-husband argued that he had discharged his duty according to Muslim law. The Supreme Court, in reaching their decision, cited Section 125 of the Criminal Procedure Code that requires husbands with means to support destitute ex-wives.[88]

---

[85] Saumitra Banerjee, "Women against Rape," *Sunday* (March 30, 1980), pp. 40–3; Subhadra Butalia, "Taking it to the Streets," *The Times of India* (March 2, 1980), p. III.
[86] Agnes, *Protecting Women*, p. ws19.   [87] *Ibid.*
[88] Zoya Hasan, " Communalism, State Policy, and the Question of Women's Rights in Contemporary India," *Bulletin of Concerned Scholars*, 25, no. 4 (October–December, 1993), pp. 9–10; Zoya Hasan, "Minority Identity, State Policy and the Political Process," *Forging Identities*, ed. Zoya Hasan (New Delhi, Kali for Women, 1993), pp. 59–73.

Very quickly what had been perceived as a women's issue became a communal issue as Muslims challenged the right of the courts to interfere in their law. Shah Bano's ex-husband stated that he had done whatever Muslim law required. Throughout India, conservative Muslims argued that this decision was an attack on their identity as a religious minority.[89] Feminists, liberals, and conservative Hindus denounced Muslims for their backward laws. Just as the British had judged their treatment of women superior to that of Hindus so, in the mid-1980s, Hindus argued that their women were treated better than Muslim women.

In 1986 Rajiv Gandhi's Congress government introduced the Muslim Women's (Protection of Rights in Divorce) Bill denying Muslim women redress under Section 125 and naming the natal family responsible for support in cases of destitution.[90] Outside parliament, Muslim women's groups and Indian women's organizations, notably, the National Federation of Indian Women, the All-India Democratic Women's Association, and the Mahila Dakshata Samiti, protested against the bill. But inside parliament Begum Abida Ahmed, a Muslim woman in the Congress Party, expressed her shock that a self-respecting woman would want to beg maintenance from a husband who had divorced her. Begum Abida Ahmed was no different from her female, or male, colleagues in her acceptance of the party line.[91]

Zoya Hasan argues that Rajiv Gandhi's government deliberately supported this bill in an effort to pacify Muslims angry about the reopening of the disputed Ayodhya site. The consequence, for women, was denial of the distinction between minority identity and gender identity.[92]

The Ayodhya mosque referred to above was a sixteenth-century mosque allegedly constructed on the site of the god Ram's birthplace. The original temple, so Hindu militants contend, was destroyed during the reign of the Mughal emperor Babar. The Ram Janambhoomi movement, a movement to destroy the mosque and rebuild a Hindu temple, was led by the Rashtriya Swayamseval Sangh, a militaristic Hindu organization. In 1986 they were given permission to hold prayer meetings at this site. The Bharatiya Janata Party (BJP), a Hindu nationalist

---

[89] Hasan, "Communalism," p. 11.
[90] *Ibid.*; Madhu Kishwar, "Pro Women or Anti Muslim? The Shahbano Controversy," *Manushi*, 32 (January–February, 1986), pp. 4–13.
[91] Rita Manchanda, "Women in Parliament," *Manushi*, no. 47 (July–August 1988), p. 29.
[92] Hasan, "Communalism," p. 14.

party, took advantage of this situation to garner support for itself. Tension escalated, communal clashes increased, and on December 6, 1992, Hindu militants destroyed the Ayodhya mosque. December of 1992 and January 1993 witnessed a series of riots and bombings.

Women belonging to the Rashtra Sevika Samiti, the women's wing of the Hindu right, have been at the forefront of attacks on Muslims.[93] Amrita Basu has focused her attention on two important leaders of Hindu nationalism: Uma Bharati and Sadhvi Rithambara, both "single, militant, young women of modest backgrounds" skilled at inciting crowds to violence.[94] Appropriating the rhetoric of the feminist movement of the 1980s, the BJP has made violence against women its rallying call. Unfortunately even this issue has been given a communal twist as Muslim men are accused of raping Hindu women.[95] Tanika Sarkar warns observers of the Indian scene about the "dazzling visibility" of Sadhvi Rithambara, Uma Bharati, and Vijayraje Scindia. These women, she observes, come out into the streets and engage in violence only when men determine their presence useful.[96] The activist roles assumed by these women do not challenge or violate conventional norms defining dutiful daughters and faithful wives.[97] What is the impact of the public roles of these women on Indian women generally and on the women who participate? Tanika Sarkar's answer to the first question is negative: "No feminist can possibly argue that the movement can contribute anything to the broad rights of women."[98] However, she concedes that individuals engaged in protest might gain bargaining power within their homes. Sarkar ends with a word of caution about valorizing the activism of right-wing women: "this limited yet real empowerment leads them to a complicity with fascist intolerance and violence, towards the creation of an authoritarian, antidemocratic social and political order."[99]

The new visibility of women in the right-wing movement, appropri-

[93] One of the first serious articles to appear on this topic was Tanika Sarkar's "The Woman as Communal Subject: Rashtrasevika Samiti and Ram Janambhoomi Movement," *EPW*, 26, no. 35 (August 31, 1991), pp. 2057–62. In 1993 Amrita Basu was guest editor for a special issue of the *Bulletin of Concerned Scholars* (October–December, 1993) on women and religious nationalism in India, which included articles by Zoya Hasan, Tanika Sarkar, Amrita Basu, and Paola Bacchetta.

[94] Amrita Basu, "Feminism Inverted: The Real Women and Gendered Imagery of Hindu Nationalism," *Bulletin of Concerned Scholars*, p. 26.

[95] Basu, "Feminism Inverted," p. 29.

[96] Tanika Sarkar, "The Women of the Hindutva Brigade," *Bulletin of Concerned Scholars*, p. 20.   [97] Basu, "Feminism Inverted," p. 36.   [98] Sarkar, "The Women," p. 23.

[99] *Ibid.*

ating the issues of the contemporary feminist movement in their demonstrations against Muslims, is disturbing. It has had a dampening effect on the women's movement that was so buoyant and optimistic in the 1980s. It demonstrates that the present-day availability of women for a variety of causes is also part of the historical legacy. There is now a complicated mix of women playing public roles – leftist women, moderates, conservatives, right-wing women – all appropriating the trappings of feminism but without commitment to a vision of gender justice and human rights voiced by the authors of *Toward Equality*. The outcome remains to be seen.

CONCLUSIONS

There would have been no women's movement in India if Indian men in the nineteenth century had not been concerned with modernizing women's roles. They focused their attention on certain issues: sati, child marriage, widow remarriage and, most important of all, female education. They saw the world through a particular caste/class lens and the net effect of their efforts was to bring women, especially women from their own families, into the new world created by colonial rule. The decisions made by these men meant that women, whether they wanted to or not, would become part of the new society.

Those women who liked this new world thrived in it and began to develop worlds of their own. Sex segregation and norms of female seclusion offered them an opportunity to form their own organizations relatively free from male tutelage though not free from patriarchy. They explained their organizations, their work, and their demands for a greater say in policy-making with an ideology I have labeled social feminism.

The first-wave feminist movement, motivated by this ideology and working through women's organizations, presented demands for women's rights. The involvement of many of these women in the nationalist struggle tied women's rights to the freedom movement through a uniquely Indian feminist nationalism. It was an ideology that both Gandhi and Nehru supported and which, officially at least, became Congress policy.

After independence from British rule, the Indian Constitution and basic doctrines promised equality, participation in nation building, and a new valuation of women. This did not mean women had attained equality. Rights, Jawaharlal Nehru warned women, are rarely given away, they must be won.

In the aftermath of Independence many women were pleased with what they had gained. The ruling Congress Party paid lip service to women's concerns, set up the National Social Welfare Board to parcel out money to a host of social welfare projects, and looked to the all-India women's organizations for help in carrying out its mission. When asked to send representatives to planning committees, women from main-stream organizations assumed the problems of their own class had been solved and only poor women needed help. Simplistic schemes, overly dependent on volunteerism, were developed without detailed knowledge of the groups to be served. Women in communist and socialist parties echoed the party line regarding the alignment of power and the need for revolution but they too succumbed to their male leaders. Despite their participation in these organizations and parties, there were many women who remained clear-headed about the actual conditions of women and what needed to be done.

Toward Equality was the wake-up call. The women who wrote it asked how a country that called itself democratic could continue to live with worsening conditions for half its population. This report and the subsequent studies alerted educated, middle-class women to the worst inequities in their society. And as these newly awakened women carried out research projects, wrote and spoke about these problems, and attempted to institute new programs, they too faced new challenges. Their own institutions and families were less supportive than expected and the recipients of this attention were not always grateful.

The contemporary feminist movement, beginning in the late 1970s and still alive today, has brought women's issues to the attention of all Indians. Feminists, galvanized by endemic violence against women, developed new organizations and new institutions in the 1980s.

Violence against women was not a new issue but whenever it had been raised in the past, it was recast to serve a male political agenda. Sati in the nineteenth century became a religious issue. Whether or not husbands were entitled to conjugal rights with prepubescent girls became a debate about the fitness of Indians to govern themselves. Katherine Mayo was purportedly concerned about the health and well-being of India's females but her diatribe against Indians supported British officials opposed to responsible government for Indians. When Indian women freedom-fighters were sexually molested, these incidents were portrayed as attacks on Indian manhood. The facts and consequences of violence against women were systematically ignored as men fought men in the political arena. But domestic violence was not an invention of the colonial debate. Historical evidence suggests an earlier version of dowry murders in the "accidental" burnings of women in kitchen fires and the "suicides" of women who jumped down wells. During the struggle for independence from British rule, whenever Indian women raised issues of domestic violence, male leaders urged them to give priority to the nationalist struggle. After Independence, women leaders were asked to give priority to nation-building. Finally, these issues have had a hearing.

It would be naive to write as if all were well with the women's movement in India. The separatist movement in the Punjab, the cycles of terrorist acts and repression in this state and other parts of India, the revived communalism and pogroms against Muslims, and the rise of the Hindu right have all disrupted the women's movement. Some feminists have found it necessary to put these issues first and these movements have created ideological divisions between women. After the euphoria of the 1980s Indian women who worked with the new organizations entered the 1990s disappointed in the new legislation and troubled by ethnic and communal conflict.

Indian women at the end of the twentieth century would argue that they still have a long way to go to attain gender justice. The issues of the moment and the unsolved problems must not be allowed to negate the victories of the past. It is important to temper the interpretation of the present with an appreciation of the enormous sacrifices Indian women have made to bring about change. This is not the first time that legislative measures have been found wanting or that women's concerns have been set aside in favor of other issues. As I have tried to indicate in previous chapters, women's education and political action have altered India's social and political landscape. Women have moved from being objects of legislation to initiators. For many women the family no longer exercises total control over their destinies. A general awakening has begun and it cannot be permanently suppressed.

BIBLIOGRAPHIC ESSAY

The sources used for writing this book include official government records, newspapers, collected speeches and writings, reports and minutes, memoirs and autobiographies, oral histories, personal letters, diaries, and songs, as well as monographs and articles with Indian women as their subject. It is particularly significant to note that women's history is being written now and gender is fast becoming as much a tool of analysis as class, caste, and race. Articles and books are published daily offering new and fresh insights about women's lives and how gender shapes and is shaped by the wider social and political context.

The critical year for the history of Indian woman was 1975. Between 1975 and 1979 thirty books on women were published, as many as the total produced over the previous several decades. A bibliography of works on Indian women in English published in 1976 incorporated 800 references; four years later Carol Sakala's *Women of South Asia: A Guide to Resources* (Millwood, N.Y., Kraus International Publications, 1980) registered 4,627 entries, and the literature has continued to proliferate. Unfortunately the new literature on Indian women and questions related to gender in India is not readily available. Much of it is published in newer, and sometimes inaccessible journals, presented at conferences, or published in collected works.

There are a few bibliographies which focus specifically on women in India: Kalpana Dasgupta, *Women on the Indian Scene* (Delhi, Abhinav Publications, 1976); Carol Sakala, *Women of South Asia*; Harishida Pandit, *Women of India: An Annotated Bibliography* (New York, Garland, 1985) but these works are all sadly out of date. Barbara Ramusack's "Women in South and Southeast Asia," in *Restoring Women to History* (Bloomington, Ind., Organization of American Historians, 1988) is extremely useful as a summary of the main periods and issues, and includes a bibliography. This has been revised and will be published as "Women in South and Southeast Asia," in Barbara Ramusack and Sharon Sievers, *Women in Asia* (Indiana University Press). In "From Symbol to Diversity: The Historical Literature on Indian Women," *South Asia Research*, 10, no. 2 (November, 1990), Ramusack discusses the development of both women's history and feminist history in South Asia and discusses key works. Aparna Basu's "Women's History in India: An Historiographical Survey," was published in *Writing Women's History: International Perspectives,* ed. Karen Offen *et al.* (London, Macmillan, 1991). Still, there is a crying need for a comprehensive bibliographic work to guide readers to the many articles and papers now available.

There are very few histories of Indian women. For years A. S. Altekar's *The Position of Women in Hindu Civilization* (Delhi, Motilal Banarsidass, 1959, first published in 1938), was the only such book available. Phallocentric in the extreme, this book discussed male texts on and male attitudes towards women. Neera Desai's *Woman in Modern India* (Bombay, Vora and Co., 1957) was the first social history of Indian women with women as its subject. Padmini Sengupta's *The Story of Women in India* (New Delhi, Indian Book Company, 1974) offered a journalist's panoramic sweep of Indian history from ancient times until the 1970s. Although not a narrative, the *Dictionary of National Biography*, 4 vols., ed. S. P. Sen (Calcutta, 1972), is valuable for its short biographies of prominent women.

International Women's Year, 1975, stimulated and reinforced a growing interest in women's history. As a consequence a number of books were published focusing on women with some attention to their history. Tara Ali Baig, *India's Woman Power* (New Delhi, Chand, 1976); B. R. Nanda, ed., *Indian Women: From Purdah to Modernity* (New Delhi, Vikas Publishing, 1976); Devika Jain, *Indian Women* (New Delhi, Publications Division, Ministry of Information and Broadcasting, GOI, 1975); and Alfred deSouza, *Women in Contemporary India: Traditional Images and Changing Roles* (New Delhi, Manohar Book Service, 1975) all suit this genre. The three later books, collections of papers by women and men who study India, all include useful historical articles.

Toward Equality, the report of the Committee on the Status of Women in India (New Delhi, Government of India Ministry of Education and Social Welfare, 1974) is not a history but employs an historical perspective in assessing women's status. The impact of this report on the research done on women in India has been significant. First, the report made scholars aware of the extent to which they had ignored the lives of ordinary women. Much of the scholarship that followed this report sought to compensate by focusing on the lives and labor of women from the lower socio-economic strata. Very little historical writing was done between 1975 and the late 1980s while economic and sociological studies flourished.

The late 1980s and the 1990s have seen the publication of a number of historical works on women. *Economic and Political Weekly* (*EPW*) began its bi-annual "Review of Women's Studies" in April, 1986. In April and October of every year since then, *EPW* has included five or six articles on women, many of them treating historical topics. Throughout the last twelve years *EPW* has provided a valuable forum for the discussion of new research in women's studies. The publication of *Recasting Women: Essays in Colonial History*, ed. Kumkum Sangari and Sudesh Vaid and *"We were Making History": Life Stories of Women in the Telangana People's Struggle* by Stree Shakti Sanghatana, in New Delhi by Kali for Women, both in 1989, signaled the directions that women's history would take. *Recasting Women* is a collection of articles by historians turning new theoretical perspectives on conventional questions and *"We were Making History"* gives voice to women participating in the Telangana struggle. *Women and Culture,* ed. Kumkum Sangari and Sudesh Vaid, a valuable collection of seventeen short articles by historians addressing questions of women's role in Indian history, was first published in

1985. It had been extremely difficult to find until it was republished in 1994 by the Research Center for Women's Studies at SNDT Women's University in Bombay. 1995 saw the publication of two new valuable collections of articles on women: *From the Seams of History: Essays on Indian Women,* ed. Bharati Ray (Delhi, Oxford University Press, 1995), and *Indian Women: Myth and Reality*, ed. Jasodhara Bagchi (Hyderabad, Sangam Books, 1995).

Throughout the writing of this book I drew heavily on two general histories of modern India, Sumit Sarkar, *Modern India, 1885–1947* (Delhi, Macmillan India, 1983) and Judith M. Brown, *Modern India* (Delhi, Oxford University Press, 1985).

In writing chapter 1, I used a variety of sources. The British view of India as backward because of its gender ideology is best presented by James Mill, *The History of British India,* 2 vols. (New York, Chelsea House, 1968). There are numerous missionary accounts of the degraded condition of Indian women such as Revd. E. Storrow, *Our Indian Sisters* (London, The Religious Tract Society, n.d.) and Mrs. Marcus B. Fuller, *The Wrongs of Indian Womanhood* (Edinburgh, Oliphant, Anderson and Ferrier, 1902). Equally instructive are the journalist Mary Francis Billington's *Woman in India* (London, Amarko Book Agency, 1895) and the ethnographic volume *The People of India,* by Sir Herbert Hope Risley, 2nd edn. edited by W. Crooke (Delhi, Oriental Books Reprint Corp., 1969).

Among studies of reform in nineteenth-century India, Charles H. Heimsath's *Indian Nationalism and Hindu Social Reform* (Princeton, N.J., Princeton University Press, 1964) is valuable for its attention to reforms affecting women. Kenneth W. Jones' *Socio-Religious Reform Movements in British India* (Cambridge, Cambridge University Press, 1989) is a regionally based history of religious reform movements in India. David Kopf's *The Brahmo Samaj and the Shaping of the Modern Indian Mind* (Princeton, N.J., Princeton University Press, 1979) is the most thorough analysis of the Brahmo Samaj. Meredith Borthwick's *The Changing Role of Women in Bengal, 1849–1905* (Princeton, N.J., Princeton University Press, 1985), looks at topics salient to women to assess the changes experienced by the women in the Brahmo Samaj. Ghulam Murshid, *Reluctant Debutante* (Rajshahi, Rajshahi University, Bangladesh, 1983) treats the same topic. Judith E. Walsh looks closely at the late nineteenth century "advice" literature to Bengali women in "What Women Learned When Men Gave Them Advice: Rewriting Patriarchy in Late-Nineteenth Century Bengal," *Journal of Asian Studies,* v.56, no. 3 (August 1997), pp. 641–677. Vina Mazumdar's article, "The Social Reform Movement in India – From Ranade to Nehru," in *Indian Women: From Purdah to Modernity,* ed. B. R. Nanda, considers male social reformers concerned with women's issues in the nineteenth and twentieth centuries.

There are numerous studies of Indian reformers. S. N. Mukherjee's "Raja Rammohun Roy and the Status of Women in Bengal in the Nineteenth Century," in *Women in India and Nepal,* ed. Michael Allen and S. N. Mukherjee (Canberra, Australian National University, 1982), is a superb article on the "father of modern India." For Rammohun Roy we are fortunate in having translations of his writings, *Raja Rammohun Roy Letters and Documents,* ed. Rama Prasad Chanda and Jatindra Kumar Majumdar (Delhi, Anmol Publications, 1987). Isvarachandra Vidyasagar's *Marriage of Hindu Widows* (1855) has been translated by K. P. Bagchi (Calcutta, K. P. Bagchi and Co., 1976). Two studies of this reformer are Asok Sen's, *Iswar Chandra Vidyasagar and his Elusive Milestones* (Calcutta, Riddlu-India, 1977), and S. K. Bose, *Iswar Chandra Vidyasagar* (New Delhi, National Book Trust, 1969). The *Autobiography of Kandukuri Veeresalingam Pantulu,* trans. Dr. V. Ramakrishna Rao and Dr. T. Rama Rao, 2 parts (Rajamundry, Addepally and Co., n.d.) is complemented by Karen I. Leonard and John Leonard's "Social Reform and Women's Participation in Political Culture: Andhra and Madras," *The Extended Family,* ed. Gail Minault (Columbus, Mo., South Asia Books, 1981) and "Rao Bahadur Mr. K. Virasalingam Pantulu and His Wife," *ILM,* 2 (September, 1902). Neera Desai's *Social Change in Gujarat* (Bombay, Vora and Co., 1978) focuses specifically on Gujarati reformers in the nineteenth and twentieth centuries. Pratima Asthana's *Women's Movement in India* (Delhi, Vikas Publishing House, 1974) takes as its subject both the principal male reformers and some of the women pioneers.

The literature assessing the colonial experience is especially rich. I have always liked Francis G. Hutchins, *The Illusion of Permanence: British Imperialism in India* (Princeton, N.J., Princeton University Press, 1967) for his discussion of British motives. Mrinalini Sinha's "'Manliness': A Victorian Ideal and Colonial Policy in Late Nineteenth Century Bengal," Ph.D. dissertation, SUNY Stonybrook (1988), published in 1995 by Manchester University Press as *Colonial Masculinity: The "manly Englishman" and the "effeminate Bengali" in the late nineteenth century,* affords a feminist's view of the role of gender in the making and carrying out of colonial policy. Tapan Raychaudhuri's *Europe Reconsidered* (Delhi, Oxford University Press, 1988) shows us Europe through the eyes of nineteenth-century Bengali intellectuals. Partha Chatterjee's *Nationalist Thought and the Colonial World* (Delhi, Oxford University Press, 1986) discusses the interaction between Western and Indian ideas in the development of Indian nationalism. Sudipta Kaviraj's article, "On the Construction of Colonial Power: Structure, Discourse, Hegemony," *Contesting Colonial Hegemony,* ed. Dagmar Engels and Shula Marks (London, German Historical Institute, 1994) is a fascinating discussion of the interplay between consent and coercion in colonial India. Although none of these books is about women, they define the setting for reforms aimed specifically at women. Partha Chatterjee's influential article, "The Nationalist Resolution of the Women's Question," in *Recasting Women: Essays on Colonial History,* focuses on the waning of the woman question in nationalist politics. His *The Nation and Its Fragments: Colonial and Postcolonial Histories* (Princeton, NJ, Princeton University Press, 1993) includes two excellent chapters: "The Nation and Its Women" and "Women and the Nation."

What we know about women's lives before the nineteenth century is primarily textual. A significant contribution to our literature on the traditional role of women is I. Julia Leslie's *The Perfect Wife* (Delhi, Oxford University

Press, 1989). A feminist article challenging the class orientation of such documents is Uma Chakravarti's "Whatever Happened to the Vedic *Dasi?*" in *Recasting Women.*

Women Writing in India, vol. I: *600 BC to the Early Twentieth Century*, ed. Susie Tharu and K. Lalita (New York, The Feminist Press, 1991), translations of writings by women, makes a valuable contribution to our study of history. Malavika Karlekar, *Voices From Within* (Delhi, Oxford University Press, 1991) selects from nineteenth-century writings by Bengali women. Tanika Sarkar has written about Rassundari Devi in "A Book of Her Own. A Life of Her Own: Autobiography of a Nineteenth-Century Woman," *History Workshop Journal*, 36 (autumn, 1993). There are also memoirs and autobiographies of women reformers and social workers, for example, Ramabai Ranade, *Himself, The Autobiography of a Hindu Lady* (New York, Longman, Green and Co., 1938) and Shudha Mazumdar, *Memoirs of an Indian Woman*, ed. Geraldine Forbes (New York, M. E. Sharpe, 1989).

The literature dealing with sati has flourished since Roop Kanwar's death in 1987. One of the most direct and readable articles is I. Julia Leslie's "Suttee or Sati: Victim or Victor?" *Bulletin,* Center for the Study of World Religions, Harvard University, 14, no. 2 (1987/1988). V. N. Datta has written *Sati, A Historical, Social and Philosophical Enquiry into the Hindu Rite of Widow Burning* (Delhi, Manohar, 1988). A. Yang's "Whose Sati? Widow Burning in Early Nineteenth-Century India," *Journal of Women's History*, 1, no. 2 (1989) is an interesting interrogation of the documents available on sati. The most recent book on this topic is John Stratton Hawley's *Sati, the Blessing and the Curse* (New York, Oxford University Press, 1994). Lata Mani's writings on sati have focused attention on the discourse surrounding this custom; see "Contentious Traditions: The Debate on *Sati* in Colonial India, in *Recasting Women.*

Other topics of social reform have not yet received the attention that has been lavished on sati. However, Rosalind O'Hanlon's work on Tarabai Shinde, *A Comparison Between Women and Men: Tarabai Shinde and the Critique of Gender Relations in Colonial India* (Madras, Oxford University Press, 1994) offers new insights into the problems of women and women's consciousness about their own oppression. O'Hanlon also discusses Tarabai Shinde's writings in "Issues of Widowhood: Gender and Resistance in Colonial Western India," *Contesting Power*, ed. Douglas Haynes and Gyan Prakash (Delhi, Oxford University Press, 1991). Lucy Carroll's work on law is a welcome and significant contribution to social history. For this period see her "Law, Custom, and Statutory Social Reform: The Hindu Widow's Remarriage Act of 1856," *Women in Colonial India*, ed. J. Krishnamurty (Delhi, Oxford University Press, 1989). Sudhir Chandra's *Enslaved Daughters: Colonialism, Law and Women's Rights* (Delhi, Oxford University Press, 1998) is an exhaustive study of the Rukhmabai case.

Research for chapter 2 was difficult because so few histories of women's education have been written. Of value in establishing a baseline view of the status of female education in the early nineteenth century are William Adam's reports on vernacular education in Bengal and Bihar, submitted to the government in 1835, 1836, and 1838. Joseph Diamond's *One Teacher, One School* (New Delhi, Biblia Imper Private Ltd., 1983) includes Adam's second report on Rajshahi and his third report on Bengal and Bihar. One of the few books on women's education is Karuna Chanana, ed., *Socialisation, Education and Women: Explorations in Gender Identity* (New Delhi, Orient Longman, 1988). This collection of essays includes a number of historical works: Aparna Basu, "A Century's Journey: Women's Education in Western India, 1820–1920"; Karuna Chanana, "Social Change or Social Reform: The Education in Pre-Independence India"; Mrinal Pande, "Women in Indian Theatre"; and Meenakshi Mukherjee, "The Unperceived Self: A Study of Nineteenth Century Biographies." Two books on education generally were useful: Syed Nurullah and J. P. Naik, *History of Education in India* (Bombay, Macmillan, 1943) and Aparna Basu, *Essays in the History of Indian Education* (New Delhi, Concept Publishing Co., 1982). Glendora B. Paul has written about women's education in "Emancipation and Education of Indian Women Since 1829," Ph.D. dissertation, University of Pittsburgh (1970). J. C. Bagal's *Women's Education in Eastern India: The First Phase* (Calcutta, The World's Press Private Ltd., 1956), is limited to Bengal. Meredith Borthwick's *Changing Role* is another important source on this topic but also limited to Bengal. Michelle Maskiell has written about students of Kinnaird College in *Women Between Cultures* (Syracuse, South Asia Series, Syracuse University, 1984). Two additional books of a general nature are Minna S. Cowan, *The Education of the Women of India* (Edinburgh, Oliphant, Anderson and Ferrier, 1912) and Premila Thackersey, *Education of Women: A Key to Progress* (New Delhi, Ministry of Education and Youth Services, 1970). There are articles on female education in two very useful collections: Evelyn C. Gedge and Mithan Choksi, *Women in Modern India* (Bombay, D. B. Taraporewala, 1929) – a book called the "authentic voice of modern Indian womanhood" – and Syam Kumari Nehru, ed., *Our Cause: A Symposium by Indian Women* (Allahabad, Kitabistan, 1938). The *Indian Social Reformer*, begun *c.* 1894, includes numerous articles on female education.

The missionaries were very active in female education in India and there are valuable accounts of their schools in missionary archives located in England and the USA. I used the collection of letters, magazines, and official reports at the United Society for the Propagation of the Gospel in London (formerly Society for the Propagation of the Gospel in Foreign Parts) to write my article on zenana education: "In Search of the 'Pure Heathen': Missionary Women in Nineteenth Century India," *EPW*, 21, no. 17 (April 26, 1986). Aparna Basu has written a fine article covering almost two centuries of missionary work in "Mary Ann Cooke to Mother Teresa: Christian Missionary Women and the Indian Response," *Women and Missions: Past and Present,* ed. Fiona Bowie, Deborah Kirkwood and Shirley Ardener (Providence, R.I./Oxford, BERG, 1993). One of the few people working on Indian Christian women is Dr. Padma Anagol. Her article, "Imperialism and the Question of Subaltern Women's Agency: Indian Christian Women and Indigenous Feminism, c.1850–1920," is included in Claire Midgley (ed.), *Gender and Imperialism* (Studies in Imperialism Series) (Manchester, Manchester University Press, 1998), pp. 79–103.

There are a number of books on English women, other than missionaries, who became involved in promoting female education. One example is Mary Carpenter's *Six Months in India* (London, Longman, Green and Co., 1868); another is Sister Nivadita's [Margaret Elizabeth Noble] *The Complete Works of Sister Nivedita* (Calcutta, Ramakrishna Sarada Mission, Sister Nivedita Girls' School, 1967–8). Annette Beveridge's career as a teacher in India is related by her husband in *India Called Them* by Lord Beveridge (London, George Allen and Unwin, 1947). Annette Beveridge also wrote a diary and letters which are available at the Indian Office and Oriental Library Collection (IOOLC).

In the late nineteenth and early twentieth centuries, the Theosophical Society in Madras attracted English and Irish women who became interested in women's education. Most notable among them was Annie Besant, the subject of a two-volume biography by Arthur H. Nethercot. It is the second volume, *The Last Four Lives of Annie Besant* (Chicago, University of Chicago Press, 1963) that deals with her life in India. There are also a number of writings and lectures by Besant dealing with education that have been published. Two such works are *Ancient Ideals in Modern Life* (Benares, Theosophical Publishing House, 1900) and *Wake Up, India* (Madras, Theosophical Publishing House, 1913). On her views on women and politics, see Annie Besant, *The Political Status of Women*, 2nd edn. (London, C. Watts, 1885), (pamphlet).

For the Arya Samaj's efforts on behalf of women's education I have relied on Kenneth W. Jones, *Arya Dharma* (Delhi, Manohar, 1976), Madhu Kishwar, "Arya Samaj and Women's Education: Kanya Mahavidyalaya," *EPW*, 21, no. 17 (April 16, 1986), and Kumari Lajjavati, "A Pioneer in Women's Education," *ISR*, 45 (June 1, 1945).

Pandita Ramabai's letters to her spiritual preceptor at Wantage have been published as: *The Letters and Correspondence of Pandita Ramabai,* compiled by Sister Geraldine, ed. A. B. Shah (Bombay, Maharashtra State Board of Literature and Culture, 1977). We also have Pandita Ramabai's own polemical work designed for sale in the USA and Canada: *The High-Caste Hindu Woman* (New York, F. H. Revell, 1887). There are a number of sympathetic biographies of Ramabai by Christians, for example: Rajas Krishnarao Dongre and Josephine F. Patterson, *Pandita Ramabai* (Madras, Christian Literature Society, 1969), Nicol Macnicol, *Pandita Ramabai* (Calcutta, Association Press, 1926), and Muriel Clark, *Pandita Ramabai* (London, Paternoster Bldg., 1920). Meera Kosambi's article on Ramabai, "Women, Emancipation and Equality: Pandita Ramabai's Contribution to Women's Cause," *EPW*, 23 no. 44 (October, 1988), is especially insightful. This article as well as Kosambi's, "An Indian Response to Christianity, Church and Colonialism: The Case of Pandita Ramabai," have been published, together with her article on the Age of Consent Bill, in *At the Intersection of Gender Reform and Religious Belief*

(Bombay, Research Center for Women's Studies, SNDT University, 1993). Pandita Ramabai is one of the subjects of Padma Anagol's dissertation, "Women's Consciousness and Assertion in Colonial India: Gender, Social Reform and Politics in Maharashtra, c.1870–1920," (University of London, 1994), which traces the emergence of feminism among women in Western India in the late nineteenth and the early twentieth centuries. Antoinette Burton treats Ramabai's years in England in *At the Heart of the Empire: Indians and the Colonial Encounter in Late-Victorian Britain* (Berkeley, University of California Press, 1998). Jyotsna Kapur, "Women and the Social Reform Movement in Maharashtra," M.Phil. thesis, Delhi University (1989), is a valuable piece of work for putting these issues into perspective. There is a significant (and neglected) collection of yearly reports, pamphlets, and correspondence at "Mukti," Ramabai's last school at Kedgaon, Maharashtra.

Material on the Mahakali Pathshala is difficult to locate although I have interviewed some women in Calcutta who attended this school in the early years of this century. M. M. Kaur in *The Role of Women in the Freedom Movement (1857–1947)* (New Delhi, Sterling, 1968) discusses the founder as a niece of the Rani of Jhansi, the heroine of 1857. Most of my information came from newspaper articles, for example, "The Mahakali Pathshala," *The Statesman* (February 3, 1985) and journals such as the *Indian Ladies Magazine* in 1903.

The educational institutions developed by (Maharshi) Dhondo Keshav Karve in Poona are discussed in his own memoir, *Looking Back* (Poona, Hinge Stree-Shikshan Samastha, 1936), and in his life story, written in Marathi. This has been translated and included with his wife Anandibai's memoir in *The New Brahmins*, ed. and trans. D. D. Karve, with editorial assistance from Ellen E. McDonald (Berkeley, University of California Press, 1963). The one biography of D. K. Karve was written by G. L. Chakravarkar, *Dhondo Keshav Karve* (New Delhi, Publications Division, Government of India, 1970). An extremely valuable account of Karve's work on behalf of widows is included in the autobiography of his sister-in-law, a teacher in his school, Parvati Athavale. Her book is entitled *My Story, The Autobiography of a Hindu Widow,* trans. Revd. Justin E. Abbott (New York, G. P. Putnam, 1930). Karve's Women's University was renamed Shreemati Nathibai Damodar Thackersey Indian Women's University (or SNDT) and relocated in Bombay. SNDT Women's University is India's premier institution for women's higher education. An article that discusses the transition is "Thackesay [*sic*] Women's University Convocation," Sir Visvesvaraya's Convocation Address (June 29, 1940), *The Indian Annual Register,* vol. 1 (January–June, 1940) (Calcutta, Annual Register, 1940).

Gail Minault has been at the forefront of uncovering the history of education for Muslim women and her book, *Secluded Scholars: Women's Education and Muslim Social Reform in Colonial India* (Delhi, Oxford University Press, 1998) is rich in detail. Her article, "Other Voices, Other Rooms: The View from the Zenana," in *Women as Subjects,* ed. Nita Kumar (Charlottesville, University Press of Virginia, 1994), is an interesting reading of male reformers' texts to understand zenana life. She has translated Khwaja Altaf Hussain Hali's work (1874) on education for women in *Voices of Silence* (Delhi, Chanakya Publications, 1986). She has also written the following articles on Muslim educators of women: "Shaikh Abdullah, Begam Abdullah, and *Sharif* Education for Girls at Aligarh," *Modernization and Social Change among Muslims in India,* ed. Imtiaz Ahmad (New Delhi, Manohar Book Service, 1983); "Sayyid Mumtaz Ali and 'Huquq un-Niswan': An Advocate of Women's Rights in Islam in the Late Nineteenth Century," *Modern Asian Studies,* 24, no. 1 (1990); and "Purdah's Progress: The Beginnings of School Education for Indian Muslim Women," *Individuals and Ideals in Modern India,* ed. J. P. Sharma (Calcutta, Firma K. P. Mukhopadhyaya, 1982). Sonia Nishat Amin has written extensively about Muslim women, their education, family life, and literary activity in "The World of Muslim Women in Colonial Bengal: 1876–1939," Ph.D. dissertation, University of Dhaka (1993) published as *The World of Muslim Women in Colonial Bengal 1876–1939* (Leiden, E. J. Brill, 1996). Among other useful articles for this topic by Amin are: "The Early Muslim Bhadramahila," in *From the Seams of History* and "Filling the Gap: Women's History – The Case of Muslim Bhadromohilas in Bengal," *Journal of Social Studies,* 62 (October, 1993). For information on Begum Rokeya I relied on Roushan Jahan, ed. and trans., *Inside Seclusion* (Dhaka, BRAC Printers, 1981), Murshid, *Reluctant Debutante,* Sonia Amin's two articles: "Rokeya Sakhawat Hossain and the Legacy of the 'Bengal' Renaissance," *Journal of Asiatic Society,* Bangladesh, 34, no. 2 (December, 1989) and "The New Woman in Literature and the Novels of Nojibur Rahman and Rokeya Sakhawat Hossain," *Infinite Variety: Women in Society and Literature,* ed. Firdous Azim and Niaz Zaman (Dhaka, University Press Ltd., 1994), and articles in journals such as the *Indian Ladies' Magazine.*

Sources on Sister Subbalakshmi include Monica Felton's *A Child Widow's Story* (London, Victor Gollancz, 1966); *Women Pioneers in Education (Tamilnadu)* (Madras, Society for the Promotion of Education in India, 1975); an interview with Mrs. Soundarain (Madras, January 22, 1976); note by Sister Subbalakshmi (n.d.) enclosed in a letter from Rabindranath Tagore to Miss M. F. Prager, Eur. Mss. B 183 (IOOLC); Malathi Ramanathan's biography, *Sister R. Subbalakshmi: Social Reformer and Educationalist* (Bombay, 1989), and the interview with Sister Sublakshami [*sic*] (December 10, 1930), Ruth Woodsmall Collection, box 28. The Ruth Woodsmall Collection is housed at Smith College, Northampton, Mass.

To convey some sense of what education meant to women I have relied heavily on *Women Writing in India; From Child Widow to Lady Doctor: The Intimate Memoir of Dr. Haimabati Sen,* translated Tapan Raychaudhuri, ed. Geraldine Forbes and Tapan Raychaudhuri (New Delhi, Roli, in press); and other first-person narratives. An interesting article suggesting how this new educational agenda weaned women away from popular culture is by Sumantha Banerjee, "Marginalization of Women's Popular Culture in Nineteenth Century Bengal," *Recasting Women.* Nita Kumar's "Oranges for the Girls, or, the Half-Known Story of the Education of Girls in Twentieth-Century

Banares," in *Women as Subjects* looks at curricula for girls in three schools in Benares.

To write chapter 3 on women's organizations I was able to use the records of the three major women's Indian associations: the Women's Indian Association (WIA), the National Council of Women in India (NCWI), and the All-India Women's Conference (AIWC). Records for the WIA are scattered. Some are located in the AIWC Library in New Delhi, some are at the old WIA headquarters in Madras, and some are in the Reddy Collection in the Nehru Museum and Memorial Library (NMML). Records for the NCWI were located in a New Delhi garage and have since been deposited in the NMML. Other records of the NCWI were in the private library of Mrs. Tarabai Premchand in Bombay. I first began to read AIWC records in the library of their former building. I continued my research while the present building was under construction. In the process of moving to the new building it appears some of the earlier files may have been lost.

Aparna Basu and Bharati Ray have written a history of the AIWC from 1927 to 1990: *Women's Struggle* (New Delhi, Manohar, 1990). Comparable histories for the other major organizations do not exist. There are a growing number of articles and books which treat women's organizations, for example, Dagmar Engels, "The Limits of Gender Ideology," *WSIQ*, 12, no. 4 (1989). I have written the following articles on the women's movement in India: "Women's Movements in India: Traditional Symbols and New Roles," *Social Movements in India*, 2 vols., ed. M. S. A. Rao (New Delhi, Manohar Publications, 1978), vol. 1; "Caged Tigers: First Wave Feminists in India," *WSIQ*, 5, no. 6 (1982); "The Indian Women's Movement: A Struggle for Women's Rights or National Liberation?" in *The Extended Family*; "From Purdah to Politics: The Social Feminism of the All-India Women's Organizations," in *Separate Worlds*, ed. Hanna Papanek and Gail Minault (Delhi, Chanakya Publications, 1982). Monographs which explore the linkage between the women's organizations and socio-political change include: Jana Matson Everett's *Women and Social Change in India* (New Delhi, Heritage Publishers, 1981); Radha Krishna Sharma, *Nationalism, Social Reform and Indian Women* (New Delhi, Janaki Prakashan, 1981); Vijay Agnew, *Elite Women in Indian Politics* (New Delhi, Vikas, 1979); and Latika Ghose, "Social and Educational Movements for Women and by Women, 1820–1950," *Bethune School and College Centenary Volume, 1849–1949*, ed. Dr. Kalidas Nag (Calcutta, S. N. Guha Ray, 1950). Barbara Southard's *The Women's Movement and Colonial Politics in Bengal: The Quest for Political Rights, Education and Social Reform Legislation, 1921–1936* (New Delhi, Manohar, 1995) was not available when this book went to Press.

Fewer records are available for studying the earlier women's organizations. For male-initiated women's organizations in the Brahmo Samaj I used both Meredith Borthwick's *The Changing Role* and Sivanath Sastri, *History of the Brahmo Samaj*, 2nd edn. (Calcutta, Sadharan Brahmo Samaj, 1974). On the Parsee organization my main source was *Golden Jubilee Stri Zarthosti Mandal, 1903–1953, and Silver Jubilee Sir Ratan Tata Industrial Institute, 1928–1953 Volume* (Bombay, n.p., 1953). For information on the Arya Mahila Samaj I drew upon K. J. Chitalia, ed., *Directory of Women's Institutions,* Bombay Presidency, vol. 1 (Bombay, Servants of India Society, 1936); "Arya Mahila Samaj," (n.d.), notes by Mrs. Leela Joshi (received from the author); and "Arya Mahila Samaj: An Appeal" (n.d.), a cyclostyled sheet received from Sarojini Pradhar. The *Indian Ladies' Magazine,* begun by Mrs. Kamala Satthianadhan (b. 1879) in 1901, was an English publication designed to inform women about women's issues. This magazine is an excellent source for information on the role of women in the Indian Social Conference and the early women's organizations. Some volumes of this magazine are available in the National Library, Calcutta, but the only complete collection I could locate belonged to Padmini Sen Gupta (now deceased), Mrs. Satthianadhan's daughter.

Early organizations for Muslim women are discussed in Gail Minault, "Sisterhood or Separation? The All-India Muslim Ladies' Conference and the Nationalist Movement," in *The Extended Family,* Sonia Amin's dissertation, "The World of Muslim Women," and Jahan Ara Shahnawaz, *Father and Daughter: A Political Autobiography* (Lahore, Nigarishat, 1971).

The first all-India organization begun by women for women was the Bharat Mahamandal. There is an account of its origins by its founder Saraladevi Chaudhurani: "A Women's Movement," *MR* (October, 1911). J. C. Bagal's "Sarala Devi Chaudhurani," in *Sahitya Sadhak Charitmala,* 99 (Calcutta, Bangiya Sahitya Parishad, 1964) includes information on her organization. Also, articles in *ILM* and *MR* elaborate the workings of the Mahamandal. Saraladevi's memoir, *Jibaner Jharapata,* in Bengali, was published in Calcutta in 1958. Tapati Sengupta of Jadavpur University, Calcutta, is presently writing her doctoral dissertation on Saraladevi Chaudhurani.

To gain some understanding of how these organizations actually operated and what they meant to the women who belonged, it is instructive to look at memoirs. Three memoirs are particularly valuable for this topic: Kamala Bai L. Rau, *Smrutika: The Story of My Mother as Told by Herself,* trans. Indirabai M. Rau (Pune, Dr. Krishnabai Nimbkar, 1988); Manmohini Zutshi Sahgal, *An Indian Freedom Fighter Recalls Her Life,* ed. Geraldine Forbes (New York, M. E. Sharpe, 1994); and Shudha Mazumdar, *Memoirs of an Indian Woman.* A related book is *The Position of Women in Indian Life* (New York, Longman, Green and Co., 1911) by H. H. the Maharani of Baroda about what India needed to borrow and assimilate from the West in the quest for a modern identity. An interesting account of women in the World War I era is included in Ruth Woodsmall's notebooks, 1916–17, and diaries, 1913–17, in the Ruth Woodsmall Collection. Ruth Woodsmall went to India with the YWCA and made a serious effort to get to know the "new women" joining organizations and attempting to effect social change.

Two Irish women intimately associated with the development of the WIA were the two theosophists Margaret Cousins and Dorothy Jinarajadasa (married to a Singalese theosophist) who settled in Madras. Margaret Cousins and her husband James wrote a joint autobiography: J. H. Cousins and M. E. Cousins, *We Two Together* (Madras, Ganesh and Co., 1950). Margaret E. Cousins wrote *Indian Womanhood Today* (Allahabad, Kitabistan, 1947) and there is an account of her work by Dr. (Mrs.) S. Muthulakshmi Reddi, *Mrs. Margaret Cousins and her Work in India* (Madras, Women's Indian Association, 1956). Catherine Candy, Loyola University, Chicago, is now writing a biography of Margaret Cousins.

There is much less information available on Dorothy Jinarajadasa even though she played a major role in the development of the WIA. There are a number of her letters in the Dr. Reddy Papers but I have only been able to find one article by her: Mrs. D. Jinarajadasa, "The Emancipation of Indian Women," *Transactions of the Eighth Congress of the Federation of European National Societies of the Theosophical Society,* held in Vienna, July 21–26, 1923, ed. C. W. Dijkgraat (Amsterdam, Council of the Federation of European National Societies of the Theosophical Society, 1923). The limited appeal of theosophy, because of its identification with brahminism, has been explored by C. S. Lakshmi in *The Face Behind the Mask: Women in Tamil Literature* (Delhi, Vikas, 1984), and by Prabha Rani in "Women's Indian Association and the Self-Respect Movement in Madras, 1925–1936: Perceptions on Women," a paper delivered at the Women's Studies Conference, Chandigarh (October, 1985). C. S. Lakshmi has also discussed the Self-Respect Movement's manipulation of gender issues in: "Mother, Mother-Community and Mother-Politics in Tamil Nadu," *EPW*, 25, nos. 42 and 43 (October 20–27, 1990).

Barbara Ramusack has written extensively on the role of British women in India: see "Cultural Missionaries, Maternal Imperialists, Feminist Allies: British Women Activists in India, 1865–1945," *Western Women and Imperialism,* ed. Nupur Chaudhuri and Margaret Strobel (Bloomington and Indianapolis, Indiana University Press, 1992); "Catalysts or Helpers? British Feminists, Indian Women's Rights, and Indian Independence," in *The Extended Family;* and "Embattled Advocates: The Debate over Birth Control in India, 1920–1940," *JWH,* 1, no. 2 (fall, 1989). Antoinette M. Burton in "The White Woman's Burden: British Feminists and 'The Indian Woman,' 1865–1915," *Western Women and Imperialism* and her new book *Burdens of History* (Chapel Hill, University of North Carolina Press, 1994) has explored the ways the Indian woman question featured in the writings and activities of British feminists. Janaki Nair has analyzed the writings of some English women in her article, "Uncovering the Zenana: Visions of Indian Womanhood in Englishwomen's Writings: 1831–1940," *JWH,* 2, no. 1 (spring, 1990). A special issue of *Women's History Review,* ed. Barbara N. Ramusack and Antoinette Burton, 3, no. 4 (1994), was devoted to a discussion of feminism, imperialism, and race – a dialogue between India and Britain.

Veronica Strong-Boag has written about the International Council of Women in *The Parliament of Women* (Ottawa, National Museum of Canada, 1976). An excellent book on one of the founders of the NCWI is Lady Tata, *A Book of Remembrance* (Bombay, J. B. Dubash, 1933). This book is valuable in that it includes some of Lady Tata's letters and speeches. To help explain the interest of some of these elitist women in British-dominated women's organizations, I found Douglas E. Haynes' article, "From Tribute to Philanthropy: The Politics of Gift Giving in a Western Indian City," in *Journal of Asian Studies*, 46, no. 2 (May 1987) especially interesting. The Bombay Presidency Women's Council, which has its headquarters in the same building as the Asiatic Society in Bombay, has retained its annual reports and some additional papers. These are the only regional papers of the NCWI that I was able to locate.

To gain some understanding of Indian women who were involved in the reform movement I used a variety of documents given to me by families, interviews, and published and unpublished papers by other historians. Cornelia Sorabji's private papers are at the IOOLC. Cornelia Sorabji has written the following books about her life and work: *Between the Twilights* (London, Harper, 1908), *India Recalled* (London, Nisbet, 1936), and *The Purdahnashin* (Calcutta, Thacker and Spink, 1917) as well as a number of articles on Indian women and social reform issues. Antoinette Burton has written about Cornelia Sorabji's years in England in "Cornelia Sorabji in Victorian Oxford," in *At the Heart of the Empire: Indians and the Colonial Encounter in Late-Victorian Britain* (Berkeley, University of California Press, 1998). My sources on Maniben Kara were "Life Sketch of Maniben Kara," (unpublished) received from the Western Railway Employees Union (Bombay, 1979); an interview with Maniben Kara (Bombay, April 24, 1976); and "Maniben Kara" (September 17, 1969), s-14, South Asian Archive, Centre for South Asian Studies, Cambridge.

Accounts of the AIWC are included in its own records (mentioned above) as well as in an article by M. Cousins, "How the Conference Began," *Roshi*, special number (1946).

For my discussion of the child marriage debate I used numerous articles written on the age of consent issue in 1891 including: Tanika Sarkar, "Rhetoric against Age of Consent, Resisting Colonial Reason and Death of a Child-Wife," *EPW*, 28, no. 36 (September 4, 1993); Dagmar Engels, "The Age of Consent Act of 1891: Colonial Ideology in Bengal," *South Asia Research*, 3, no. 2 (November, 1983); and Mrinalini Sinha, "The Age of Consent Act: The Ideal of Masculinity and Colonial Ideology in Late Nineteenth Century Bengal," *Proceedings of the Eighth International Symposium on Asian Studies* (1986), Padma Anagol-McGinn, "The Age of Consent Act (1891) Reconsidered: Women's perspectives and participation in the child-marriage controversy in India," *South Asia Research*, 12: 2 (1992), pp. 100–118.

I have also written on child marriage: "Women and Modernity: The Issue of Child Marriage in India," *WSIQ*, 2, no. 4 (1979). For that article and this work I used Legislative Assembly Debates; Government of India, Home Department Judicial and Political files; the *Report of the Age of Consent Committee, 1928–1929* (Calcutta, 1929); records of the women's organizations; and a number of articles. Barbara Ramusack has published "Women's Organizations and Social Change: the Age-of-Marriage Issue in India," *Women and World Change*, ed. Naomi Black and Ann Baker Cottrell (Beverly Hills, Sage Publications, 1981). Katherine Mayo's book, *Mother India* (New York, Harcourt Brace, 1927) turned the child marriage issue into a debate about whether or not Indians were fit for self-government. For an insightful review of Mayo in her pre-India days see Gerda W. Ray, "Colonialism, Race, and Masculinity: Katherine Mayo and the Campaign for State Police" (1992) unpublished paper. Mrinalini Sinha has written two excellent articles on Katherine Mayo's work: "Reading *Mother India*: Empire, Nation, and the Female Voice," *JWH*, 6, no. 2 (1994) and "Gender in the Critiques of Colonialism and Nationalism: Locating the 'Indian Woman,'" in *Feminists' Revision History,* ed. Ann-Louise Shapiro (New Brunswick, N.J., Rutgers University Press, 1994). Mrinalini Sinha is presently writing a monograph on the Indian responses to Katherine Mayo.

British women became involved in this controversy and some of the letters exchanged can be found in the Rathbone Papers in the Fawcett Library in London. Eleanor F. Rathbone wrote *Child Marriage: The Indian Minotaur* (London, Allen and Unwin, 1934) a book which summarized the failure of efforts to enforce a minimum age of marriage.

Chapter 4 was written primarily from records of women's organizations; Government of India Public Home Department files; British parliamentary reports; records of the Indian National Congress; private letters, especially in the Rathbone Papers in the Fawcett Library and in the Theosophical Society archives at the Theosophical Society Library in Adyar, Madras; and articles in the *Indian Ladies' Magazine, New India,* and *Modern Review.* I used the following parliamentary papers: *Report on Indian Constitutional Reform* (1918); Joint Select Committee on Government of India Bill, vol. II, *Minutes of Evidence* (1919); Joint Select Committee on Government of India Bill, vol. I, *Report and Proceedings of the Committee* (1919); Report of the Indian Franchise Committee (1932); Indian Round Table Conference (Sub-committee Reports) (1931); Minutes of Evidence given before the Joint Select Committee in the Indian Constitutional Reform (1934); and Joint Committee on Indian Constitutional Reform, vol. I, *Report* (1934).

In writing about the first franchise debate I have used accounts written by participants, pamphlets, letters, and newspaper clippings. "A Copy of the Address Presented by the All-India Women's Deputation to Lord Chelmsford (Viceroy) and Rt. Hon'ble E. S. Montagu (Secretary of State)," is in pamphlet form in the Suffrage-India collection in the Fawcett Collection. The Suffrage-India collection is the best source for pamphlets, clippings, and letters referring to the first franchise campaign by Indian women. Among these materials is Mrs. Herabai Tata's "A Short Sketch of Indian Women's Franchise Work." Herebai's daughter, Mithan Lam, wrote "Autumn Leaves: Some Memoirs of Yesteryear" (unpublished manuscript). The AIWC also kept files on the work done on behalf of the franchise issue by these women. For Cornelia Sorabji's involvement in the franchise issue see Cornelia Sorabji Papers, Eur. Mss. F/165/5, IOOLC, especially her newspaper clippings, letters, memoranda, and "Social Service" file. Mrinalini Sen, the Indian woman who borrowed suffragette tactics, wrote "Indian Reform Bill and Women of India" (first published in *Africa and the Orient Reviews,* 1920), reprinted in *Knocking at the Door* (Calcutta, Samir Dutt, 1954).

Muthulakshmi Reddy (sometimes written "Reddi") wrote an autobiography: *Autobiography of Dr. (Mrs.) Muthulakshmi Reddy* (Madras, M. Reddi, 1964) and Dr. (Mrs.) S. Muthulakshmi Reddy, *My Experiences As a Legislator* (Madras, Current Thought Press, 1930). Her papers, including her views on franchise and her speeches, are in the NMML. *Dr. Muthulakshmi Reddy, the Pathfinder*, ed. Aparna Basu (New Delhi, AIWC, 1987), also includes a number of her speeches. I have also used some secondary accounts already mentioned, especially Dr. (Mrs.) Muthulakshmi Reddi, *Mrs. Margaret Cousins and Her Work in India.*

There are very few scholarly articles written on the franchise issue. Barbara Southard, "Colonial Politics and Women's Rights: Woman Suffrage Campaigns in Bengal, British India in the 1920s," *Modern Asian Studies,* 27, no. 2 (1993) and Gail Pearson's "Reserved Seats – Women and the Vote in Bombay," *Indian Economic and Social History Review,* 10, no. 1 (1983) are among the few regional studies. I have written more generally on the franchise issue in "Votes for Women," *Symbols of Power,* ed. Vina Mazumdar (Bombay, Allied Publishers, 1979).

The second franchise debate is discussed by Mrs. P. Subbarayan, *The Political Status of Women Under the New Constitution* (Madras, n.p., n.d.), letters in the Fawcett Collection, and the AIWC files. Especially significant are documents such as "Memorandum of the All-India Women's Conference" (1932) found in these files.

Newspapers and journals, specifically *The Hindu, Indian Ladies' Magazine,* and *Stri Dharma* (the magazine of the WIA), include numerous articles on this topic. The Suffrage-India collection at the Fawcett Library is a rich source for this period as well as the earlier campaign. It includes some rare documents such as Mrs. P. K. Sen, "Supplementary Memorandum on the Franchise of Women." Mary Pickford went to India with the Lothian Committee. Her account of that experience is in her papers Eur. Mss. D, 1013, IOOLC.

Renuka Ray's influential tract, "Legal Disabilities of Indian Women," first published in *Modern Review* (November 1934), led to the demand for a universal law code for women. Records of the government response can be found in Government of India Home Department (Judicial) files. The best source for the development of the Hindu Code is the Report of the Hindu Law Committee, B. N. Rau Papers, file 11, NMML. Harold Levy's Ph.D. dissertation "Indian Modernization by Legislation: The Hindu Code Bill," University of Chicago (1973) is an important work on this topic. Lotika Sarkar has written about Nehru's role in "Jawaharlal Nehru and the Hindu Code Bill," in *Indian Women*, edited by B. R. Nanda. Janaki Nair's *Women and Law in Colonial India: A Social History* (New Delhi: Kali for Women, 1996) examines the transformation of the law.

The Indian National Congress involved women in its planning efforts: see National Planning Sub-Committee of Women's Role in the Planned Economy, AICC, file no. G-23/1640. Information on the formation of a women's department within Congress is in "Scheme of the Work of the Women's Department," AICC files (1940–2); Sucheta Devi, secretary, Women's Department, AICC, "The Aims of the Women's Department of the AICC," AICC files. NMML.

Chapter 5 draws heavily from personal accounts, oral interviews, newspaper articles, Government of India Home Political Department files, and Congress documents. Although there are many accounts of the freedom movement that mention the role of women, few of them do so with any specificity. Manmohan Kaur, *Role of Women in the Freedom Movement, 1857–1947* (New Delhi, Sterling, 1968) was the first book on the freedom struggle to focus on women. Unfortunately, it is not entirely reliable. Kamaladevi Chattopadhyay has written a participant's account: *Indian Women's Battle for Freedom* (New Delhi, Abhinav Publications, 1983). Vijay Agnew has written on women in the freedom movement in *Elite Women in Indian Politics*. One of the best accounts of this period is the regional study by Gail O. Pearson, "Women in Public Life in Bombay City with Special Reference to the Civil Disobedience Movement," Ph.D. thesis, Jawaharlal Nehru University (1979). Gail Pearson has also written "Nationalism, Universalization, and the Extended Female Space in Bombay City," in *The Extended Family*. J. C. Bagal has written on Bengali women in the freedom struggle in *Jattiya Bangla Nari* (Calcutta, 1361 B.S. [1954]) as has Dr. Niranjan Ghosh, *Role of Women in the Freedom Movement in Bengal* (Calcutta, Firma K. L. Mukhopadhyay, 1988). Another regional study is K. Sreeranhani Subba Rao, "Women and Indian Nationalism: A Case Study of Prominent Women Freedom Fighters of the East Godavari District of Andhra Pradesh," a paper given at the Third National Conference of Women's Studies (Chandigarh, 1985). *Manushi* carried a number of short and valuable articles on women who played a role in the independence movement. I have written about women and the Indian National Congress in "The Politics of Respectability: Indian Women and the Indian National Congress," *The Indian National Congress*, ed. D. A. Low (Delhi, Oxford University Press, 1988). Kumari Jayawardena included a chapter on "Women, Social Reform and Nationalism in India," in *Feminism and Nationalism in the Third World* (New Delhi, Kali for Women, 1986). Aparna Basu wrote an article on "The Role of Women in the Indian Struggle for Freedom," in *Indian Women*, ed. B. R. Nanda. Bharati Roy has focused specifically on Bengal in "The Freedom Movement and Feminist Consciousness in Bengal, 1905–1929," in *From the Seams of History*. Geeta Anand, "Appeal of the Indian Nationalist Movement to Women," senior thesis, Dartmouth College (1989) includes interviews and songs. Gail Minault treats Muslim women in "Purdah Politics: The Role of Muslim Women in Indian Nationalism, 1911–1924," in *Separate Worlds*.

I have also drawn heavily on interviews I have conducted, transcripts of oral interviews and private papers in the Nehru Memorial Museum and Library, and transcripts in the collection of oral histories in the South Asia Archive, Centre for South Asian Studies, Cambridge. My own interviews were with Helena Dutt (Calcutta, September 25, 1975); Latika Ghosh (Calcutta, February 29, 1978); Jaisree Raiji (Bombay, May 2, 1976); Dr. Sushila Nayar (New Delhi, April 6, 1976); Santi Das Kabir (New Delhi, March 25, 1976); Kamala Das Gupta (Calcutta, July 12, 1973) Kalyani Bhattacharjee (Calcutta, March 14, 1976); Santi Das Ghosh (Calcutta, February 24, 1976); Smt. S. Ambujammal (Madras, January 19 and 25, 1976); Ambabai (Udipi, May 24,

1976); Santi Ganguly (Calcutta, February 8, 1976); Ujjala Mazumdar Rakshit-Roy (Calcutta, February 8, 1976); and Suniti Choudhury Ghosh (Calcutta, February 15, 1976). I have also interviewed many other women and their ideas informed this work but I have not directly used their interviews in the writing of this chapter. Among the oral history transcripts at NMML on which I drew were those of Smt. Sucheta Kripalani, Kamala Das Gupta, Mrs. S. Ambujammal, and Smt. Durgabai Deshmukh. The NMML also has collections (often very limited) of papers of the following women: Smt. Ambujammal, Raj Kumari Amrit Kaur, Smt. Durgabai Deshmukh, Hansa Mehta, Rameshwari Nehru, Vijayalakshmi Pandit, S. Muthulakshmi Reddy, Rukmini Lakshmipathi, Mridula Sarabhai, and Madame Bhikaji Cama. I also relied on the interview with Goshiben Captain (May 16, 1970) in the South Asia Archive in Cambridge.

There are numerous memoirs and autobiographies for this period. Among them are Manmohini Zutshi Sahgal, *An Indian Freedom Fighter*, Kamaladevi Chattopadhyay, *Inner Recesses/Outer Spaces: Memoirs* (New Delhi, Navrang, 1986), *Smrutika: The Story of My Mother*. Also of value were short pieces: S. Ambujammal, "Face to Face," a lecture delivered at Max Mueller Bhavan, Madras (January 22, 1976) and Bimla Luthra, "Nehru's Vision of Indian Society and the Place of Women in it," unpublished paper (n.d.), NMML. Unfortunately Aparna Basu's *Mridula Sarabhai: Rebel with a Cause* (New Dehli, Oxford University Press) was not available when this book went to Press.

Most important for the study of Gandhi is the *Collected Works of Mahatma Gandhi* 90 vols. (Delhi, Publications Division, Ministry of Information and Broadcasting, 1958–84). Judith Brown has written three books on Gandhi: *Gandhi's Rise to Power, 1915–1922* (Cambridge, Cambridge University Press, 1972), *Gandhi and Civil Disobedience, 1928–1934* (Cambridge, Cambridge University Press, 1977), and *Gandhi, Prisoner of Hope* (New Haven, Yale University Press, 1989). Many of Gandhi's speeches and writings on women have been collected in M. K. Gandhi, *Women and Social Justice,* 4th edn. (Ahmedabad, Navajivan Publishing House, 1954). Gandhi's letters to women in his ashram were published as *To the Women* (Karachi, Anand T. Hingorani, 1941). Sujata Patel examined Gandhi's representations of women in "Construction and Reconstruction of Woman in Gandhi," *EPW,* 23 (February 20, 1988). Madhu Kishwar has written the best single article on "Women and Gandhi," published in *EPW,* 20 (October 5 and 12, 1985). I also used Gandhi's newspapers, for example, *Young India,* and Gandhi's private letters to Saraladevi Chaudhurani, which were given to me by her son Deepak Chaudhury.

The most important newspaper for this chapter was the *Bombay Chronicle* which carried more articles on women than any other newspaper in India. I also used *Forward, Amrita Bazar Patrika, Modern Review, Indian Social Reformer, Stri Dharma, The Hindu,* and *The Tribune.*

I was able to access records of some of the women's political organizations, particularly Gandhi Seva Sena and Desh Sevika Sangha. These papers are in private hands or in the All-India Congress Committee files, NMML. Accounts of the Mahila Rashtriya Sangha by Latika Bose (following her divorce Latika resumed use of her maiden name Ghosh and preferred to be known as Latika Ghosh) are in *Banglar Katha,* 11 (Ashwin and Jaitha, 1335 [1928]).

General works on the revolutionaries include David M. Laushey, *Bengal Terrorism and the Marxist Left* (Calcutta, Firma K. L. Mukhopadhyay, 1975); *Terrorism in India, 1917–1936,* compiled in the Intelligence Bureau, Home Department, GOI (Simla, GOI Press, 1937, reprinted Delhi, Deep Publications, 1974); and Kali Charan Ghosh, *The Roll of Honour, Anecdotes of Indian Martyrs* (Calcutta, Vidya Bharat, 1965).

For women in the revolutionary movement see Kamala Das Gupta, *Swadinata Sangrame Banglar Nari* ["Bengali Women in the Freedom Movement"], (Calcutta, Basudhara Prakashani, 1970). I have written about women revolutionaries: "Goddesses or Rebels? The Women Revolutionaries of Bengal," *The Oracle,* 2, no. 2 (April 1980). Since then Ishanee Mukherjee presented "Women and Armed Revolution in Late Colonial Bengal," at the National Conference of Women's Studies (Chandigarh, 1985) and Tirtha Mandal has written *Women Revolutionaries of Bengal, 1905–1939* (Calcutta, Minerva, 1991). For this book I have used Ishanee and Mandal's work as well as interviews, private documents, official records, and works of fiction. *Pather Dabi,* published serially between 1923 and 1926, was the first popular novel in Bengali on revolutionary activities and inspired at least two of the women revolutionaries. Rabindranath Tagore's novel, *Char Adhyaya* (1934), translated as *Four Chapters* (Calcutta, Visva-Bharati, 1950) is interesting as a comment on how revolutionary women were viewed by respectable society.

Kalyani Das Bhattacharjee shared with me "A Short Life Sketch of Kalyani Bhattacharjee," (unpublished), lists she kept of women who were in prison with her, and transcripts of a taped interview. Akhil Chandra Nandy, who helped plan Santi and Suniti's shooting in Comilla, wrote "Girls in India's Freedom Struggle," *The Patrika Sunday Magazine* (September 2, 1973) and spoke with me about his revolutionary activities on a number of occasions. I received a copy of Bina Das's "Confession" from the author.

Topics related to women's role in the freedom movement continue to attract scholars. There is a great deal of work being done on their activities as well as how they were represented in writings and speeches of the time. A new series of writings and speeches of prominent women includes books such as the *Selected Speeches and Writings of Rajkumari Amrit Kaur,* ed. G. Borkar (New Delhi, Archer Publications, 1961). Some of the participants are now engaged in writing their memoirs and collecting their papers for libraries.

Writing chapter 6 presented immense problems. There are very few articles or books written on women's work in India and many of the official reports on labor have omitted women. Census data is also limited for this topic. I have drawn on a wide variety of sources for this chapter: official reports, memoirs and autobiographies, government files, the records of women's organizations, and some articles and monographs.

I began with women's entry into the professions, the most visible result of education for women. I have chosen to focus on the medical field because we have some excellent autobiographies by and articles on medical women, for example, *From Child Widow to Lady Doctor*; *Autobiography of Hilda Lazarus* (Vizagapatnam, SFS Printing, n.d.); *The Autobiography of Dr. (Mrs.) Muthulakshmi Reddy*; and *The Life of Anandabai Joshee* (her name is spelled Anandabai and Anandibai and Joshi and Joshee in different accounts) by Mrs. Caroline Healey Doll (Boston, Roberts Brothers, 1888). There is a fictionalized account of Anandibai's life by S. J. Joshi, *Anandi Gopal*, translated by Asha Damle (Calcutta, Stree, 1992). Malavika Karlekar has written on Dr. Kadambini Basu, the first Indian woman to complete a medical degree in India, in "Kadambini and the Bhadralok," *EPW*, 21, no. 19 (April 26, 1986).

At present there are a number of studies on medical issues in India. Roger Jeffrey, *The Politics of Health in India* (Berkeley, University of California Press, 1987), David Arnold, *Colonizing the Body* (Berkeley, University of California Press, 1993) and Mark Harrison, *Public Health in British India* (Cambridge, Cambridge University Press, 1994) are all significant contributions to this topic but say little about women. Four recent articles: Dagmar Engels, "The Politics of Child Birth: British and Bengali Women in Contest, 1890–1930," *Society and Ideology: Essays in South Asian History Presented to Professor Kenneth Ballhatchet,* ed. P. Robb (Delhi, Oxford University Press, 1993); Maneesha Lal, "The Politics of Gender and Medicine in Colonial India: the Countess of Dufferin's Fund, 1885–1888," *Bulletin of the History of Medicine,* 68 (1994); Geraldine Forbes, "Medical Careers and Health Care for Indian Women: Patterns of Control," *Women's History Review* (1994); and Chandrika Paul, "Uncaging the Birds: The Entrance of Bengali Women into Medical Colleges 1870–1890," a paper presented at the Mid-West Conference on Asian Affairs (Cleveland, 1993), are characteristic of the new research on women and medicine in colonial India. Chandrika Paul has now completed her dissertation on medical women in Bengal at the University of Cincinnati and Supriya Guha her dissertation, "A History of the Medicalisation of Childbirth in Bengal in the Late Nineteenth and Early Twentieth Centuries," at the University of Calcutta. Dr. Hilda Lazarus' "Sphere of Indian Women in Medical Work," in *Women in Modern India,* provides us with an insider's view. The sources available for further work of this nature seem extremely rich.

The literature on women in professions other than medicine is scanty. Cornelia Sorabji wrote about her legal work in *Between the Twilights, India Recalled,* and *The Purdahnashin* and Mithan Lam wrote about her education in "Autumn Leaves." Calcutta University Commission, 1917–1919, *Women's Education* (Calcutta, Superintendent Government Printing, 1919), centenary and other special celebratory volumes on women's colleges, such as Bethune College and SNDT Women's University, provide us with some information about women in the teaching profession.

For general works on women's labor I turned to J. C. Kydd, *A History of Factory Legislation in India* (Calcutta, University of Calcutta, 1920); Morris D. Morris, *The Emergence of an Industrial Labour Force in India* (Berkeley, University of California Press, 1965); Janet Harvey Kelman, *Labour in India*

(London, George Allen and Unwin, 1923); D. R. Gadgil, *Women in the Working Force in India* (Bombay, Asia Publishing House, 1965); Jaipal P. Ambannavar, "Changes in Economic Activity of Males and Females in India: 1911–1961", *Demography India*, 4, no. 2 (1975); A. R. Caton, ed., *The Key of Progress* (London, Humphrey Milford, 1930); Shyam Kumari Nehru, ed., *Our Cause: A Symposium of Indian Women* (Allahabad, Kitabistan, 1938); and Evelyn C. Gedge and Mithan Choksi, eds., *Women in Modern India* (Bombay, D. B. Taraporewala Sons and Co., 1929). One of my best sources was Dagmar Engels' "The Changing Role of Women in Bengal, *c.* 1890–*c.* 1930," Ph.D. dissertation, School of Oriental and African Studies, University of London (1987) published as *Beyond Purdah: Women in Bengal, 1890–1939* (New Delhi, Oxford University Press, 1996). Samita Sen's doctoral dissertation, "Women Workers in the Bengal Jute Industry, 1890–1940: Migration, Motherhood and Militancy," University of Cambridge (1992) is an important contribution to the history of laboring women.

There are only a few articles which have tried to probe women's economic roles under colonial rule. Although they are few in number these articles, for example, Mukul Mukherjee, "Impact of Modernization on Women's Occupations" *IESHR*, 20, no. 1 (1983) and Radha Kumar, "Family and Factory: Women in the Bombay Cotton Textile Industry, 1919–1939," *IESHR*, 20, no. 1 (1983) are models for rereading the records that exist. Both these articles have been reprinted in *Women in Colonial India: Essays on Survival, Work and the State*, ed. J. Krishnamurty (Delhi, Oxford University Press, 1989). A more recent article by Mukherjee, "Women's Work in Bengal, 1880–1930: A Historical Analysis," was published in *From the Seams of History*.

I was able to use a few official reports in writing this chapter. Among them were the *Report of the Textile Factories Labour Committee* (Bombay, 1907); Dr. A. C. Roy Choudhury, *Report on an Enquiry into the Standard of Living of Jute Mill Workers in Bengal* (Calcutta, Bengal Secretariat Books Depot, 1930); and *Report of the Royal Commission on Labour in India* (Whitley Report, 1930–1) all in IOOLC. On women in mines I was limited to records found in the West Bengal Archives, Calcutta.

I also drew upon my own interviews, interviews conducted by others, and writings by women involved with the issues of women's work in India. Miss G. Pimpalkchare, research worker with the Industrial Department, Government of Bombay, was interviewed for a report Ruth Woodsmall was completing for the YWCA. This interview is located in the Ruth Woodsmall Collection. I was able to interview Godavari Parulekar (Bombay, February 24, 1980), and Renuka Ray on a number of occasions between 1973 and 1989. I used Renuka Ray's *Women in Mines*, tract no. 2, AIWC (Arunch, AIWC, 1945) for her views on the issue of female labor in the coal mines. The annual reports, files, and correspondence of the women's organizations were used extensively in writing this chapter.

Records on prostitutes are difficult to trust because they originate with people rescuing women from the streets. There is a Box-Bombay in the

Josephine Butler Collection in the Fawcett Library which includes papers of
the Bombay Social Service Conference, the Social Purity League of Bombay,
and the Bombay Vigilance Association. B. Joardar, *Prostitution in Nineteenth
and Early Twentieth Century Calcutta* (New Delhi, Inter-India Publications,
1985) is a regional study which draws primarily on official records and literature. In the last few years feminist scholars have suggested the possibility of
new interpretations. *Women Writing in India* has included an excerpt from the
prostitute-actress, Binodini Dasi, that allows us to hear her voice. Veena Talwar
Oldenburg has written a tantalizing article, "Lifestyle as Resistance: The Case
of the Courtesans of Lucknow," *Contesting Power,* urging us see the extent to
which courtesans may have been empowered by their profession. Amrit
Srinivasan's, "Reform and Revival: The Devadasi and Her Dance," *EPW,* 20,
no. 44 (November 2, 1985) is an excellent article on *devadasis.* Philippa Levine,
"Venereal Disease, Prostitution and the Politics of Empire: The Case of British
India," *Journal of the History of Sexuality,* 4, no. 4 (1994) focuses on the
construction of the prostitute as the source of venereal disease and the treatment of both soldiers and women in late nineteenth-century India.

Unfortunately we do not even have biased literature to inform us about the
work of women on plantations, in agriculture generally, as petty traders and
domestic laborers. Swapna Banerjee completed her Ph.D. dissertation on
"Middle-Class Bengali Women and Female Domestic Workers in Calcutta,
1900–1947" at Temple University, Philadelphia in 1997. Her article,
"Exploring the World of Domestic Manuals: Bengali Middle-Class Women
and Servants in Colonial Calcutta," was published in *South Asia Graduate
Research Journal,* 3, no. 1 (Spring 1996) pp. 1–26.

Chapter 7 more than any other part of this book uses accounts by women
who participated in the action described. Unfortunately, the post-
Independence period has been neglected by people writing histories of women.
To discuss women's role in politics from 1937 on, I used AIWC and WIA correspondence, memoranda, and records of meetings; the Jawaharlal Nehru
Papers (NMML) for his correspondence with women and with others on
women's issues; M. Reddy Papers; clippings on this issue from various newspapers sent to Eleanor Rathbone; my own interviews; and oral history transcripts in the Nehru Library.

Assessing the role of Muslim women at this time is most difficult. There is
one broad history of Muslim women: Shahida Lateef, *Muslim Women in India*
(London, Zed Books, 1990) but it is very general. Begum Shah Nawaz was a
major player at this time and she has written: "Women's Movement in India,"
Indian Paper no. 5 (New York, International Secretariat Institute of Pacific
Relations, 1942). Interviews with prominent women, especially Muslim
women, are included in Ruth Woodsmall's Survey of Women's Interests and
Distinctive Activities, 1930–1932. I was able to meet Kulsum Sayani in
Bombay and talk with her about her work. She gave me a copy of "My
Experiences and Experiments in Adult Education," by Kulsum Sayani
(unpublished) and showed me copies of her newspaper for women. She was
interviewed by the Centre for South Asian Studies, University of Cambridge

(July 30, 1970) and for the Ruth Woodsmall project. Information on Hajrah Begum came mostly from AIWC records, an interview (New Delhi, April 2, 1976), and Hajrah Begum's article, "Women in the Party in the Early Years," *New Age* (December 14, 1975).

Aruna Asaf Ali has written about her own life and political activities in *The Resurgence of Indian Women* (New Delhi, Radiant Publishers, 1991). A biography by Dhan, *Aruna Asaf Ali* (Lahore, New Indian Publications, 1947), is extravagant in its admiration for her. Some of her writings and speeches have been collected in *Aruna Asaf Ali, Great Women of Modern India*, ed. Verinder Grover (New Delhi, Deep and Deep, 1993). For Sucheta Kripalani we have *Sucheta: An Unfinished Autobiography*, ed. K. N. Vasvani (Ahmedabad, Navajivan Publishing House, 1978), published after the author's death, and her letters and memoranda as head of the newly created women's department of the Indian National Congress. These records are in the All-India Congress Committee files in the NMML.

Two studies of the Bengal famine were used in writing about this period: Paul R. Greenough, *Prosperity and Misery in Modern Bengal* (Oxford, Oxford University Press, 1982) and Amartya Sen, *Poverty and Famines* (Delhi, Oxford University Press, 1981). Kalyani Bhattacharjee talked to me extensively about her famine work and gave me copies of a journal, *Bengal Speaks*, they produced at the time. Renu Chakravartty's *Communists in Indian Women's Movement, 1940–1950* (New Delhi, People's Publishing House, 1980), is an indispensable source. I was also fortunate to be able to interview Renu Chakravartty (Calcutta, July 23 and August 15, 1972). Geeta Anand has written an interesting but unpublished paper on "The Feminist Movement in India: Legacy of the Quit India Movement of 1942," senior thesis, Dartmouth College (1989).

For my discussion of the Rani of Jhansi regiment I relied on Peter Ward Fay, *The Forgotten Army* (New Delhi, Rupa and Co., 1994) and Leonard A. Gordon's *Brothers Against the Raj* (New York, Columbia University Press, 1990). On Subhas Bose I also used M. Gopal, ed., *The Life and Times of Subhas Chandra Bose* (Delhi, Vikas, 1978) and Arun, ed., *Testament of Subhas Bose* (Delhi, Rajkamal, 1946). One of the earliest papers on the role of women in the INA was Krishna Bose's "Women's Role in the Azad Hind Movement" (unpublished, 1976). Lakshmi Sahgal wrote, "The Rani of Jhansi Regiment," published in *The Oracle*, 1, no. 2 (April, 1979). *A Revolutionary Life: memoirs of a political activist* by Lakshmi Sahgal (New Delhi, Kali for Women, 1997) includes her autobiography, an essay on the Raui Jhansi Regiment and an interview with Ritu Menon and Kamla Bhasin. My article, "Mothers and Sisters: Feminism and Nationalism in the Thought of Subhas Chandra Bose," was published in *Asian Studies*, 2, no. 1 (1984). I interviewed Lakshmi Swaminathan Sahgal, in Kanpur (March 19, 20, 21, 1976).

For information on the role of women in the radical social and political movements I used Peter Custers' "Women's Role in the Tebhaga Movement," *EPW*, 21, no. 43 (October 25, 1986) and *Women in the Tebhaga Uprising* (Calcutta, Naya Prokash, 1987); and interviews with Renu Chakravartty (see above) and Manikuntala Sen (Calcutta, February 21, 1976). Sources on

Godavari Parulekar's work with the Warlis include, Godavari Parulekar, *Adivasis Revolt* (Calcutta, National Book Agency Private Ltd., 1975); Godavari Parulekar, interview (Bombay, February 24, 1980); and Renu Chakravartty, *Communists*. Vasantha Kannabiran and K. Lalita have written about the Telangana struggle in "That Magic Time: Women in the Telangana People's Struggle," *Recasting Women*. One of the most exciting books to appear is *"We Were Making History"*, compiled by Stree Shakti Sanghatana.

The literature on women in post-Independence India, used for chapter 8, is abundant and growing daily. One of the best sources for a range of topics on women in India is *EPW*. In addition to bi-annual issues on women's studies, sometimes devoted to a single topic, articles on women and gender appear in every issue. I find this the best source for new research. A new Indian journal, *Genders*, has just begun publication. *Manushi, A Journal about Women and Society* covers a wide range of topics and is wonderfully current and relevant. *In Search of Answers*, ed. Madhu Kishwar and Ruth Vanita (London, Zed Books, 1984) is a collection of articles from *Manushi*. There have also been a number of edited books on Indian women, articles appearing in a variety of journals, and articles included in general anthologies on women. In this essay I will not attempt to give an overview of all contemporary scholarship but rather mention the sources I used in writing the chapter.

Scholarship on the fate of women during partition and the "recovery" that followed was practically non-existent until *EPW* devoted its April 24, 1993 issue (28, no. 17) to this topic. This special issue included the following articles: Ritu Menon and Kamla Bhasin, "Recovery, Rupture, Resistance"; Urvashi Butalia, "Community, State and Gender"; Karuna Chanana, "Partition and Family Strategies"; Ratna Kapur and Brenda Crossman, "Communalising Gender/Engendering Community." Urvashi Butalia has written *The Other Side of Silence: Voices from the Partition of India* (New Delhi, Penguin India, 1998) on this topic.

There has been a great deal written on the women's organizations, both the old ones that predated Independence and those formed after 1947. Valuable sources are: M. Mathew and M. S. Nair's *Women's Organizations and Women's Interests* (New Delhi, Ashish Publishing House, 1986); Neera Desai's "From Articulation to Accommodation: Women's Movement in India," *Visibility and Power*, ed. Leela Dube, Eleanor Leacock, and Shirley Ardener (Delhi, Oxford University Press, 1986); and Patricia Caplan's *Class and Gender in India* (London, Tavistock Publications, 1985). Details about the formation of the National Federation of Indian Women are included in its *Tenth Congress of the National Federation of Indian Women*, Trivandrum, December, 1980 (Delhi, NFIW, 1980).

There are three general books which take all contemporary Indian women as their subject and paint in broad strokes – Joanna Liddle and Rama Joshi, *Daughters of Independence* (London, Zed books, 1986), Sara S. Mitter, *Dharma's Daughters* (New Brunswick, Rutgers University Press, 1991), and Elisabeth Bumiller, *May You Be the Mother of a Hundred Sons* (New York, Random House, 1990).

Toward Equality was the landmark document for this period. Not only did it present a great deal of data and stimulate a new set of studies, it also challenged the very categories used to collect data. Yet with all its criticism of women's status, it focused primarily on economic and political issues, largely ignoring violence against women.

Unfortunately very little has been written on Indian women and politics. There are a number of memoirs, autobiographies, and biographies of important women, but very few are analytical. On Vijayalakshmi Pandit we have: Robert Hardy Andrews, *A Lamp for India* (London, Arthur Barker, 1967), Vera Brittain, *Envoy Extraordinary* (London, Allen and Unwin, 1965), R. L. Khipple, *The Woman Who Swayed America* (Lahore, Lion Press, 1946), and Vijayalakshmi Pandit, *So I Became a Minister* (Allahabad, Kitabistan, 1939). Kamaladevi Chattopadhyaya became a major figure in India's handicraft production and has been a favorite figure for biographers. Jamila Brijbhushan wrote *Kamaladevi Chattopadhyaya: Portrait of a Rebel* (New Delhi, Abhinav Publications, 1976) and Yusef Meherally edited *At the Crossroads,* her collected writings and speeches (Bombay, National Information and Publications Ltd., 1947). We also have Kamaladevi's own memoir, *Inner Recesses, Outer Spaces.* Sarojini Naidu died in 1949 but at least three biographies have been produced: Tara Ali Baig, *Sarojini Naidu* (New Delhi, Publications Division, Ministry of Information and Broadcasting, 1974), Padmini Sen Gupta, *Sarojini Naidu* (Bombay, Asia Publishing House, 1966), as well as Sarojini Naidu's collected *Speeches and Writings* (Madras, G. A. Natesan, 1925). In recent years we have witnessed the publication of the autobiographies of women who played significant roles in politics and social work after Independence: for example, Renuka Ray, *My Reminiscences* (Bombay, Allied Publishers, 1982), Aruna Asaf Ali, *The Resurgence of Indian Women,* and *Sucheta: An Unfinished Autobiography.*

Articles and books on women, other than Indira Gandhi, as political actors are difficult to find. There are pieces that celebrate the strength and power of Indian women, for example, Shanta Serbjeet Singh, "Shakti in Modern India," *Femina,* 14, no. 17 (August 17, 1973). Wendy Singer is one of the few historians to have written on women as participants in the contemporary political process. Her articles, "Women's Politics and Land Control in an Indian Election: Lasting Influences of the Freedom Movement in North Bihar," and "Defining Women's Politics in the Election of 1991 in Bihar," both in *India Votes,* ed. Harold Gould and Sumit Ganguly (Boulder, Westview Press, 1993), are among the few attempts to look at these questions. Singer is now engaged in a study of "'Women' and Elections in India, 1936–1996." Amrita Basu wrote about women's activism in Bengal and Maharashtra in *Two Faces of Politics* (Berkeley, University of California Press, 1992). Rajeswari Sunder Rajan's "Gender, Leadership and Representation," in *Real and Imagined Women* (London and New York, Routledge, 1993) is an interesting comment on the problems feminist scholars encounter in using feminist theory to look at women in powerful positions.

There are many books on Indira Gandhi and the following is only a sampling: Niranjan M. Khilnani, *Iron Lady of Indian Politics* (Delhi, H. K. Publishers, 1989), Raj Darbari and Janis Darbari, *Indira Gandhi's 1028 Days* (New Delhi, R. Darbari and J. Darbari, 1983), Henry C. Hart, ed., *Indira Gandhi's India* (Boulder, Colo., Westview Press, 1976), and Inder Malhotra, *Indira Gandhi* (London, Hodder and Stoughton, 1989). Ashis Nandy has written about the appeal of Mrs. Gandhi in "Indira Gandhi and the Culture of Indian Politics," in *At the Edge of Psychology* (Delhi, Oxford University Press, 1980). I found two newspaper articles on Mrs. Gandhi especially interesting on the question of whether or not Mrs. Gandhi was a champion of women: "Indira Gandhi and Women's Liberation," *The Asian Student* (November 23, 1974) and Meher Pestonji, "All Eyes on Mrs. G!" *Eve's Weekly* (October 27–November 2, 1979). Jawaharlal Nehru's letters to Indira between 1922 and 1939 have been published as *Freedom's Daughter,* ed. Sonia Gandhi (London, Hodder and Stoughton, 1989). Some of Mrs. Gandhi's speeches have been collected and published as *Indira Gandhi* in vol. VII of The Great Women of Modern India series, edited by Verinder Grover and Ranjana Arora (New Delhi, Deep and Deep Publications, 1993).

Many social scientists have wrestled with the question of why India has so many women in powerful positions while the masses of women are deprived. Ashis Nandy's view is presented in "Woman Versus Womanliness: An Essay in Speculative Psychology," in B. R. Nanda's *Indian Women,* and repeated by Sara Mitter in *Dharma's Daughters.* Susan Wadley presents a cultural explanation in her "Introduction," *The Powers of Tamil Women,* ed. Susan S. Wadley (Syracuse, N.Y., Maxwell School, 1980). I find Gerald D. Berreman's thoughts on this topic in "Women's Roles and Politics: India and the United States," in *Readings in General Sociology,* 4th edn., ed. Robert W. O'Brien, *et al.* (Boston, Houghton Mifflin, 1969) and "Race, Caste and Other Invidious Distinctions in Social Stratification," *Race,* 13 (July, 1971–April, 1972) very interesting. An article which looks at women in South Asia generally is Raunaq Jahan's "Women in South Asian Politics," *Third World Quarterly,* 9, no. 3 (July, 1987). I particularly like Imtiaz Ahmed's "Women in Politics" in Devika Jain's *Indian Women* and Mary Fainsod Katzenstein, "Toward Equality? Cause and Consequence of the Political Prominence of Women in India," *Asian Survey,* 18, no. 5 (May, 1978).

There are two general books on women in parliament. C. K. Jain's *Women Parliamentarians in India* (New Delhi, Surjeet Publications, 1993), is a useful guide to this topic. The author examines women parliamentarians and their role and women in decision-making; it includes interviews with twenty women parliamentarians and profiles of women in parliament. J. K. Chopra, *Women in Indian Parliament* (New Delhi, Mittal Publications, 1993), includes an unreliable history of women's political participation from the nineteenth century as well as a chronicle of the role played by various women parliamentarians in certain pieces of legislation.

There are some very interesting books and articles on the contemporary women's movement. Radha Kumar's *The History of Doing* (New Delhi, Kali for Women, 1993) is a beautifully illustrated interpretive history of movements for women's rights and feminism in India in the nineteenth and twentieth centuries. Half of this volume is devoted to the contemporary women's movement. Neera Desai and Vibhuti Patel have focused only on the international decade in their *Change and Challenge in the International Decade, 1975–1985* (Bombay, Popular Prakashan, 1985). Neera Desai has also edited *A Decade of Women's Movement in India* (Bombay, Himalaya Publishing House, 1988). Gail Omvedt's *We will Smash this Prison!* (New Delhi, Zed Press, 1980) is a living portrait of women engaged in struggle. Omvedt has also written an interesting history of the contemporary women's movement in a chapter in her book *Reinventing Revolution* (Armonk, N.Y., M. E. Sharpe, 1993). There are two articles which offer some special insights into the contemporary women's movement: A. R. Desai, "Women's Movement in India: An Assessment," *EPW*, 20, no. 23 (June 8, 1985) and Mary Fainsod Katzenstein, "Organizing Against Violence: Strategies of the Indian Women's Movement," *Pacific Affairs*, 62, no. 1 (spring, 1989).

The literature on women's economic and material conditions has truly blossomed and provides a contrast with the literature from the colonial period. Some interesting books on women's work are Leela Gulati, *Profiles in Female Poverty* (Delhi, Hindustan Publishing, 1981), Maria Mies, *Indian Women and Patriarchy* (New Delhi, Concept, 1980), Devika Jain, *Women's Quest for Power* (Sahibabad, U.P., Vikas, 1980), Rekha Mehra and K. Saradamoni, *Women and Rural Transformation* (New Delhi, Indian Council of Social Science Research, Centre for Women's Development Studies, 1983), and Susheela Kaushik, *Women's Oppression* (Sahibabad, U.P., Shakti Books, 1985). Prem Chowdhury's *The Veiled Women: Shifting Gender Equations in Rural Haryana 1880–1990* (Delhi, Oxford University Press, 1994), looks at women's roles – economic, marriage customs, widowhood, inheritance – and sees a worsening situation. Chowdhury notes that although modern development has transformed the face of Haryana, women have not benefited from these changes. Bina Agarwal's long-awaited *A Field of One's Own: Gender and Land Rights in South Asia* (New Delhi, Cambridge University Press, 1994), focuses on the material basis of women's subordination, especially their property rights. Srimati Basu, *She Comes to Take Her Rights: Indian Women, Property and Propriety* (State University of New York Press, in press) studies why women do not claim their rights.

Barbara D. Miller's *The Endangered Sex* (Ithaca, N.Y., Cornell University Press, 1981) provided the wake-up call about India's unequal sex ratio. Amartya Sen's widely read "More Than 100 Million Women Are Missing," *The New York Review* (December 20, 1990) discussed this problem in both India and China. I find Amartya Sen's writing on this issue and the absence of equity for females extremely sensitive. I especially like his *Commodities and Capabilities* (Amsterdam, North Holland, 1985) and his article written with Jocelyn Kynch, "Indian Women: Well-being and Survival," *Cambridge Journal of Economics*, 7, nos. 3/4 (September/December, 1983).

EPW carries numerous articles on women and economic issues. For example, see the articles in a special issue of *EPW*, 24, no. 17 (April 29, 1989):

C. Sridevi, "The Fisherwoman Financier"; Nirmala Banerjee, "Trends in Women's Employment, 1971–1981"; Jeemoi Unni, "Changes in Women's Employment in Rural Areas, 1961–1983"; Roger Jeffrey, Patricia Jeffrey, and Andrew Lyon, "Taking Dung-Work Seriously"; and Miriam Sharma, "Women's Work is Never Done." *Manushi* is an excellent source for women's voices about their work. For example see Prayag Mehta, "We Are Made to Mortgage Our Children – Interviews With Women Workers of Vellore," *Manushi*, 22 (1985).

The linking of sex-determination tests with sex-selective abortions have galvanized the attention of those studying women in India. Some of the first papers on this topic were given by Vibhuti Patel. She has published "Sex-Determination and Sex Preselection Tests in India: Recent Techniques in Femicide," *Reproductive and Genetic Engineering*, 2, no. 2 (1989). Uma Arora and Amrapali Desai wrote an essay on this topic: "Sex Determination Tests in Surat," *Manushi*, 60 (September–October, 1990) and Manju Parikh's "Sex-Selective Abortion in India: Parental Choice or Sexist Discrimination" was published in *Feminist Issues* 10, no. 2 (fall, 1990), pp. 19–32.

The topic of rape hit the popular press in 1980. For example, Subhadra Butalia wrote "The Rape of Mathura" for *Eve's Weekly* (March 8–14, 1980). Examples of other articles are "The Rape Rap," *India Today* (June 30, 1983), and "The Raped Still Tremble," *Probe India* (March 1983). The literature on "dowry deaths" is extensive: Chairanya Kalbag, "Until Death Do Us Part," *India Today* (July 15, 1982); *Saheli Newsletter*, 1, no. 2 (June, 1984); Lotika Sarkar, "Feeble Laws Against Dowry," *Facets*, 3, no. 3 (May–June, 1984); Sevanti Ninan, "At the Crossroads of the Courts," *Express Magazine* (November 27, 1983); and Vimla Farooqui, "Dowry as a Means of Acquiring Wealth and Status," *HOW* (May, 1983) are a few examples. There have also been numerous articles in *Manushi*. The *Saheli Report* (November 25, 1983) was privately circulated. Two official documents of interest are the *Report of the Joint Committee of the Houses to Examine the Question of the Working of the Dowry Prohibition Act, 1961*, C.B.(II), no. 333 (New Delhi, Lok Sabha, 1982) and the Law Commission of India's *Ninety-first Report on Dowry Deaths and Law Reform* (August 10, 1983). The best article summarizing the new legislation to protect women is Flavia Agnes' "Protecting Women Against Violence? Review of a Decade of Legislation, 1980–1989," *EPW*, 27, no. 17 (April 5, 1992).

The Roop Kanwar sati-like death was widely reported. "A Pagan Sacrifice," *India Today* (October 15, 1987) treated it as a possible suicide but many other articles glorified it as sati. Feminist writers, like the editor of *Research Center Women's Studies Newsletter*, called it: "Sati – Cold Blooded Murder," 8, nos. 3 and 4 (December 1987). Especially interesting in this controversy is Ashis Nandy, "Sati as Profit Versus Sati as Spectacle: The Public Debate on Roop Kanwar's Death," in *Sati, the Blessing and the Curse*. Veena Talwar has written a superb (and entertaining) article and rebuttal to Nandy: "The Roop Kanwar Case: Feminist Responses," and "The Continuing Invention of the Sati Tradition," also in *Sati, the Blessing and the Curse*.

Communalism has been the issue of the 1990s for women in India as well as Indians generally. Zoya Hasan has written an excellent article, "Communalism, State Policy, and the Question of Women's Rights in Contemporary India," *Bulletin of Concerned Asian Scholars*, 25, no. 4 (October–December, 1993) that discusses the Shah Bano case within the context of the larger revival of communalism. This has also been a topic for Madhu Kishwar, *Manushi*'s editor: "Pro Women or Anti Muslim? The Shahbano Controversy," *Manushi*, 32 (January–February, 1986). *Forging Identities: Gender, Communities and the State*, ed. Zoya Hasan (New Delhi, Kali for Women, 1994) includes a number of articles which further our understanding of gender and religious issues for Muslim women.

One of the first serious articles to appear on women in the Hindutva movement was Tanika Sarkar's "The Woman as Communal Subject: Rashtrasevika Samiti and Ram Janambhoomi Movement," *EPW*, 26, no. 35 (August 31, 1991). In 1993 Amrita Basu was guest editor for a special issue of the *Bulletin of Concerned Asian Scholars*, 25, no. 3 (October–December, 1993) on "Women and Religious Nationalism in India," which included articles by Zoya Hasan (see above), Tanika Sarkar, "The Women of the Hindutva Brigade," Amrita Basu, "Feminism Inverted: The Real Women and Gendered Imagery of Hindu Nationalism," and Paola Bacchetta, "All Our Goddesses Are Armed: Religion, Resistance, and Revenge in the Life of a Militant Hindu Nationalist Woman." Volume 8, nos. 3–4, of the *Committee on South Asian Women Bulletin* was devoted to "Women and the Hindu Right." It included Jyotsna Vaid, "On Women and the Hindu Right," Sucheta Mazumdar, "For Rama and Hindutva: Women and Right Wing Mobilization," Vibhuti Patel, "Communalism, Racism and Identity Politics," Paola Bacchetta, "Muslim Women in the RSS Discourse," and Madhu Kishwar, "Warnings from the Bombay Riots." *Women and Right-Wing Movements: Indian Experiences*, ed. Tanika Sarkar and Urvashi Butalia (London: Zed Books, 1995) is an excellent addition to this literature.

The scholarship on women in South Asia is almost all interdisciplinary and increasingly influenced by post-modernist theory. This has led to a spate of collected works which include articles written from different points of view and on different periods. Works that attempt to synthesize periods or movements are rare. This is a most exciting time to be researching and reading women's history, for every day brings new pieces of work with tantalizing possibilities. I view my own work as only a first attempt to provide a useful framework for new explorations.

INDEX

Hindu Widow Remarriage Act, 22
Hindu Woman's Right to Divorce Act,
 113–14
Hindu Woman's Right to Property Bill,
 113–14
Hogg, Mr., 95
Home Rule League, 93, 99
home science, 53–4, 56
Hossain, Begum Rokeya Sakhawat, 55–7
Hunter Commission (Indian Education
 Commission), 44–6
Hyderabad State, 218–20

Ilbert Bill, 122
India Act, of 1919, 99–100; of 1935, 106,
 108, 112, 190–2
Indian Civil Service, 29, 199
Indian Constitution, 223–4, 227, 229, 234,
 252
Indian Education Commission, *see* Hunter
 Commission
Indian Ladies Magazine (ILM), 43
Indian Medical Service, 166
Indian National Army, 212–14, 220
Indian National Congress (INC), 64, 66,
 89, 92, 99, 112, 150, 202, 203, 214, 252,
 253; civil disobedience movement, 154,
 156; elections of 1937, 191–6; female
 franchise, 93–4; Indira Gandhi, 232;
 Jyotimoyee Ganguli, 141; Kulsum
 Sayani, 201; Madras, 143–4; non-
 cooperation movement, 126; Quit
 India movement, 190, 203–9; Rajiv
 Gandhi, 250; reports on police violence
 against women, 150–3; Round Table
 Conferences, 107–8; Subhas Chandra
 Bose, 212; women at Congress
 meetings, 122–3, 136–7, 162; Women's
 Congress, 142–3; Women's
 Department, 117, 208; women's rights,
 115, 117, 120; women's sub-committee
 of National Planning Committee, 117,
 199–200
Indian Republican Army, 139
International Council of Women, 75, 160
International Labor Organization (ILO),
 114, 160, 168, 171–5
International Women's Suffrage Alliance,
 160
International Women's Year, 2, 226–7, 243
Irwin, Lord, Viceroy of India (1926–31),
 106–7
Iyengar, S. Srinivasa, 144

Jinarajadasa, Dorothy, 72–4, 94, 110
Jinnah, Muhammad Ali, 197, 201

Joint Select Committee on Franchise
 (1918), 95, 97
Joshi, Anandibai, 6, 47, 162–3
Joshi, Sir Morophant Visavanath, 87
Joshi Committee, 85, 88, 90, 145
journals, women's, 5, 29, 201, 227, 247, 248;
 Indian Ladies Magazine, 43; *Manushi*,
 244; *Roshni*, 82, 202, 205; *Stri Dharma*,
 74, 69
Jugantar, 123, 138
jute mills, 167–70, 173–5

Kale, Anasuyabai, 195
Kanwar, Roop, 247–8
Kanya Mahavidyalaya, 44
Kara, Maniben, 78, 91, 174–5, 187, 227
Karve, Anandibai *aka* Joshi, Godubai, 47,
 51–3, 180
Karve, Dondo Keshav, 17, 20, 45, 47, 51–4,
 119
Kaur, Amrit, 235; AIWC, 82, 108, 111, 173;
 female franchise, 128; Gandhian, 129,
 178; Rau Committee, 117; Union
 Health Minister, 231
khaddar, 164; civil disobedience movement,
 132, 135, 137, 142, 143, 146; non-
 cooperation movement, 126–7, 144
Khwaja Altaf Husain Hali, 20
Kishwar, Madhu, 8
Kripalani, Sucheta, 125–6, 206–9, 231
kulin, 22–3

labor legislation, 168–70, 172–5
labor unions, 174–5, 217, 225, 241
Ladies Recreational Club, 73
Lady Hardinge Medical College, 164–5
Lady Willingdon Training College and
 Practice School, 59
Lakshmipathy, Rukmani, 145
Lam Mithan (*see also* Tata, Mithan), 76–7
Lazarus, Dr. Hilda, 163–4, 167
League of Nations, 85, 89, 114, 160, 169,
 185
legal profession for women, 157, 158, 167,
 186; Cornelia Sorabji, 98, 98n.17;
 Mithan Tata Lam, 76–7, 100
Limayi, Anutayi, 230
Linlithgow (Franchise) Committee,
 111–12
Lok Sabha, 229, 247
Lothian (Franchise) Committee, 108–9
Lothian, Lord, 108
Lukanji, Mrs., 135
Luthra, Bimla, 147
Lynch, Christina *aka* Drysdale, Mrs.
 Christina, 58–9

Vivekananda, Swami *aka* Datta,
Narendranath, 17–18, 20, 30–1, 60
Voice of Freedom, 205

Waddedar, Pritilata, 140–1
Warli movement, 216–18, 221
White Paper of 1933 (Franchise), 109–10
Whitley Commission, *see* Royal
Commission on Labour in India
widow remarriage, 252; Dayananda
Saraswati, 20 n.35; prohibitions on, 16,
71; Ranade, 25–6; Vidyasagar, 19, 21–2;
Virasalingam, 23–5
widowhood, tragedy of, 20
widows, 167, 220; domestic labor, 53, 180;
education of, 47, 52–3, 57, 58–60; in the
freedom struggle, 152, 154;
prostitution, 182, 184; status of, 20, 22,
33, 67, 188, 189
Wingate, Iris, 178
women, enfranchised after India Act of
1919, 101
women revolutionaries, 138–42, 155, 190,
213
Women's Department, Indian National
Congress, 208
Women's Fellowship of Service, 175
women's history, 2, 4–5, 9
Women's Indian Association (WIA), 79,
105, 132; first franchise campaign, 92,
94–5, 97; history of, 72–5; Sarda Act,
87, 88; second franchise campaign,
106–8, 111; Sister Subbalakshmi, 59–60

women's legal rights, 112–19, 154
women's literacy, 200–1, 218
women's Medical Service, 164, 166–7
women's sub-committee, National
Planning Committee, 117, 199–200,
203
Women's Swadeshi League, 144–5
women's voting behavior, 229
Wood, Sir Charles, 40
work, women domestics, 7, 53, 218; in
middle-class families, 180–1; numbers
in 1921, 157; efforts to organize, 175,
179, 218
work, women in the colonial economy,
157–88
work, women in factories, 157, 158, 159,
186, 221; AIWC's concern with, 171–2;
Bombay Provincial Women's Council,
172–3; factory legislation, 168–9, 173,
175–6; jute mills, 169–71; labor leaders,
174; Open Door International, 174–5;
textile mills, 168, 169
work, women in mines, 157, 158, 159,
176–9, 186
work, women on plantations, 158–9, 186
World War I, 29, 93, 124, 142, 165
World War II, 90, 203, 220

YWCA, 64, 178

zenana education, 37, 40
Zutshi, Lado Rani, 64, 121, 129, 147, 222

THE NEW CAMBRIDGE HISTORY OF INDIA

I The Mughals and Their Contemporaries

II Indian States and the Transition to Colonialism

III The Indian Empire and the Beginnings of Modern Society

IV The Evolution of Contemporary South Asia

* Already published
† in paperback